Minoan Architectural Design

Approaches to Semiotics
63

Mouton Publishers
Berlin · New York · Amsterdam

Minoan Architectural Design
Formation and Signification

Donald Preziosi

Mouton Publishers
Berlin · New York · Amsterdam

Library of Congress Cataloging in Publication Data

Preziosi, Donald, 1941-
    Minoan architectural design.

    (Approaches to semiotics; 63)
    Bibliography: p.
    Includes index.
    1. Architecture, Minoan. 2. Modular coordination
(Architecture) I. Title. II. Series.
NA267.P7 1983   722'.61   82-22415
ISBN 90-279-3409-6

Printed in Germany.

It appears that the Minoans did not object to
disorderly planning as such; they obviously saw
no advantage in symmetry and may have been
lovers of the picturesque at all costs; in fact
their architecture resembles their other arts in
showing no sense of form.

A.W. Lawrence, *Greek Architecture*, 1957, p. 34.

Contents

List of Figures

Preface

A decade ago I completed a doctoral dissertation on the subject of Minoan architecture whose intent was in part to establish the nature of the planning and layout procedures followed by Minoan builders in the realization of their designs (*Minoan Palace Planning and Its Origins,* Harvard University, 1968). While the discoveries stemming from that study have been summarily published in various journals,[1] a full account of that project and its implications has only surfaced in my graduate seminars at Yale and MIT. In recent years I have been increasingly asked by students of Bronze Age art and architecture to make this study more widely available.

To date no serious and comprehensive study of Minoan architecture has appeared,[2] and the student of this first European civilization continues to rely upon fragmentary accounts embedded (indeed often hidden) within a labyrinthine mass of technical archaeological writing concerned, more often than not, with problems of a nonarchitectural nature. The only other recourse for the student has been writing of a superficial and impressionistic nature on the subject of Minoan art and aesthetics.

The present volume is an attempt to rectify this situation, and seeks to elucidate the network of organizational features of Minoan architecture in the light of detailed analyses of the formal spatial organization of a corpus of Minoan buildings and settlements.

Since 1968 this analytic study of Aegean architecture has continued, accelerated in 1970 with the establishment of an ongoing research project concerned with the development of adequate theories of architectonic formation and signification. Some of the results of this project to date have been published in two recent books, in which the Minoan material examined originally in my thesis has served in part as an exemplary corpus: *The Semiotics of the Built Environment: An Introduction to Architectonic Analysis* (Indiana University Press, 1979), and *Architecture, Language and Meaning: The Origins of the Built World* (Mouton, The Hague, 1979). The present book has as its substantive antecedent a volume published in New Haven in 1970, which consisted of a collection of formal and functional analyses of Minoan buildings by students in my graduate seminars at Yale (*Labrys,* New Haven, 1970). The latter collection is no longer available.

The present book is a synthesis of our research on Minoan architecture over the past decade, and comprises a re-examination of that material in the light of the theoretical principles of architectonic formation and signification elaborated in the aforementioned research project, begun at Yale in 1970, and continued more recently at MIT and S.U.N.Y. The fieldwork upon which the original dissertation was based has now been augmented by new analyses on Crete done in 1972.[3]

In the study of any architectural material – and especially of material widely removed in time and space – one of the principal problems facing the analyst is the establishment of the synchronicity of data; the state, in other words, of initial plans and subsequent alterations and modifications. In the case of Minoan architecture, and in particular in regard to the analysis of buildings such as the great 'palace' of Knossos which were occupied for half a millennium and were subject to sporadic growth and often abruptly radical change in design, this task can become enormously difficult. The immediate aim of the fieldwork on which the original study was based was in part to establish the relative chronology of construction. In this task, we brought to bear on the problem a method of analysis which had hitherto not been employed on Crete – namely the structural and metrological analysis of plans themselves.[4] Through extensive surveys *in situ* of Minoan remains, in a series of campaigns over several years,[5] we sought to elucidate the manner in which a given building was planned and laid out, so as to arrive at a clearer understanding of a building's conception and organization.

The information yielded by this study, coupled with already-existing studies of materials and construction methods, has in a variety of ways fundamentally altered our understanding of the nature of Minoan design, and the recurrent patterns of spatial organization and relationships among component forms which can only be clearly seen through close analysis have called into question not a small amount of the published writing on the subject. In seeking to discover the nature of minimal formal components in Minoan architecture, and the patterns of their association, interaction, and transformation, this work has conclusively demonstrated the existence of an orderliness and systematicity underlying the often extraordinarily intricate and complex spatial harmonics of the Minoan built environment.

After three quarters of a century of excavation, writing and speculation, it is often difficult for the person learning about Minoan architecture to fully appreciate the often heated and controversial polemics surrounding the discoveries of Minoan remains. Indeed, discussions of Minoan architecture have traditionally generated more heat than enlightenment since Arthur Evans turned his first spade at Knossos in the spring of 1900.[6] Scholarly circumspection, while far from nonexistent, has nevertheless often been buried beneath the sheer weight of spectacular discovery on Crete (and now on Thera). Indeed, it seems not unfair to say that in many respects the body of literature lying athwart the architectural remains of Bronze Age Crete is as labyrinthine in its capacity to try the patience of the serious student as are the very plans of many Minoan structures in testing one's maze-solving abilities. Not a few students simply abandon hope of making any sense of an architectural corpus in which no two plans are identical, and in which each building appears at first glance to be an impossibly complex three-dimensional aggregate of space-cells scattered haphazardly by some dark Daedalic wit.

It has long been tempting to respond to a scholarly and popular tradition which held that Minoan architecture was 'devoid of clear organizing canons of design', or that its 'agglutinative' appearance represented an unconscious attempt to recapture some troglodytic ambience, by erecting a counter-edifice purporting to demonstrate that even the most tumble-down farmstead was a marvel of arcane harmonic planning. But many of the views of early writers concerning the 'illogical' or 'irrational' nature of Minoan design, as illustrated in the following statement:

To estimate the level reached by Cretan architecture and to enjoy its charms one must forget those intellectual qualities of order, symmetry and balance which give Greek buildings their incomparable beauty.[7]

are best met with the silence they deserve. Nevertheless, the serious student must remain aware that such impressions have deeply informed our received understanding of Minoan architecture, and such bizarre judgments have strongly affected our very perceptions of Minoan culture in general.[8]

But modern scholarship alone is not at fault here, for such views have themselves been influenced by the inabilities of the later Greeks to understand their brilliant (and non-Greek) predecessors in the Aegean. Greek mythology both damns and praises the Minoans in the same breath: while paying homage to the advanced level of technology and invention of the Minoans in the stories of that ancient Leonardo, the Cretan Daedalos, Minoan building is remembered in the context of the story of the Athenian hero Theseus, Ariadne and the Minotaur and the former's escape from the *labyrinthos* – a word which in the Cretan language meant 'house of the *labrys* (or double axe)' and which to the Greeks came to mean 'maze' or 'labyrinth'. At the same time that the Greeks placed the three Minoan 'kings', Minos, Rhadamanthys, and Sarpedon, as just and wise rulers in their underworld, they also, in their patriarchal and puritanical fashion, had difficulty coping with remembrances of a society whose women were evidently (and shockingly) rather more than mere chattel – as witnessed by their titillating stories of female sexual 'excesses' – encapsulated neatly in their anecdote about Pasiphae.

It is hardly surprising that a systematic overview of Minoan architecture on its own terms has not appeared. The first generation of archaeologists to deal with Minoan remains were usually good classical scholars, accustomed to the principles of design of classical Greece and thoroughly imbued with the judgmental impedimenta regarding classical art set in motion by Roman critics and swallowed whole by later Western art history. From such a perspective, the art and architecture of the Minoans seemed baroquely unclassical, disconcerting, 'primitive', and perhaps to some degree even embarrassing. In such a framework, Minoan buildings could indeed be seen as 'illogical, disorderly growths'.

It is hard to find anyone today who takes such pronouncements seriously, and yet in the study of Minoan architecture such perspectives have deeply imbued, even unconsciously, many of the ostensibly 'objective' descriptions of remains one still finds in the literature, and the beginning student should be sensitive to this often hidden bias.

The rectification of these impressions has taken a long time, for an additional, but perhaps also partly related reason: once one finds one's 'Ariadne's Thread' through the literature, one is confronted with the remains themselves: some structures simply no longer exist, either through natural and often unavoidable decay or because the land on which they stand has reverted to private ownership for use as precious farmland. Not a few buildings remain inadequately published, in part due to early and unsophisticated excavation methods, or because their excavators were more interested in solving problems of relative ceramic chronology, or because quite simply the energies of many excavators have been necessarily spread thin in order to be able to rescue for scientific study the plethora of new sites continually uncovered to the present day. Homer's statement about Crete that it contained 'ninety cities and many men innumerable' is, if anything, an understatement. Another impediment to study is the fact that among the extant structures are some whose published plans bear scant resemblance to the actual remains themselves, as anyone who has spent more than a fleeting time with the ruins will attest.[9]

Despite these problems, there often remains, to even the casual visitor, an impression of a certain homogeneity, a certain conceptual resemblance about many Minoan buildings, often just beyond the thresholds of articulate definition. One remembers this indefinable 'ambience' of 'style' as involving certain kinds of perceptual expectations: that a given corridor, despite its size and orientation, will characteristically change direction in certain ways, or that a certain type of room will inevitably have a typical manner of entrance, or be joined to other groups of space-cells in characteristic ways, or that one's subliminal expectations that there will be a colonnaded portico at a certain remove from a court of a certain size will be fulfilled.

Such perceptual resemblances, moreover, tend to link together building types as different as the rustic farmhouse (the 'Villa Rurale') at Gortyn, the elegant and surprising townhouses of Knossos, Tylissos, or Mallia, and the great civic megastructures (called 'palaces' in the literature) at Knossos, Phaistos, Mallia, Gournia, or Kato Zakro. In addition, one often gets the impression that this stylistic ambience lingers from city to city even across more than half a millennium of transition and transformation.

The aim of this book is not to seek ways to justify these impressions, but rather to explore, in a principled and systematic fashion, the nature of whatever conceptual homogeneities (and heterogeneities) may be evidenced through a detailed structural analysis of the remains themselves. Our interest is principally with the recurrence of patterns of formation, with both patterns of invariance and variation. We seek answers to some very basic questions: what are the sets of minimal formative units in the corpus, and how is the significance of each form altered by differences in setting, context, orientation, size, and material realization? What is similar and what is different about two houses in terms of their formative organization? How are buildings functionally composed, and what is the nature of internal zoning and channeling of traffic? Are the same forms used for contrastive functions (and if so, are we to then consider them the same forms)? Are there significant formal differences between structures used for different purposes? Is there a rule-governed 'syntax' in the ways certain types of space-cells are associated both horizontally and vertically? And, ultimately, do the patterns of association among significant forms defined by the corpus constitute a 'code' or ordered system in its own right, distinct both from contemporary corpora (e.g. Egyptian architecture) and subsequent systems (e.g. Mycenaean architecture)?

This is not a 'history' of Minoan architecture in the once-fashionable sense of a diachronic and genealogical account of groups of 'monuments' linked together formally over time. Our aim is not to purport that the significance of construction Y is fully explained by its formal relation to an antecedent construction X and a subsequent construction Z. Such a method too often fosters a doubly false impression: that forms have a life of their own apart from the set of forms amongst which they are copresent, or apart from their broader sociocultural contexts; and that architectural (or, in general, artifactual) history has a linearity and developmental logic of its own, which it patently does not. Any componential system within culture is a system of *relationships,* not of forms, and its development over time (and space) is necessarily cumulative, interactive, and reciprocally interwoven with the development of all other systems which may comprise a given culture. To speak of a 'history' of architecture — either cross-culturally or infra-culturally — which is autonomous of other historical developments, is inevitably a romantic academic fiction.

Any serious study of architecture can only be firmly grounded in the synchronic contextual network of relationships which defines, and is in turn defined by, its component formations. The significance of any given architectonic form — from entire settlements to the proportions of doorways — is defined by the sum of its relationships to all the other copresent formations within which it is embedded at a given place and time. This set of relationships links forms both to their synchronous partners and those which, generated earlier, remain in present perception to continue to influence the former.

This book is devoted to the systematicity of such relationships as manifested at various periods in the life of the corpus of Minoan architecture.

We should be wary, moreover, of two additional false assumptions, which are still to be found, both tacitly and explicitly, in some contemporary writing on architecture. The first concerns a purported universality in the significative apperception of forms. Despite even recent claims to the contrary,[10] architectonic forms do not carry universal or innate connotations apart from their perceptual and significative appropriations within the conventions of given cultures. Our somatic, perceptual, or cognitive responses to given formations are as much the product of our acculturated learning as they may be due to 'innate' perceptual dispositions.[11] A given architectonic formation may be uplifting or threatening (or both) depending upon its context. It is such context-sensitivity which is a major determinant of our architectonic 'reading', played against our memory of the set of contextual variants undergone by a given formation. Every aesthetic system is, as far as can be adequately demonstrated, culture-specific and time-specific.

A second, usually tacit, assumption which must be called into question for our purposes here concerns the nature of the relationship(s) between the architecture of a time and place and other manifestations of thought and behavior elsewhere in a society. As I have argued elsewhere in some detail,[12] the architecture of an age or place is not the passive imprint of thought and action, the direct and transitive 'reflection', the mold-negative of systems of thought and value. Such a perspective (itself grounded in a further incorrect assumption, namely that architecture is a passive stage-set *for* behavior and thought) seriously misconstrues the patent fact that the built environment actively and dynamically cues and shapes our perception and action: we build *in order to* think and act.

Thus it cannot be claimed that what is revealed regarding the underlying conceptual organization of Minoan architecture can necessarily be taken as a privileged insight into all the innermost workings of the Minoan mind. Such revelations are inevitably synecdochal or fragmentary. The 'view' from other aspects of Minoan artifactual culture will present us with partly distinct and overlapped perspectives on Minoan thought and culture. Moreover, it is an unwarranted assumption that all of these different perspectives will yield a single common set of invariants. We so little understand the intricacies of connectivity between one aspect of culture and another that the positing of absolute, invariant and direct relationships between architectonic signification and other systems of social meaning and value would necessarily short-circuit our understanding.

This is not to say that the conceptual underpinnings of Minoan architectonic formation represent nothing about the Minoan mentality – rather, they do not reflect everything about the latter, any more than do other aspects of Minoan culture, such as its plastic and visual arts, its socioeconomic or political systems, or its language(s). If, as Mary Douglas writes in a poignant and lucid essay, '. . . the organization of thought and of social relations is imprinted on the landscape',[13] then we must also take into account the equally valid observation of Ulric Neisser that:

Because perception and action take place in continuous dependence upon the environment, they cannot be understood without an understanding of that environment itself.[14]

It is in this spirit that the conclusions reached by the present study should be taken: just as our understanding of the organization of the Minoan-built environment will deeply affect our understanding of other aspects of Minoan culture, so too will our increased growth in the latter areas feed back upon, and eventually alter, the implications of the following explorations.

FORMAT

Because this is not a 'history' of the 'development' of Minoan architecture, but a structural and comparative study of Minoan architectural organization as manifested in its extant corpus of buildings, the present volume is not organized chronologically. Instead, the following comprises a survey of various building types arranged in order of increasing complexity of plan and spatial syntax. Some 50 different structures are examined, chosen principally from among the hundreds extant[15] as the best preserved examples of Minoan design.

The book is divided into two main sections, to address the interests of different groups of readers. Part One comprises a general survey of the formal organization of Minoan buildings, and examines *recurrent patterns of design* in the corpus. This part concludes with a discussion of the identification and nature of the component-significative units in the corpus, and considers some of the ways in which such units combine and interact to form larger-scale units. This section includes a theoretical discussion on the nature of architectonic corpora and their organizational properties.

Part Two is addressed to the more advanced reader, and is somewhat more technical in nature, being devoted to the detailed *modular analysis* of Minoan groundplans. Several dozen buildings — essentially the same considered more generally in Part One — are examined individually in an attempt to discover the particular planning and layout procedures followed by Minoan builders in the realization or generation of their designs. This study provides additional information regarding the conception of each building, and suggests more detailed evidence for the relationships among Minoan buildings, both synchronically and chronologically. In a few cases there is some evidence for the common authorship of groups of buildings.

Included in Part One is an examination of a building type which begins to appear on Crete during and immediately after the destructions of the great 'palaces', providing concrete evidence for the assimilation by Crete of a design format with a long history elsewhere in the Aegean. In some cases the modular and metrological similarities between these Late Bronze Age Cretan buildings and buildings in the Mycenaean mainland orbit strikingly augment the external linguistic evidence for the arrival of Greek-speaking peoples in the island.

While the two parts of the book are aimed at readers with differing backgrounds, the organization of the volume is intended to provide beginning students with the opportunity to familiarize themselves with increasingly technical and detailed information about Minoan architectural design. Through extensive references, the set of analyses below may also be used as a springboard to yet more detailed study of individual buildings.

ACKNOWLEDGEMENTS

To say that the existence of this study has been largely made possible by the contributions of a very great number of individuals is neither false modesty nor polite exaggeration. So many students, friends and colleagues have informed this ongoing project to its benefit that it would be incorrect to say that it has not been a joint and collaborative venture. When I began to look carefully and critically at the subject of Minoan architecture and its literature in an undergraduate survey given by Professor David Gordon Mitten at Harvard in 1964, I became almost immediately impatient to clarify what I felt intuitively to be a number of false and misleading pronouncements in the literature on the nature of Minoan design, and I felt impelled to justify my intuitions with further study. I was fortunate to put myself under the guidance of Professor G.M.A. Hanfmann in my desire to go to Crete and make a survey of the remains, so as to quickly (as I thought) solve certain basic problems concerning the planning procedures of Minoan builders. I felt (rightly, as I was to discover) that only an exhaustive study of the remains themselves could provide a firm basis for further detailed study of Minoan design. I went to Crete under the aegis of a Charles Eliot Norton Fellowship during 1964-1965, having originally decided that all I would need to answer my questions was a couple of months of intensive field surveys. It quickly became apparent that I was just beginning to scratch the surface of the problem, and that a truly comprehensive survey of Minoan (and Aegean) buildings was imperative if my own conclusions were to be less cursory and impressionistic. My surveys were extended through the following year thanks to the support offered by a Harvard Travelling Fellowship, and I returned in 1967 to begin to make sense of my field notes and sketches. The dissertation upon which the present book is in part based was begun that year in New Haven, as I began teaching at Yale, and the synthesis of my fieldwork into a coherent account was to a significant degree aided by my interactions with my students there.

This work became the basis of an ongoing research project at Yale within the yearly context of my graduate seminars on Minoan art and architecture,[16] and its cumulative growth was crucially aided by the continuing participation of a number of students, in particular Michael Bales, Maggie Rogow, Charles Gates, and Marie-Henriette Carre. This project bifurcated into two overlapped parts in 1969-1970, one concerned with the detailed study of Minoan architectural organization, and one involved in more generic study of the nature of the formative and significative composition of architectural material *per se.* Again, the same core of students were involved in both projects, and for a period of months in 1970-1971 we met nearly every evening to thrash out increasingly crucial problems regarding the nature of architectonic meaning and formation as a result of our close study of architectural corpora of various periods, including contemporary material.

When I left Yale in 1973 to teach in the Department of Architecture at MIT, the Minoan material was put aside in my own research to concentrate on the elaboration of adequate theories of architectonic form which were sensitive to developments in cognate disciplines. These explorations were supported in part by a grant from the National Endowment for the Humanities in 1973, and were significantly aided by in-house leaves from MIT, where I benefited greatly from my conversational interactions and work sessions with many colleagues and students, in particular Wayne Andersen, Stanford Anderson, Robert Karl Manoff, Christian Norberg-Schulz, Jonathan Matthews, Hong-bin Kang, Linda Suter Robson, Ik-jae Kim, Keiko Prince, Werner Oechslin, Alexander Tzonis, Peter Eisenmann, and Arthur Steinberg. That research was itself guided and nurtured previously at Yale through my inter-actions with my colleagues Sheldon Nodelman, Vincent Scully, Jr., Neil Levine, Irving Rouse, Kwang-chih Chang, Henry Wollman, Grace Seiberling, George Kubler, Francois Guerin, and Christine Gangneux.

The completion and publication of the two 1979 books men-tioned above has left me free to undertake the present study, and has made possible a new synthesis of the two aforementioned research programmes, both of which continue. Since coming to Ithaca in 1977, the continuing stimulation and support by my Cornell colleague Linda R. Waugh, and by Roman Jakobson of Harvard have both clarified the directions of my questions and provided the impetus for further exploration.

Apart from (what will be obvious to the reader are) my own sketches and analytic diagrams, the illustrations of Minoan build-ings in this book were prepared under the expert and critical hand of Mr. David Peck, Jr. several years ago to the specifications of my own field surveys and measurements. Each isometric elevation is an entirely new description of the Minoan buildings examined below, and the laborious process of preparing these illustrations has had an important effect on the explication of my own original surveys. It is hoped that their precision and clarity will serve as an effective guide to the reader interested in a less impressionistic account of Minoan architectural design.[17]

Center for Advanced Study in the Visual Arts
National Gallery of Art
Washington, D.C.

NOTES

1. D. Preziosi, 'Formal and functional analysis of Minoan architecture', in *Labrys* (New Haven, 1970), a collection of analytic studies of various Minoan buildings, in collaboration with Douglas Connor, Martin Hoffmeister, Philip Kurland, and Peyton Helm; *id.*, 'Modular design in Minoan architecture', in *Studies Presented to George M.A. Hanfmann,* (Cambridge, Mass., 1971), edited by John Griffiths Pedley, David Gordon Mitten, and Jane Scott. During the years 1967-1971 the writer presented lectures on the subject of Minoan design to the annual meetings of the Archaeological Institute of America, published in summary outline in numbers of the *American Journal of Archaeology* for those years.

2. With the notable exception of the interesting work of Professor James Walter Graham, as reported in his introductory survey *Palaces of Crete* (1962), and in his more detailed articles appearing in the *American Journal of Archaeology* (*AJA*) 60 (1956): 151ff; 61 (1957): 255ff; 63 (1959): 47ff; 64 (1960): 329ff; 65 (1961): 165 ff; 74 (1970): 231ff.

3. Done in collaboration with Michael Bales and Maggie Rogow, members of my graduate seminar on Minoan architecture at Yale. This work involved remeasurement of some remains and extensive photographic documentation.

4. In the original survey, some 330 structures were studied both on Crete and elsewhere in the Aegean and on the Greek mainland. The survey included both tombs and fortifications as well as public and private buildings. Of the original sample, some 170 yielded reasonably clear modular profiles (the majority of those which didn't were tombs); of these about one-half are Minoan buildings, comprising the best preserved of those extant. A somewhat similar study of Egyptian architecture has been undertaken over the years by Dr. Alexander Badawy, some of the results of which are published in his monograph *Ancient Egyptian Architectural Design* (Los Angeles, 1965).

5. Survey campaigns were made in the Aegean in 1964, 1965 and 1966 in connection with the aforementioned doctoral dissertation (Harvard University, 1968); this work was supported by a Charles Eliot Norton Fellowship and a Harvard Travelling Fellowship during those years, and my principal advisors at Harvard were G.M.A. Hanfmann and Kenneth Conant. Cloth and steel measuring tapes of 25-meter and 100-meter lengths were employed in most of the detailed work, with the assistance of Patricia Getz, Robert Hahn, Nicholas Hahn, Philip Pappas, and Krista Pappas. Throughout this work I was graciously aided by the American School of Classical Studies in Athens, where I was a resident Fellow from 1964-1966, and by invaluable conversational and bureaucratic assistance from Dr. Doro Levi, then head of the Italian School of Athens. The work was also aided through my interactions with members of the British School at Athens, and its Villa Ariadne at Knossos. Mr. Joseph Shaw of the joint American-Greek excavation team at Kato Zakro provided welcome and invaluable advice concerning the details of Minoan constructional methods.

6. As reported in the monumental set of volumes published between 1921 and 1936 by Sir Arthur Evans, *The Palace of Minos at Knossos* (Volumes I through IV).

7. G. Glotz, *The Aegean Civilization:* 119.

8. See especially A.W. Lawrence, *Greek Architecture* (1957): 34, 41, 291; and Snijder's *Kretische Kunst*: 89-90, for typical pronouncements on Minoan art and architectural design.

9. A typical example is the crucially important structure built during the Early Minoan II period at Vasiliki in eastern Crete, termed the 'House on the Hilltop' by its early excavator Richard B. Seager. The structure, which would have been important as a possible predecessor to the design of the later (Middle Minoan) 'palaces', was published in a form which is grossly in error, both in layout and in orientation. A complete discussion will be found in my aforementioned dissertation (hereafter *MPPAO*), pp. 150 and 494.

10. Notably R. Arnheim, *The Dynamics of Architectural Form* (Berkeley, 1977); see also the otherwise insightful book by C. Moore et al., *Body, Memory and Architecture* (1977).

11. See in this regard the second edition of *Perception* by J. Hochberg (1978). For an extreme view in the opposite direction, see Yi-fu Tuan, *Topophilia* (1975).

12. D. Preziosi, *The Semiotics of the Built Environment* (Indiana University Press, 1979b): 61-73; *id., Architecture, Language and Meaning* (Mouton, 1979a): Chapter VI, 'Communication and culture'.

13. Mary Douglas, 'Symbolic order in the use of domestic space', in *Man, Settlement and Urbanism*, ed. by Ucko and Tringham (1974).

14. Ulric Neisser, *Cognition and Reality* (San Francisco, 1976): 183.

15. See above, Note 4.

16. An early synthesis of this work was published as the volume *Labrys* (New Haven, 1970): see above, Note 1.

17. Not included in the present study are analyses of the buildings currently being excavated in the remarkable Minoan city on the southern coast of the island of Thera (Santorini), begun in May, 1967 by Dr. Spyridon Marinatos, and the Greek Archaeological Service. Buried under many meters of volcanic sediment, this Minoan 'Pompeii' promises to strikingly augment our picture of the Minoan culture. In some cases, houses remain largely intact up to their second storeys, and many of the structural members which have disappeared in Cretan ruins are here present. Because excavation is still in progress, and published plans are still largely provisional, the Theran material has not been included in our survey. An examination of the plans published to date (for which see our bibliography below) has revealed formative organizations which support the conclusions reached in the present study.

Abbreviations

The following is a list of frequently cited journals, articles, and volumes with reports of excavations and studies pertaining to Minoan Crete and the Bronze Age Aegean areas.

AA	Archäologischer Anzeiger
AAA	Arkhaiologika Analekta ex Athinōn
AE	Arkhaiologiki Ephemeris
AEAD	Ancient Egyptian Architectural Design (A. Badawy 1965)
AJA	American Journal of Archaeology
AM	Mitteilungen des Deutschen Archäologischen Instituts/Athenische Abteilung
Ann	Annuario della Scuola archeologica italiana di Atene
ArchRep	Archaeological Reports (Society for Promotion of Hellenic Studies)
AS	Anatolian Studies
BCH	Bulletin de Correspondence Hellénique
BdA	Bolletino d'Arte
BSA	Annual of the British School at Athens
CAH	Cambridge Ancient History
Dheltion	Arkhaiologikon Dheltion
DMG	Documents in Mycenaean Greek (M. Ventris and J. Chadwick 1956)
Ergon	To Ergon tis Arkaiologikis Etaireias
EtCret	Etudes Crétoises
GBA	Greece in the Bronze Age (E.T. Vermeule 1964)
GerasKer	Geras Keramopoulou
CFFC	Guide des fouilles françaises en Crète (Tire and van Effenterre 1966)

Guida	Guida degli scavi italiani in Creta (L. Pernier and L. Banti 1947)
Gournia	Gournia, Vasiliki and Other Prehistoric Sites in Eastern Crete (H. Boyd et al. 1908)
Handbook	A Handbook to the Palace of Minos at Knossos (J.D.S. Pendelbury, 1933)
Hanf	Studies Presented to George M.A. Hanfmann (1971)
Hesp	Hesperia
ILN	Illustrated London News
JdI	Jahrbuch des Deutschen Archäologischen Instituts
JHS	Journal of Hellenic Studies
JRIBA	Journal of the Royal Institute of British Architects
KrKhr	Kretika Khronika
MMA	Mycenae and the Mycenaean Age (G. Mylonas 1966)
MonAnt	Monumenti Antichi
MPPAO	Minoan Palace Planning and Its Origins (D. Preziosi 1968)
MRIL	Memorie delle Reale Istituto Lombardo
Mycenae	Mycenae, An Archaeological History and Guide (A. Wace 1949)
OpArc	Opuscula Archaeologica
OpAth	Opuscula Atheniensis
PAE	Praktika tis en Athenais Arkhaiologikis Etaireias
PAPS	Proceedings of the American Philosophical Society
PC	The Palaces of Crete (J.W. Graham 1962)
PM	The Palace of Minos at Knossos I, II, III, IV (A.E. Evans 1921, 1928, 1930, 1936)
PMF	Il Palazzo Minoico di Festos I, II (L. Pernier and L. Banti 1935, 1951)
PN	The Palace of Nestor at Pylos (C. Blegen et al.: I, 1966; ff.)
RT	Royal Tombs at Dendra near Midea (A. Persson 1931)
SME	The Swedish Messenia Expedition (N. Valmin 1938)
StMedArch	Studies in Mediterranean Archaeology
TPR	Town Planning Review

Troy	Troy I-IV (C. Blegen et al. 1950-1958)
TuI	Troia und Ilion I, II (W. Dörpfeld 1902)
Tylissos	Tylissos: Villas Minoennes = Etudes Crétoises III (1934)
VTM	Vaulted Tombs of Mesara (S. Xanthoudhidhes 1924)

PART ONE

Formal Organization

Introduction

GENERALITIES

Destroyed over three millennia ago, Minoan structures have been subject to break-up and dispersal of their members, settling and realignment of walls, and obliteration of nearly everything of a non-mineral nature. In many cases, even stone wall pieces of great size and weight have been removed and reused elsewhere. Apart from the Minoan city currently being excavated beneath the volcanic soil of the island of Thera, no more than two dozen examples can be cited of structural walls remaining to a height of over a meter.[1] With precious few exceptions, our picture of Minoan architecture is almost exclusively horizontal.

The student of Minoan architecture, faced with this basic material set of circumstances, is further subject to other obstacles in the attempt to reconstruct a building's original plan and elevation. In not a few cases, latter-day restoration of the remains has taken place. This varies from simple rebuilding and cementing of ruined walls back into place so as to hold together what faint traces might exist of sections of a structure, to wholesale reconstruction of large sections of a building, complete with hypothetical upper storeys, wall-decoration, and imitation half-timber frameworks. Reconstruction varies, in other words, from the very careful rebuilding of walls with extant fallen material by the skillful eyes and hands of the Greek Restoration Service under the guidance of a structure's excavators, to the transformation of a structure into something very like a tourist museum (as with the great palatial compound at Knossos).[2] In the case of the latter, it is not so much the character of the 'reconstitutions' which hinders the student of Minoan architecture (all of the details of which can

— and have been — debated at great length)[3] as the loss to future study of whole sections of the building by having been effectively cemented over.

Nevertheless, we can reasonably piece together a picture of what Minoan buildings (generally) may have looked like by weighing various fragments of comparative evidence against each other: the structural disposition of the plans themselves, new three-dimensional evidence from the Thera excavations, and pictorial evidence from the Minoan visual arts regarding the appearance of typical buildings and cityscapes.[4] To this evidence may be added broader inferences from our knowledge both of contemporary architecture outside of Crete — for example the Aegean area, or Egypt and the Near East — as well as from our general understanding of architectural composition, including the traditions of building which have a long history in the Aegean of today.[5]

We know, for example, that Minoan buildings were almost invariably *multi-storeyed,* having two or three floors (and in some exceptional cases, such as the palatial compound at Knossos, perhaps four or five). It is clear from extant plans that the exterior surfaces of Minoan structures were rarely entirely flat or lying in a single plane, but rather were highly articulated into alternating recesses and projections. We can also reasonably infer, on the basis of differing thicknesses of various interior walls, that their roof lines may well have been stepped: higher flat roofs over sections of a building with thicker walls, lower flat roofs over those sections with thinner walls. It is also apparent from the extant remains that Minoan buildings were *materially composite,* having been constructed out of combinations of stone (either finely hewn and squared or as piled, irregular rubble), wood (often used as a 'half-timber' framework arranged horizontally and vertically, with stone filling between, not unlike the familiar construction of mediaeval Europe), and clay or plaster (used as filling between rubble stone, and to provide a finely smoothed surface on the inside and outside of walls).

It seems evident that lighter materials (such as timber) were sometimes used to build upper storeys, and the (often staggered) flat roofs of buildings may not have been devoid of light construction in articulating verandas, clerestories, tented summer sleeping quarters, and work surfaces (for example for the drying of olives and dates).

The typical Minoan building, then, was not only multiform in its material composition, but it was also visually complex as a geometric formation. Only a very few Minoan freestanding buildings were simple rectangular boxes; invariably they were highly complex three-dimensional formations.

In addition, there is strong evidence for the fact that Minoan buildings were highly colorful, particularly on the inside. The new evidence of wall painting from Thera indicates that the Minoans painted almost any conceivable interior surface — walls, ceilings, floors, door jambs and window sills — in bright, contrastive colors, with figured scenes and/or geometric decoration. This decoration, moreover, does not seem to be confined to great mansions and 'palaces', but is characteristic of relatively modest houses. Our evidence for the external coloring of buildings is less secure: while visual representations of houses normally show facades highly articulated with contrasting colors, the evidence from the remains themselves generally indicates that exterior wall surfaces were mostly washed over with simple white or beige plaster. Nevertheless, some painting should have been used as a preservative for exposed timber in walls, and if such a procedure was consistent with the multicolored painting of interior wall timbers, then the outer facades may also have been multicolored to a certain extent. Analogous practices are found in contemporary Egypt,[6] as well as later Greece.[7]

The plans of Minoan buildings are similarly complex, often resembling a jigsaw puzzle of rooms of various sizes, corridors, light-wells, courtyards, and stairwells (often two or three in houses of relatively modest size). A characteristic feature of many Minoan buildings is that it is often the case that only a portion of ground-floor rooms are accessible from that level. Some rooms have no apparent access from immediately contiguous rooms, but must be reached (either by ladders or wooden stairs no longer extant) from a second storey. In effect, such ground-floor rooms form appendages to a higher storey but at a lower level. Such rooms may have served as 'basement' storage cells. A striking example of this arrangement may be seen in the 'Villa Rurale' at Gortyn, where more than a third of the rooms on the ground floor are annexes of the second storey (Figure I.1).[8]

These complexities of plan arrangement are not the result of the agglutinative addition of space-cells to each other over periods of time, as was once thought, but are the result of intentional initial design and construction, as detailed structural and modular analyses have shown.[9]

Minoan interior spaces tend to be squarish in plan, except for corridors, or rooms given over to storage (which are rectangular, and often long and narrow), or some internal courtyards. Ceiling heights tend to be uniform as far as the evidence allows us to judge, normally between three and four meters. In general, rooms open into each other, or jointly open onto common interior chambers; corridors become more numerous in large buildings. It is frequently the case that rooms have multiple entrances, and in a typical house plan there will exist many choices of passage, and a variety of ways of getting from one part of a building to another, even in houses of modest size.

Almost without exception, Minoan ground plans are not bilaterally symmetrical (in contrast to contemporary Egyptian buildings, where the reverse is the case[10]). Upon entering a building, one is normally confronted with a choice of movement to various parts of the structure. Rooms within tend to be clustered into zones or suites of common function: residence, storage, work space, etc. These clusters of space-cells themselves describe complex configurations when taken as a whole, each configuration or aggregate of cells interlocked with the next. It is normally the case that each cell-cluster is controlled by one doorway. Figure I.2 strikingly illustrates the internal functional zoning of a typical Minoan house, the 'House of the Chancel Screen' at Knossos, in comparison with an Egyptian house of the Amarna period.

THE MINOAN GROUNDPLAN

No two Minoan houses are identical in plan.[11] A good illustration of this characteristic of the corpus may be found in the plan of part of the settlement at Tylissos, consisting of three contemporary structures (Houses A, B, and C) (Figure I.3).

Houses A and C include extensive residential quarters, whereas

B may have served as a storage/warehouse for House A. Indeed, it may have been joined to the latter at the level of the second storey, as shown in the inset diagram in Figure I.3.[12]

The similarities among Minoan houses lie in details of organization and in relationships among components rather than in identity of overall ground plans and geometric configuration of members. Even in Minoan towns, closely packed and contiguous houses are not 'row houses' as such – in other words, more or less identical structures aligned together along a street – but rather tend to be strikingly different in internal arrangement. Nor is this characteristic necessarily the result of piecemeal in-filling of an urban fabric, as illustrated in the plan of Quarter Delta at Mallia (Figure I.4).

The house along the street were built at the same time (as indicated by the uniform facade articulation along the street, itslef semi-autonomous of the internal spatial subdivisions of the houses behind), but each house reveals different internal arrangements.[13]

The kind of internal spatial complexity exhibited by the Minoan house is well illustrated by the following example, House C at Tylissos (shown in Figure I.3 in relationship to its immediate context).[14]

Entrance is gained at *E* in Figure I.5, the only means of access to the building. One enters into a square vestibule (cell 0) to the right of which is a porter's room (cell 1). The vestibule gives onto a long corridor (cell 2), off which are seven doorways. These doorways, otherwise identical in formation and size, control very different functional zones beyond: *a* opens into a rectangular room serving as a work space, with an interior storage-closet (cells 3 and 3a); *b* is a door to a closet under the stair; *c* opens into an L-shaped corridor beyond which is the central room of the house, perhaps a shrine (cells 4 and 5); door *e* opens onto a stairway to the second floor; *g* and *f* open into a series of storage magazines. Only door *d* gives access to the private living quarters of the house, opening first into a second long corridor which descends a few steps to an additional door straight ahead (*h*). The latter opens into yet another corridor. The latter has two doorways: *k*, to the left, giving access to a large stairwell, and *i*, leading into the main living halls of the house. There is another means of entrance into the domestic quarter via a corridor perpendicular to that beyond door *d*, leading to doorway *j*, which opens onto a room with a raised hearth/platform. The latter room has two doorways on its right side, one leading into a second chamber illuminated by a large window in its wall, opening onto the light-well portion of the hall system (cell A), and a second door (*1*) leading via a long corridor to a third stairwell, and, beyond door *m*, to a latrine.

The main hall system of the house (cells A, B, C) consists of the aforementioned light-well (cell A), an antechamber beyond two columns (B), and, beyond two square piers flanking three doors, an interior hall (C).

Two oddities of the plan may also be mentioned. Cell 11 is a narrow room enterable only from outside the house, with no interior communication beyond this. Cells X and X' are large square rooms, most likely storage cellars, with access only from the second storey.

While the overall plan may be inscribed within a square, its outer trace consists of deeply recessed planes alternating with squarish projections, all of which are aligned, at their edges, with continuations of perpendicular internal walls.

A notable feature of initial entrance into the first corridor is the fact that none of the seven doorways gives any patent clue as to the functional distinctions of the zones beyond: all seven doors are of equal size and configuration (and, presumably, of similar material construction, most likely painted wood with metal fittings). Unless each of the doors were painted contrastive colors or otherwise decoratively distinguished, the stranger to the house would be at a loss to know what lay behind a given closed door.[15] No other Minoan house has an identical arrangement, and, as we have noted above, each Minoan house was strikingly different from all others. Indeed, the house immediately next door (House A), built at the same time and presumably by the same builders, has a strikingly different internal arrangement. While most of the same elements are present, they are composed and aligned to each other in different ways.

No trace of the second storey is extant, and the three stairways are preserved only partially. We may reasonably assume that this upper storey was somewhat simpler in plan, possibly (though not necessarily) of lighter construction, with larger columned halls. The existence of three separate stairwells would attest to functional differences on the upper floor: the innermost stair (near door *m*) was most likely a private family stair, leading down to the latrine; the second (and largest) stairway, off door *k*, possibly was only semi-private; and the outermost stair, off door *e*, was most likely used largely for service, being closest to the storage magazines in which would have been kept various foodstuffs: supplies of wine, oil, grain, meat and vegetables.[16]

The following diagram illustrates the division of the plan into separate functional zones, each of which consisted of a cluster or matrix of cells, controlled by a single threshold (Figure I.6).

That this is the house of a well-to-do nuclear or extended family is clear, and we may justifiably imagine that the residents were supported by groups of servants assigned to a variety of tasks, concerned with gathering, storage, transport and preparation of food, cleaning and upkeep of the house, small manufacture of tools, utensils and implements, recording of various aspects of the house economy, and control of visitors.

The function of cell 11 is unknown, but may possibly be concerned with the storage of domestic animals, by analogy with houses elsewhere.[17] Also by analogy, the cell at the geometric center of the plan may have been a family or house shrine.[18]

The existence of so many internal doorways was patently a guarantee of privacy and security, not only by their number, but more importantly by their disposition: the entrance to the private quarters is in no way marked *vis-à-vis* other doorways, existing simply as the second door on the right of a corridor with seven identical doors.

A glance at the diagram in Figure I.7 will give some idea of the relative proportions given over in the house to spaces of various function.

A good deal of space is devoted to the complementary functions of circulation among cell-clusters and their separation. Functional zones, in other words, do not directly open into each other, but are separated by corridors and the distances they afford. Each cell cluster functions semi-autonomously, and we may imagine that the business of each area was carried on with minimal intrusion from that of another area.

The differences in the size and proportions of the three stair-wells are of interest. The smallest 'back stair' near door *m* contrasts with the significantly larger private stair beyond door *k*. The latter may be considered the 'main' family stair as well as a possible passage for guests. Of intermediate size is the outermost stairway, off door *e*, the one most likely used for service.

The latter stair stands in contrast to the two stairs of the residential quarter as public vs. private, whereas the two private stairs are graded iconically by the contrast larger : smaller :: more public : more private.

The domestic quarter contrasts with all other quarters on the basis of the nature of its internal circulatory arrangements. All other quarters or cell-clusters are dead-ended appendages to the main circulatory corridor; each is a cul-de-sac. The living halls are distinguished from these by the fact that there are multiple circulatory connections among space-cells. Emphasis is given to greater circulatory freedom. Cell D contains four separate doorways, each giving onto a different room or corridor. Whereas the major hall system (cells A, B, C) is accessed to the remainder of the cluster only through cell C, the latter has two doors, one onto the primary corridor, one onto cell D. The light-well cell (A) provides visual connection and ventilation to interior cell E by means of a window running the full length of one of its walls. Only cell F (the latrine) is a cul-de-sac proper. As we shall see in the discussions below, it is the character of these *relationships among cells,* and their contrasts to other kinds of relationships within other cell-clusters, which tend to remain constant across otherwise widely different house plans in the Minoan corpus.[19]

House C at Tylissos has been looked at in some detail in order to begin our demonstration that close analysis of these highly intricate and labyrinthine Minoan buildings reveals carefully structured patterns of spatial organization and functional composition. As we shall see below, everything about an architectonic formation is significant in some way, but not everything is significant in the same way. But we can only learn a limited amount by the study — no matter how detailed — of any one structure, or of only a small sample of structures, no matter how seemingly 'typical'. Certain fundamental patterns of formal organization can only be perceived by the comparative study of many buildings. In this way we will learn to distinguish what is invariant and constant from what is a contextual variation of some common pattern.

In looking back at Tylissos C, for example, we may well ask a number of important questions, which, while obvious, may not necessarily be immediate in our perusal of the plan. For example, are there fixed patterns of spatial positioning of various functional cell-clusters? Will it be the case that the main alignments of one cluster (e.g. the hall system matrix) are always perpendicular to another (e.g. the storage magazine group) or others? Is the placement of the hall system invariantly on the northern side of a house, and is the storage area usually on the west? Is the hall system always the 'innermost' cluster of a house? Are the functional distinctions among stairways in a house always correlated to distinctions in relative size or in orientation or in placement?

As we shall observe below, only some of these patterns are replicated elsewhere. For example, there tends to be a high probability that storage areas are found on the western side of houses, whereas by contrast the domestic quarters may occur anywhere. And yet the latter reveal their own invariances of placement, not strictly tied to cardinal direction, but rather to manner of entrance with respect to other cell-clusters, no matter where they appear in a house.[20]

PLANNING AND CONSTRUCTION

As we shall see in more detail below (Part Two), the plan of Tylissos C was laid out and executed with great care and precision on a modular grid of ropes and pegs whose proportions determined the placement and alignment of individual walls.[21] As is now apparent from extensive field surveys and measurements, Minoan buildings in general were laid out with great care and often remarkable precision, and this degree of attention given the realization of a design extended both to public and private construction, to vast compounds as well as more modest houses.[22]

In this section we shall look at the evidence derived from surveys for the planning and execution of buildings. We will examine the layout of several relatively simple structures, and discuss the implications of this evidence for our understanding of the formal spatial organization of Minoan groundplans.

Excavated in a two season campaign by Spyridon Marinatos in

1925-1926, the simple structure at Tou Vrakhnou O Lakkos (here-after TVOL) stands near the village of Kouse, about an hour's walk south of the great palatial compound of Phaistos (Figure I.8).[23]

In outline, the house is very nearly a perfect square, some 11 meters on a side. What remains today is a rubble wall foundation enclosing a large square main chamber (possibly an open court), surrounded on two sides by subsidiary rooms, and the trace of a two-flight stairwell at the southeastern corner. The walls are preserved to heights of slightly less than a meter, and are con-structed of large irregular stones with small stone packing in the interstices. Originally, these rubble walls were brought out to a uniform surface plane by means of a clay stucco, traces of which remain in fragment.

At the four corners of the structure are fairly well-squared corner stones, probably set in place first in the construction of the house. Within, there are four ground-level doorway thresholds, including the only exterior entrance, to the southwest. Passage between the main room and the stairway would have been made over a step above ground level. There is no clear way of telling if the two northeastern chambers (cells 4 and 5) communicated with other ground floor rooms: access may have been possible only from the second storey. Outside the main entrance is a finely hewn square block 0.40 EW by 0.50 NS.

In general, it appears that this simple house was very carefully laid out. The north-south length is ±11.00, the east-west length ±10.95, an error of ±0.05. The plan in Figure I.9 gives the measurements of the walls and interior spaces.

The walls themselves exhibit two thicknesses: ±0.80 for the exterior walls and all interior walls except those separating cells 2 and 3, and 5 and 6a, and 6a and 6b; the latter average 0.50-0.55 in width. The three interior doorways measure ±0.80 square, whereas the main door is ±1.00 wide.

As indicated in the plan above, the dimensions suggest a simple fractional modularity in the disposition of the structural frame: within a square of ±11.00, there is an internal square of ±6.00 (the main chamber). If we include the two outer walls of cell 1 in this division of the plan, the north-south length of the structure divides at ±6.80 + ±4.20, while the east-west width divides at ±6.75-6.80 + ±4.15-4.20.

Considering the care by which the building was constructed, we take it as a reasonable assumption that these regularities are not fortuitous. In other words, to a certain extent the dimensions of walls and interior spaces should have been the result of a clarity and economy in the realization of the design. By such an assumption, the dimensions of the building should represent some simple fractions and multiples of each other.

Thus, ±4.20 : ±6.80 :: 21 : 34, or a ratio of approximately 3 : 5. If the overall length and width, then, are taken to be 8x, the smaller chambers would be 3x in depth, and the main cell 5x in length and width. What then is 'x'? If 8x = ±11.00, x = ±1.375.

We may then assume that the basic module employed in layout and construction would have been ±1.375, a dimension which itself may have been some simple fraction (or, more likely, some simple multiple) of whatever unit of measurement had been employed by the builders.

Let us look closely for a moment at the implications of these dimensions for understanding the procedures of layout. We must first ask what the relationship of the assumed module (±1.375) is to the two smaller dimensions exhibited by the structure: namely, the two wall widths of ±0.80 and ±0.50 (as well as the width of ±1.00 of the entrance way). In the case of the wall widths, these dimensions of course are rough averages,[24] considering the ruined nature of the rubble walls; but for the moment let us consider the reasonable assumption that the wall widths would have been made to some close approximation of a simple modular length (for reasons of economy and structural consistency). If the wall-widths are simple whole number modular values, then:

1. If ±1.375 = 2 modular units, the module = ±0.68750 (0.690)
2. If   „   = 3   „   „   , „   „   = ±0.45630 (0.460)
3. If   „   = 4   „   „   , „   „   = ±0.34375 (0.340)
4. If   „   = 5   „   „   , „   „   = ±0.27500 (0.275)
5. If   „   = 6   „   „   , „   „   = ±0.22917 (0.230)

All of these latter are possible units and yield the same proportions for the overall dimensions of the structure. But what of the wall widths (±0.50, ±0.80) and the main door width (±1.00)?

Following the implications of our initial assumptions, these dimensions should be expressive of simple fractions of the modular length, i.e. simple unit lengths. Calling the larger wall width A and the smaller width B, note the following:

1. A = 0.8625 or 1¼   x 0.690; B = 0.5175 or ¾   x 0.690
2. A = 0.86   or 1¾   x 0.460; B = 0.46   or 1   x 0.460
3. A = 0.86   or 2½   x 0.340; B = 0.51   or 1½ x 0.340
4. A = 0.825 or 3   x 0.275; B = 0.55   or 2   x 0.275
5. A = 0.855 or 3½   x 0.230; B = 0.46   or 2   x 0.230

We must reject all solutions except number 4 for the following reasons: (1) All others involve fractional quantities or combinations of whole numbers and fractions; (2) All others express the ratio between A and B (which, by our assumption, should be simple) in complex terms; and (3) the ratio between A and B expressed in modular terms by solution 4 is simple and congruent with that between the smaller and larger squares of the overall design, i.e. there is a simple homogeneity expressed by this solution: large square : smaller length :: width A : width B. In other words, 8 : 5 :: 3 : 2.

Figure I.10 illustrates the modular solution.

The modular length deduced from the overall layout, ±1.375, thus equals exactly four units. The overall square is 40 units on a side; the 'inner square' is 25 units, the width of the peripheral cells is 15 units. The main door opening, ±1.00, may have been intended to be reduced to a simple unit width of three (i.e. 0.825) when the wooden door jambs were set in place. Each jamb would then be ca. 0.10 thick, a dimension consistent with that of extant jamb traces.[25] A similar situation might have existed with the emplacement of the wooden jambs of the interior doors, reducing their ±0.80 width to two modular units or 0.55, again allowing for jambs of c.0.13 in thickness.

In this analysis we have assumed two things: first, that the house should have been conceived in simple modular terms, and secondly, that the execution of the design followed a layout procedure not unlike the grid-planning evidenced elsewhere, both in contemporary Egypt, as well as more generally in later Western architectural practice.

The evidence for the former assumption comes directly from the clarity and consistency (and economy) of the construction itself, which is patent even in the ruined state of the remains. We may surmise that the design of the building was executed in the simplest and most economical fashion as follows:

1. Lay out a square of ropes between four pegs put into the ground at a distance of 40 units apart. This may be done most simply in the following manner: first, stretch a cord of 40 units north-south between 2 pegs, defining the east side of the construction. So as to make the east-west extensions of 40 units parallel, do the first step at sunrise so that the first 2 pegs cast long east-west shadows, whose trace can be followed. Second, having made these two east-west lengths of cord exactly 40 units, join the two western pegs with a cord again 40 units north-south. So as to assure that the four cords are exactly perpendicular to each other as well as parallel to their opposites, as a third step either use a wooden 90° template to align the corners and/or stretch two diagonals joining opposite corner angles of equal length. These diagonals would have had to be roughly 56 units long.[26]

2. It would be most economical to have the original 40 unit cords divided into eight sections either by chalk marks or knots. An internal secondary grid would then make up a grid of 64 squares each five units square.

3. Using such a grid as a guide, lay walls along the inner edges of the overall square, forming the outer walls.

4. All interior walls would then follow the lines of the grid at points indicated in Figure I.10.[27]

The result of such a planning procedure indicates that the actual *internal* dimensions of space-cells arc *not necessarily* of simple modular lengths, being in effect metrological 'remainders' of the initial grid layout: a wall would be built on either side of a grid-cord, depending upon original design decisions or *ad hoc* decisions made by builders in the allotment of spaces.

In the actual construction of walls, we may surmise that the four carefully squared blocks would have been first set within the corners defined by the outermost angles of the grid. Next, the four outer rubble walls would have been laid to join together each of the corner blocks. The circumferential walls of the main cell (1) would be built perpendicular to the outer walls being constructed, at a distance of 25 units from the southern and western outer edges of the latter. Next (or partly concurrently) the walls dividing what was to become the L-shaped rank of peripheral rooms would be constructed.

No trace of timber remains in the ruins, but we may expect that door and window frames (apart from thresholds) would have been of squared timber. The stairway was evidently entirely of wood above the first riser, and the top course of rubble masonry of the walls would have had longitudinal beams above, to which would be secured the transverse beams which spanned each room.

The second storey outer walls may have been somewhat thinner than those below, perhaps half-timbered. On this floor the plan of rooms would most likely have followed that of the ground floor, although the thinner wall separating cells 2 and 3 may indicate either no partition at the second storey above, or a wooden column or two rather than a wall proper.

As mentioned above, cell 1 may not have been roofed over; at any rate no trace remains of foundation supports for internal columns or piers. Cell 1 may thus have consisted of an interior courtyard roughly 17 units square, which would serve to increase the ventilation and lighting of the peripheral cells: judging from evidence elsewhere, Minoan buildings tended to have fewer (and smaller) exterior windows on their ground floors than on upper storeys, no doubt for reasons of security and privacy.

As also noted above, it is unclear whether cells 4 and 5 communicated directly with either cell 1 or cell 3, although they communicate directly with each other. Either they were accessed only from the second storey (perhaps by means of a descending flight of wooden stairs contiguous with cell 6a and internal to cell 5), or we must assume that their thresholds into either cell 1 or cell 3 were a step or two above the other ground-floor thresholds: such a practice is not uncommon in traditional Cretan construction today.

According to its excavators, there is some evidence that cells 4 and 5 were used for food preparation and storage, probably comprising a kitchen and pantry; although if cell 1 was a court, we would expect that a certain amount of food preparation took place there, again a not infrequent practice today on the island. Cells 2 and 3 may then have served either for storage or daytime living and dining purposes, while the major 'hall system' found commonly in other construction on ground floors may have been found (if it existed here) on the second floor. The thinner wall separating cells 2 and 3, as noted above, may have supported a column or two partitioning two cells, in the manner of colonnaded hall systems elsewhere.

The roof of the house would have been flat, and accessible (probably by a continuation of stairwell 6a/6b) under a wooden clerestory, a practice for which evidence has been seen in the representation of Minoan houses in visual art[28] and by what is evidently a house model of terracotta now in the Herakleion Museum.[29] The roof itself would have been constructed by alternating registers of beams of increasingly smaller diameter, covered over by reed matting itself impregnated by a thick sheet of waterproof clay and clay aggregate.

The modular analysis given above represents what is felt to be one of the simplest and internally coherent models for the generation both of the formal design and composition of spaces, as well as the technical procedures of its material realization. This is not to claim in any conclusive sense that this was precisely the manner of the building's design and generation, but rather that our scenario is the most economical and straightforward model.

What has been suggested above is a holistic approach to solving the problem of how TVOL was planned and laid out. As will become evident below, in the detailed comparative analyses of Part Two such an approach may be employed successfully in such an inquiry. As will also be seen in that section of the study, the detailed modular proposals arrived at in the present building are supported by similar analysis of a large number of structures of various types.[30]

Our interest in the present Chapter is focussed principally upon the formal organization of the design of Minoan buildings, and our aim is to elucidate patterns of invariance and variation in such design conception. As will become evident below, there were a number of different constructional approaches employed by Minoan builders in the realization of their designs. But standing beneath these variations in material construction are certain consistencies of pattern in the formal organization of spaces, and it is the latter which is our concern here.

We have seen that TVOL was evidently conceived, formally, as a simple square-within-a-square, around the inner portion of which were deployed an L-shaped register of space-cells. This formal conception, as will become evident below, was but one of a series of structural patterns employed by Minoan designers. But as we shall presently see, this same structural framework was employed in a number of other buildings.

PATTERNS OF INVARIANCE AND VARIATION

Illustrated in Figure I.11 are the remains of a small structure at Rousses (hereafter RSS) excavated by Nicholas Platon in 1957, and dated by him to the Middle Minoan III period.[31] It is far removed from TVOL (which stands in the south central part of the island), built in the eastern part of Crete.

It will be immediately evident that at RSS we are dealing with a groundplan essentially identical to that of TVOL, only its mirror-reversed image. RSS consists of a rectangular frame ±10.95 NE-SW and ±8.10 NW-SE.[32] Like TVOL, it comprises a large squarish cell (1), surrounded by an L-shaped register of four smaller cells (2, 3, 4, 5). Cell 5, like the similarly numbered cell at TVOL, is fairly large, but here there are no traces of a stairwell. Unlike TVOL, RSS had a squared central pillar in cell 1, attesting to the existence of a ceiling.

Both houses are similar in the sense that the deployment of smaller chambers is identical: two small cells stand at the back side of cell 1, and two along its flank. But unlike TVOL, there are unambiguous traces of direct communication between the lateral cells (4 and 5) and both cells 1 and 3.

The structure is badly ruined on its left flank, although the position and direction of the original walls is clear. The western end of the northwestern wall abruptly thickens, as indicated in the plan, near the partition between cells 3 and 4, revealing a characteristic feature of Minoan exterior surfaces; although as we shall see it is not always correlated directly with perpendicular internal wall-ends.

Another possible distinguishing feature of the building is a conjectural second door along the front (southeastern) side, into cell 5. The evidence, however, is not secure enough to fully assert its existence, for the wall is badly denuded at this point.

The structure at RSS was built essentially in the same manner as that of TVOL, using similar materials, although it is doubtful whether it extended beyond a single storey. In addition, close modular analysis has revealed that it was planned and laid out in the same manner as the house at TVOL (see below, Part Two), employing the same modular divisions: recall that TVOL was 11 meters square (= 40 by 40 units). RSS is approximately 11 by 8.10-8.40 meters, or 40 by 30 modular units.[33]

However, the excavators suggest that the structure was not a private house (at least at the time of its destruction),[34] but rather a *hieron* or building devoted to religious purposes: a number of patently religious artifacts were found in the ruins. Such buildings are extremely rare in Minoan architecture, where there are few 'temples' as such (in the sense of major public monuments familiar in the Near East and Egypt at this time), only fairly small sanctuaries of limited number.[35] By and large, Minoan worship appears to have been admixed with secular construction, e.g. small shrines within private domestic structures. As we shall see below, while the great 'palaces' in the major cities of Knossos, Phaistos and Mallia incorporated shrines and areas of worship, these are relatively small in size and visually secluded within an overwhelmingly secular[36] context. Apparently a good deal of Minoan religious activity centered on sanctuaries high in the hills and mountains, and in caves already hallowed for many centuries.

What is of immediate interest here, however, is the fact that at RSS we are dealing with a formative pattern essentially identical to that of the (domestic) structure at TVOL. Both have an identical structural framework pattern of walls and cells, the major difference between the two being the mirror reversal of the layout. As noted above (and explored in detail in Part Two) the modular organizations of the two buildings are also similar.

It would seem that we are dealing here with some type of standard pattern common to these two structures (of different size and, more significantly, of different basic function), and we may well imagine this 'square-within-a-square' pattern as one of a series of standard pattern-book designs employed by Minoan designers for a variety of purposes. Such a situation is entirely consistent with architectural practice of other places and periods.

We may also consider the emergent fact that in the conceptual organization of the Minoan corpus, there existed a certain semi-autonomy with respect to various levels of architectonic structure. Note that in our explorations thus far we have examined something of the nature of material (constructional) organization, formal spatial order, and modular organization. As we broaden our view of the corpus, it becomes evident that these three aspects of architectural organization are *not necessarily* directly tied to one another in an invariant manner. In other words:

1. The same modular unit is employed in structures of different absolute size, orientation, and internal order;

2. the 'centripetal' plan-pattern can be employed under similar contrastive circumstances, and that moreover:

3. this structural frame pattern remains topologically constant despite geometric mirror reversal;

4. the same structural frame of walls and cells can be employed to different spatial and communicative effect by employing different connections among cells. As is evident by a perusal of both TVOL and RSS, their circulatory patterns are in part contrastive;

5. the same structural frame can be employed (and, we may presume, evidently successfully) for quite different functional purposes.

These are concretely obvious yet very crucial points to bear in mind as we extend our view to encompass greater portions of the Minoan corpus.

If we look, for example, at the house plan in Figure I.12, we shall find essentially the same kind of structural frame as that employed by the designers of TVOL and RSS:

Pictured is a farmhouse discovered by Dr. Platon in 1952 at a place called Riza about a half-hour's walk from the village of Akhladhia. Called by its excavators Akhladhia A (hereafter AKHL),[37] it is one of two structures on the upper flank of a hill: structure B is separated from A by a narrow corridor/passageway, and both are constructed within terracing walls on their outer flanks. Only part of structure B is extant.

The plan of AKHL is essentially complete, and describes a rectangle approximately 14 by 19 meters with its longitudinal axis oriented NE-SW. Unlike TVOL, the house's outer facade is not uniplanar, but has three projecting wall curtains. One to the southwest divides that wall roughly in half along its extent; one to the northeast has a return jog between the two back registers of rooms, and one to the east jogs between the entrance cell (h) and the large cell i to its north. In all three cases, the indentations are aligned with interior perpendicular walls.

Cells a-b-c comprise a pillared and columned hall system, divided into two sections by a pier-and-door partition (PDP) with four openings. The larger cell (a-b) has a row of columns (bases only are extant) parallel to the latter, across the room's middle: in effect these comprise three distinct cells. Cell c has two stone benches along its southeastern and northwestern walls, joined into an L: these seating arrangements suggest a possible dining area. Immediately behind cell c are two small chambers (m and n) which according to the building's excavators may have served as kitchen and pantry.

The hall system proper, with its three aligned cells, communicates externally onto the central corridor space to the right by means of four contiguous doorways, of which three open into cell b and one into cell c.

The entrance vestibule (cell h) opens beyond into an L-shaped corridor which is partially paved with flagstones (g) (and hence may perhaps have been an open light-well); beyond this corridor are two small cells, rooms f and e. The latter has an internal window opening back into the largest cell of the house, room i, where remains of a centrally placed pillar base are found. The principal entrance to cell i is by means of a doorway immediately adjacent to the main entrance into the house, to the south.

Beyond cells g, f and e are three interconnected cells (o, p, q) which are only accessible from the outside back flank of the house: it is possible that this cell-cluster was a stable.

It will be evident that cells h, g, f, e, i are similar in their relative disposition to the plan of TVOL: in both cases we may see the same pattern of a large square cell surrounded on two flanks by a register of four smaller cells. But while the pattern is realized as a square, as at TVOL, the absolute position of the bank of small cells replicates that of RSSS. But the plan of AKHL differs from both in its circulatory pattern: here the main house entrance is not into the large cell, but into one of the small cells (here, cell h). In addition, the connection between the large cell and its subsidiaries is singular, occurring only with cell h, the entrance vestibule, although there is visual connection between cells i and e by means of the large internal window shown on the plan.[38]

It is of note that the absolute sizes of the square plan of TVOL and the square cell-cluster forming a portion of AKHL are very nearly identical: the overall sizes here are ±10.75-11.00. Furthermore, the proportions of the square cell to its peripheral register of cells is the same as at TVOL, namely 3 : 2.[39] These proportions are clear despite the occasional misalignments of walls: AKHL was clearly not as carefully laid out as either TVOL or even RSS.[40]

But at AKHL this structural pattern was put to uses largely different from those at TVOL: here, the living quarters of the house, consisting of a traditional hall system,[41] are appended to the square cluster h-g-f-e-i, the latter at least in part given over to work space.[42]

Thus it may be seen that this structural pattern is employed in yet a third functional manner, and yet a third circulatory fashion; moreover it serves as but a section of the overall house, a semi-autonomous cell-cluster in its own right.

There appears to have been no second storey in the house, although room for a stairwell does exist within the L-shaped corridor g, and precedent does exist for stairwells in similar places elsewhere.[43]

Yet another example of the structural frame appearing in the three structures above may be seen in Figure I. 13, illustrating the plan of House Zeta Alpha (hereafter ML ZA) at Mallia, dated to the Middle Minoan IIIb/Late Minoan Ia Period.[44] The house consists of two major internal zones, and three entrances; the western third of the structure comprises the residential cluster proper, while the remainder to the east is devoted to work space, storage and other functions.[45]

The overall plan bears an interesting resemblance to that of AKHL above: the western third of ML ZA corresponds to the southwestern domestic quarter of AKHL, while the eastern section consists, in both cases, of a square compound divided into larger and smaller cells. In both houses, entrance to the domestic cluster is gained by means of a north-south corridor from the street entrance and a left turn (to the west) into this area.

The plan of ML ZA is considerably more complicated than that of AKHL, and there is evidence for alteration and internal change in the original plan, particularly on the eastern side. ML ZA is much larger in size than AKHL, being ±17.50 by ±24.30 along its outer trace. But a careful modular analysis of the building's dimensions indicates that ML ZA was conceived as a 2 : 3 rectangle. As indicated in the measured plan shown in Figure I.14, the builders constructed the northern and southern outer walls on the outer (rather than the inner) face of the original planning grid. Lengths a – a' and b – b' are, respectively, ±16.10 and ±16.15. Note that 16.20 : 24.30 :: 2 : 3.

The eastern two-thirds of the structure forms a very nearly perfect square, ±16.00 by ±16.05, and the western domestic quarter's width is one-half this dimension, as indicated in the plan. The major divisions of the eastern quarter are thus isomorphic with the plans of the three buildings examined above (TVOL, RSS, AKHL). Indeed, there are similarities also in absolute size: the 'inner square' of ML ZA is equal in size to the 'outer' squares of the other buildings:

1. ML ZA : ±10.75 NS x ±10.75 EW
2. TVOL : ±11.00 NS x ±10.95 EW
3. RSS : ± 8.10 NS x ±10.95 EW[46]
4. AKHL : ±10.75 NS x ±11.00 EW

In addition, both ML ZA and AKHL are 2 : 3 rectangles. The overall modular dimensions of ML ZA are 60 units NS by 90 units east-west (the unit here again being ±0.270);[47] the domestic quarter is 30 by 60 units; the hall system proper is 20 by 30 units; the eastern square is 60 by 60 units, with an inner square of 40 by 40 units. The rectangular room at the southeastern corner of the building approximates 20 by 30 units, the size of the covered portion of the hall system at the northwestern corner.

Figure I.15 indicates the modular organization of the building, as realized by means of the standard modular planning grid. It is of interest that whereas the major through-walls of the structure are positioned along major modular subdivisions of the grid, a number of smaller internal walls are not so fixed. Measurements indicate that the latter walls were laid out *after* more major partition walls were already in place, their positioning taken from the faces of already existing walls. In the case of the three storage magazines on the northeastern corner of the building, it is clear that the builders measured out 10 + 10 + 10 units from the face of the adjacent major wall. As shown in Figure I.16, a number of sections of the house were erected in similar fashion.

Here it is clear that there is evidence for some of the procedural details followed by Minoan builders in laying out structures, and this evidence points to an internal chronology of construction. The builders of ML ZA may thus have used the initial planning grid to fix the position of major load-bearing and boundary walls only, and then, having constructed those walls (at least up to the level of their bottom courses), used their existing faces to lay out subsidiary walls.

This kind of modular information, coupled with an examination of the material details of wall-bonding, can provide us with a more detailed scenario of the chronology of construction, as well as evidence for later alterations to existing structural frameworks.

Before returning to a consideration of the significance of the centripetal structural framework pattern seen here at ML ZA, let us consider briefly the formal organization of the domestic cluster of cells in the structure.

A look at the isometric reconstruction in Figure I.13 above indicates the presence of characteristic features of Minoan house organization. In addition to the hall system proper in the north-western corner of the building — consisting of two internal cells separated by a pier-and-door-partition (PDP), and opening onto what was evidently a private garden or court[48] — we find a small stairway adjacent to the entrance to the hall system, an internal sunken cell across an intermediary vestibule (of a type referred to in the literature as a 'lustral basin'),[49] and to the south of this an additional series of halls or rooms partitioned again by PDPs. This latter quarter was originally an L-shaped cluster of cells; the thin wall fragments in the angle of the hall system are evidently a later modification. Beyond this angle is a small projection from the southwestern corner of the house, serving as a narrow latrine.

The main entrance to the house opens into a vestibule perhaps serving as a position for a *concierge*; before the doorway straight ahead is a stairwell to the second storey. Beyond that door, the north-south corridor is bordered by two open cells, evidently used for workspace and storage. The corridor ends at two doors to the north: that to the left controlling access to the domestic quarter, and that straight ahead leading to a large cell within which is a rectangular sunken pavement, of unknown function.[50] At the southeastern corner of the latter is a small door leading to the area of the storage magazines,[51] to the south of which, beyond the traces of ruined walls and later intrusions is a curious rectangular cell at the southeastern corner of the building.

The latter is entered through a PDP, and comprises two main sections: an upper section containing a single column at the center of its western side, and beyond this a sunken area. The entire cell is bordered by stone benches on all four walls. We do not know what function this chamber served; it may well have been a meeting place of some kind, a club house or a site for some group performance. The fact that this chamber was most likely semi-public in function is indicated by its closeness to two doorways leading to the outside, a larger door opening southward onto the public street, and a smaller entrance in the eastern wall, perhaps communicating with a side alley or courtyard between ML ZA and whatever structures may have existed further to the east.

The tight controls afforded various clusters of cells in ML ZA is reminiscent in spirit of the house at Tylissos looked at above (TYL C): one door only controls access to the entire domestic quarter in both houses, and a single doorway connects the area of the storage magazines with the remainder of the house. Both ML ZA and TYL C reveal a major long entrance corridor to which are appended various contrastive functional zones. Similarly, the outermost stairway of ML ZA, near the entrance vestibule, recalls the stairway off the entrance corridor at TYL C, and both may have provided a means for immediate service of the second storey without disturbance of the domestic quarter proper on the ground floor.

The outer facade of the building is not uniplanar. In the area of the major entrance the street facade is set back in a wide recess. This curiously resonates with a correspondingly positioned projection in the facade of the northern side, beyond the north central room: where the southern facade is recessed, the northern facade projects. Such resonances of planar harmonics are familiar in Minoan construction (a very nice and more striking example is found in a contemporary house at Mallia, House Delta Alpha, looked at in detail below): while some writers have sought to explain their occurrences as due to a desire to provide a long length of wall with greater stability,[52] I think the reasons for their existence are multiple. Whatever stability may have been conferred in a material sense (and this is itself arguable), I think that their existence is simpler and more self-referential: they provide visual interest to an otherwise uniplanar and unarticulated surface, and such shallow recesses and projections resonate consistently with general tendencies in formative organization, manifest both in coloration and sculptural morphology (see above, 'Generalities').

Of principal interest in this section has been the particular structural framework seen in various transformations at TVOL, RSS, AKHL and ML ZA. Underlying these four transformations is a *domain of spatial relationships per se,* in which a cluster of space-cells is composed in hierarchical fashion (with respect to relative size) and in geometric fashion (with respect to the positioning of cells of different size). We may characterize this set of relationships as follows.

Within a structural frame of rectilinear formation (normally, in the examples we have seen, square) there are composed five cells of which one is significantly larger and the others are appended to it in an L-shaped register, occupying two sides of the former. The remaining two sides of the larger cell form the corner boundary of the overall structure itself.

This structural framework may stand alone, or may comprise a portion (in the two examples we have, the right side) of a larger construction. Moreover, this spatial patterning is semi-autonomous of specific functional usages, and, in addition, its component space cells may intercommunicate in any number of ways.

What then is invariant to this pattern of formal organization? And what is variable?

To a certain extent, there is a constancy of absolute size: with the exception of one of the dimensions of RSS, all are ± 11.00 square. A second constancy involves the relative proportion of the larger cell to its subsidiaries: the smaller cells are to the larger, generally, as 1 is to 2.

Another apparent invariant is the geometric relationship between the larger cell and the smaller cells: in all cases, the latter are positioned around two flanks of the former. In addition, the smaller cells invariably number four.[53]

This structural frame is *not necessarily* tied to (a) the absolute position of the L-register *vis-à-vis* the large cell; (b) the absolute size of each of the smaller cells; (c) the internal nature of the cells (note that the large cell at TVOL was apparently an open court, and that at AKHL one of the small cells was probably a light-well); or (d) the distribution of functions among the cells.

It is apparent, then, that the descriptive definition of this 'centripetal' structural pattern must focus upon underlying *sets of relationships* with respect to which each of the examples we have examined is a specific *contextual variant* rather than an increasingly more complex elaboration of some single fixed material pattern. This structural pattern is a pattern of association among cells of two size types, and comprises a matrix of relationships among cells. It is this matrix of relationships, just decribed, which is invariant behind the multiple realizational variants examined above.

As we seek to define the sets of constancies manifested in Minoan architecture, we shall find a variety of invariants governing the formative organization of cell-matrices, as well as other aspects of Minoan design. This centripetal matrix, dwelled upon in some detail, is but one such syntactic pattern.

NOTES

1. Notable examples are the palatial compounds of Knossos and Phaistos, the houses at Knossos and Tylissos, portions of the 'Little Palace' at Haghia Triadha near Phaistos. On the Thera material, not specifically examined in the present study because excavation is still continuing, see the reports begun by Dr. Spyridon Marinatos in *AAA* I(1) (1968): 3-9; I(3) (1968): 213-220; II(3) (1969): 374-375; III(1) (1970): 1-5, and continuing, and also the volumes entitled *Thera* (Volumes I, 1968 *et seq.*), appearing annually. Good plans and photographs may be found in Volume VI: 197.

2.   The discovery and excavation of Knossos by Sir Arthur Evans, beginning in 1900, is documented in the volumes *The Palace of Minos at Knossos,* Volumes I-IV (1921-1936), where detailed and extensive justifications for the Knossian restorations are given. See the bibliography below on Knossos. By contrast, the restorations of the similar compounds at Phaistos and Mallia, excavated concurrently by Italian, French and Greek archaeologists are extremely modest. In the latter cases, the visitor will find reconstruction dates stamped into the cement of rebuilt sections.

3.   Many of Evans' reconstructions were imperative if a clear picture of this multi-storied compound were to be read unambiguously: see the sensible remarks of J.W. Graham in his survey *The Palaces of Crete* (1962): 26, 117-119.

4.   At Knossos, for example, there were found the fragments of what may have been a mosaic depicting buildings in a (Minoan?) town (see below under Knossos), and a number of Minoan frescoes depict facade portions of Minoan buildings. A recently discovered fresco from Thera depicts townscapes on islands, but it is unclear whether these are intended as Minoan (Theran) or foreign: see *Thera VI.*

5.   As we shall have occasion to observe in the analyses below, a number of constructional details found today in Cretan and other island buildings replicate practices dating from Minoan times. References to such practices will be found in the general bibliography below in volumes and articles dealing with contemporary island architecture.

6.   On Egypt, see the remarks in I.E.S. Edwards, *The Pyramids of Egypt* (1961): 73-76. A good introduction to Egyptian planning and construction methods may be found in A. Badawy, *Ancient Egyptian Architectural Design* (1965): 'Introduction'.

7.   In particular the evidence from early Hellenic temple construction and clay models of early temples; see A.W. Lawrence, *Greek Architecture* (1956).

8.   The structure was discovered in 1958 by the Italian School of Archaeology under the direction of Dr. Doro Levi, and is located in the south central Messara plain in a locale known as Kannia, two kilometers from the acropolis of Greco-Roman Gortyna. It is dated to the Late Minoan I period. See D. Levi, 'La Villa Rurale minoica di Gortina', *BdA* 44 (1959): 237-265, plan, figure 2, p. 238. We shall look in more detail at this interesting structure below.

9.   See our analyses of Gortyn below, Part Two.

10. As a perusal of Egyptian plans will reveal. See A. Badawy, *Egyptian Architecture,* 1966b, and our comparative study of Minoan and Egyptian house design later in this Chapter. The contrasts are clearly shown in Figure I.2 below.

11. In contrast to the situation evident in contemporary societies elsewhere (Egypt, Mesopotamia, mainland and Aegean Greece). This characteristic may very well be due to the accidents of survival.

12. Discussed in detail in our analyses of Houses A and B below in Part Two. Whether such a formal connection existed between the two buildings or not, the internal organization of House B (at least on its ground floor) suggests that it was given over almost completely to storage. Were House B a separate household would depend on whether or not it contained residential suites on its second storey. If there were such suites, the structure would then be unique in organization in the corpus.

13. A detailed analysis is given for Quarter Delta of the city of Mallia in Part Two below. An excavation report of the quarter appears in *Et. Cret.* IX: 48-54, and a plan is given as plate LXVII in that report. See also *CFFC:* 57-58.

14.   Tylissos C, like its neighbors, was built in the Middle Minoan IIIb/Late Minoan Ia period. It was excavated by J. Hazzidhakis, whose description appears in *Et. Cret.* III (1934): 32-47. Discussed also by J.W. Graham, *Palaces of Crete* (hereafter *PC*): 61-2; and D. Preziosi, *Labrys* (1970): 68-108. A detailed discussion of its planning and construction is given in Part Two below.

15.   There is no direct evidence for such contrastive color coding, but the myth of Ariadne's red thread which helped Theseus find his way out of the Knossian labyrinth may find an archaeological support in the red painted border of the extant portion of the Western Corridor of the Knossian palace, leading from the area of the Central Court to the main western entrance to the compound.

16.   The relative position of these storage magazines, not far removed from the household entrance, is compatible with the placement of the ranks of great storage magazines on the western flanks of the palatial compounds of Phaistos, Knossos and Mallia, similarly close to external access without direct disturbance of other business within.

17.   See for example the set of cells on the northeastern corner of the house at Akhladhia (Figure I.12), similarly unconnected to the remainder of the house. The Tylissan room, however, is fairly small and narrow, and its usage may have related to other matters external to the household proper.

18.   The centrality of location of rooms used as shrines both in houses and palaces (e.g. at Knossos, Phaistos and Mallia, the so-called 'pillar crypts') is one of the constancies of Minoan design, and (in the palaces, at least, as we shall see below) this positioning may be in part ritually commemorative of the acts of foundation, much like our own 'cornerstones'. The evidence at Knossos for such practices is especially strong.

19.   See our discussion below in the section 'Patterns of Invariance and Variation', this Chapter.

20.   A detailed analysis of the Minoan hall system is presented in Chapter II.

21.   Such a layout procedure appears to have been common to societies in the eastern Mediterranean during the Bronze Age. The most detailed work on this subject has been carried out in Egypt, where there also exists textual and graphic evidence for grid planning (see Badawy, *Ancient Egyptian Architectural Design*, 1965). The existence of such a methodology for Crete is evidenced by detailed analysis of the dimensions of plans, as illustrated by Part Two below, where the identity of Minoan builders' modules is established. No Minoan measuring rods have been identified in Cretan remains, and it is unlikely that any such rods would have survived, since it seems reasonable to suppose that they were of wood. However, a wooden measuring rod found in Egypt at El-Lahun by Flinders Petrie, and (possibly) in connection with fragments of Minoan pottery made at that site — attesting perhaps to the presence of Cretan masons contributing their skills to the erection of the pyramid complex of Sesostris II during the Middle Kingdom — may in fact be of Minoan origin, for its dimensions and divisions replicate what has been separately deduced from the study of Minoan remains themselves (see D. Preziosi, *MPPAO*: Conclusions, and Part Two below). The El-Lahun rod is definitely not Egyptian, although whether it is in fact of Cretan origin and design remains unclear. At present it is in the collection of University College, London.

Perhaps coincidentally, the name of one of the three wise Minoan rulers — Sarpedon — remembered by the later Greeks, may be an allusion to Minoan foundation rituals: in later Greek, the term *harpedonaptae* is a title given the 'stretchers of the cord', i.e. in the layout of a building. Taken in connection with the glotto-chronological conjecture that the initial aspiration of certain Greek words of the historical period represents a loss of prevocalic initial sibilant *s-*, the two words may be connected. This is, of course, a tantalizing conjecture, but it may not have any secure foundation. Nevertheless, the conservatism and long-term preservation of builders' methods and terminology (discussed by Badawy, *op. cit.*: Introduction) is well known, and the phonological similarity between the two words may not be entirely coincidental.

22.   The precision of layout of major public construction on Crete matches the evidenced precision in layout of contemporary Egyptian monumental architecture, once the synchronicity of the plans of major Minoan buildings such as the palaces is firmly established.

23.   S. Marinatos, 'Mesominoiki Oikia en Kato Mesara', *Dheltion* IX (1924-1925): 53ff, plan given on p. 54. See also D. Preziosi, 'Harmonic design in Minoan architecture', *Studies Presented to Professor G.M.A. Hanfmann* (1972), edited by D.G. Mitten, J.G. Pedley and J. Scott.

24.   There exists one wall section, at the southern end of the western wall of the house, which consists of a single large block out smooth on three sides (west, south, east), measuring 0.80 in width.

25.   Alternatively, following the line of the argument, the opening itself might represent four modular units, i.e. 1.10.

26.   More exactly, the length of the square root of 32. There is abundant evidence that Egyptian builders were familiar with such diagonal calculations (see Badawy, *op. cit.*), and even had a name for such a diagonal rule – the *remen* – to be employed in the 'squaring of a grid'. It is not unreasonable to suppose that Minoan builders shared in this technology. Once again, there is a tantalizing bit of material which might have to do with this phenomenon. As we shall see in detail in our analysis of the palace at Knossos below (Part Two), there were found in the Foundation Deposit of the palace, adjacent to the geometric center of one of the major modular grid squares defining the west central block, several jars (originally containing some foundation offering) whose faces bore the incision of a rectangle with two diagonals etched within. It may be that such unique incisions served to catalogue the intended location of these jars in the original foundation deposit. On the other hand, such a conjecture must be weighed against a thorough and systematic study of the distribution of 'masons' marks' found in the remains.

27.   Presumably the grid-net would remain in place long enough for most major interior partitions to be begun. For evidence of relative chronology in the layout of walls, see the discussion of Mallia's House Zeta Alpha below in the next section of the present Chapter. As will become evident later in this study, there appears to be some correlation of the geometric subdivisions of a planning grid with a certain standardization in the proportional allotment of functional space within a structure. In other words, these constant ratios tend to follow the idealized portions of the modular grid rather than (overtly and directly) the actual square footage of rooms.

28.   See above, Note 4.

29.   Not included in the illustrations of this volume, and seen by me and photographed in 1972. A full account of the model has not yet been published as of this writing.

30.   See above, Preface, Notes 1, 4 and 5.

31.   A report of the excavation of this building, near Khrondhrou Viannou will be

found in *BCH* (1958): 778-779; *id*. (1960): 826ff, plan p. 826.

32. As indicated in our plan, portions of the eastern corners are in ruins, but the trace of foundations is secure enough to reconstruct the position of the walls at these points.

33. A detailed analysis of the modular organization of the building is given below in Part Two.

34. N. Platon, *BCH* (1960): 826.

35. In other words, there are no monumental temples on Crete of the type so characteristic in other contemporary societies: where Egyptian and Mesopotamian temples and ritual constructions were relatively gigantic compared to more secular construction, the reverse is the case on Crete, where compounds of religious function (assuming in most cases that certain buildings and rooms were religious) are comparatively small, informal, hidden, or remote from habitations.

36. Assuming, of course, that such an opposition of 'secular' to 'religious' was viable in the framework of Minoan society.

37. N. Platon, *BCH* LXXXIV (1960): 822ff, plan, p. 824.

38. A similar type of window frame was seen above at Tylissos C.

39. The structure was laid out as 40 by 60 units on a module of 0.340; see below, Part Two, for details.

40. But, importantly, its misalignments have a consistency about them: misaligned walls tend to be parallel to their opposite number. These errors in layout may possibly be connected with irregularities in the terrain of this hill.

41. Namely, the three cells in the lower left corner. See the next Chapter for a discussion of the formative organization of the hall systems.

42. Here, as in most of our functional attributions, we rely directly upon the material evidence from excavation, along with the conclusions of the building's excavators. There are, however, certain problems with such evidence, most notably the fact that the finds within a given cell represent the *latest* use of a room, at the time of a building's destruction. There is no guarantee that the room had the same usages when the building was first built. Hence we must weigh the material evidence carefully, comparing it with a broad spectrum of construction elsewhere, all of which must itself be balanced against an understanding of the society derived from other sources. In addition, we should bear in mind that it is more likely in a society such as the Minoan that certain functional appropriations of space would tend to be conservative, with houses used from generation to generation in similar ways. A number of invariant patterns in the spatial relationships among functions will become clear in the next Chapter, and these patterns, themselves, will also affect how we evaluate the functional conclusions (or lack thereof) of given excavations.

43. For example in House Zeta Alpha at Mallia, discussed next.

44. *Et. Cret.* IX: 63-79, plan Plate LXV; *GFFC*: 63-66; Graham, *PC*: 64-66.

45. The plan as a whole, and in particular the latter section, is partly overlain by later intrusions and alteration to the original plan. There is, however, as we shall see, some evidence for the chronology of internal construction, evidenced by modular analysis.

46. It is of interest that the smaller dimension of RSS, ±8.10, is the same as that of the western section of the present structure. As discussed in Part Two in the modular analysis of ML ZA, this dimension is apparently intended as one-half the overall east-west width of the house.

47. The same as that derived for TVOL and RSS.

48. The western limits of this garden or court have not been fixed; we may conjecture that its boundary was aligned with the outer (western) wall of the latrine projection to the south, but this need not have been the case.

49. This is Sir Arthur Evans' term, derived from his observations at Knossos. Whether such sunken chambers served purely ritual (and/or lustral or purification) purposes, or whether they were more secular bathing areas, has remained unclear. Some show traces of waterproof Minoan cement, others do not. All known feature balustrades around their perimeters, surmounted in some extant examples by thin columns, thus allowing visual connection to surrounding portions of the rooms or corridors within which they are embedded. At the palace of Kato Zakro there is a circular sunken construction, with evidence for peripheral columns, in an eastern courtyard; it may have been a pool or well.

50. It may not be unreasonable to assume that this cell was used in food preparation and/or storage, considering its adjacency to the living quarters and position intermediate to living and service areas. The associated finds are ambiguous, however.

51. Note that the storage magazines here number three (as at the house Tylissos C). In both houses, one of the magazines is separately accessed, and two are controlled by a single entrance. This may not be entirely fortuitous, and might possibly be attributed to differences in what was stored, e.g. grain and other dry (or dried) foodstuffs in the double magazine, wine, oil and other liquids in the single magazine. Similar groupings of storage magazines, again no doubt relating to differences in the nature of what was stored, may be seen elsewhere.

52. Discussed by Graham (*PC, passim*), and suggested by a number of excavators, including Sir Arthur Evans. The theory holds in general that a long wall trace is more apt to be stable under frequent earthquake conditions if it is partially self-supporting by means of recessed and projected facade sections which depend upon each other (as well as perpendicular walls within). Crete is certainly in an earthquake zone, and various excavators have pointed to evidence that buildings have periodically been wrecked for such reasons. But such an explanation is only partially convincing, for the simple fact that such a practice can only, in many cases, be due to more directly decorative motivations, where the static structural benefits would be minimal or nonexistent.

53. Except for ML ZA, where there has been structural alteration to the building in this area which may have erased such an original pattern, if indeed it did exist here. Nevertheless, at ML ZA we may see the equivalent 'square-within-a-square' arrangement. Similar formal arrangements may be observed in Houses G and J at Kato Zakro, to be discussed below in Chapter II, third section.

Formal Organization

INTRODUCTION

In Chapter I we saw that there exist certain patterns of formative organization in the planning and layout of Minoan buildings, in particular that there exist a number of constancies in the ways in which spaces of various function are related to one another. In the present Chapter we will explore the patterns of invariance and variation exhibited by the broad range of Minoan construction, from relatively modest houses to the great palatial compounds of the principal Minoan cities.

We will begin with an examination of the format of the Minoan hall system, the principal cluster of cells around which the standard Minoan house is organized, and then pass on to a consideration of the relationship of the hall system to other component sections of the house. This will include a comparative analysis of the ways in which the various functional compounds within domestic structures are related to each other.

These analyses will be followed by a study of the organization and planning of the major Minoan palatial compounds, and their formal and functional relationships to the cities they dominate.

A final section will be devoted to a series of changes in formation taking place in the Late Minoan period, and evidently representing the influence of practices originating outside of Crete.

THE MINOAN HALL SYSTEM

Many Minoan houses incorporate a set of halls, normally three in number, and partitioned from each other by a row of columns and a set of square piers. The latter include sets of double doors which fold back flat onto these piers, or into specially designed shallow recesses. Referred to as pier-and-door partitions (hereafter PDPs), these pier systems allow a great deal of flexibility in the admission of light and ventilation. In effect, they serve either as solid walls (when the entire row of doors is closed), or as colonnades (when all the doors are open and folded back). The most famous example of a hall system is the so-called 'Hall of the Double Axes'[1] and its subsidiary 'Queen's Megaron' in the eastern quarter of the palace at Knossos (Figure II. 1); (Figure II.2 illustrates the operation of the PDP system). The 'Hall of the Double Axes' thus serves either as a long colonnaded single hall, or as a series of separate rooms, depending upon the disposition of the doors. The hall system, which is unique to Minoan architecture, normally includes at one end an open court or light well. In the case of the hall system at Knossos, this light well, on the inner (W) side of the system, rises several storeys to the roof of the building, and is adjacent to an elegant stairwell rising in perpendicular stages up to the level of the central courtyard (and presumably beyond).[2]

At its eastern end, the hall system at Knossos opens onto a colonnaded porch or veranda looking out across a descending ravine to the hills beyond. Very similar hall systems exist, as we shall see, at the great palatial compounds of Phaistos and Mallia, as well as in the so-called 'small palaces' near Phaistos (at Haghia Triadha) and elsewhere in the city of Knossos.[3] A particularly interesting hall system has been uncovered in the recent excavations of the palace of Kato Zakro on the eastern end of the island, and similar material is in evidence on Thera.[4]

The hall systems of private domestic structures are usually smaller in size, but nevertheless incorporate the same basic features as their palatial counterparts. They are normally wholly internal to a house plan, although there are several examples where a hall system will open directly onto a private garden or exterior courtyard (see ML ZA, Figure I.13 above, Chapter I).

To get some sense of the variation possible in the construction of the Minoan hall system, we might compare the organization of a series of plans taken from several towns on the island (Akhladhia, Knossos, Mallia and Tylissos), and begin to specify their invariant properties.

Figures II.3 through II.10 below illustrate eight domestic hall systems dating approximately to the Middle Minoan III-Late Minoan I periods. In each case we will discuss the relationship of the hall system to the other sections of a house.

Figure II.3 is a plan of House A at Akhladhia (AKHL), discussed previously in Chapter I. The hall system proper comprises cells denoted in the plan as (a-b-c), connected to the vestibule (h) by means of a double door at the northeastern juncture of (a) and (b), and to cell (g) both at (b) and at (c). Cell (b) thus gives access both to (h) and (g) through its northeastern wall, which consists entirely, then, of a PDP system in its own right. Cell (a) is separated from (b) by a colonnade consisting of two columns flanking a central pillar, while (b) is separated from (c) by a PDP system with three pillars adjacent to four double doors. Only the bases remain as indications of original pillars and columns, which would have been of timber.

It is unclear as to whether one of the cells was a light well; if one did exist, it would most likely have been cell (a), on the analogy of other hall systems. It is possible, however, that either adjacent cell (g) or cell (h) may have served as a light well: as was noted above in Chapter I, a portion of cell (g) is paved with flagstones, a probable indication that the cell was a light well.[5] In either case, conditions for internal lighting would have been met.

It was noted above in the previous Chapter that cells (m) and (n) may have served as a kitchen and pantry, and that the western portion of cell (c) might have been used for dining, assuming that the L-shaped stone bench in this corner could be used for collective seating, possibly around a wooden table.

The three cells of the hall system are of equal size and proportions, and each communicates with cells beyond: none is a cul-de-sac. With respect to the outer entrance of the house, the hall system is behind two doorways: the outer house door, most likely a large double door across the threshold at the southeastern entryway, and the PDP system forming the right flank of all of cell (b) and part of cell (a).

The next structure, the so-called 'House of the Chancel Screen' (KN HCS) at Knossos, is built against the eastern flank of the terracing adjacent to the eastern side of the palatial compound of Knossos (Figure II.4).[6]

Whereas AKHL was a fairly straightforward farmhouse, KN HCS may not have been an ordinary house, as indicated both by its internal appointments and its close proximity to the palatial compound itself. Sir Arthur Evans termed it the 'House of the Chancel Screen' because of the unique cell (d) adjacent to cell (c), separated from the latter by a balustrade with two columns, and comprising a stepped platform surmounted by two centrally placed slabs, possibly a raised dais or statue base.[7] Its function is unknown.

The entrance to the house is at the southeast, incorporating a long narrow corridor beyond the outer doorway, leading to a flight of nine steps rising to the west (cell (g)). The stair leads to a landing beyond which is a door opening onto the central cell of the hall system (b). The longitudinal axis of the system is perpendicular to the direction of entrance, as at AKHL.

To the south of cell (b) is a door leading to an L-shaped corridor beginning at cell (e), beyond which, after another 90° turn, is a sunken 'lustral chamber', cell (f).[8] The great thickness of the wall separating cells (e) and (f) is inexplicable: there may have been a stairway at this point, but no trace of such a construction remains. That there was a second storey in the structure is indicated by the partially extant stairwell off cell (i) on the western flank of the house.

The hall system proper (cells a-b-c) is partitioned by two PDP systems (in contrast to AKHL, where cells (a) and (b) are separated by an open colonnade). Beyond the shallow cell (a) is an additional room, whose shape is reminiscent of storage magazines elsewhere. As was the case with AKHL, cell (b) has one of its perpendicular flanks taken up by a PDP system with two double doors; its opposite flank is composed of two separate doors. Cell (c), the northernmost cell, is flanked to its left by the two columns opening onto the room of the dais, while its right flank consists of a row of windows. First floor windows are rare in Minoan remains; this set is sufficiently high off the ground level beyond to assure privacy within, since the house itself is built into a slope on partly terraced foundations.

It is possible that cell (a) was a lightwell, by analogy with examples elsewhere, although the windows of cell (c) would have admitted a good amount of light and ventilation to the system as a whole.

To the west of cell (b) is a separate cell cluster at whose center (h) stands a so-called 'pillar crypt', beyond a circumferential corridor (i). At the extreme ends of the corridor are two storage magazines. The pillar crypt evidently had some ritual function, on analogy with similar cells elsewhere (see discussion on the palace below). The house also contains a 'cellar' room beyond the southern corner of corner of corridor (i), accessible only from the second storey above.

Because of the slope into which the house is built, the building may possibly have had a second entrance at the second floor level, on the western side. A second-storey western entrance evidently also existed in the house below, also at Knossos.

Located some 100 meters northeast of the northeastern corner of the palace of Knossos, the so-called 'Royal Villa' was uncovered and named by Sir Arthur Evans in 1903; a new survey of this remarkable building was made by him in 1926.[9] The building stands in a cutting made into the descending slope of a hill overlooking the ravine of the Kairatos stream (Figure II.5).

The structure originally had two or possibly three storeys,[10] and was probably also accessible on its western flank by a second-storey entranceway. It is most probably not a simple domestic structure: there are no standard storage magazines – at least on the extant ground floor – and the structure contains a number of features which suggest that its use was (at least in part) of a ritual nature. These include a very fine 'pillar crypt' (cell (e)) and a cell behind the hall system, (d), featuring a raised balustrade and a niche at its back incorporating a stepped platform which may have been the site of a seat, statue, or some religious emblem. That the pillar crypt was used for votive offerings seems evident from its articulated floor, consisting of a circumferential channel around the pillar, into which were sunk two deeper cists, perhaps for the collection of liquid offerings.[11]

The main entrance at this ground floor level was into a corridor (cell (f)), leading directly into cell (a), the first portion of the hall system. Beyond cell (a) is a doorway leading into a triangular enclosed space, quite possibly a garden. The hall system proper, cells (a-b-c), consists of a light well (a), a central cell or porch (b) beyond two columns, and an inner room (c) beyond a PDP system with three double doors. As noted above, the balustraded back cell

(d) stands beyond; it is conceivable that it too was open to the second storey.

The patterns of circulation in the structure are remarkable and unique in a structure of modest size, for one can pass from one end of the building to the opposite end by several possible means. From the entrance corridor (f), one has a choice of passage into the light well beyond (a) through a PDP wall, or, to the left, through another PDP system, leading into a chamber of which part was used for the storage of fresco panels (area (h)). Beyond this cell are two doors. That to the left (S) opens into a rectangular cell with a back door leading into corridor (g). The right-hand door of the former cell also leads to the same corridor, which also gives onto cell (c) of the hall system.

The stairwells occupy an unusually large amount of the area of the plan. Corridor (g) leads in a single flight to a landing (with a window beyond), serving as the intermediate stage between the first and second floors. The landing gives onto two flights on either side: that on the left undoubtedly led across the back flank of the building into a corridor or vestibule, which itself must also have connected with a second stairwell at the far corner of the building. This latter then led back down to the pillar crypt, cell (e). Thus it is possible for one to disappear from cell (c) on its left side and reappear again on its right side, by going up the left stair and descending on the right.

The set of controls and system of internal traffic suggest multiple usages for this building, perhaps allowing certain guests or visitors access to selected portions at certain times. Thus, one could visit the innermost pillar crypt without passing through the hall system, by entering from the second level, or one could visit the area of cell (d) either through the length of the hall system or by means of the bypass to the left of cell (f). Or one could enter corridor (g) without passing through the cell beyond (h).

It is possible that there was an additional stairway beyond the L-shaped stair leading down to the pillar crypt. At this point is a deep enclosed cell which could have served as a storage cellar, later filled in with rubble to serve as the support for a corridor or stair leading to a third storey.

If this were a structure devoted in large part to ritual practice and performance, the triangular open area beyond cell (a) might also have been the site for an open-air shrine, a carefully tended tree (such as those standing in lined pits in the western court of the Knossian palace, adjacent to the triangular area in the western court delimited by raised causeways, as depicted in a fragmentary Knossian fresco).[12] The latter is shown as a site for public dancing by women.[13]

It may well be that this remarkable building was a combined residence and religious offices, serving in part as the dwelling for a priest(ess) or family devoted to maintainance of one or more Minoan religious cults.

A structure which takes its name from a series of stored fresco panels is the 'House of the Frescoes' at Knossos, excavated by Evans in 1923-1926 (Figure II. 6).[14]

This small house stands in the northwestern quarter of the city of Knossos, just off a major street (the so-called 'Royal Road') leading from the northwestern corner of the great palace at a distance of some 35 meters.[15] Barely 120 square meters in area (c. 11½ by 16 meters), it appears to have served principally as a domestic structure. Portions of fresco panels were found stacked in cell (i). Although no sure trace of a stairway was found, Evans conjectured that a small wooden stair stood in cell (h).

The only entrance is into cell (f), to the left of which is a room most likely serving as a porter's lodge, cell (g). The entrance vestibule gives onto two doorways: that immediately inside the front door leads to cells (h) and (i), which served as work space and storage rooms. Cell (i) leads onto the central hall of the hall system, room (b). The second door in the entrance vestibule leads into a narrow corridor divided by an intermediary door into two smallish cells (i-d). The latter cell also give acccss to the hall system, at its light-well end, cell (a).

The hall system resembles the others seen above by its division into three chambers (a-b-c), and their separation by PDP systems. The innermost cell (c) is separated at present by two doors at opposite ends of a wall. It is possible that the central wall-piece is a later modification, transforming a tripartite PDP system into a two-door wall system.

An unusual feature of the central room (b) is a window on its outer flank, unusual for a ground floor, at a low and exposed position, contrasting with the window in cell (c) at KN HCS. The central section of cell (a) is paved, indicating the likelihood of a clerestory roof over part of this light well, no doubt at the second storey roof level.

The outer trace of the structure shows standard wall recesses and projections. The long wall along the corridor jogs slightly at the point of separation between cells (e) and (d), and the outer wall at cell (a) projects in contrast to the recessed portion at the opposite side of the building, at cell (c). We have already seen similar examples of such opposed recesses and projections above, notably at ML ZA, and TYL C (to be examined again in this section).

The next house, House Delta Alpha at Mallia (ML DA), is fairly modest in size, and can be inscribed within a square some 13½ meters on a side (Figure II. 7).[16]

The entrance to the structure is into vestibule cell (e), to the left of which are the remains of a two-flight stairwell leading to the second storey. At the narrow end of cell (e) is a PDP wall system, with two doors opening onto corridor (d), a U-shaped area which in part surrounds a sunken 'lustral chamber' (f), which is entered beyond a set of double doors at the end of the left arm of the corridor. At the opposite end of that arm of (d) is a doorway to the right of the entrance, leading into a suite of rooms used for storage and work space. The latter area includes a small stairway, traces of which are shown in cell (g).

The wall separating cells (d) and (g) may have been a later modification of the original plan, possibly indicated by the two upright pillar segments along its length. If this wall is in fact a later alteration, (d) and (g) may have been a single cell partitioned by a set of square pillars.

The hall system (a-b-c) stands beyond a PDP system running along the inner flank of cell (c), and providing access into both adjacent cells: the three double doors on the left open into cell (d), the single one to the right communicates with cell (g). The lack of precise alignment of the fourth PDP pier with the wall separating cells (d) and (g) may be a further indication of the latter's lateness of appearance. At any rate, such a misalignment is unusual in an otherwise precisely laid out structure.[17]

In the hall system proper, cell (c) is twice the length of either cell (b) or (a). It is separated from cell (b), the porch, by a PDP of three piers and four doors. The porch itself opens onto the light well (cell (a)), and is separated from it by a single, centrally placed column.

The outer trace of the structure is deeply indented and articulated, and, as discussed in detail in Part Two below, its various facades resonate proportionally with each other in modular dimensions. Each of the four faces of the building is differently articulated, and there is strong evidence that the trace of the groundplan was generated by means of modular subtractions from an original square grid. The structure was erected near the crossroads of two major streets in the section of the city of Mallia named by the excavators Quarter Delta.[18]

House Zeta Alpha (ML ZA) at Mallia is already familiar from our examination of it in Chapter I above; it is contemporary to House ML DA just looked at.[19] Here we might note its similarities to the organization of House ML DA (Figure II.8).

The major entrance is into vestibular cell (f), off one side of which is a stairwell (as at ML DA, cell (e)). In both houses, a corridor lies beyond the vestibule door (cell (e) here, cell (d) at ML DA). In both houses a left turn leads to access into the 'lustral chamber', cells (g) at ML ZA and (f) at ML DA. Directly ahead of cell (d) here is a small stairway, close to the entrance of the hall system proper. The small stair in cell (g) at ML DA occupies an equivalent position *vis-à-vis* the hall system entrance. In both cases, the hall system is accessible at cell (c).

The hall systems proper are essentially identical in internal organization: cell (c) is partitioned from cell (b) in both houses by means of a three-piered PDP system with four flanking doors. The outer end of this porch cell is defined in both cases by a single central column. But whereas cell (a) at ML DA is a small lightwell, area (a) at ML ZA was most likely a more open court, and possibly even a small garden (see our discussion above in Chapter I).

ML ZA is of course a much larger house, and yet its internal deployment of spaces is equivalent to that seen above at ML DA, and there is a certain constancy of *relationship* manifest among cells, despite differences in absolute size and placement. In addition to what has been just noted, we may see in the general arrangement of the pillared hall system beyond the 'lustral chamber' (cell (g)) at ML ZA a certain similarity to the set of pillared halls at ML

DA to the right of cell (g) there, despite the modifications to the original plan suggested above. In discussing ML ZA in Chapter I, it was noted that a cell on the plan served as a latrine: it is not known for sure if such an accomodation existed at ML DA.

ML ZA is a house built onto a main city thoroughfare, while ML DA, also in a crowded portion of the city (Quarter Delta; see Figure I.3) is a freestanding structure, built at a crossroads, its left corner set back to accomodate a turn in the sidewalk. Both are entered at the middle of one of their sides.

Despite these differences, the organization of spaces within, and the topological (and to a certain extent geometric) relationships among their component parts are equivalent. With respect to the position of the hall systems, note that both occupy the upper left corner of their houses, both are oriented in the same manner, and both communicate with other portions of their houses only through cell (c).

The next plan shows the large and complicated house A at Tylissos (TYL A), excavated by J. Hazzidhakis in 1909-1913, and dated to the Middle Minoan III-Late Minoan I period.[20] It was built at the same period as houses B and C at Tylissos; its relationships with the latter are portrayed in Figure I.3 in Chapter I. TYL A is the largest of the three structures, some 35 meters north-south by 22 meters east-west. As was conjectured above in Chapter I (and as illustrated by the aforementioned figure), it may very well be that House B was an annex to House A (since the former consists, at least on its ground floor, entirely of storage magazines). The two houses may have been connected by a short bridge at the second storey, which would directly connect the adjacent stairwells of both buildings.[21]

Apart from the break in part of the western wall of TYL A (possibly a later destruction),[22] the only entrance to the structure is at vestibule (cell (1)), which is enclosed on its inner flanks by an L-shaped set of piers. There may have been double doors between the piers, although no trace remains. On the left flank of cell (1) is a low double step, which quite possibly may have allowed direct access through a low window or doorway into the porter's chambers. At any rate, the wall opening at this point would at least allow for visual and auditory control of the entranceway.

Beyond cell (1) is an L-shaped cell (2), serving as a central lobby of the structure, and permitting access in three directions. In the upper left corner is a stairway turning immediately up to what would become a long corridor on the second storey. In the northern corner of the lobby is a door leading to two storage magazines with central pillars. On the left flank of the first magazine is a door leading to a small cell at the right end of which is another stair, reminiscent of the tripartite stair at KN RV: a central ascent bifurcating at a mediate landing into two flanking flights. The right flank stair would return southward to meet the corridor or cells which connect with the outermost stair of the building just noted. The left flank stair may have returned back down to the series of storage cellars on the ground floor, hidden away at the northwestern corner of the building. The stair would have come down parallel to the central riser, but behind a wall, perhaps into a perpendicular corridor. The adjacent cellars might be accessed through doors a step or two above grade.

The cell giving access to the tripartite stair also leads southward into a long narrow corridor ultimately running into cell (p), evidently a room with religious usages, possibly a pillar crypt.[23] If the break in the western wall represents a ruined entrance rather than a later intrusion, then this corridor would provide direct access to storage and work areas from the back side of the house (which, perhaps not coincidentally, is adjacent to House B a few meters beyond): a building which we conjecture may be a storage annex to House A.

Returning to the entrance cell (2), it will be seen that the remaining doorway leads into corridor (x) to the south, the only access to the domestic quarter of the building. On the eastern side of cell (x) is the entrance to the guard's suite of rooms, consisting of two square cells connected by a narrow corridor. At the southern end of the corridor is a second door, beyond which is the central hall system of the house.

The hall system (cells a-b-c) runs east-west, and the central cell (b) serves both as a porch between cell (c) and the lightwell (a) and as a continuation of corridor (x) to rooms further south. Cell (c) has five small cells surrounding it on three sides, of which one — cell (d) — is a stairway, and may also have included a closet under the stair.[24]

Cell (b) wraps around two sides of light well (a), and gives further access to the 'pillar crypt', cell (p). The latter is part of an independent cluster of cells, of which one − cell (n) − features a central column. As noted above, access to the long north-south corridor on the western flank of the house may be gained here.

To the south of cell (b), beyond another door, a corridor continues and turns 90° to the west. Off the latter part of this corridor are three small cells, and, at the end − in the southwestern corner of the house − another stairwell.

The hall system itself is essentially the same in plan to those already seen, although the lightwell is partly enclosed by L-shaped cell (b). On the western flank of cell (a) is an internal window, providing light and ventilation to cell (n) beyond, in a manner equivalent to TYL C (see below).[25]

The outer trace of this large mansion is indented and recessed in a familiar fashion, and no two flanks are similar in articulation. As will be discussed below in Part Two, there is evidence for a proportional harmonics in the modular dimensions of the various planes: for example, the southern facade of the building is divided into three projecting sections, measuring respectively 10 + 15 + 25 units, a ratio of 2 : 3 : 5. The entire plan was generated by subtractions from an overall modular grid forming a 3 : 5 rectangle.

The plan of TYL C (Figure II.10) is already familiar from our discussions above in Chapter I, and so we will dwell here principally on its similarities with TYL A.[26] In both houses, entrance is into a vestibular area to one side of which is a porter's room (cell (k) at TYL C, cell (x) at TYL A). Entrance into the hall system proper is, in both cases, by means of a corridor which meets the system perpendicularly (cell (x) at TYL A, cells (l, m) at TYL C).

Although both hall systems run east-west (parallel to the initial direction of entrance into the house), their internal positions are reversed: at TYL C the lightwell is at the eastern end, at TYL A on the west side. In both cases, however, the lightwells communicate internally with adjacent cells by means of windows.

Taking the group of examples above as a whole, let us now attempt to define their common properties.[27]

From the discussions above, it is evident that we are dealing here with a series of invariant features of cellular association. Not only are the hall systems themselves similar in internal organization, but it also appears that to a certain extent the manner whereby they are related to other cell clusters is generically similar. As may also be evident from a comparative study of the plans above, the relationships among cell types underlie variations in size, orientation, and material composition.

It may be useful to clarify these impressions by comparing directly the various organizational features examined above.

The following list (Table II.1) compares the individual components of the eight hall systems:

Table II.1. *Hall system: Components*

	a		b		c
AKHL A	lightwell (?)	/C/	porch	/PDP/	hall
KN HCS	lightwell	/PDP/	porch	/PDP/	hall
KN RV	lightwell	/C/	porch	/PDP/	hall
KN HF	lightwell	/PDP/	porch	doors*	hall
ML DA	lightwell	/C/	porch	/PDP/	hall
ML ZA	garden	/C/	porch	/PDP/	hall
TYL A	lightwell	/C/**	porch	/PDP/	hall
TYL C	lightwell	/C/	porch	/PDP/	hall

*Apparently originally a /PDP/.
**L-shaped colonnade, or "/C/".

The internal syntactic organization of the hall systems is the same in each case, but there are alternative formal realizations:

1. the boundary between cells (a) and (b) may be *either* /C/ or /PDP/;
2. cell (a) is invariably unroofted (or may have had a clerestory covering), but may be *either* an enclosed open area such as a garden (ML ZA) or court, or a lightwell entirely within the boundaries of the structure proper;
3. the boundary between cells (a) and (b) may be realized formally as a linear colonnade (/C/) or an L-shaped set of columns (as at TYL A);
4. The boundary between cells (b) and (c) may not be a full /PDP/ system, but (as at KN HF) a double door.

What of the relative *sizes* of the cells comprising the hall system?
It is apparent that in absolute size the hall systems differ; but is
there a consistency in the relative sizes of cells *within* each system?
In the following Table, '1' = the largest cell; '2' = middle sized cell;
and '3' = smallest cell:

Table II.2.   *Hall system: Cell sizes*

	a	b	c
AKHL A		all equal in size	
KN HCS	3	2	1
KN RV	2	2	1
KN HF	2	1	3
ML DA	2	2	1
ML ZA	1	3	2
TYL A	2	3	1
TYL C	2	3	1

Evidently, then the relative sizes of the cells are not invariant,
although a greater number of (c) cells are larger than any of the
others.

In terms of internal proportions, the overall system invariably
forms a rectangle which, with the exception of AKHL A, is at least
twice as long as it is wide.

The absolute orientation of the hall system varies considerably,
because of differences in house alignment, although in general the
tendency is for the longitudinal axis to run roughly east-west. As
we shall see below in discussing the major palaces, this east-west
alignment generally holds even when it is the case that one of the
lateral flanks of the hall system (as at Mallia and Phaistos) opens
out into a northerly garden or veranda: at Knossos, the outer
veranda of the Hall of the Double Axes is at the longitudinal outer
edge of the system, to the east.

It is important to bear in mind also what is *not* characteristic
of the hall system in this sample: the lightwell never stands
between two adjacent cells.

What of the relationship of this cell-matrix to other clusters of
cells in a structure? Is there a pattern in its connectivity to other

parts of a house? Is it invariably, for example, the 'innermost' section of a building?

One invariant pattern is already clear from a perusal of the plans: the system is always entered on one of its lateral flanks. In other words, *the alignment of the system is always 90° to the direction of its entrance.* Inversely, we can state that the system is never entered on its short end. This is true both of the examples seen here and of the larger hall systems of the great palaces.

But is there a consistency as to *which* of the three cells is entered from elsewhere in a house?

Table II.3.   *Hall system: Primary access*

	a		b		c
AKHL A	x	and	x		
KN HCS			x		
KN RV	x			or	x
KN HF	x	or	x		
ML DA					x
ML ZA					x
TYL A			x		
TYL C					x

As table II.3 illustrates, no one cell type serves as primary access in all examples, even in the same town. Access may be gained to the system through any of the three cells, from the area of primary entrance into the house. In two cases (AKHL A and KN HF), primary access is equally into two cells (cells a and b in both houses).

It will be noted in the plans that *no* hall system opens directly onto the exterior of a house (although one, ML ZA, opens onto a garden at the back of the structure); invariably the systems are beyond some vestibular space, however minimal.

Table II.4.   *Hall system: Separation from entrance*

	Number of thresholds including house door	
AKHL A	2	(= 1 cell separation)
KN HCS	2	(1)
KN RV	2	(1)
KN HF	4	(3)
ML DA	3	(2)
ML ZA	4	(3)
TYL A	4	(3)
TYL C	4	(3)

Table II.4 indicates that there is invariantly a *minimum of one cell* between a hall system and the front door of a house, no matter how small the house.

Thus far, we can state that the formative features of the hall system are as follows:

1. A cluster of 3 cells of types (a, b, c);[28]
2. aligned longitudinally (a) + (b) + (c);
3. lateral to direction of access;
4. positioned at least one cell removed from house entrance;
5. with initial primary access at not more than two points.

With regard to the relative position of other prominent features of a house, we have noted the presence nearby of stairwells giving access to a second storey. These stairwells, where they exist, are appended close to the following cells in the system:

Table II.5.   *Hall system: Stairway access*

	stair	off cell	in cell no.
AKHL A	*	c	g
KN HCS	x	b	i
KN RV	x	c	g
KN HF	**	b	i
ML DA	x	c	g
ML ZA	x	c	d
TYL A	x	c	onto c
TYL C	x	c	m

*At AKHL A, it is conjectured that there was a stair in cell (g).
**At KN HF, there may have been a stair in cell (i).

In all cases, the stairway is closely associated with cells (b) or (c) — never cell (a) — and is, morever, distinct from stairwells which serve more public portions of a house, or areas which need more constant servicing. With the exception of TYL A, whose plan reveals a stair opening directly onto cell (c) (and which may be a later alteration),[29] nearby stairways are invariably located outside the system itself, usually opening onto an adjacent corridor. In several cases (TYL A and C, KN RV) there are two stairways within easy reach of the halls, although KN RV may not have been a strictly domestic structure, as we have seen above.

The houses also have several other types of cells, often closely associated with the hall systems, although there is a flexibility in their relationship, when they are present:

1. 'pillar crypts' or shrines:
   KN HCS (h), off (i), off (b)
   KN RV   (e), off (c)
2. pillar rooms, possibly shrines:
   AKHL A (i), off (h), off (b/a): workshop?
   TYL A   (p), off (b)
   TYL C   (p), off (k): workshop?
   TYL C   (central room), off (K)[30]
3. hygiene/lustral cells/latrine:
   AKHL A (f) = latrine?
   KN HCS (f) = bath?[31]
   KN RV   (h) = latrine?[32]
   ML DA   (f) = bath?
   ML ZA   (g) = bath?
   ML ZA   (h) = latrine
   TYL A   (d) = latrine?[33]
   TYL C   (f) = latrine

We have also noted that the hall system is never a cul-de-sac, even when it stands at the innermost end of a structure, for invariably there exists multiple access to other cells, either physically behind, or off in another direction. Consequently, several cells in a system may serve dual functions: serving, in other words, as a component hall in the system proper, and as a passageway to other sections of a house. For example, in TYL A, cell (b) serves on its way to the southern end of the house. Therefore, we may simultaneously as a porch cell between light well (a) and hall (c), and as a continuation of corridor (x), which bisects the hall system add an additional feature to our list of five given above:

6. not forming a cul-de-sac.

In summary, then, it has become clear that the examination of the houses above has revealed a number of apparently invariant properties in the organization of the Minoan hall system. Our sample is limited to the best preserved non-palatial structures, but a perusal of other houses below, as well as of the great palatia compounds and the so-called 'little palaces', will support the present conclusions. What is of interest to our inquiry into the formative principles of Minoan architecture is the emergent fact that such principles have to do primarily with patterns of relationship among component elements, rather than properties of absolute size, orientation, alignment, position, and of constructional details.

What has emerged, in other words, is a consistency of underlying syntax in the relationships among cells of a certain type. As we broaden and deepen our analyses below, it will become evident that there is a certain orderliness or systematicity to these kinds of relationships, which indicate those properties of Minoan architecture which differentiate it from other architectonic systems, and simultaneously give it a particular identity.

MINOAN HOUSES

In the previous section we examined the formative organization of one type of cell-cluster, the standard Minoan hall system, which served as one of the primary components of the Cretan domestic structure. The analyses have also revealed that there exist certain consistent patterns of association between the hall system taken as a unit, and other portions of a house.

Thus far we have observed *two* principal patterns of formative organization. In Chapter I, we saw that underlying the organization of certain structures there existed a pattern of formal structure — the square-within-a-square pattern — which was constant despite other patterns of spatial connection among cells defined by this structural frame. As we shall see in the present section, other Minoan buildings reveal a similar structural framework.[34]

In the previous section, we observed a different pattern of organization in the association of cells forming the hall system of some Minoan houses. One example, AKHL A, revealed the presence of these two patterns together, side by side.[35]

In the present section, we shall look more broadly at the design and layout of Minoan houses, adding to our survey some ten additional structures from various parts of the island. As with most of the buildings looked at above, the following were originally constructed, according to their excavators, in the span of time traditionally designated as the Middle Minoan III — Late Minoan I periods.[36] We will discuss each structure individually, and then compare their formal organizations more directly, integrating our analyses with the observations in the sections above.

The following structures, all freestanding houses, will be looked at sequentially:

1. AMNISSOS (AMN): The 'Villa of the Lilies' (MM III)
2. GORTYN (GRT): 'La Villa Rurale' (LM I)
3. KNOSSOS (KN S): South House (MM IIIb/LM Ia)
4. KNOSSOS (KN SE): Southeast House (MM IIIa)
5. MALLIA (ML ZB): Mallia House Zeta Beta (MM IIIb/LM Ia)
6. NIROU KHANI (NK): 'Minoan Megaron' (MM IIIb/LM Ia)
7. SKLAVOKAMPOS (SKLV): Large House (LM I)
8. PALAIKASTRO (PLK B): House B (LM I)
9. PALAIKASTRO (PLK X): House X (LM II)
10. TYLISSOS (TYL B): House B (LM IIIb/LM Ia)

Amnissos

Figure II.11 shows the extant, excavated portion of a large house called 'The Villa of the Lilies', dating to the Middle Minoan III period. The structure stands on the eastern foot of a hill known today as Palaiokhora, the site of a port city during Minoan times, some seven kilometers east of the city of Herakleion on the northern coast of the island.[37] Amnissos was excavated by Marinatos from 1932-1938, and recently restudied and partially restored by N. Platon.[38]

The eastern quarters of the house have been destroyed, but enough of the plan remains to give a reasonably clear picture of its original composition in the western areas.

The Villa of the Lilies (so named after the fine fresco fragments of lilies found fallen into the debris of the room with two columns) includes a number of features characteristic of other Minoan houses we have seen. Most noteworthy is the hall system (cells 3-4-5) along the northern flank of the building, facing the coastline beyond. These three cells are separated by PDP systems running perpendicular to each other. This perpendicular arrangement is reminiscent of the hall systems of the palatial compounds at Phaistos, Mallia and Kato Zakro. In the two former cases, the halls lie on the northern flank of the building, and additionally reveal a line of columns along the outer border: no such columns are extant here, although it is reasonable to suppose that a colonnade ran along this northern side of the building, not unlike that at Mallia.[39] That the original northern boundary of the structure was beyond the trace of the present remains is indicated both by the extensions of walls to the east (on the lower left corner of Figure II.11), as well as by the presence of a threshold block beyond the line of the western wall of the hall system. In this regard, the outer trace of the building may have resembled the indented northern facade of the palace of Phaistos.[40]

It is unclear where the original entrance may have been. On the southern side of the house is an entrance stair leading down into a long narrow corridor (cell 1). The western extension of this corridor may have formed a stairway leading up to a second storey. Cell 2 may have served as a porter's lodge.

Not indicated in the published plan of the building, nor in the present plan, is a doorway connecting cell 1 with cell 6: there is an opening here in the remains themselves, revealed clearly in Graham's photograph.[41] Cell 6 is considered to have been a sanctuary by the building's excavators, who also place an additional stairwell in this chamber. Cell 6 opens into room 7, partially paved with flagstones, and containing two columns aligned north-south. It is not known if there were additional columns here. The pavement suggests that this chamber may have been in part unroofed, perhaps comprising a small court or lightwell.

To the north of cell 7 are two additional rooms (cells 8-9). The northerly cell opens out to the north, in line with the veranda of the hall system, by means of a doorway nearly three meters wide. These two cells are connected by a doorway which has been restored in the remains as a double door.[42]

To the west of these rooms is a corridor joining cell 7 with the northern border of the house. Its southern terminus is in the area of cell 11, most likely a rubbish pit.[43]

It is possible that there was a direct second-storey entrance to the house ,from the flank of the hill to the west; the western wall of the structure is a retaining wall. We may conjecture that the second level entrance would have been in the southwestern corner of the structure, possibly connecting with the upper level of the stairwell-corridor leading up from cell 1, and connecting with the hypothetical stairwell in cell 6 as well. Such an arrangement is similar to that seen above for KN RV and other Knossian hillside houses.[44]

It is likely that the veranda of the hall system opened out into a walled court or garden, as with the similar cell clusters at the Phaistian and Mallian palaces. A similar arrangement is suggested for Mallia House Zeta Alpha above, although in that case the canonical triple-cell hall system opens to the outside on its short side: the present arrangement more closely resembles the palatial clusters.

Despite the incompleteness of the remains, the regularity in the dimensions of spaces suggests a systematic modular layout, discussed in detail in Part Two below.[45]

Gortyn

Dated to the LM I period, the 'Villa rurale' was discovered and excavated in 1958 by the Italian School of Archaeology under the direction of Doro Levi. It stands in an area known as Kannia, some two kilometers from the acropolis of the Greco-Roman city of Gortyn, southwest of the present village of Mitropolis (Figure II.12).[46]

In plan, the building is a multiplanar rectangle some 20 by 23 meters in size, with its longer axis oriented east-west. The workmanship of the extant walls (preserved to a height of less than one meter) is in general quite good, particularly on the exterior, where the facades are constructed of carefully hewn ashlar masonry blocks of limestone. As the plan shows, however, many walls, while themselves straight, often do not meet at true right angles, particularly on the interior.

Evidently a farmhouse, the building was undoubtedly part of a larger agrarian compound which would have included animal pens and outbuildings, suggested by the traces of additional walls to the northeast (part of which is shown in dotted outline on the plan).[47]

There are two entrances, to the west and south. The latter entrance (the larger of the two) consists of a paved court some 3 by 4 meters, with a great stone threshold opening out to the terminus of a raised stone causeway or sidewalk approaching the house diagonally from the southeast.[48] To the immediate left of this entrance cell 1 is a bicameral porter's lodge (cells 4,5), which simultaneously communicates with the western entrance of the house via cell 7 to the north. Cell 6, also to the north of cell 2, may have served for storage and record-keeping.[49]

Cell 1 also gives onto a series of circulatory passages (2, 3, 9) and, from 2, to a two-flight stairway leading to the second storey (cells A A'). The position of this stairwell, immediately adjacent to the entrance cluster, finds many parallels; see for example houses ML Za, TYL A, TYL B, TYL C, as well as AMN above.

There are no living halls on the ground floor (cf. TVOL), which is given over almost exclusively to storage and work areas. Storage rooms, 10, 11, and 12, with central pillars, recall the similar cells to the right of the entrance of the house TYL A. This cell cluster is accessed solely by a single doorway opening off cell 12.

Much of the remainder of the house is accessible only from the second storey. While there is evidence that cell 8 originally communicated directly with cell 13, at some point in the history of the building this doorway was walled up. Even in its original state, however, only cells 13, 14, 15, 16, and 17 were accessible from the ground floor: the remainder were always appendices of the second storey.

Within this western area, only cells 17 and 16 had non-storage functions; it has been suggested by the structure's excavators that these tiny chambers were the household shrine. Cell 13 was evidently a stairwell, whose return flight was partially supported by the unusually thick wall foundations to the west. This stair would have opened onto a north-south corridor on the second storey, over cell 14 below. It is possible that cells 17 and 16 may have been open through the second storey, at least in part: a similar situation may be seen at KN RV.[50]

Cells 20, 21, and 22 form a single cluster. It is likely that these were accessible from the second storey at a point adjacent to the stairwell A: at the first landing over the southern flank of the latter two flights, a downward return might have been built into cell 20, either along its eastern flank, or in an L-shaped return along that cell's southern and western flanks. The remaining cells in this western area of the building (18, 19) probably had their own individual stairs or ladders.

It is not clear where the main living halls would have stood on the second storey, we may conjecture that they were positioned over cells 10, 11, and 12, at least minimally. The ground floor pillars would thus have supported a row of columns and/or PDPs above, providing room for a balcony-veranda facing north over the estate.

The multiplanar facade of the 'Villa rurale' is articulated in a familiar fashion (see ML DA above). The northern facade comprises a tripartite plane with a central recess. Its opposite, the southern facade, is the reverse: a central projected plane between two recessed sections. On the longitudinal axis of the building, the western facade is a reversed image of that to the east: a longer north-south facade projected on the northwestern corner balances a longer north-south facade recessed on the southeastern corner. Similar articulations have already been seen above at ML DA and TYL C, although both are different in overall size and in the depth of recession. Closest in design is ML DA, where opposite facades reflect each other such that the northern and southern facades are tripartite, the east and west divided into two reversed planar sections.

A detailed modular analysis of GRT is given in Part Two, highlighting the differences in planning between this building and ML DA.

Knossos: South House

This three-level house stands adjacent to the stepped portico and bridgeway forming the southwestern entrance to the great palatial compound at Knossos. Excavated by Evans, the building is some 19 by 13 meters in overall size, and reveals a characteristic indented outer trace.[51] The South House is one of the best preserved Knossian structures, and was built at the beginning of the Second Palace Period.

Figure II.13 is a composite reconstruction in which the disposition of the third level (the principal area of entrance) is omitted, standing above cells 10 and 11. The house entrance was above cell 11, and was immediately adjacent to the stairwell on the northwestern corner of the house. This stair led down into cell 11 (a pillar crypt), on the main storey,[52] as well as up to a fourth level. A window in the northern facade illuminated the stair on its flank.

The plan is partially cut away, revealing a pillared basement with three pillars beneath columns on the first storey; the eastern-most column was supported beneath by the north-south retaining wall of the basement, invisible in the section here. The pillar basement communicated with a chamber directly under cell 7, a store room in which was found a hoard of bronze tools. These two chambers comprise the only subterranean section of the house.

The main floor illustrated by our isometric plan consists of the pillar crypt (11), a large adjacent cell (10), a squarish central room (7) leading onto a four-columned hall (6) to the south, and a lavatory and latrine (8-9) to the north. The columned hall opens onto a stairway with a double landing, leading to a storey above and, in cell 4, to the pillared basement below. Cell 5 is a sunken 'lustral chamber'.

The main entrance to the hall system (cells 3-2-1) from cell 4 comprises a PDP system (as at ML DA). The hall is of the familiar form, with a large chamber (3) separated longitudinally from a porch (2) by a PDP system. At the southern end is a light well (cell 1). Our plan conjecturally restores an exterior entrance at this point at the suggestion of the excavators, but no secure evidence of such an entranceway has been found, and we shall omit it in our discussion below.[53] Traces of an inset window were found in the inner chamber (cell 3). Evans conjecturally restored windows in the southern walls of cells 10 and 6,[54] the former of which is reconstructed here.

In all respects, the South House resembles the freestanding houses examined above, with its hall system occupying one flank of the building, connected closely with a 'lustral area' and a stairway communicating with storage basements below and living areas on the second storey above. The pillar crypt, constituting the household shrine, stands adjacent to one of the principal stairwell entrances to the building (as at KN RV). The central area, cells 7 and 6, may have served respectively as kitchen/pantry and dining area, together with cell 10, although no evidence to support this conjecture exists.[55]

The overall plan was conceived as a 2 : 3 rectangle (like the Knossian House of the Frescoes)[56] and the southern facade was progressively stepped back toward the east, along a diagonal line corresponding to the traces of an ascending, paved roadway rising from west to east. The entire building is aligned with the NE — SW extent of the bridgeway leading from the southwestern entrance to the palace itself. The latter road stood at the level of the main western entrance to the house, at the storey above the floor shown in our plan.

Knossos: Southeast House

Built during the MM IIIA period, the Southeast House at Knossos is somewhat earlier in date than the South House.[57] It nevertheless shares a number of organizational features with the latter, as well as with the Knossian Royal Villa and House of the Frescoes (Figure II.14).

The structure was built up against terracing that was later to support the construction of the House of the Chancel Screen.[58] The lower entrance level of the latter corresponds to the contiguous upper-level entrance of the Southeast House. The alignment of the former house corresponds to that of the palace immediately adjacent to its western flank, whereas the Southeast House was constructed at a slight angle to the former.

KN SE was approximately 17 meters north-south and at least 15 meters east-west. Its eastern boundaries are badly denuded: the plan indicates in dotted outline a likely completion, in part following Evans' reconstruction.[59] The plan underwent some remodelling and modification during the LM IIIB period.[60]

The hall system of the house (cells 9-10-11) occupies the southern flank, furthest removed from the main entrance stairwell in the northwestern corner. Its position recalls that of KN HF, KN S, ML DA (with respect to its relation to the entrance system), while its southerly position replicates that of KN HF. Its internal arrangements, however, differ slightly from these later buildings, for the light well stands not at one of the ends of the cluster, but at the center. This chamber (cell 10) does not, moreover, occupy the entire middle zone of the cluster, but constitutes a smaller rectangular area defined by an L-shaped portico. In this regard, it replicates the internal arrangement of the light well of TYL A, although the latter stands at one end of the system, not at its center (see above, Figure II.9).

A customary PDP system separates cells 10 and 9, and incorporates three double doors. The inner (W) cell features a raised U-shaped platform along its inner flank. The hall cluster communicates with the entranceway to the northwest through two small cells (8-7), in a manner similar to KN HF, while an alternative route connects the entrance to cell 11 via cells 1, 2, and 5.

Immediately to the east of the entrance stair is a pillar crypt, cell 4, whose position replicates that of the pillar crypt of KN RV. The latter, however, is connected directly to the northwestern entrance stair: here access to the crypt is indirect, passing through cells 1 and 2 (see above, Figure II.5).

The position of the pillar crypt here may have been influenced by the presence of a cave-sanctuary used during Neolithic and later times: a block in the southwestern corner of cell 4 covered an aperture of this cave.[61] But the entire arrangement of a pillar crypt adjacent to an entrance stair replicates arrangements seen elsewhere, at KN RV, as just noted, and also KN S (above, Figure II.13).

The crypt opens into a long storage magazine (cell 3) to the east, an arrangement recalling that of the pillar crypts in the Knossian palace itself (to be examined below), as well as that seen above at KN HCS.[62] Cell 2 evidently served as an anteroom to the crypt, and no doubt was also connected to storage and preparatory functions. It is unclear how large this cell was.

Cell 2 opens into cell 5 to the south, of unknown function. It contained a slightly raised platform in its northeastern corner. On its western flank is a niche set deep into the wall, and on its southern side is a PDP door system, probably originally comprising two double doors. Seen from the inside of the hall system, the northern walls of cells 10 and 11 consisted of four double doors, those to the right (E) opening back into cell 5, those to the left opening into cells 6 and 6a. Cell 5 may have been a kitchen, although no secure evidence for this has been unearthed.

It appears that the central section of the building, cells 6 and 6a, may have originally served as a central light well, judging from the lining of the walls of cell 6, finely hewn limestone blocks of a type, according to Evans,[63] normally found in exterior or exposed positions. These blocks, however, end at the point where the very narrow wall separating cells 6 and 6a begins, on the northern flank. This latter wall, made up entirely of thin gypsum, divides the central area into a larger rectangular room (6) and a narrow chamber barely a meter in width. The function of the latter is unknown. It may have initially served as a bypass corridor between cells 10 and 5, although given the contiguity of cells 10, 11 and 5 we would be hard put to imagine the purpose of this bypass route. It seems unlikely that 6a was the foundation of a narrow stair, for the gypsum slabs would be ill-suited to support such a stairway. Evans considered that 6a might have been a small bed-chamber,[64] but this seems unlikely (although certainly not impossible). It is also unclear if the gypsum slabs originally stood to the height of the ceiling – they may have merely been a low partition – but the presence of door jambs at the southern end suggests complete enclosure. The orientation of the door jambs in both cells 6 and 6a indicates that the narrow double doors would have folded down to the southern side when closed, suggesting that these doors could be locked from within.[65]

Despite the enigmatic central zone, KN SE is organized in ways which are already familiar: the presence and position of the house's main clusters and cell-types is closely reminiscent of the houses of the MM IIIB/LM I period already examined.[66]

Mallia: House Zeta Beta

House Zeta Beta stands diagonally across the street from House Zeta Alpha examined above (Figure II.8) in Quarter Zeta, to the east of the Mallian palace.[67] Its northern flank is aligned with the direction of the paved causeway and street leading eastward from the eastern entrance to the palace, which passes south of ML ZA, and at ML ZB turns northeasterly. The northwestern corner of ML ZB is directly across the street from the southeastern corner of ML ZA. The house is bordered on its western flank by a paved plaza which extends westward to the palace, and is bordered to the east by a transverse north-south street (Figure II.15).

The house changes its internal alignment toward the south, bringing this facade more in line with house Zeta Gamma,[68] whose northeastern corner stands very close to the southwestern corner of ML ZB, at cell viii. The southern facade of the latter is aligned with the orientation both of House Zeta Gamma and the north-south street to the east of ML ZB. The relative disposition of the three houses of Quarter Zeta is shown below in Figure II.16.

The main entrance to the house is by means of a doorway off the sidestreet, in the northeastern corner (cell 1). This vestibule bifurcates into an L-shaped corridor to the south, and a passageway to an L-shaped stairway to the north. There may have been doors separating cell 1 from both passages. Under the return of the stairway was cupboard (cell 3).

The entrance way opens into a central chamber, cell 8, which features a single central column. The position of this columned cell and its relation to an entrance to the northeast replicates an arrangement to be seen below in the very large Maison E (Le Petit Palais) elsewhere in the city. In the latter structure, to be examined below, this central area is much enlarged, and shows evidence of having been a courtyard (Figure II.22).[69]

Cells 4, 5, and 6 served as storage magazines, as did cell 13, whose triangular space was generated by the change in orientation of the house at the point. Cells 9, 10, 11, and 12 were evidently service areas, and there is some indication that cell 12 may have been a kitchen.[70] Dotted lines in our plan indicate conjectural doorways connecting several cells.

The primary hall system of the house is cells 20 and 21; there are traces of PDP foundations separating these two cells. A third cell of the system, cell 7, opens off cell 21 through what may have been a double door. There is no recognizable light well here, although cell 20 opens to the south onto a paved exterior porch giving access to what might have been a small private garden; a somewhat similar arrangement occurs in ML ZA across the street.

The position of the hall cluster is the same as that of Mallia House E, namely, at the southwestern corner of the building, beyond the central chamber of the building.

The structure also includes a latrine (cell 19) adjacent to the living apartment, and a window onto the main east-west street to the north, in cell 4. The latter, however, may have been a second doorway, for the sill is rather low for a window onto a public street.[71] The function of cell B at the southwestern corner of the building is unknown, and it may well have been closed off on its western side.

As will be seen in our discussion of House E below, the organization of the house is replicated elsewhere through various transformations of position and relationship among cell-clusters, and its resemblance to other Mallian houses is notable.

The northern facade of the structure, along the main east-west street of this quarter, is divided into three planes of roughly equal length, only partially corresponding to the position of interior transverse wall-ends. This tripartite arrangement recalls a number of houses looked at above, particularly GRT, ML DA, KN S, KN SE, KN HF. The house contrasts with the other two Mallian houses examined in having no sunken 'lustral chamber' and no second stairwell adjacent to the living halls.[72]

Nirou Khani

This large mansion, excavated by Xanthoudhidhes in 1918,[73] stands on the northern coast of the island, some 13 kilometers east of Herakleion (Figure II.17). Part of a settlement which included a port at nearby Haghia Theodhoroi,[74] this structure is built upon a large paved courtyard whose furniture included an assemblage of ritual objects, including a large 'horns of consecration' and a tripartite shrine platform. It is not known if the large courtyard was entirely surrounded by construction; only its southern, western, and eastern boundaries remain. The present coastline is only a few meters beyond the northern section of the building. Both the size of the structure, and its excellent craftsmanship, indicate that this was no ordinary domestic establishment, and both the excavator and Sir Arthur Evans considered its purposes to be largely religious in nature.[75] Nevertheless, its internal organization suggests that whatever other functions the structure served, it was also a residence.

The major (extant) entrance is to the southwest, through a long courtyard (cell A), leading into a passageway (B) separated from the former and from the main court beyond by doors.[76] The southern boundary of these cells is formed by a retaining wall, through which descends a short flight of steps, into cell B.

At the juncture of cells A and B there is a projection southward by the house proper, at which point cell 28, with two openings, served as a porter's lodge for the control of traffic coming from the west and south.

The main courtyard, cell C, has traces of flagstone paving to a distance of roughly ten meters east of the eastern facade of the house. Within this area was a reserved section of pavement (now obliterated) extending between two circular pits some 2½ meters deep, as indicated on our plan. Two southward projections of this section focus upon objects standing along the southern wall of the court: a large 'horns of consecration' to the west, and a tripartite shrine platform to the east. The latter recalls the general outline of the tripartite shrine on the western facade of the central court of the palace of Knossos (q.v.),[77] the circular pits recall similar objects in the western courts of the palaces of Knossos and Phaistos (which may have been the sites of specially planted [or preserved] trees),[78] and the reserved section of paving recalls several similar sections in the central court of the palace at Mallia.[79]

There are two entrances into the structure from court C: that to the north leads to a large storage area lined with magazines, while that to the south leads to the hall system of the building.

The latter is of a familiar type, consisting of a porch (cell 1) and a hall (cell 2) beyond a PDP system with four double doors.

The plan of this hall system superficially resembles a simple Mycenaean 'megaron' with its opening onto a (semi?)-public courtyard,[80] but Minoan analogies also exist: see the plan of ML ZA above, Figure II.8.[81]

Appended to the hall system are the remaining cell-clusters of the building. A door in the northern side of cell 2 opens into the major storage areas, cells 15-19, and a door in the southern side of that cell opens into a corridor leading to a stairwell to the west and, to the east, to a cluster of small chambers (cells 24-28). Cell 28 in this cluster served as a guard's station, while in cell 24a were found a set of large bronze double axes.

At the western end of cell 2 is a door opening into a corridor (cell 3) which communicates with the rest of the extant portions of the building. To the south of the corridor is a PDP entrance to a room with a bench (cell 4), which opens to the east to a room (cell 5) containing lamps, and a room to the south which served to store small altars. To the west of cell 4 is a light well (cell 8) bordered by square pillars. Storerooms are appended to the light well to the south (cells 9-10).

To the north of corridor 3 are two small chambers (6-7); that to the west contained three small altars while that on the east (6) featured a stone bench along its northern wall. To the west of corridor 3 is a north-south corridor which communicated with the area of the storage magazines to the north (through cell 15), and two narrow corridors running westward (cells 12-13). How far the building extended here is unknown; it is possible that at least part of the cell system (12-13-14) may have been a stairwell, particularly if there was a western entrance to the building at this point.[82]

Although superficially unlike many of the houses we have looked at so far, NK is organized topologically in a familiar fashion. The central position of the hall system recalls KN RV; its closeness both to a stairwell and service areas resonates with many other examples. The stairwell internal to the storage area is not unlike TYL A and C, and the strategically placed porter's lodge is echoed in both these houses (especially TYL A, with its external window). The separate entrance to the storage magazines from the exterior (via cell 17) recalls TYL A's back door.

The presence of many stored objects of patent ritual function, as well as the large paved courtyard with its shrine(s), nevertheless place Nirou Khani among a group of structures more 'palatial' or semi-public in type, and we shall consider this aspect of the building in our examination of the palatial compounds below.[83]

Sklavokampos

Some 18 by 24 meters in size, this large house was excavated by Marinatos in the 1930s; most of the remains were obliterated during World War II.[84] The following account is based principally upon published reports (Figure II.18).

The building consists of two major zones which do not communicate on the ground floor level. The area to the north, evidently the principal residential zone, featured a hall (cell 2), an entrance vestibule and porter's lodge(?) (cells A, 1), a long east-west corridor a stairwell under which was a latrine, a shrine(?) (cell 5), and two interconnecting rooms (3-4), possibly sleeping chambers. The corridor terminates to the west at a door leading to storerooms (7, 6) and a fine four-bayed veranda formed by three square pillars cell 8. The latter recalls the northern veranda at AMN, although the latter opened off a hall system (see Figure II.11).

Cell 2 was evidently the main living hall, revealing characteristic PDP arrangements on one flank. It is not known what the internal arrangements were (i.e. if the hall was subdivided into smaller cells); most of this part of the house was accidentally destroyed before excavation. The closeness of the hall to a latrine, stairway, and porter's lodge(?) is a familiar composition.

We have already seen another house wherein major zones on a ground floor do not intercommunicate: Gortyn. There, however, most of the entire ground floor was given over to storage, while here no such functional division is evident. The southern half of the house includes a separate entrance (into cell B), and is largely given over to service (cells 11 and 12 may have been a kitchen and pantry). At the center of the area (cell 9) is a fine courtyard surrounded by three squared pillars and a wall-corner on the northeastern side. This wall angle incorporates a built pillar, but it is unclear if this is an indication that the connecting walls were a later addition. In other words, it is conceivable that cell 3 originally connected with this peristyle court, whose disposition resembles those found at Mallia (ML E) and Palaikastro (House B and others).[85] Such an arrangement would be consistent with peristyle houses elsewhere, but there is no evidence on which to base such a conjecture.

There was no doubt a second stairway in the house in this southern quarter, probably within or adjacent to corridor B, rising westward beyond the southern doorway of the house. The ground on which the house stands rises gradually toward the south, and the floor level of this quarter is roughly half a meter above that of the living quarters to the north.

Palaikastro: House B

Figure II.19 is a plan of the portions of the city of Palaikastro excavated by the British Scool between 1902 and 1906, now almost totally obliterated by activity during World War II.[86] Shown in heavy outline in our plan are the traces of two houses, B and X, which incorporate features seen elsewhere in Minoan construction. The larger house (B) is approximately 21½ by 43 meters in size, and fronts on a major east-west street. It features a peristyle court at its center, bounded by four columns, recalling the house at Sklavokampos just examined; it was probably roofed by a clerestory.[87] To the right of this is a sunken 'lustral basin', a familiar feature in Knossian and other houses in the central section of the island.

That this was a two-storey house is indicated by the presence of two stairways: one to the immediate north of the courtyard, and one adjacent to the southeastern entrance. To the north of the latter are traces of a columned (hypostyle) hall, with pillars alternating with columns, recalling the cluster of cells to the north of the central courtyards of the palaces of Knossos, Phaistos, Mallia, Karo Zakro and Gournia.[88] Beyond this hall was a courtyard bounded by a wall on the north and east; it is not known what other construction originally existed in this area.

The original house entrance may have been through the columned portico at the southern central flank, indicated in hatched outline on our plan.

Whether the central court area was originally structured like a more familiar hall system is problematical; if so, it would have been L-shaped rather than rectangular. The presence of two additional courts of similar formation has been detected in two houses across the main street to the south, but these do not seem to have been extended further.[89] That such hall systems did exist at Palaikastro may be seen in House X, at the right of the plan.

Palaikastro: House X

This very interesting (and now no longer extant) house stood at the eastern limit of the excavated portion of the city of Palaikastro, at the juncture of three streets. Rectangular in shape with several projecting facades, the house is approximately 17 by 25 meters, exclusive of a unique raised exterior porch at the south-eastern corner (Figure II.20).

The site is very much a jumble of foundations dating well back into the Early Minoan II period,[90] and the walls reveal few threshold blocks, making it difficult to discern the network of internal connections. What remains indicates the following.

The house was entered through the stepped porch into a vestibule (cell 1), to the west of which was a stairwell (cell 2). The central chamber, cell 3, contains two columns across its axis, with a third base (square) to the north: the latter may have fallen from an upper storey.[91]

To the east of cell 3 is the hall system of the house, a bicameral suite divided by a PDP system with three double doors. The inner section opens laterally, to the south, to another cell (5). It is unclear whether any of these three chambers was a light well, or if in fact cell 6 may have been a light well, later walled up and connected elsewhere. Had the latter been the case, then we may conjecture that two columns stood where the western wall of cell 6 stands. The resultant arrangement would then be identical to arrangements elsewhere.

The entire western wing of the house, entered through cell 7, consists mainly of foundations of cellars of an earlier building, incorporated in the new building to the east.[92] As indicated by our plan, the entire eastern half of the structure is of uniform alignment and homogeneous construction, contrasting with the older western zone. The modular grid superimposed upon the plan indicates the eastern quarter's simplicity and homogeneity (discussed in detail below in Part Two). Of note here is the position of the hall system and the configuration of the outer trace.

With regard to the latter, the tripartite eastern facade is similar to house facades built during the MM III/LM I period elsewhere; for example, ML DA, KN S, KN SE, KN RV. The position of the hall system—occupying the central third of the plan — recalls that of KN RV and KN HCS.

A unique feature of Palaikastro X is the stepped porch, consisting of four columns upon a platform whose outer steps extend out into the street, and curve around to the northeast along the turn in the road. A small bench stands in the porch, against the back wall. It is likely that the second storey of the house extended out over the porch at this point, providing a commanding view down the three confluent streets. This upper level may have been entirely enclosed, or may have simply been an open balcony. Similar porticoes may have existed along the second level of the west facade of the major palaces (Knossos, Phaistos, Mallia), or along other palace facades such as the eastern facade of the central court at Kato Zakro. The only other example of a veranda opening out to public view in a private house might have been cell 8 at Sklavokampos (Figure II.18), although the latter is enclosed by end walls, unlike the present example.

Tylissos: House B

Located barely 1.2 meters to the west of the projecting western stairwell bastion of TYL A, the present structure is, by contrast, a simple rectangle. In plan (at least at the extant ground floor level) it bears little resemblance to house plans already seen. It is most likely that the structure was a storehouse annex to TYL A.[93] Houses A and B together make for an establishment as large as any of the so-called 'little palaces' of Knossos, Phaistos and Mallia (Figure II.21).

As a freestanding structure, TYL B would be unique, with its ranks of storage rooms around a central series of circulatory passageways, themselves enclosing a paved central chamber (cell 21). But as a warehouse annex to House A, the best analogue is in fact the western magazine block of the Second Palace of Phaistos (q.v.), constructed around the same time. The latter contrasts strongly with the north-south ranks of long magazines remaining from the First Palace Period at Knossos and Mallia, and probably represents a rethinking of storage and circulatory requirements in major buildings.

Like the western magazine block at Phaistos II, TYL B stands to the west of a residence compound (TYL A). While evidently connected with the latter at the second storey (as indicated in our reconstruction inset in Figure I.3), the structure is also entered at the ground floor level by a doorway in the center of the eastern facade (cell 1). To the north of this vestibule is the stairway, and to the south is an antechamber (cell 3) leading to a guard's room (4). Vestibule 1 leads straight on to cell 2, to which are appended the remaining cells of the structure. At this point are three doors. That to the north controls access to cell 6, antechamber C, and cells 19, 18, and 20 beyond. That to the west leads into the central chamber, a paved hall with a columned balustrade dividing it into a larger and smaller area (cell 21). The latter also communicates with cells 19 and 18 to the north. The southern door in cell 2 leads to the U-shaped corridor (cell 7) to which are appended eight storage rooms. The largest cell in the building is 8 which, like cells 5 and 6, is closely connected with the outer passageways of the structure.

The function of cell 21 is unknown. Cells 18 and 19 contained offering tables, and it is not inconceivable that cell 21 may have been part of a small shrine, although there is no evidence to support this.[94] Nothing remains of the second storey to indicate its functions. It may simply have consisted of an annex to the living halls on the second storey of TYL A, combined with servants' quarters and service areas. It is not unlikely, also, that part of the ground floor of this structure housed part of a service staff.

The fact that Houses B and A are not exactly aligned with one another is of interest (see above, Figure I.3). While evidently planned and laid out with a uniform module (and contrasting in this with House C to the northeast),[95] the two structures may have been constructed in sequence. House B is, however, in alignment with House C, and it is conceivable that these two were laid out prior to House A. Considering the care with which each building was itself laid out and constructed, these misalignments must be due to topographic adjustments and/or the disposition of preexisting walls and property lines on the site.[96] But despite the overall misalignment of Houses A and B, their alignment is very nearly exact in one area only: the respective outer flanks where our proposed bridge would have stood, connecting the adjacent stairwells. Indeed, the curious diagonal jog of the southwestern wall of the stairwell bastion of House A follows the orientation of its partner across the alleyway, rather than the orientation of its own house. This might suggest that TYL A was built after TYL B.

OTHER RESIDENCES

The previous examples provide a good sample of the best preserved Minoan houses. A few other house plans are looked at in Part Two, but the information they have yielded is principally of value in considering detailed questions of planning and layout,[97] rather than questions of formative and functional organization.

The remaining sections of this Chapter will be devoted to larger constructions, including the so-called 'little palaces' in the three cities of Knossos, Mallia and Phaistos, and the major 'palaces' of those cities, as well as Kato Zakro, Gournia, and Plati.

Mallia: House E ('Le Petit Palais')

One of the largest non-palatial Minoan structures known, ML E is located some 170 meters south of the Mallian palace.[98] In its extant state, it is approximately 54 by 34 meters in size, its long axis running east-west. The plan is partially confused on the eastern side, owing to the intrusion of later walls and structural modifications, indicated by lighter walls in our plan, Figure II.22.

The house stands along the southern front of a city street, and the remains indicate that it was bordered (at least in part) by a north-south street to the east. It is unclear whether the western facade was contiguous with an adjacent structure, and to the south the house may have opened onto private open ground.

ML E is essentially a larger version of ML ZB (Figure II.15), and its internal organization replicates that of the latter building, notably in the relative placement and positioning of functional zones.

The major entrance is at the northeastern corner (as at ML ZB), into a square vestibule (cell 1) with an off-center column. Directly ahead to the west is a narrow chamber which was most likely a stairway.[99] To the southeast is a doorway leading to a north-south corridor (cell 2) which leads into a paved central courtyard (cell 2 *bis*) which may have featured a partly circumferential colonnade. The position of this court is identical to the central (covered) cell of ML ZB, which also reveals the trace of (one) supportive column.

The courtyard is bounded to the north by cell 3, of unknown function. At the northeast is a door leading northward to a second colonnaded chamber opening into a hall to the south (cells 4-5-6). Cells 5 and 6 were evidently separated by a PDP system, although only threshold blocks remain of the multiple doorway.

The zone of cells to the east of courtyard 2 *bis* comprised service areas given over to food storage and preparation (similar to ML ZB), while the cells to the northwest of the central court and halls comprised a series of storage magazines. The position of the latter recalls that of ML ZB.

The domestic quarter of the house is located along the entire southern flank. Apart from whatever connections may have existed on the second storey, the living halls are accessible on the ground floor only through courtyard 2 *bis*, at the latter's southwestern and southeastern corners. To the southeast is a PDP system, and a similar entrance way may also have existed on the southwest. Again, the placement of the living halls is the same as at ML ZB; at the far flank of the house, on the side of the building opposite the major entrance, and across a central courtyard or chamber. In this regard, the system resembles all of the Mallian houses we have seen thus far: ML ZA has its hall system at the far side of the building (in this case on the northern flank), and ML DA's hall system is also opposite the position of entrance, to the west: see above, Figures II.7 and II.8.

Closely associated with the hall systems of all four houses is a bathroom/'lustral chamber', here cell 9. As at the other three Mallian houses, the 'lustral area' is separated from the halls by its position off an adjacent corridor. Although the other three houses reveal the trace of a nearby stairwell, ML E's plan is too ruined to confidently ascertain where such a stairwell would have stood: likely candidates are cells 12 and 25.

The best preserved section of the domestic quarter – or at least the most recognizable portion – is the peristyle court, cells 14 and 13, toward the southeast. Cell 15 was undoubtedly an associated hall. As at ML ZB, the southern central flank of the house opens out to a secondary entrance, probably into a private garden (cell 20). It is likely that cell 8 was an additional hall, as was cell 26 to the southwest.

If it was in fact the case that the hall systems occupied most of the long flank of the building, then there would be a resemblance to the so-called 'Little Palace' at Knossos (see below), the latter consisting of a series of interconnecting halls including a square peristyle court. The Knossian halls, however, are raised to a second-storey level, and evidently all faced upon a continuous veranda. It is possible that there was a similar arrangement here at Mallia on a second level. The southern facade of ML E, and the corresponding eastern facade of the Knossian mansion, are of approximately equal length.[100] Both mansions, moreover, incorporate a 'lustral chamber' nearby.

Despite its very great size, ML E is organized in a manner similar to ML DA, ML ZA, and ML ZB. Its resemblance to ML ZB is striking, being essentially an enlarged version of a familiar house type, rather than a smaller version of the great palace.

Knossos: 'Little Palace'

Some 43 by 27 meters in size, the Knossian 'Little Palace' (KN LP) is slightly smaller than ML E. Its long axis runs north-south, in contrast to the latter. The structure, which rivals the Knossian palace in the elegance of its appointments, stands at the western terminus of the paved avenue running out from the northwestern entrance of the palace (Evans' 'Royal Road').[101] Like ML E,

KN LP is a large private residence embedded in the urban fabric, bounded by streets and alleyways (Figure II.23).

It is not entirely clear whether KN LP comprises the entirety of a large compound. If, as Evans suggested, it was connected at a second storey to the 'Unexplored Mansion' across an alleyway to the west,[102] then we may be dealing with a compound not unlike TYL A/B.[103] Until we know the nature and disposition of the 'Unexplored Mansion', any speculation in this area is premature.

Figure II.23 shows Evans' isometric reconstruction of the building, indicating that KN LP was probably a three-storey structure. The entire southwestern quadrant stands one storey below the remainder. Of the latter, only the southeastern projection — the set of columned halls — has a basement, consisting of a crypt with five square pillars. Everything to the east conjecturally restored; there is no secure evidence for the complex entrance porch along the eastern flank of the building. The latter is omitted in C.C.T. Doll's 1910 plan (Figure II.24).[104]

The most notable feature of the building is the long series of halls along the eastern flank, comprising in effect a doubled hall system fronting, at center, on a square peristyle court. The latter most likely had a clerestory roof above the third level. The entire hall system is bordered to the east by a long colonnade, making for a veranda or balcony not unlike the smaller examples of Amnissos and Sklavokampos, and similar in design to the outer verandas of the palatial hall systems of Knossos, Phaistos, and Mallia.[105] The arrangement also recalls the hall systems of the great mansion at Haghia Triadha near Phaistos, to be examined below. If our conjecture regarding the original disposition of ML E is correct, the latter system may have resembled KN LP on its upper storey: in both cases, a square peristyle court is situated within the system of halls.[106]

The principal extant entrance to the structure is within a recess of the southern facade, next to a bicameral porter's lodge. To the west of the latter is a rectangular room with two square pillars. This chamber was a cul-de-sac. To the north of this entrance portico is a door leading to a stepped east-west corridor, to which are appended two separate stairwells. That to the west may have led in part to the hypothetical bridge connecting KN LP with the 'Unexplored Mansion' to the west. The stair on the east constituted the main stairwell of the building.

The southeastern projection of the building consists of several pillared chambers sunk below grade, connected to the outside by a doorway in the northwestern corner. Evidently devoted to ritual usage,[107] the cluster connects, by means of a stairway on the southwestern corner, with a set of columned halls on the second level. The area then gives access to the hall system to the north.

The western zone of the mansion is divided into several cell-clusters. In the area of the main stairs are a series of small storage chambers, and a paved court immediately to the west of the stair. Opening off the peristyle court are five small cells bordering the sunken 'lustral chamber' (bathroom). The latter is entered from a square anteroom to the north, and was apparently transformed at a later date into a shrine, according to Evans.[108] North of the anteroom is a latrine, drained out to the north of the building.

The alignment of this northwestern quarter follows the line of a street to the west, itself bounded by a wall to the west. This may indicate that the latter is anterior in date to the construction of the northwestern section of KN LP.

The mansion has about one half the number of cells appended to its hall system as ML E. This *may* be indicative of an associative or auxiliary function of the 'Unexplored Mansion' to the west. In other words, if it is not unreasonable to assume that KN LP and ML E were households of similar type, then we may expect that the 'Unexplored Mansion' might have served as a storage annex to KN LP, not unlike TYL B.

To term this structure a 'Little Palace' we must justify a number of auxiliary assumptions. We must question whether this was the residence of a socially prominent household which was also involved to some degree with the business of the great 'palace' itself. If the latter were an 'official' palatial compound, would KN LP then constitute a private governmental residence?

It is patent that we have no such evidence upon which to base such speculations. The fact that KN LP stands at the 'terminus' of a 'royal road' – Evans' term for the paved avenue leading from the northwestern corner of the Knossian palace to the eastern flank of the present structure – is unconvincing. There is nothing about this structure, either in its organization or appointments, to suggest that it was other than simply a large private residence, similar to ML E, embedded in the fabric of the town. It exhibits all the familiar features of a private house, with its (albeit grand) hall system, pillar crypts, 'lustral chamber', latrine, and storage magazines and porter's lodge, all of these elements deployed in a manner identical to other Knossian houses. It is only the accident of discovery which makes this structure appear unique and special; there were undoubtedly other similarly large and finely built mansions around the city of Knossos.[109]

Haghia Triadha

Larger than either KN LP or ML E, the elegant mansion of Haghia Triadha stands at the western or coastal end of the great hilly promontory at whose eastern end stands the palace of Phaistos, three-quarters of an hour's walk away. The structure is built along the western and eastern flank of the hill, and extends east-west for about 85 meters. The inner portion of this L-shaped building evidently featured a paved courtyard at a second level. At the eastern end of the excavated area, additional construction bounded this inner court. It is unknown if this open area was bordered to the south by additional construction as well.

While a detailed discussion of HTR's organization must await final publication, we may make a number of observations based upon the state of the plan.

As indicated by Figure II.25, the mansion was accompanied by additional construction to the north, at a level lower than the former. During the Late Minoan III period, HTR was a palatial citadel of Mycenaean type, replicating components of the mainland citadel of Tiryns.[110] These remains are indicated in outline on the plan.

Of the Minoan villa itself, we may note the inclusion of two extremely fine hall systems: one standing at the northwestern corner of the building (cells 3, 4, 11, 12, and 14), and one at the eastern end, adjacent to a stairway rising to the inner courtyard (cells 1, 2, 19, 20, and 21).

The stairway at the northeastern corner rises from the north, just inside a doorway. At this point a stepped rampway ('rampa dal mare') rises to the west along the northern border of the structure. The latter evidently led to entrances at or near the northwestern corner of the villa, and probably continued south-ward along the eastern side of the structure ('via a Festos'). Along the latter side are found a cluster of rectangular cells resembling in their disposition a rank of storage magazines not unlike the western magazines of other Minoan houses and palaces. This set of rooms was appended to a long north-south corridor/light area to the east, and traces of windows were found at the eastern end of four of these magazines. The western facade comprised a series of closed set-backs resembling the indented trace of the western facades of the palaces of Mallia and Knossos.

The hall system to the north, one of the largest known, includes several PDP halls plus a peristyle court (?) in the northwestern angle (cell 11). The cluster commands a fine view out toward the coast of the bay to the west, a view enhanced from the second (courtyard) level (no doubt) by a long veranda or colonnaded balcony, recalling KN LP and the conjectural second-storey veranda of ML E. An inner cell in the system (4) includes a stone bench around three sides, while in cell 13 were found storage niches for clay tablets.[111]

The organization of this northwestern hall system, as well as that to the northeast, recalls most closely the hall systems of the palace of Phaistos. Indeed, the northeastern hall system is very nearly a replica of the Phaistian hall system, consisting of a double rank of halls, a porter's room (?) on the northeastern corner (cell 20), and an appended stairwell to the immediate south of the southern halls. In addition, on the eastern flank of both systems is a peripheral north-south corridor, providing a by-pass entrance on this side of the building. While the HTR hall system is bounded by an east-west wall to the north, that of Phaistos opens out through a veranda, in a manner similar to the hall systems of AMN or SKLV. At the second storey here we may well imagine an arrangement similar to the latter, and to the colonnaded system at KN LP, raised above grade.

The area between the two hall systems at HTR is filled with storage and work areas, although we would expect on comparative grounds that there existed a 'lustral chamber' immediately to the west of the northeastern hall system (as at Phaistos or KN LP). Cell 17, used in its extant condition as a storage room, is in form a pillar crypt, consisting of a square paved chamber with a central square pillar. If this area was part of a household shrine, we may imagine that its principal focus was on the second storey, at the level of the courtyard to the south. This would place a hypothetical pillar crypt in the body of the building at a position resonating with the pillar crypts of the major palaces, viz. at the center of the long flank of construction fronting on a rectangular courtyard.[112] The pillar crypt is also directly to the north of a stepped construction in the court considered by the building's excavators as the area of an open-air shrine, west of E in the plan. As we shall see below in our discussion of the palaces of Knossos, Phaistos and Mallia, their principal ritual chambers or pillar crypts stand at the center of the body of construction along the long flank of their central courtyards.

The remains of this part of the building are overlain and disturbed by the foundations of the Late Minoan III period Megaron (walls A-B-C-D and area *E*), and our picture of the internal arrangements of the courtyard is incomplete. A squarish chamber just north of wall A in our plan, consisting of a room with four square pillars, is similar in disposition to a cell at the northeastern corner of the palace at Phaistos. The latter, to be discussed below, was a First Palace Period construction incorporated into the Second Palace and serving as an entrance portico to the northeastern quarter of the later palace.[113]

It is not known if the construction at the eastern end of the court should be counted as part of the mansion itself. It features a series of storage magazines at its western flank, and two PDP halls to the east, which evidently opened into a courtyard running north-south. This construction may in fact have constituted a private and separate house, not unlike the houses adjacent to the palaces of Knossos (KN S, KN SE), or those forming part of the boundary of the courtyard of the provincial palace compound at Gournia (q.v.). At the southeastern corner of this area is a small rectangular building which the excavators suggest may have been a shrine during the Late Minoan III period, built after the destruction of HTR, and forming part of the 'Mycenaean' citadel.[114]

The question as to the relationship of HTR to the Phaistian palace compound has no easy answer. While the mansion would indeed comprise a fine 'summer palace' for the 'rulers' at Phaistos, this need not have been its sole function. And yet its organization and appointments, the prominence of its position, and its (at least partly) incorporated large courtyard strikingly contrast with the large urban houses of KN LP and ML E. Its courtyard is as long, and may have been as wide, as the central court of the large palaces. In overall area, it is larger than the palace of Gournia. Indeed, of the three large mansions called 'little palaces', its organization is the only one which would suggest that this is a smaller version of the great palaces; KN LP and ML E are simply blown-up private residences.

But if HTR was a 'small palace' (let alone a 'Royal Villa'), what in fact is its relationship to the contemporary great compound at Phaistos? Is the latter more of an official, governmental compound in which the rulers of this south Cretan city-state periodically 'held court' or did their business, with HTR comprising a more residential 'palace' in its own right?

Many of the discussions of Minoan governmental organization are based on remarkably flimsy conclusions and on assumptions which derive from superficial impressions. From the outset of Cretan excavation, Evans and others formed conclusions as to the societal functions of the buildings quickly termed 'palaces' on the basis of purported resemblances to palatial compounds elsewhere in the eastern Mediterranean during the Bronze Age. We simply do not know how the Minoans governed themselves in the period before mainland hegemony (LM III). While it is clear that the great compounds of Knossos, Phaistos and Mallia housed large and complicated bureaucracies, we do not know whether those bureaucracies supported a royal household or a general commonwealth. Was 'Minos' a king, pharaoh, or Mycenaean-type warlord, or is 'Minos' the title of an elected official? Was Crete 'ruled' from Knossos, or was the island a federated commonwealth of city-states? Could there have been separate 'kings' at Knossos, Phaistos, Mallia, Gournia, Kato Zakro, Plati, and Haghia Triadha? Why does each major city have a 'palace'? Until such questions are seriously addressed, we shall not understand the functional interrelationships of these Minoan constructions.

It is patent that HTR — unlike KN LP and ML E — is a 'palatial' compound, if by 'palatial' we mean resembling its larger but similar cousins at Knossos, Phaistos and Mallia. But whether the latter were in fact 'palaces' in our sense of the term is quite unclear. Indeed, as we shall see below, their very architectonic organizations make it plain that they are different kinds of constructs than their purported counterparts in Egypt, Mesopotamia, or mainland Greece.[115]

URBAN MEGASTRUCTURES: THE PALACES

Gournia: Palace

Shown in the plan are the remains of the inland quarters of the town of Gournia, excavated in the first decade of the century by Harriet Boyd-Hawes.[116] Situated near a sheltered cove within the Bay of Mirabello on the northeastern coast of the island, Gournia consists of a densely packed group of houses covering a hill, at the uppermost part of which is a large mansion or palatial compound. The town originally extended northward along the flat land to the cove, several hundred meters to the north.[117] Settlement remains from the Middle Minoan period have been found, but the greatest bulk of the construction dates from the LM I period. After the town's destruction, a mainland-type megaron house was built to the southwest of the ruins of the palace, as at HTR, during the LM III period (Figure II.26).[118]

The remains revealed the presence of a score of contiguous but separate houses built to approximately the same NS-EW orientation, all fronting on the paved and partially stepped streets traversing the hillsides. Each house is squarish or rectangular in outline, and many reveal the traces of small paved courts or light wells. Each house would normally have had a second storey, and the roof lines of the houses would have risen in stepped fashion toward the summit of this hill town. Open spaces at the interior of several blocks suggest the incorporation of private garden plots accessible from the rear of the houses, and in some cases opening onto small alleyways which joined the main street grid (e.g. areas A, B-37, C, D-33). Such a pattern resembles the densely packed organization of scores of present-day Greek island towns. If House Ab is taken as typical, most of the houses were squarish in plan where the topography permitted, and each was entered roughly at the center of its street side, often into a paved vestibule.[119]

The streets of the town eventually converge on the area of the summit of the hill, dominated by a large palatial compound (G). Unlike its more urban cousins, the Gournia palace is tightly embedded in the town fabric, contiguous with other buildings except for its southern frontage on a rectangular courtyard or plaza running north-south.

The courtyard itself is directly accessible by means of a public street ('East Ascent D' in the plan), and most likely by other public streets to the south, which is presently denuded. It is not known how far the court extends to the south, but if it comprised a 1 : 2 rectangle, like the courtyards at Knossos, Phaistos and Mallia, its southern boundary would have been approximately a dozen or so meters south of the East Ascent.

The eastern and western flanks of the court are made up of the walls of what the excavators take to be separate, private houses; construction probably not part of the palace itself to the north. If this is the case (and of course we have no sure way of knowing), the disposition of the compound would resemble that of HTR. The 'courtyard' of the Gournia palace, in other words, is evidently a public or semi-public plaza, rather than an interior court.

A more detailed plan of the palace proper is shown in the next plan, Figure II.27.

Standing as it does at the top of the hill, the structure is greatly ruined, and it is difficult to trace the position of many of its original interior walls. But from what is readible, we may discern a number of features which resonate with other palatial compounds on Crete.

There are several entrances to the structure: East Ascent D, leading up to the plaza or court, a second court entrance to the west, adjacent to cells 15, 16, and 17, a doorway in the western facade into the area labelled 'storerooms' in Boyd-Hawes' plan, adjacent to a zone to the north labelled 'men's apartments' (pure fantasy), and an entrance somewhere on the eastern facade, accessible either from East Ascent C or the East Ridge Road in Figure II.26. The latter street either entered the structure near cell 31, or else ran along the eastern facade to the south, to join the stepped street East Ascent C in its approach to the northeastern corner of the courtyard.

Along the western facade of the building, the public street widens into a small court, and terminates at a double doorway. The western door opens onto a narrow corridor ('terrace' in the plan), the eastern door to another paved corridor. Both cells terminate to the south at doorways. The arrangement resembles the main western entrance to the palace at Knossos, with the continuation of the corridors into an eastward passage to the court reminiscent of the 'Corridor of the Procession' at Knossos. But the doubling of the passageway along the western facade is a puzzle. Why an alternative passageway here?

Note that the western facade walls to the north of this double corridor, and those to the south and east, beyond the corridor, are faced with finely hewn ashlar limestone masonry, recalling the fine workmanship of the western facades of the major palaces, which front on (public) western courts. The section to the north of the corridors also reveals a finely articulated indented trace, identical to those of the major palaces. It has been suggested[120] that at the time of its destruction, this facade was being remodelled and spruced-up to resemble its more urban cousins. I would suggest, however, that the reason for not including in this remodelling scheme the portion of the western facade along the double corridor is that the latter was considered as interior to the fabric of the mansion itself. In other words, the public portions of the streets terminated to the north and south at this corridor system. This would make sense if we assume that the so-called 'terrace' to the west was in fact the foundation of a double stairway leading to a central landing and crossing eastward onto the second storey of the mansion, possibly to a vestibule and hall system over the area of the western magazines (cells 4 through 12), and the pillared hall at the center of the structure (cell 20). The hypothetical east-west corridor would pass over the central jog in the lower corridor facade, into the area over cell 7 to the east.

Such a situation might also imply that the palace fabric covered over the double corridor, and may even have extended westward. In other words, it is not inconceivable that the palatial compound included construction to the west of the streets (recall TYL A and B, and KN LP). It also recalls the area to the west of the West Porch of the palace of Knossos. The area beyond the western wall of the 'terrace' was only partly excavated, and the suggestion that the compound included a structure to the west cannot be supported.

While it does seem evident that the palace extended at least to the western wall of the western corridor, this does not necessarily mean that the latter had to have been a stairway. Another plausible explanation may be given, namely, that the 'terrace' was in fact a porter's chamber, with a double entrance so as to control access from the ends of the public streets beyond. Such an explanation rests upon the resemblance of these cells to the western entrance at Knossos, namely, an entrance corridor to the east, a porter's lodge to the west, both fronting side-by-side onto an entryway to the north. And, just as the eastern corridor here not only leads to the area of the western entrance to the palace court or plaza but also provides continuity with the north-south street beyond, to the south, so also does the 'Corridor of the Procession' at the Knossian palace evidently connect with the bridgeway-bypass to the southwest of that building. The topological identity of the two situations underlies their geometric dissimilarities.[121]

Gournia resembles the Knossian palace also with respect to the placement of storage magazines along the western facade. In both cases we find narrow rectangular cells aligned east-west, from the position of the entranceways, and up to the north. Here, however, the magazines stop near the western entrance through the ashlar facade; it is not known what the disposition of rooms to the north was.

The latter area, fancifully termed 'men's apartments', may possibly have been a residential zone, for the small cell 28 was a latrine. There was evidently a stairway at 26 in the plan, at the eastern end of the destroyed area on whose western flank was an additional stair. The latter opens down to the area next to the western entrance, a situation seen above in many Minoan houses.

Cells 23 and 24 comprised storage magazines, and the former was bounded on its eastern side by a stair rising to the north (22 on plan). To the south of this area is a pillared hall, featuring alternate rows of square pillars and round columns. Such a hall is replicated in the major palaces of Knossos, Phaistos, Mallia and Kato Zakro, and in each of those cases the hall stands to the north of the courtyard. In its alternation of pillars and columns, the

Gournia hall resembles Phaistos most closely.[122] Taken as a cluster of cells, Gournia 20, 24, and 23 closely resemble both Phaistos and Mallia. Despite detailed differences in plan, all three cases feature a pillared hall, adjacent storerooms of various sizes, and a stairway to the second storey. Whether the pillared hall itself served the same function as those elsewhere is unknown.[123]

It is not known what stood to either side of the hall, or if this hall was in fact a central component in a traditional hall system. To the southeast of cell 21 ('central hall' on plan) is a small cell opening on the latter through a central column. It contained a stone bench within, similar in kind to cell 4 at HTR, which stood at the eastern end of a large hall system, in an identical relationship to a larger set of cells to the west.

But there is simply no way of knowing if this central zone of the palace comprised a hall system of the familiar type. Judging from the fact that in the other cases where a pillared or 'hypostyle' hall occurs, it is always separate from a hall system cluster, we may suggest that the residential halls at Gournia stood elsewhere. The most likely sites would be area 27-28-29 or 32, both of which were considered likely residential zones by the building's excavators. My own suggestion would be area 32, on the eastern flank of the building.[124]

To the south of the pillared hall, at 19 in the plan, is an L-shaped corridor which opens to the south onto a stepped portico bordering the northern side of the court. The L-shaped steps seem like a miniature version of the so-called 'theatral area' at Knossos or Phaistos, although in actual size they are reminiscent of the stepped shrine of the courtyard at HTR. That this northwestern corner of the court was in some way devoted to religious ritual is suggested by the find of a 'horns of consecration' just south of area 18, near the pillared portico fronting on the western side of the court, just east of cell 17. This portico is similar in general form to the 'tripartite shrine' on the western flank of the Knossian central court. Directly to the west, along the western facade of the structure along cell 15, was found an incised double-axe symbol, possibly another indication that the portico to the east was a shrine. As we shall see below, the positioning of double-axe (labrys) symbols in the palaces appears to be connected to rituals of worship.[125]

Cells 14, 15, 16, and 17 are confused. Evidently also used for storage, their heavy walls might also have supported a stairwell to an upper storey, and possibly, if quarter H to the south were functionally part of the palatial compound, connecting with a second storey over that area.

Gournia thus presents many of the major functional and structural components of the great palatial compounds, but in miniature. It is about a tenth the size of the Knossian palace, but preserves, in its compactness, a syntax of cellular relationships manifested by the great urban megastructures. It is to these latter that we shall now turn.

Knossos: Palace

Figure II.28 presents the final published plan of the vast palatial compound of the city of Knossos copied from Sir Arthur Evans' four-volume treatise on Minoan civilization.[126] Virtually a city-within-a-city, the Knossian megastructure was originally constructed at the beginning of the Middle Minoan period, and was remodelled and rebuilt over a period of nearly half a millennium. The plan shows the compound as it appeared more or less at the time of its final destruction, during the Late Minoan period.[127]

The southern and eastern flanks of the compound are built up against the sides of a valley formed by the confluence of two small streams. To the south, this valley is spanned by a bridge which terminates at the southwestern corner of the structure, connecting with the circulatory fabric of the palace through a series of corridors.[128]

The published plan is somewhat misleading, for it does not incorporate topographical contours. In fact, the entire eastern half of the building is two storeys below the level of the central court, and from this point the hill slopes down to the stream bed to the east. The two houses at the southeastern corner of the compound, KN HCS and KN SE, are at a lower level than the adjacent palace construction, and the second storey of the latter house is at the ground floor level of the former. At the southwestern corner of the compound, the South House is two storeys below the grade of the adjacent bridgehead, and the South Corridor is at a level lower than the Corridor of the Procession to the north.

The remainder of the megastructure stands at approximately the same level: the central court is a few steps higher than the west-central block of cells to its west. The ground gradually slopes downward over the area toward the northwest, and the pillar hall at the northern end of the building, approached from a ramp sloping downward from the courtyard, is about a storey lower than the latter.

The western court is of uniform height between the West Porch entrance at the south to the Northwest Treasure House (NWTH) at the north. Between the latter and the northwestern corner of the palace, a raised causeway opens onto a series of steps which descend to the north, to meet an east-west causeway forming the southern boundary of the 'Stepped Theatral Area.', a stepped platform of unknown function. This structure stands at the eastern terminus of a paved walkway at whose western end is the so-called 'Little Palace' discussed above (KN LP).

The stepped platform or 'theatral area' consists of a lower paved court entered both from the western end of the east-west walkway, and from the south by wide steps perpendicular to the stairs leading up to a squarish platform to the east. Within the angle formed by the two flights is a square stone bastion. It is not known if the upper platform contained any construction, whether, for example, it was roofed over, featured benches, columns, or any appointments such as a shrine or other ritual focus.

This stepped platform is essentially a freestanding version of the so-called 'grand stairway' built into the northwestern corner of the palace at Phaistos, to be discussed below. Both constructions feature a perpendicular flight of steps, of which the eastern stair leads to an upper platform. At Phaistos, the platform is surmounted by a central large pillar between two projecting walls, and a PDP system behind.

Indeed, taken as a whole, the northwestern corners of the two palatial compounds are identical in organization, and similar in arrangement, as a cursory comparison with Figure II.43 below will reveal. Both contain (1) an upper platform; (2) a longer and narrower east-west flight of steps rising to the east; (3) a shallower and wider north-south flight of steps (at Phaistos rising to the north, at Knossos rising to the south); and (4) a third stair connecting this area with another section of the northwestern court system (at Knossos rising to the south, at Phaistos rising to the north). At Knossos, this latter stair is thought to give access to a 'Northwest Porch', leading to a higher level of the palace proper, while the stairway at Phaistos leads to a higher western court, at the second storey of the palace fabric to the east, and evidently connecting with an entrance at that storey.[129]

While there is no patent equivalent at Phaistos to the NWTH of Knossos, the west courts of both palaces reveal the presence of a tripartite walkway forming a triangular paved area within: that at Knossos is further to the south, in the area of the West Porch; that at Phaistos, dating to the First Palace Period, is immediately contiguous with the stepped platform construction. Both courts also reveal the presence of sunken circular walled pits (*koulouras*). The three at Knossos and the four at Phaistos (q.v.) are immediately contiguous to one of the shorter western sides of the triangular paved area, and it is tempting to see in this construction the model for a figured fresco of dancers found at Knossos,[130] depicting a public dancing scene within the triangle, adjacent to three planted trees on one side and the boundary of the western facade of the palace on the other.

The Knossian stepped platform may well have served as the focus of the climax of some processional celebration or performance, which might have included public group dancing within or around the triangular *chorós* or dancing-area.[131] The importance of this set of celebrations to the palatial compound is augmented by the inclusion of a stepped platform into the very fabric of the second palace of Phaistos, the latter representing in architectonic standardization of behavioral patterns more loosely incorporated into the series of constructions at Knossos.

A similar triangular *chorós* is to be found in the southern part of the western court at Mallia, as we shall see, but at that site no evidence has been found for a 'stepped platform' area. At Mallia, such a structure would have to be entirely built up from the flat topography, whereas at Knossos and Phaistos the changes in ground level afford easier inclusion of such a construction into the sloping land. If such a structure existed at Mallia, it may have been incorporated into part of the western facade of the palace, rising above some part of the western magazine areas.[132] No evidence for a similar structure has yet come to light at Kato Zakro, and the miniature L-shaped stepped area in the northwestern corner of the Gournia court may be more coincidental than isomorphic.[133]

At both Knossos and Phaistos the long arm of the triangular walkway in the western court leads to the principal western palatial entrance (assuming, as we believe correctly, that the Phaistian 'grand stairway' is oriented outward rather than directed inward).[134] At Knossos, this entrance is at the West Porch, a portico on whose southern, inner end are two doorways. That to the east opens into the Corridor of the Procession: a paved causeway leading into the palace, similar to the causeway entrance within the western facade of Phaistos. The western door opens into a porter's lodge. The disposition of the portico recalls the bifurcated entranceway at Gournia, discussed above. At an earlier date, conjectured Evans, the palace entrance may have simply continued eastward, in the area of magazines 2 and 3 on his plan.[135]

The West Porch stands between the magazine portion of the palace and construction flanking it to the west, evidently an annex to the palace itself.[136] As at Gournia, the West Porch area would have given access not only to the Corridor of the Procession which led to the palatial interior, but also to some continuation of the raised bridgehead to the south. In other words, the West Porch also controls a bypass route along the southwestern edge of the palace, no doubt one of the main routes through the city of Knossos (as at Gournia).

The other construction on the periphery of the palace which is of note is the Northwest Treasure House (NWTH), a plan of whose ruined state is given in Figure II.29.

The building was evidently a storehouse-annex to the palace itself,[137] and consists of about 28 rooms, most of which are mere storage-cellars. Some of these are barely a meter wide. The eastern facade of the building had a series of shallow recesses and projections echoing the western facade of the palace proper, adjacent to the stepped causeway leading up from the 'theatral area' to the north. The northern facades of the building are aligned to the east-west walkway forming the boundary of the latter structure.

Indeed, the northwestern half of the building has this alignment, while the southeastern half aligns with the palace itself. The northern facade projects out toward the southwestern edge of the 'theatral area', and included two large cells flanked to the west by an entrance corridor. At point Z on the plan were found traces of a relief fresco which evidently stood on the outer surface of the wall here, facing the entrance to the stepped platform.

At area Y on the plan, Evans conjecturally restores a stepped porch leading up to the northwestern corner of the second storey of the palace (shown in Figure II.30). It is certainly possible that this stairway incorporated a bridge over to the second level of the NWTH, whose southeastern corner is aligned with the northwestern projection of magazine 186. We may thus imagine that the NWTH originally had a series of larger halls and cells on its second storey, over the storage cells below. Apart from the apparent ground floor entrance to the NWTH to the north, no other traces of entrances are found (see Figure II.29).

The NWTH serves as the northern boundary of the West Court, whose western boundary probably continued in a terraced arc down to the area near the western angle of the triangular *chorós* to the south. This western section of the West Court is built over the remains of earlier houses, trances of which can be seen in the *koulouras* or walled pits to the south. The southern facade of the NWTH forms a series of setbacks echoing and continuing the northwesterly projections of the palace facade proper.

Entrance to the West Court, then, would have been at three key points of controlled access: to the northeast, in the (covered?) angle of the NWTH and the palace's northwestern corner, to the southeast, at the West Porch (which, as we have suggested, provided entry from the viaduct passageway from the south), and somewhere on the western side of the court, possibly at its south-western corner. There was probably a porter's lodge built under the Northwest Porch, fronting on the stepped causeway rising between the angle of the NWTH and the northwestern corner of the palace.

It is patent, then, that the West Court served as a controlled interface between the city and the palace (as at Phaistos),[138] and we may reasonably conjecture that its functions were of a collective nature, and (at least semi-) public. Taken in connection with the 'theatral area' beyond the NWTH to the north, the western front of the palace may be considered to be the major central plaza of the city of Knossos, an urban 'central court' or commons, so to speak.

It is evident that Knossos resembles Phaistos and Mallia in this regard, and in all three palaces it is the western facade section which receives the most articulatory attention. Here the outer palace walls are most finely built and composed, facing on a large public paved plaza, itself evidently the site of major civic celebrations.[139]

At Phaistos, as we shall see, the eastern side of the palace is devoted to more private use in connection with residence and service support of palace activities proper. Similarly, at Knossos, the quarters to the east of the Central Court contain residence halls, storage magazines, workshops, and other auxiliary spaces. At both Knossos and Phaistos, the eastern facade faces out over a descending and less publicly accessible slope. But even at Mallia, where the eastern facade of the palace faces onto a large paved court, the latter facade receives less attention in its articulation, in contrast to the more formal facade on the West Court. We may thus consider the western facades of the great palaces as their more formal public 'front'.

Two additional primary entrances to the palace are approached from the West Court area. One of these is at the terminus of the east-west causeway bypassing the NWTH and stepped platform, giving access into a large pillared hall to the north extremity of the building (Figure II.28). The entrance itself consists of a double door beyond which is a vestibule. The eastern side of the vestibule has a second double door, and to the south is a porter's lodge. A similar entry system occurs at Phaistos, although there the double entryway and flanking porter's lodge is at the central portion of the western facade, rather than at its northern end.[140]

There is a second northwestern entry into the building, adjacent to the latter. This gives onto a long narrow cell whose eastern end might well have served as a station for a guard, before opening through a double door onto a two-columned cell labelled on the plan the 'North West Portico'.

Both entries provide alternative passages to the Central Court by means of ramps. The North West Portico has a second double door at its southern end, beyond which is a dog's-leg ramp to the courtyard beyond. On its western flank is a door leading to a cell which evidently served as an antechamber to an open area at whose center is a familiar sunken 'lustral chamber', which Evans termed an 'initiatory area'. The great pillared hall to the northeast, with ten pillars and columns in a north-south double row, provides further access to the east, into storage and workshop areas comprising the entire northeastern quadrant of the building. Its southern end opens onto a ramp rising steeply to the Central Court between flanking porticoes or verandas projecting northward from the latter. At the northeastern end of the ramp is another small cell which has been taken to be a porter's lodge or guard station. The pillared hall itself will be discussed below.[141]

By contrast, the remaining four entrances to the structure, with the exception of the 'East Bastion', are less highly marked. On the southern face of the structure is a small entryway (the 'South Porch'), with a porter's lodge, connecting with the South Corridor and the two ramps ascending to the Central Court. In the southern angle of the building, behind the retaining wall forming the western flank of the House of the Chancel Screen (KN HCS), is an inconspicuous door eventually connecting with a staircase at the southeastern angle of the easternmost ramp ascending to the Central Court. There is no obvious porter's lodge here, although there does exist a sunken 'lustral chamber' (as at the northwestern entrance of the palace), and a suite of rooms taken as a small shrine.

In the center of the eastern facade, immediately north of the portico of the Hall of the Double Axes is a conjectural stepped entry, giving access to the latter, and probably to the east-west corridor bisecting this part of the building. This entrance stands within a slope bounded to the east by heavy retaining walls, possibly the site of a private garden connected to the hall system. Such a terraced garden may find an echo with the conjectural garden outside the hall system at Mallia,[142] and the ruins here make it uncertain whether the stepped entry communicated with the exterior of the building proper, or merely with an enclosed garden terrace.

The remaining entrance is the East Bastion, further to the north on the eastern flank of the structure. The Bastion consists of an

S-shaped set of flights enclosing two central bastions, giving entry onto a conjectural ascending east-west stair within. This stair or corridor evidently gave access to the storage and work areas of the northeastern quadrant of the palace.[143]

As discussed previously, several separate residential structures are built up against the walls of the palace proper: the South House (KN S), Southeast House (KN SE), and the House of the Chancel Screen (KN HCS). In addition, there are traces of other structures, of which the largest is the Northeast House, built against the northern wall of the eastern palace quadrant, and some remains of earlier buildings to the north of KN SE. Of these houses, only the Northeast House reveals a plan which is partially readible, but the ruined state of the latter makes it difficult to trace its original structure.

It is significant that these auxiliary structures front only on the northern, eastern and southern sides of the building. In its present state, the plan reveals no subsidiary structures of residential form to the west.[144] The relationship of the three houses studied above to the life of the palace is unclear. KN HCS and KN SE might possibly have served as residences for governmentally prominent individuals or families, or as guest apartments of some kind. KN HCS stands up against a terrace upon which stands the small southeastern palace entrance noted above, and it is evident that there was an entry to the house at this second storey. It seems reasonable to suppose that the two structures were residential appendages of the palatial compound, although we have no way of determining their precise relationship.

The South House (KN S) looks like an appendage of the great viaduct-street leading to the southwestern entrance to the palace, and its upper storey entrance is attached to the latter immediately adjacent to the conjectural South West Porch. Although the structure is clearly residential in its appointments and internal organization, it is conceivable that its occupants may have performed some community function in connection with regulation of palace traffic. But of such a function we have no clue.

Across the bridge and surmounting the opposite slope of the ravine is a unique structure dubbed by Evans the 'caravanserai,' because of its seeming resemblance to a hostelry for travellers arriving at the city from the south of the island.[145] It seems evident that the route on which the 'caravanserai' stands was the terminus of one of the principal cross-island roads leading from Knossos to Arkhanes and ultimately to the Messara valley in which stands the city of Phaistos.

The Overall Plan of the Palace. The palace presents a contiguous mass of construction surrounding a large Central Court. The latter, some 50 meters in length and half as wide, is oriented north-south, a pattern repeated at the palaces of Phaistos, Mallia, Kato Zakro, and Gournia, and contrasting with the east-west orientation of the courtyards of Haghia Triadha and Plati.[146]

Despite the fact that there are some 250 separate cells to the structure on its ground floors, not all of these cells are fully interconnected with each other. In fact, the mass of cells divides into a jigsaw of cell-clusters numbering only two dozen. In other words, the palace comprises a set of distinct functional zones with controlled access at particular points between zones or cell clusters. This organization is diagrammed in Figure II.30.

In this diagram, the fabric of the palace divides up into block-like clusters fronting upon the Central Court (C-1) like so many city blocks opening onto a public plaza. Because of such an organization, no one interior cell is so deeply embedded in the structural fabric that it is very far removed either from the Central Court, a major transverse corridor, the exterior of the building, or a stairwell. In this regard, the cell-cluster organization of the Knossian palace is perfectly consistent with the organization of the ordinary residential structure into distinct and semi-autonomous functional zones (as we have seen above and will examine again below).

Evans believed that the original palace construction, dating from the beginning of the Middle Minoan period, comprised a series of separate blocks or 'insulae' whose coalescence over time around a central core gave the resultant mass the aspect of a city-within-a-city.[147] While it is no doubt true that the entire palace was built over a period of time, it is not correct to say that the palace grew 'by accretion'; there is no longer any doubt that the structure was planned as a whole, and its component parts were laid out according to a predetermined scheme, as we shall see in our analyses in Part Two below.

Figure II.30 illustrates the cluster organization of the compound. Each distinctly recognizable cell is assigned a number; courts are denoted by C-1 through C-3b, and stairwells by Za through Zp. Horizontal interconnections among cells are shown by connecting lines (multiple in the case of double doors or PDP systems), entrances by E-1 through E-8. Major connections between cell-clusters are shown by heavy lines, and cells which do not communicate horizontally with adjacent cells are crossed out diagonally. Necessarily, some cellular interconnections are conjectural, particularly in the northeastern quadrant, where all that remain are foundation walls.

Looking first at the western clusters, it will be seen that the structural frame of each of the major projecting magazine blocks does not correspond to separate cell-clusters. Thus, a portion of the two northwesterly magazine blocks comprises a single cluster (cells 186-189), while the northernmost block comprises two clusters: a set of cells accessible from the second storey only, and a cell (186) which is part of a larger system including half of the block to the south. While cells 190-204 are all appended individually to north-south corridor 181, the latter is divided into two parts, making cells 190-199 a separate zone from cells 200-204. At some point in the history of the building, corridor 181 was divided into two parts by means of a doorway adjacent to cells 199 and 200.

A similar situation will be observed below at Mallia, whose western magazine block undergoes a major remodelling in the later history of the palace.[148]

The position of the magazine blocks replicates that of the palaces of Phaistos, Mallia, and Gournia by comprising the western flank of the building. The closest parallel is Mallia, where much of the entire western flank of the building consists of storage magazines aligned east-west, fronting upon a long north-south corridor to the east. But in general, there are many examples in Minoan design where the western flank of a structure is given over to storage, despite the size and function of the building involved. Notable comparisons include KN LP, ML E (magazines to the northwest), HTR, TYL A/B, and KN HCS.

The Knossian magazine block as a whole is appended to a circulatory corridor (cells 181a-b-c) which separates it from the rest of the building. At the northern end is a stairway (Z1) leading to a second storey. There is a storage chamber beneath the stair, enterable from the northern side, at which point the corridor turns back down to the south (cell 181a), to join corridor 180 through a doorway, leading eastward to the northwestern corner of the Central Court (C-1). At the southern end, the north-south corridor leads into an area next to the so-called 'South Propylaeum' and the eastward extension of the Corridor of the Procession (cell 1a). The only direct access from the magazine zone to the west central block is at cells 233a and 240. The former connects with a stair-well (Zp) as well as to the area of the pillar crypts (230 and 231). Cell 240 leads into a cell-cluster wrapped around the bastion forming the 'Grand Staircase'.

The plan is much confused in this area, and its original state is the subject of recent controversy.[149] The evidence for a 'Grand Staircase' at this point is quite flimsy. It has no parallel in any of the other palaces, and appeared in Evans' plans shortly after the 'Grand Stairway' was uncovered at the palace of Phaistos (which, as we have seen above, was most likely part of a 'theatral area' rather than a major palace entryway). Unfortunately, Evans' reconstruction of the object in concrete has sealed off for study the remains of this controversial area, which may have been part of a hall system.

Evans saw his 'Grand Staircase' as part of a great formal entrance, through his 'South Propylaeum', between the 'Corridor of the Procession' and a 'piano nobile' on the second floor. In other words, he conjectured that, like many European palazzi, the palace of Knossos had its main living and state halls above the level of the western portion of the palace. Accordingly, he (and others) reconstruct a series of pillared halls over the western magazine blocks.[150] While it is reasonable to suppose that on a second storey the cells were larger, each covering several cells of this 'basement' floor below, there is no evidence for a monumental grand stairway system leading up to this area at this point, and such a system is based on assumptions regarding the monarchical nature of Knossian government which are probably unwarranted.

At any rate, the magazine area comprises a functional zone separate from the rest of the palace, appended to its own north-south corridor. As noted above in connection with the West Court, its outer western facade is finely constructed and articulated, comprising the public monumental 'front' of the structure. By its very fineness of construction and its great size, it would have no doubt been symbolic to the citizenry of the wealth and power of the government and/or commonwealth. The same may be claimed of the equivalent western fronts of other palaces and large mansions.

What is puzzling about the magazine block is its lack of easy access to the outside, at least if we are to follow Evans' published plan. In every other case of a large storage area, both in the palaces and in large mansions, easy access is provided to the exterior, to facilitate the transport of goods and raw materials. As it stands, the easiest access is through cells 1 a and 5, via corridor 17 and vestibule 11a, ultimately coming through the 'light area' of the 'South Propylaeum', at cell 18. While it is certainly feasible that such a 'grand' entryway might have served such a dual function (namely, transport of goods as well as providing official public entry to a 'piano nobile'), this is out of keeping with the situations we find in other palaces and large mansions. It is likely that access to the north-south magazine corridor was provided directly from corridor 1a to corridor 17, an area of uncertain original formation due to the state of the remains.[151] The latter area would be positionally well suited for the control of such traffic, recording of goods transfer, and the imparting of instructions as to the destination of quantities of grain, oil, wine, and other foodstuffs.

Similar control stations probably existed to the east of the great pillared hall to the north (cells 141-140), and in the area of the East Bastion (E-6/Zi).

Except for what was evidently a service connection with the north-south magazine corridor, the west central block turns its back on the latter and faces onto the Central Court (C-1). This group of four major cell-clusters evidently comprises the principal ritual chambers of the palace. The southern zone, cells 234-242a, is uncertain both in plan and function, as we have noted above. Evidently consisting of a series of halls, it is fronted on the court side by a colonnade of six square piers.[152] It provides internal lateral access to the central zone to the north at cell 235.

This central zone, cells 221-233b, consists of the major shrine area of the palace – the Tripartite Shrine fronting on the Central Court, and the pillar crypts (cells 231-230) within – plus auxiliary storage and service rooms to the north. The Tripartite Shrine stands at the geometric center of a square formed by the Central Court and west central block together, and the eastern pillar crypt (cell 231) stands at the geometric center of the block itself. Beneath the floor adjacent to the latter was uncovered the 'Vat Room Deposit', considered by Evans to be a collection of offerings comprising the foundation deposit of the palace as a whole.[153]

The position of the pillar crypt in the Knossian palace — at the center of its west central block, and on the east-west axis of the entire building — is replicated in the palaces of Mallia and Phaistos.[154] The significance of this positioning in the layout grid of the structure (and of the other palaces) is discussed in detail below in Part Two, along with the significance of the placement of double-axe symbols in palatial construction. The pillars of the Knossian pillar crypts are covered with incised double-axe symbols, and jars of the foundation deposit found nearby bear a related symbol.[155] The disposition of the central portion of the planning grid of the palace is shown in Figure II.31.

The Tripartite Shrine, standing at the center of the western facade of the Central Court, faces across the court to what would originally have been an entrance to the east-west corridor opposite. Near the center of the court, some 2½ meters north of this east-west axis, and directly south of the Northern Entrance ramp, an early plan of the excavation placed the foundations of a squarish 'altar base', which has disappeared in the final published plan by Evans.[156] The position of this object is shown in Theodore Fyfe's plan, reproduced here as Figure II.32.

A similar structure, also interpreted as an altar base, occurs in an equivalent position at the center of the court at Mallia.[157] Similar altar bases occur at Knossos, in the 'Court of the Altar' on the plan above, as well as at two points in the West Court. Only the two latter appear in Evans' later plan (above, Figure II.28).

The significance of these bisection axes and central points of the palace plan is unclear, but it is not unreasonable to suggest that they exist at least in part to commemorate or mark significant points in the planning and layout of the great structure; a phenomenon well known in contemporary Egyptian design, and similar to traditional practices in contemporary societies.[158]

At any rate, it is clear that this central zone of the west central block comprises a primary religious and ritual focus of the palace compound. The entire western facade of the Central Court consists of a more or less continuous colonnade, interrupted only by the structure of the Tripartite Shrine, and a large stairway with a central column just to the north (stairway Zn). The present appearance of this facade is the result of later remodelling, and there is evidence that the original facade was set back to the west a meter or two. Its disposition is shown below in Figure II.33:[159] To the north of the Tripartite Shrine, stairway Zn leads up from the Central Court to a second storey, whose disposition is unknown. The stairway replicates a similar one in an equivalent position at Mallia. In both cases, the stairways are immediately adjacent to the central 'temple' areas, flanking them to the north.

The northern zone of the west central block is dominated by the so-called 'throne room' system (cells 212-220), one of the most familiar portions of the Knossian palace.[160] This entire area, as well as the L-shaped rank of cells to the north (205-211 and stairway Zm) dates from the latest period of the palace, and in its organization replicates the form of megaroid compounds such as have become familiar during the Mycenaean period in mainland Greece and the Aegean islands. Both in its overall form and position with respect to the Central Court (northwestern corner), the Knossian 'throne room' is very nearly identical to a structure incorporated in the Late Minoan III period palatial compound at Plati, on the Lassithi plateau to the east of the island. This cell cluster at Knossos was most likely the seat of the (mainland?) rulers of the Knossian palace during its final phase, at a time when much of the remainder of the palace was in ruins. Its significance will be discussed in a later section of the present Chapter.[161]

The hall system, comprising cells 216-214-215, consists of an anteroom to the east (216) fronting on the Central Court by means of a quadruple PDP system of doors. A double door leads westward into the 'throne room' hall proper (cell 214). The stone 'throne' stands against the right-hand wall, in a position identical to the throne in the great Mycenaean palace at Pylos on the mainland,[162] and a stone bench flanks it on both sides, continuing around to the south on the western wall of the hall. Directly opposite the throne is a sunken 'lustral basin', entered by means of steps on its eastern side (cell 215), and open to the hall on its northern side through a balustrade. Were this a Mycenaean palatial megaron, this inner hall would have had a central raised hearth at the center of the room, on axis with the flanking throne. Above the hearth would have been a clerestory roof above a second storey gallery.

The 'throne room' thus combines Minoan and Mycenaean architectonic features (as at Plati, as we shall see below), inserted into the structural frame of a former Minoan palace compound. Annexed to the hall system are a series of smaller chambers (cells 212, 213, 217, 218, 219, and 220), used in part for storage. Wrapped around the northern and western sides of the cluster is an interconnected rank of cells (205-211), used for storage; at its eastern end is a small stairwell entered from an eastern portico as well as from a side door in the anteroom of the hall system (at cell 216). This stair (Zm) evidently served as access to private residential quarters on the second storey, over the megaroid compound.

To the north of the west central block are a series of corridors (180-160), magazines, and most likely a stairway (at cell 178?). Cell-cluster 164-169 is accessible from the northwestern corner of the Central Court, and stands over the site of earlier storage basements excavated by Evans.[163] It stands between two major palace entrances, corridor 160, to the west, leading down a dog's-leg shaped ramp to the North West Portico, and corridor 150, the principal northern entrance to the Central Court.

The latter consists of a steep ramp leading down to the pillared hall to the north (cell 141), set between flanking porticoes. It is unclear whether this entry ramp was roofed over or not; in its present reconstructed state it is open to the sky.

The pillared hall is a familiar feature in the palaces of Phaistos, Mallia, Kato Zakro, and Gournia, standing in each case to the immediate north of the Central Courts. A similar structure was seen above at the large mansion at Palaikastro, House B. Its usage is unknown, although recent excavation at Kato Zakro has suggested evidence for that hall being involved with food preparation, and it has been assumed that a fine columned dining hall existed above on the second storey.[164]

Whatever its purported functions in other palaces, the Knossian pillared hall makes for an unlikely kitchen. It stands at a point of major public entry to the palace, and is quite far removed from the major residential halls of the palace, on the eastern side of the building. Despite the fact that its position to the north of the Central Court resembles the pillared halls of the other palaces, it is in fact a principal interface between the palace fabric and the outside, and contrasts with all others known by being along an exterior flank of the building; all others are internal to the building, and not far removed from a hall system. In fact, the Knossian pillared hall can only have been a major nexus of palace traffic. It stands between the northwest propylon entrance from the northwestern court, the North East Entrance Passage (cell 140) to the east, giving access to the workshops, courts and magazines of the northeastern quadrant, and the northern entrance ramp to the Central Court, to the south. At these three entry points are cells which have been interpreted as porter's lodges (145, 141a and 140a?). The hall provides a place where traffic can be shunted to various palace areas (in contrast to Mallia and Kato Zakro, where the purported equivalents are appended to circulatory areas).

In the face of supportive evidence, then, we would have to assert that the formal resemblance between the Knossian pillared hall and those at other palaces probably does not correspond to a similarity of function.[165]

The northeastern quadrant, as noted above, stands on sloping ground some meters below the level of the Central Court. Surrounded to the north and east by a great retaining wall, it is apparent that only portions of the quadrant were roofed over, the remainder consisting of open courts and outdoor work areas. Its principal components are the Northeast Magazines (cells 120-133, and stairways Zh, Zj, and Zk), appended to the Corridor of the Draught Board (cell 103); the area of the 'Royal Pottery Stores' to the east (cell 109 and appendages); a cluster of cells to the south (cells 80-90, 98, and 99), and rooms to the east (cells 91-97, and 105-108), from which area entry to the outside is gained via the East Bastion (stair Zi).

The northeastern quadrant evidently comprises these four cell-clusters, but their interconnections are not easily readable since most of what remains are foundation walls. In particular, the East

Bastion cluster reveals no obvious connections with the two to the west, although it is reasonable to expect there to have been several. The evident connections shown above in Figure II.30 make it apparent that the four cell-clusters were semi-autonomous.

The northeastern magazine cluster is appended to the North Pillared Hall at cell 140, and it appears that the primary circulation within the cluster comprised corridor 140-136-Zk-103. It looks as if the whole cluster was roofed over. The northeastern hall (cells 119-120-121) evidently had a light-well at its center (cell 120). The connections of this cluster with the Central Court are unknown, but we might expect a stepped connection somewhere in the northeastern corner of the court, adjacent to stair Zh-3.

The northeasterly cluster was probably only partly roofed over, at least in the area labelled by Evans the 'Royal Pottery Stores', in our Figure II.28 (area 109 in Figure II.30). The latter consist of storage cellars considered to be 'Early Buildings Partly in Continuous Use'.[166] Magazines containing large storage jars (*pithoi*) occupy cells 110, 111, and 112.

It is possible that the latter were appended to the east-west corridor (cell 108) forming the northern boundary of the East Bastion cluster, although in the present state of the plan they are accessible from the northeasterly cluster. They stand within the eastward return of a great retaining wall which bisects the eastern quarters of the palace, running southward to meet a similar great wall at the east-west axis of the quarter (the latter forming the northern boundary of the residential quarter).

At the southeastern flank of the East Bastion cluster is a reconstructed veranda facing over the ravine to the east (cells 95 and 96), aligned with the veranda of the hall system to the south. It is likely that this section (including westerly cells 91-97) was an appendage of the residential quarter, to which it is connected at two points. The frontage of cells 96 and 62, porticoes of equal length bisected by the lower east-west corridor 79, augment this impression that the two clusters were part of the same building program. As noted above, this combined veranda most likely looked out onto a broad terraced garden to the east, access to which was gained through the east-west stepped corridor on its central axis. It may be suggested, then, that the East Bastion cluster was at least in part a portion of the residential quarter of the palace.

To the west of this cluster lie a series of storage magazines with heavy foundations (Corridor of the Bays; Magazine of the Medallian Pithoi); a more likely site for a second-storey dining hall, assuming it to be the case that such halls consisted of rooms with six or eight columns in a double row: such a hall would easily fit over the foundations of this area.[167]

The hall system of the palace and its appendages comprise an autonomous cell-cluster in its own right (cells 54-79 and stairwells Ze, Zf, Zg). It is connected (at this ground floor level shown on the plan) only to the southeastern quarter of the East Bastion cluster to the northeast, across the great east-west corridor 79. The latter corridor and stairwell Zg is the major entry to the system. The 'grand stairway' (Zg) leads up in several flights wrapped around a light-well/clerestory system to the Central Court to the west.

Evans found this residential area remarkably intact, though collapsed and compressed, and has reconstructed the area in detail so as to provide a clearer picture of the disposition of this elegant apartment system. In addition to the great stairway to the west, the residential quarter consists of two hall systems (the 'Hall of the Double Axes' and the 'Queen's (?) Megaron'), a colonnaded veranda, bathroom ('lustral area'), latrine, and storerooms.

As shown in Figure II.30, the quarter consists of four major zones, plus three cells accessible (separately) from an upper floor (54, 55, 56). Figure II.34 below is Evans' plan of the quarter.

The hall systems replicate systems seen elsewhere, though on a grander scale than most. The larger hall, the 'Hall of the Double Axes', so named after the proliferation of double-axe symbols carved into its walls, is the more northerly of the two, and is entered from the lower east-west corridor at the room to the east of the western light-well. The manner of entry, on the lateral flank of the system, is identical to that seen in hall systems of private residences. At the southern side of this cell (76) is a door opposite the first, leading into an S-shaped corridor which gives access to the smaller hall system.

The Hall of the Double Axes is aligned east-west, with a light-well at its western end. It consists of three chambers (including the latter) plus an L-shaped portico of columns on the eastern end, wrapped around to the south. The third chamber (cell 77) has but one solid wall; the remaining flanks are composed of PDP systems. Those on the east-west axis of the system have four double doors, while the one on the south has three. This cell is the only one in the system that can be completely shut off from adjacent cells. An identical room may be seen in the hall system at Mallia (q.v.); it too opens onto a colonnaded portico.[168] Indeed, as we shall see, the hall system of Mallia is very nearly identical in design to the Hall of the Double Axes.

Beyond the colonnade is a veranda or patio bounded to the east and south by a wall whose upper limit is not known, it may have been above sight-lines, or simply a low parapet, providing a view across the ravine to the east. The latter arrangement seems to be the one at Mallia.

The second hall system, fancifully named by Evans the 'Queen's Megaron', is half the size of the former, and lies to the south along the same east-west axis. The two halls are separated by a passage-way and stairwell, a situation replicated at Phaistos. The stairway (cell Ze) opens onto the smaller hall, and thus the northern flank of the latter consists of two adjacent doorways. In form, the smaller hall system resembles the simpler hall systems of private residences, consisting of three chambers: a light-well on the eastern end, a 'porch' cell (64), and an inner hall (65). In contrast to residential examples, however, the porch and hall (cells 'b' and 'c' of Chapter I above) are partitioned not by a full PDP system, but by a low balustrade/window: the doorway between the two is a single opening, to the north. On the southern side of the porch cell is a doorway leading to an antechamber opening back onto the veranda fronting the Hall of the Double Axes around to the north. West of the latter is a narrow cell, possibly a light-well, as indicated in Figure II.34.

On the western end of the inner hall are two doors. That to the north opens onto a bathroom or 'lustral area' (not sunken), to which light is also admitted across a balustrade to the northwest of the hall. The southern door leads into a corridor (cell 57) giving access to a cluster of service rooms standing behind both hall systems. The first chambers reached via this corridor are toilette rooms, including a latrine. To the north is a light-well which admits light both to the toilette and an adjacent eastern corridor through windows (cells 60, 70, 71). Corridor 71 leads back east to a doorway at its northeastern corner, beyond which is a continuation of the corridor (cell 71a) and, off the latter, a stairwell. Corridor 71a leads north back to the Hall of the Colonnades, adjacent to the grand staircase leading up to the Central Court (cells 74, 72, and Zg). The light-well (72) evidently had a window on its upper southern wall, illuminating stairway Zf.

The significance of this doubled hall system is unclear: why two halls? Is there a functional distinction between the two systems? The entire quarter makes for a complete residential apartment: living halls, latrines, bathrooms, storage chambers, access to private quarters above. Apart from size, the two hall systems differ principally in their interface with the outside: the Hall of the Double Axes can be completely open to sun and air, while the smaller hall system (surely not a 'Queen's' hall) is a completely interior apartment, more suited to colder and more inclement weather. Thus we may conjecture that the larger hall might have been a warm-weather apartment, and the smaller winter living chambers.

But this attribution is not entirely convincing, for the Hall of the Double Axes can itself be completely shut off from the outside; note that simply closing the eastern and southern PDP systems renders the apartment an entirely interior space. An exactly parallel situation exists at Phaistos, as we shall see.

The answer may be more patent if we consider the aspect of interiority and privacy afforded by the smaller hall system: it is simply deeper in the palace fabric than the Hall of the Double Axes, standing 'behind' the latter with respect to major public access. In addition, its only immediate access to the outside (i.e. the veranda to the east) is gained only through a double-cell vestibule, a likely spot for a porter's lodge. Its position behind the larger hall is not highly marked perceptually; there is no obvious entrance, apart from the otherwise undistinguished door in the southern flank of the inner hall of the larger system (cell 76). There is nothing patent to the visitor to the larger hall that anything significant lies beyond: no monumental or highly articulated major doorway.

These constraints on circulation, and the 'hidden' nature of the smaller apartments, suggest that the larger hall system functioned at least semi-publicly at times, possibly constituting a reception suite, room of assembly, or official hall where visitors and guests might be received, entertained, or more officially encountered.

Of course it need not have been the case that the larger hall system only served semi-public functions; it may well have also served functions similar to the smaller, but at a different season or under special circumstances. It may have also served as a more formal living (and dining?) hall for the residents of the quarter when such needs arose.

Such attributions would also make sense at Phaistos, where the palace has a similar organization of halls. We may also see a possible later parallel with the later practices evident on the (Mycenaean) mainland, where the palaces of Pylos, Mycenae and Tiryns have two megaroid hall systems: a larger, more formal 'hall of state', and a smaller domestic hall system, also of megaroid form, hidden 'behind' the former, and not as easily accessible as the larger megaron. We will consider these non-Minoan hall systems in a later section of the present Chapter.

To the south of the residential cluster at Knossos, and comprising the southeastern quarter of the palace, are a series of rooms which are autonomous of the latter, and appended to the circulatory system of the structure at the southern ramp (cell 10 on Figure II.30). It is unclear what role they play in the life of the palace. At the southern end of the cluster is a large stairway bastion lit by means of an adjacent light-well (cells 35, 36, 37, and stair Zb), which is accessible at the southwestern corner of the cluster.

The northeastern corner of the cluster is a second large stairwell, probably leading up to the level of the Central Court, exiting onto the latter at its southeastern corner (Zd). It is not clear what connection this latter area had with the remainder of the cluster. At the southeastern corner of the zone is a small exterior palace entry (discussed above), which gives onto a long vestibule (cell 41). The latter leads to a series of small chambers and corridors. To the immediate left of the entrance is a sunken 'lustral chamber', recalling the position of a similar, but considerably larger, cell at the northwestern corner entrance to the palace.

Also reached from corridor 41 is a tiny shrine (44), beyond two doors. It is unclear why in this southeastern corner of the structure there should exist a lustral chamber without associated living halls, or a 'bath' (cell 48) and a shrine-room. The entire cluster, small though it is, contains three stairwells, of which two at least are quite large and well articulated, suggesting major public access to the interior of the palace. But unlike the other major entrances to the palace to the west and northwest, the southeastern entrance system is quite unmarked — no protruding bastion or portico is identifiable (unless a portico did exist in the angle between the projecting bastion of stairwell Zb and the western wall of KN HCS to the east) — and the doorway proper is quite small. Nor is there any clear evidence for a porter's lodge, unless it too were external to the present outer trace of the building.

The series of circulatory controls in this cluster is of interest, for it provides us with a detailed picture of the ways in which Minoan designers functionally zoned their buildings. The south-eastern entrance (E-4) gives access to a vestibular corridor (41). To the latter are appended three doors. To the southwest, the door opens onto a small corridor, within which, to the south, is the entrance to the sunken 'lustral chamber'. Directly ahead is a second door leading to a continuation of the corridor, 42b, and beyond a third door is a corridor (46b) which leads, through yet another door, to the stairwell Zb.

The second door to the west of corridor 41 opens into a small corridor (43a), leading into a passage way beyond another door (43b). Beyond another door, to the north, is the shrine, cell 44. To the north of corridor 41 is a door leading to a vestibule (46c), which controls access both to a sub-cluster to the north, with its own stairwell (Zc), bathroom (48) and storeroom (47).

In other words, the multitude of door controls allows entry to the cluster at specific depths, and those only. Thus, entry to the 'lustral area', or the shrine, can be gained without passing through other areas in the cluster, and also without revealing stairwell-access to more interior parts of the palace. The system also works in the reverse direction: access from upper parts of the palace to the 'lustral chamber' can be made without going through the outer vestibule corridor (41).

This complex system of circulatory controls is a principal feature of Minoan architectural design in general, and is manifest both in large palatial compounds and in smaller private residences:

recall KN RV above. We shall meet it again in the palaces of Mallia and Phaistos.

But this system of controls contrasts very sharply with the systems of one-way controls in contemporary architecture in the eastern Mediterranean during the Bronze Age, as illustrated above in Figure I.2, Chapter I. In the Egyptian house, by contrast, the system of interior controls is such as to increasingly close off graded zones of privacy from their interiors. Minoan designers seem preoccupied with the consequences of multifunctional usage of spaces, and the circulatory patterns of Minoan buildings resemble railway shunting-yards which allow the maximum and most economical interactions between zones. This southeastern cluster of the Knossian palace is a good example: its multiple door systems allow residents and visitors to use the same functional areas without interference with each other.

Indeed, much of the fabric of the palace at Knossos is a multi-usage interface between inside and outside, and the structural frameworks of its cell-clusters allow a maximum of penetration with a minimum of interference among groups of users. Despite the great size of this megastructure, one is seldom very far from an entrance either to the periphery or to the Central Court. Measured in thresholds, the most interior cells are rarely more than a half-dozen thresholds from an exit to the outside, despite the fact that on its ground floor the structure contains some 250 cells.

The carefully designed complexity of its traffic networks provides the contents of the palace, and its inhabitants, with a maximum of security, within a compact and spatially dense framework. In this regard, the great Knossian palace is similar in organization to the most modest private house (as we have seen above).

But the contrast of Minoan structures such as the palaces with the simpler geometric lucidity of contemporary Egyptian structures — for example the great palace at Amarna, illustrated in Figure II.35 — is more superficial than real.[169]
Where the Egyptian structure calls attention to its weak points by means of monumental gateways and pylons, the Minoan structure controls access through carefully calculated surprise and illusion. Unless you know in advance where you're going in the Knossian palace (or in any private house such as TYL C), or unless you're a

native, the perceptual cues forming a *koiné* in architectonic organization elsewhere in the eastern Mediterranean will mislead. One is continually changing direction; corridors suddenly turn 90° and then back again; doorways which seem to bisect a structure and promise interior penetration turn out to be culs-de-sac. Rather than the bilateral symmetry and mirror-reversal symmetry so common elsewhere, Minoan design is deliberately anti-symmetric: its harmonies (as discussed in detail in Part Two) are perceptually more complex than those manifest elsewhere.

These complexities are the result of deliberate planning and careful layout, and permeate every aspect of Minoan design, as we shall see below. Indeed, there is some indication that Minoan ritual itself was deeply imbued with an architectonic awareness.

The principles underlying Minoan architectural design will become increasingly patent as we begin to compare the organization of the palace at Knossos with its megastructural cousins in other cities. We shall next look at the palatial compound in the city of Mallia, some 30 km east of Knossos, along the northern coast of the island.

Mallia: Palace

Figure II.36 is a plan of the central excavated portion of the city of Mallia, whose ancient name (unlike Knossos) is unknown. Mallia is a coastal city, built adjacent to sheltered coves serving as part of the Minoan port. The palace stands a mere 500 meters from the shoreline, and the entire city is built on flat land.

The plan shows the palace itself, its paved western and northern courts, and an adjacent section of the city (Quarters Delta, Kappa, and Lambda). More detailed plans of Quarter Delta are given above in Chapter I (Figure I.4), and in the present Chapter (Figure II.7 and II.16, in connection with our examination of construction in that area. Quarter Zeta is to the east of the palace, beyond the extent of the present plan.[170]

The palace stands in the midst of its city, as at Knossos, and is surrounded by construction on all sides. To the north is a great plaza (*cour nord*), of unknown function. It is bordered by exceptionally thick walls which may have served as the foundations for stepped seating, suggesting a 'theatral area' or stadium of some kind, an arena for public celebration. It is entered at its south-eastern and northeastern corners through large doorways, and possibly also on its northwestern and southwestern corners, although the remains on this western side are unclear. The columned hall to the west may be associated in function with the court.

Whatever its original disposition, the placement of the large courtyard by the palace replicates the position of the 'theatral areas' of Knossos and Phaistos. Its orientation and construction tie it to the enigmatic building in Quarter K to the southwest, the so-called *crypte hypostyle*. The latter may well have been a place of assembly of some kind, and its main sunken hall on the northern flank features a circumferential stone bench. Connected with this building are a series of long magazines, to the southeast accessible only from the hypostyle crypt.[171]

The West Court of the palace resembles those of Knossos and Phaistos with its incorporation of a paved walkway running north-south, terminating in a triangular area to the south (the *chorôs* of Knossos discussed above). The court is bounded on its western side by traces of house walls running north-south, at least along its northern half.[172] The pavement continues along to the south-west in front of a structure whose orientation follows the buildings to the north in Quarter K, and which has been interpreted as a religious structure.

As at Knossos, the western court is the major public 'front' of the palace, and constitutes one of the principal public plazas of the city. The greater bulk of the palace is on its northern and western sides (in contrast to Knossos, but similar to Phaistos), and the central court of the building is less 'central' than the former.

In Figure II.37 is given a detailed plan of the palace in its extant state. Discovered by J. Hazzidhakis, who began excavation in 1915, the city of Mallia has been excavated since 1922 by the French School, whose work still continues. Because no later buildings were constructed over the site of the palace, its plan is remarkably intact, and provides us with a more homogeneous picture than does its Knossian cousin.

It is readily apparent from a cursory glance at the plan that the palace of Mallia replicates many of the essential features of

Knossos: the long rank of magazines to the west, indented western facade finely built of squared limestone blocks, a long north-south corridor separating the magazine block from the west central block, the west central block itself with its pillar crypt at its center, a fine hall system to the northwest, a colonnaded Central Court, and a pillared hall to the north of the Court.

In its dimensions also, Mallia reveals the same principles of planning and layout (discussed in detail in Part Two below): the west central block and adjacent north-south corridor is equal in width to the Central Court, and both comprise 1 : 2 rectangles, being twice as long north-south as they are wide east-west.

The Mallian palace reveals two principal building periods, but unlike Phaistos, which was entirely rebuilt, at Mallia the second building period mostly saw minor modifications, leaving the original Middle Minoan I period plan essentially unaltered.[173] The major alterations to the original plan include an opening up of its western magazine blocks to incorporate direct external access at several points, and the insertion of a large hall system similar to the Hall of Double Axes system at Knossos in the northwestern corner of the building, taking over part of the original northern magazine area.

Mallia is a much plainer building than either Knossos or Phaistos, and few traces of fine wall frescoes are apparent here. But its construction was as carefully executed as its two replicas in the central part of the island, and it was certainly an impressive building.

The western flank of the palace is given over to long narrow storage magazines like those of Knossos. But at the southwestern corner is a unique feature: a double row of round grain silos open to the outside. This construction, which has no patent Minoan parallel,[174] covers an area which at an earlier period may well have formed one of the principal entrances to the building, to judge by the positioning of the triangular causeway at Knossos adjacent to its West Porch. No clear trace of such an entry remains in the present state of the building, however.

The silos were cylindrical (possibly conical) in shape, with central pillars supporting a roof cover. The trace of walls on the northern edge of the cluster suggests an upper platform from which grain may have been poured into the cylinders, to be removed from openings near ground level. It is unclear if the silos were walled off from the outside, and if the grain held here were supportive of the palace proper, we might expect some interior access, but none exists, at least on ground level. There may have been a connection at an upper level, though such a connection would be cumbersome and awkward, at least by our standards.[175]

The western magazine block evidently originally extended the entire length of the palace to the north, as indicated by magazine(?) foundations in the northwestern corner, describing wall-lines identical to those to the south. But during the second period of the palace, the entire northwestern quadrant was taken over by a hall system opening out to what was evidently a walled garden, thus significantly reducing the storage capacities of the palace (or perhaps relocating part of this function elsewhere).

In its present state, the magazine block is zoned off into several clusters, created by blocking off the north-south corridor at several points. At least two new palace entries were created in the western facade, cutting through pre-existing walls. Both entries are in the area of the largest magazine block, at the center of the western facade. The southern half of this block was taken back from its original trace to create what looks like a strong bastion in its southwestern corner – possibly a tower of some kind. Other such 'bastions' may be identified elsewhere on the periphery of the palace, perhaps serving to provide visual control over the surrounding (flat) cityscape – notably on the southeastern and northeastern corners. It is unclear whether the breach in the magazine walls in the block to the immediate north of the silo compound is to be taken as intended; I suspect that during the life of the palace these magazines were accessible only from within.

The effect of the placement of a blocking wall across the north-south corridor is to shunt traffic around and through two adjacent cells to the east. In fact, this entire cluster of cells at the west-central section of the west-central block consists of a maze of short corridors and passageways whose function can only have been to serve as a controlled interface between the pillar crypt zone and service corridors leading on its southern flank to the Central Court, and the storage areas of the western part of the building. The effect of this 'shunting-yard' is strikingly apparent in the following plan, diagramming the cellular interconnections in the palace (Figure II.38).

Cells 120-124, 132-134 comprise a circulatory cluster which is, in effect, the obverse of a courtyard standing between functional zones. It provides carefully controlled interconnections between four peripheral areas: (1) the cluster appended to corridor 77a, leading from the two western entrances; (2) the triple magazine cluster to the southwest, appended to corridor 77b; (3) the magazine system to the south (cells 88-93, and 136-138); and (4) the pillar crypt cluster (125-129) and its corridor-bypass on its southern flank, leading directly to the Central Court (cells 131, 131a, and 135).

Because of the variety of alternative routings, traffic to various functional areas may be directed through different doors and passages with a minimum of reduplication and interference. From corridor 77a, the northeastern door leads around to the area of the pillar crypt (via cells 120 and 123), while the southeastern door leads back around to the area of the magazines serviced by corridor 77b, via cells 121 and 122. But cell 123a also provides through passage from the pillar crypt area to the magazines off corridor 77b. In order to enter the Central Court from the western entrances without passing through the pillar crypt complex, the appropriate route would be cells 77a-121-122-124-134-(either 131 or 135).

This labyrinth of doorways and passages calls to mind the entrance corridor of TYL C (Figure I.5, Chapter I) with its seven doorways, each giving access to distinct functional zones in that house. The similarity here exists with respect to the multiplicity of choice in passage, and the resultant security in camouflage, or, more accurately, *non*-markedness or *non*-distinction.

In order for such a traffic network to function effectively, entrants must know where they are headed beforehand, or there must be some system of denotation acting to control and shunt passage. In the southeastern cluster of the palace at Knossos, it is likely that such a control would be passive, effected simply by the locking from within of certain non-publically accessible passages. Here, the system of control was more likely active as well as passive, with transporters of goods being directed verbally by a porter to selected areas by means of specific routes.

Control over access to entrance itself would no doubt have been facilitated by the bastion and its personnel (cell 82). The bastion may in fact have consisted of a high platform or tower, whose existence may be surmised by the strength of the foundations, and such a vantage point may have been accessed by a stairway built into cell 83 or 84. Such a stair may well have turned back eastward to allow entry access to the second storey over the area of the north-south corridor 77a. Cells 79-80 may be a guard's lodge.

The entry to the north (E-11) gives access to the north end of corridor 77a. Directly ahead of the entrance passage (cell 76) is a stairway to the zone above the west central block, assuming the extant steps rose over cells 108 and 109. Alternatively, the small cluster may have served as storage.

The zone of cells to the east at this point is only accessible to the Central Court. Standing in the position of the 'throne room' cluster at Knossos, this area was evidently used for the storage of cult objects in connection with the pillar crypt cluster to the south.[176] It is possible that cell 176 was also a shrine. The latter opens to the Court down a flight of shallow steps between a central pier. At its back (west) is a low stone base which is taken to be an altar or table for offerings. Behind this is a small stairway descending between two columns to a storage room behind (cell 104). Also to the west are two rows of magazines standing behind the large stairway Zc ascending from the court. The position of these cells (110-113, 117, and 118) is identical to cells 217-220 at Knossos, similarly behind a large stairway from the Court. The latter cells were appended, during the later history of Knossos, to the 'throne room' compound discussed above. It is conceivable, then, that the Knossian megaroid zone was built into the frame of a cluster of cells resembling these at Mallia.[177]

The Mallian pillar crypt (cell 125), evidently the principal ritual focus of the structure, stands in a position identical to the crypts at Knossos, differing only in orientation. Here there are two pillars (incised with double-axe symbols, as at Knossos) aligned north-south in a single cell, while at Knossos the two pillars are aligned east-west, each standing in a discrete but interconnected cell.

In both palaces, the pillar crypts communicate with cells to the west, and lead back to the north-south corridor of the magazine blocks. As at Knossos, there is also a bypass route connecting the Central Court with the magazine corridor (here doubled: cells 131 and 135). There is a stairway to the south of this bypass corridor at Knossos, but none is easily readible here at Mallia (cell 131 or cell 138?). Standing to the east of the pillar crypt, and extending several meters southward, is a north-south colonnade within the western facade of the Central Court. The facade itself is formed by a narrow wall, perhaps a low parapet of some kind. It is breached at the southeastern corner of cell 129.

To the south is a flight of four shallow, broad steps rising from the Court to the west, near the southwestern corner of the latter. It is unclear whether these steps represent the first risers of a large stairway extending over the foundations to the west up to the second storey, or whether they terminate against the eastern flank of the latter, perhaps forming a kind of stepped altar. It is also conceivable that these steps (Zd) may simply have been a small set of seats, a miniature grandstand for the observance of activities in the Court.[178]

If these were indeed steps which rose to a second storey over the foundations to the west, the angle of their rise would have rendered the cells within unusable, except for those at the western side (cells 141, 142, and 146). But it is unclear how the latter were accessed, along with the entire cluster to which they evidently belong (cells 147, 149, 150, 151, and 140). Our plan in Figure II.37 suggests, by means of dotted lines, an entry from the area of the magazines, to the west (136, 137).

South of this area are two clusters, one appended to the southern entrance to the Court (169) and one accessible only from the exterior, at least at ground level (E-7). The latter cluster calls to mind the southeastern cluster of cells at Knossos. It seems likely that there was a small stairway over cell 164a, extending over cell 167 to the north. The cell-cluster to the east reveals traces of a larger stairway (Zf), rising from the south. As we have seen in several private houses, it is not unusual for a structure to have a cell or cell-cluster entered solely from the outside, not communicating directly with the rest of the interior (TYL C, AK L). A palatial parallel may be seen at Phaistos, below, just to the south of the west-central palatial entrance (which, like entrance

E-6/169 here, consists of a corridor leading directly ahead to the Central Court).[179] The cluster was evidently a sanctuary.

Corridor 169 is the largest entrance to the interior of the palace, and leads directly to the Central Court, barely a dozen meters to the north. It is finely paved (unlike the Court itself), and gives lateral access to cell-clusters on both sides before reaching the doorway at the western end, opening onto the Court. The paving ends at a point corresponding to the original southern facade of the Court, which was later remodelled by means of a fine wall composed of shallow recesses and projections.[180]

The maze of cells to the east of the entrance system is in a quite ruinous state, and is difficult to read. Access is gained to the area via cell 174, at the southern end of which (cells 175-176) may have stood a stairway. In the fill of cell 182 were found fragments of perfume vases, evidently fallen from the upper storey. The large cell 196 has no communication with adjacent cells. Might this have been a bastion or tower like cell 82 on the western facade?

Occupying the southeastern corner of the palace is a cluster of cells entered directly from the southeastern corner of the Court (at cell 191). The entrance consists of a small flight of steps which rises into the doorway only to descend again down to the floor level within. The function of this cluster is unknown. A stairway (Zb) leads to the second storey, in the northeastern corner of the cluster.

This area is bounded to the north by the principal eastern entrance of the palace (cell 197/E-5). This entrance corridor, even shallower than the southern entrance, leads directly to the Central Court. Evidently closed off by doors at either end, this entry has no obvious porter's lodge associated with it (unless we take cell 201 for such a lodge, but this is rather far removed from the point of entry, ca. 10m). The latter recalls a similar exterior cell at TYL C (Figure I.5, Chapter I), in having no trace of internal communication.

The entire eastern facade of the Central Court is taken up by a colonnade of alternating columns and pillars, apart from wall-projections at the northern and southern corners. Behind the colonnade is a magazine block, a shallower and smaller version of the great magazine system on the western facade of the palace. The magazine block comprises two distinct clusters, both with a single entry point in their northwestern corner: cells 200, 199, 198, and cells 210-203. The latter group consists of six magazines opening to the east on an interior north-south corridor. The vases within, standing on raised benches along the walls, evidently contained liquids such as wine and oil.

To the north is a vestibule (212) through which access may be gained to the exterior of the palace once again, at cell 218. This vestibule is the center of a cluster of cells (34, and 212-218) with controlled access to the northwest into the northern portico of the Court, and to the southwest, into portico 211 on the eastern side of the Court, leading to the magazine block.

The Central Court comprises the eastern half of the central grid-square of the palace, as at Knossos (Figure II.31, above), as illustrated below in Figure II.39.[181]

As shown in the diagram, the Mallian pillar crypt was built as the center of the western half of the grid square, in a fashion similar to Knossos. While there is no equivalent here to the Knossian Tripartite Shrine at the center point of the overall planning grid, the east-west bisection axis of the pillar crypt is aligned with a structure at the center of the open space of the courtyard considered to be the foundation of a shrine or offering table or altar. At Knossos we noted the similar position of an 'altar base' occurring only in Evans' earlier published plans.[182]

The grid squares of the two palaces are identical in size, 200 modular units on a side, a dimension which is also repeated at Phaistos.[183] Other major dimensions of the palace compound are simple fractions or multiples of the same standard.

The Mallian Central Court presents a somewhat less urban aspect than its Knossian or Phaistian cousins, being essentially unpaved except for four neatly paved sections indicated in our Figure II.37 above. The significance of these pavements (if indeed their disposition is intentional and not the sparse remains of an originally fully paved courtyard) is unclear. The four pavements are more or less adjacent to the four corners of the Court, or at least bear a relationship to the Court's four main entries from outside. It is possible they may have been involved with significant positions in some public ceremony, although we have no evidence whatsoever for such a practice. While a reasonable case might be made for the triangular causeway areas of the palatial West Courts as foci of public group celebration,[184] there is nothing to support such a suggestion here. While it is the case that the exact position of the peak of Mount Dikte among the range of mountains to the south of the palace may be gotten by aligning oneself along the NW-SE diagonal axis of the Court (and equivalent phenomena may be observed at Phaistos and Knossos),[185] the preserved pavements here do not appear to relate directly with such a significant ritual sight-line.

The northern facade of the Central Court consists of a colonnade, with eleven extant columns. There is some evidence that during the first period of the palace the colonnade extended several meters to the west, to return southward within cell 103. It has been conjectured that there may have been a barrier of some kind between these northern columns, and perhaps a doorway in advance of the northern entrance to the Court (cell 30).

To the east of cell 103, cell 102 may have been a bathroom or 'lustral area'. It is unclear to which cluster it was appended, the shrine area to the south (at cell 104) is likely, since the hall cluster to the northwest already contains a sunken 'lustral chamber' on its western side (cell 62).

Behind the northern colonnade is a pillared hall (32) with an antechamber with a single pillar (31). Resembling the pillared halls of Knossos, Phaistos and Kato Zakro, one theory holds that this pillared hall supported a large banquet hall on the second storey.[186] Entry to such a hall would have been by means of stairway Zb, rising from the northern colonnade. Stair Za, to the north of the hall, would then have been a service stair. Both stairs may have joined at a common landing over cell 29. Between the two stairways are three storage magazines (25-27). Stair Za would have returned westward over magazine 25.

The northern entrance to the Court (30) leads to a portico with a single central column. This vestibule was evidently closed off by doorways to the north and south (in which case cell 27 may have served as a checkpoint/porter's lodge).

The northern cluster of the palace is clearly a service area, with groups of magazines surrounding a central peristyle court. There is an eastern entrance from the outside, via a corridor with doors at both ends (cell 13/E-2). In contrast to this smaller passage, on the northwestern corner stands a more highly marked entrance (E-1), no doubt one of the principal public passageways into the palatial compound. This entrance is approached from the west along a paved causeway of the same character as the north-south causeway in the western court (the two walkways may have joined near the northwestern outer corner of the palace, but the entire pavement of this area is missing). Cell 1 is a paved vestibule.

In a generic manner, the northern entrance recalls the northern entrance at Knossos. Both are approached via a raised walkway leading from the west, leading into a projection of the northern part of the structure (at Knossos the pillared hall serves this vestibular function). Passage then turns at a 90° angle to the south, to join a corridor leading to the northern end of the Central Court (at Knossos, the great north-south ramp). There is no patent tight control point at Mallia to match the propylon/porter's lodge at Knossos, although cell 1 here would have been closed off at both ends by doors. Evidently, cell 1 served both as a porter's station and as an entrance vestibule. Excavators found wear-marks on the vestibular thresholds, suggesting that this entrance was the most used during the life of the palace.

Cells 9/10 (originally a single chamber), opening onto the peristyle court to the east, were evidently used for the storage and processing of olive oil.[187] Cells 21, 22, and 23 were also originally part of a single cluster. Traces of a 'horns of consecration' were found within, apparently fallen from a shrine on the second storey.

A large open area (cell 20) bordered by thick walls to the west and southeast serves as the principal access to the residential quarter of the palace, focussed upon a hall system (cells 54-55-56-64-67). The latter was built during the second period of the palace (as was the Hall of the Double Axes System at Knossos), and overlies a large magazine block of the first period whose disposition resembled those still in use to the south.

The organization of the Mallian hall system replicates that at Knossos, while differing from it in size and orientation. The main hall (cells 55-64-67) opens to the north onto a veranda with columns running east-west (cell 52). To the north of the veranda there was most likely a private garden, cells 43 and possibly part of cell 50. The main chamber of the system, cell 55, is identical in disposition to the outer hall at Knossos: both are made up of three walls which consist entirely of PDP systems, plus a fourth solid wall. In both palaces, the solid wall is to the left as one faces outward to the veranda.

To the south is an inner hall and a light well beyond two columns (as at Knossos): cells 64 and 67. But here, the inner hall and light well are together equal in size to the outer hall. At Knossos, the inner hall is of the same dimensions as the outer. The disposition of the hall to the east of the outer hall, cell 56/57, is unclear. Our plan (Figure II.37) shows a single chamber, while on our cell-cluster diagram (Figure II.38) we reconstruct two cells. There exist faint traces of a division in the remains, running north-south, along the line of what may have been two columns, not unlike the two columns of the light-well to the south (cell 67). It is possible, then, that cell 56 was a narrow hall, with cell 57 being a light-well. This cell may have been walled along its northern front, and its reconstructed two columns would in fact align with the square pier of the veranda colonnade to the north. This light-well has a door in its northeastern corner, leading to cell 40, one of the entrance corridors of the system (the other hall system entrance from area 20 is via cells 65-68-69-39, of which the latter is a porticoed vestibule).

To the west of the outer hall (cell 55) is a side hall, cell 54, paved with fine flagstones like the main halls. Its position recalls the 'Queen's Megaron' halls at Knossos, here reduced to a single chamber. The southern side of cell 54 also replicates the Knossian system in that its western side gives onto a sunken 'lustral chamber', while its eastern side gives onto a corridor leading to a series of back rooms. Cells 70/71 may have been the foundation of a stairway. Behind this (to the south) is a small back chamber on whose western wall was found a double-axe symbol.[188] Directly to the east of this cluster is a cell which was evidently a pillar crypt (cell 75). A small vestibular chamber to the north of the latter, opening onto light-well 67, apparently served as the palace archive, for Linear A and hieroglyphic tablets were found here (cell 67a).[189]

While lacking the fineness of the Knossian hall system, the Mallian residential cluster is clearly built to the same pattern, and its internal organization replicates the latter to a remarkably detailed degree. The two systems are evidently contemporary, and were most likely designed by the same craftsmen, or at least by designers working from the same pattern.

If we take cells 55-56-59 as a lateral hall system, then we may observe a double hall system very much like those of Knossos and Phaistos, the principal difference being that here the main hall is shared by both systems, forming its northwestern corner. In this regard, two observations must be made. First, the lateral system clearly replicates the northern hall system at Phaistos both in orientation, the relative size and positioning of cells, as well as its lateral relation to a northerly colonnaded veranda running across the length of the two inner halls: this is patent by a comparison with Figure II.43 below.[190]

Secondly, our observations of the doubled hall system at Knossos with respect to a contrast between warmer and colder weather living halls may be augmented here. At Mallia, the northern hall system (cells 55-56-57) has two of its halls (55-56) opening out to the veranda on their northern flank, and this openness recalls the openness of the Hall of the Double Axes at Knossos. The north-south hall system (cells 55-64-67) is the more interior living hall system, with only its northern face opening onto the veranda. More of it, therefore, can be sealed off from exterior exposure, and it penetrates further into the interior of the structure.

The Mallian hall systems are unique, moreover, in using a single cell (hall 55) as the focus of a doubled, perpendicular living apartment.

The Mallian residential zone may be seen to further resemble that of Phaistos if we broaden our focus to include the peristyle courtyard diagonally adjacent to both. In each palace, the latter was undoubtedly incorporated into some primary entrance system serving as an interface between the residential apartments and a major palace entryway. The court at Phaistos, however, is at a second-storey level, to the southwest, and would have given access to the hall systems down a stairway leading eastward. But it is itself approached, as we shall see below, from the south, up a fine flight of steps leading up from the portico of the western colonnade on the Central Court. The latter connects with the major public entrance to the palace, the wide east-west paved corridor to the south of the magazine block. As with the corresponding entrance at Mallia (the northern entrance, E-1), the Phaistian entrance is the terminus of a raised causeway coming in from the western court area.

As noted before, the residential apartments at Mallia overlie a magazine storage area dating from the foundation of the palace. Traces of this system may be seen at the northwestern corner of the building (cells 45-47-49), and excavators found traces of magazine walls beneath the hall system itself, below cell 54. To the east of the aforementioned magazine cells is a corridor running north-south between two doorways (cell 48), which appears to turn westward toward the western facade of the palace (cell 50). Corridor 48 is directly in line with the great north-south magazine corridor to the south of the hall systems (cells 77a and 77b), and during the period of the first palace may have been continuous with the latter. Traces of (West Court?) pavement are to be seen along the western end of cell 50, and there may have been a recess in the original western facade at this point.

To the west of cell 53 is a small portico opening out to the West Court, enclosing two columns, dating to the time of the first palace. Its function is unknown. To the south of this is an enclosed bastion (cells 59-60-61) which may well have been the foundation of a stairway, access to which would be gained from corridor 53 to the north. This bastion may in fact have been one of a series of bastions/towers at various points on the periphery of the palace.[191]

It is likely that the northwestern quarter of the palace was at least in part a private garden facing the veranda of the residential apartments. It is unclear, however, if there was a palace entry in this area (possibilities: cells 46 and 43), for the northern face of the palace wall is denuded, as indicated in our plan. In the face of lack of evidence, we shall assume that the only connection between the residential zone and the rest of the palace was through cells 40 and 69 to the east. Immediately to the east of the latter are two cells whose form suggests the position of a stairwell. This would make three stairways in the domestic quarter, a situation paralleled at Knossos. The latter stairway would connect closely with the 'banquet hall' area across the northern entry passageway to the Central Court.

It is clear that the palace of Mallia shares a great many organizational features with its Knossian counterpart; features which are also present through various kinds of transformations at Phaistos, Gournia, and Kato Zakro. This is patent once we understand the nature of the formative elements with which the Minoan designer was working, and their morphological variations. And as we shall see in Part Two below, Mallia shares with its brother palaces invariances of planning, layout and construction.

Phaistos: First Palace

Figure II.40 is a site plan of the palatial compound and adjacent construction on the hill of Phaistos. The palace stands at the eastern edge of a promontory at the western end of the great Messara plain in the southern central part of the island. At the western end of the same outcrop of hills stands the large mansion of Haghia Triadha,[192] three-quarters of an hour's walk away.

The palace at Phaistos is the most spectacularly situated Minoan megastructure, commanding picturesque views of the mountains and valleys of the southern fringe of Crete: to the east, the buildings face directly down the east-west length of the Messara plain, beyond which is the high range of Mount Dikte; to the south is the Asterousia range of mountains, which separate the Messara plain from the Libyan Sea. To the north, the palace faces over valleys against the southern flank of Mount Ida, toward whose double peak the Central Court is aligned.[193] The palatial compound is bordered to the west by the peaks of the outcrop of hills on which the settlement stands: Haghia Triadha is hidden behind the latter, to the west.

The palatial compound itself spreads over four distinct terraces, ascending from south to north. The southernmost level is some four meters below the West Middle Court, itself about five meters below the West Upper Court. The level of the central portion of the palace, at the Central Court, is some two meters above the level of the West Middle Court.

The destructions wrought during the Middle Minoan III period, bringing to a close the life of the First Palace, evidently left the latter in such a ruinous state that an entirely new palace was built in its place. These two palaces are indicated on the plan as follows: walls in black belong to the first palace period, while the second palace is shown in outline. Traces of a settlement of the Hellenistic period are shown on the plan at two points: a large residence on the southern flank of the West Upper Court, and a rectangular building, possibly a temple, at the southern end of the palace. Both of these are oriented NW-SE, in contrast to the cardinal orientation of the construction of the Minoan period.

When the first palace was destroyed, the new palace was built on a vast concrete platform over the ruins. The latter raised the level of the West Courts, covering over their pavements and adjacent walls. Built on fewer levels than the first palace, the southwestern sector of the second palace has its ground floor level at the second level of the first palace. Everything shown in the western part of the plan in black was covered by the new western court system of the second palace. Within the body of the palace to the east, only the heavy walls shown in black to the north of the Central Court were re-used in the second period of construction, along with the Central Court pavement itself, and some walls on the northeastern fringe of the compound. Although traces of first palace construction were known during the earlier excavation of the second palace, the peripheral constructions of the first palace not sealed off by later construction were substantially revealed by the Italian School of Archaeology at Athens under Prof. Doro Levi between 1950 and 1966. Our plan is taken from the final excavation report of the School, published in 1967.

Both palaces reveal features of design seen at Knossos and Mallia, and the fineness of construction in both instances is only rivalled by portions of the palace at Knossos. Most impressive to the visitor is the area of the West Middle Court, with its triangular raised causeway connecting a stepped 'theatral' area built up against a retaining wall to the north with an east-west causeway leading into the major palace entrance in the middle of the palace's west facade, through a columned portico. The West Middle Court is bordered to the south by a diagonal line of four stone-lined round pits (*koulouras*) possibly, as at Knossos, containing a planted tree. This 'colonnade of trees' served as a wind-break to the exposed southern flank of the West Middle Court, beneath which stood a paved causeway ramp leading down from the west to the level of the West Lower Court, along a heavy retaining wall.

To the southeast of this row of *koulouras,* in a recess of the palace facade adjacent to the West Portico, is a heavy bastion projecting to the northwest, most likely the foundation of a grand stairway connecting the two court levels. The West Lower Court was evidently smaller in area than its partner to the north, and probably extended originally within the area designated as A in Figure II.41, which shows the extent of the first palace remains. The recent excavations have revealed traces of its pavement adjacent to the southwestern quarter of the first palace, and it most probably extended to the west not much beyond the western end of the stairway bastion, to be bordered by the eastern face of private houses. Remains of the latter are seen in Figure II.40 further to the northwest.

The West Middle Court was bordered to the west by a north-south wall separating the Court from hosue remains beyond. The West Upper Court (C in Figure II.41) was also finely paved, although only its western and eastern sides are distinct: the pavement to the south ends at the area of the Hellenistic residence, and it is unclear whether or not it extended to the retaining wall to the south. It is also broken off to the north. The eastern boundary of this Court is formed by a row of paving blocks which may have served as a raised causeway running north-south; the latter is aligned with the western facade of the first palace on the West Middle Court below. At the southeastern corner is a stairway connecting the two Courts. The western boundary of the Court consists of a retaining wall running SW-NE along whose eastern flank are a row of round holes in the Court pavement, suggesting a colonnade. But unlike other Minoan colonnades, there is no raised support pavement, and if in fact there were small columns inserted into the pavement holes, the resultant 'colonnade' would have been too shallow to permit passage behind. The original disposition of this construction remains enigmatic.

Of the first palace fabric itself, nearly all of the extant cells comprised storage magazines along the western facades to the north and south. Excavations between 1950 and 1966 have revealed that construction of this earlier building began at the level of the West Lower Court. These rooms are shown in Figure II.42.

These chambers run east-west and reveal several outer entrances to the west. The largest entrance consists of a flight of steps rising into a storage room at the southwestern corner. The southern wall of the palace here is nearly three meters thick, and would have borne the weight of several stories above. Its second storey would have been at the level of the West Middle Court to the north, and at this level the southwestern quarter was entered from the area of the West Portico on its northern flank. The cells to the east of the bastion are consequently at this upper level.

The West Porch stood at the center of the entire western facade of this multileveled building, and in fact its northern wall is equidistant from the southern and northern termini of the first palace facade,[194] as indicated in the diagram above. A large central column occupies what would have been the western end of the portico. Within are four doorways of which three are on the eastern side. Only the northern opening leads directly to the area of the Central Court to the east, and this passageway contains the inward extension of the raised causeway system of the West Middle Court. The two doors to the south lead into interior cells which, if the second palace entrance system replicated this here, were probably culs-de-sac.[195]

The wall aligned to the south of the column ran along the eastern edge of the stairway bastion, to connect with the upper level of the western facade of the southwestern quarter below, as indicated in heavy outline in Figure II.41. This facade returned to the west to join the outer facade of the rooms to the south; the outer plane of the latter is aligned with the outer plane of the western facade along the West Middle Court above.

The western facades along both terraces reveal the system of shallow recesses and projections characteristic of palatial construction elsewhere. These recessed planes would have most likely corresponded with the placement of windows at upper levels of the building.

Along the eastern side of the West Middle Court are remains of storage rooms comprising additional magazine blocks. The magazines themselves probably consisted of long narrow chambers running east-west, although in the present extant state of the remains, these latter appear to have been subdivided into smaller cells adjacent to the western facade (as visible in Figure II.40 above). The West Middle facade is divided into two sections at its mid-point, where the wall returns to the east by a few meters. The plans shows that there were a few breaches of the wall along this northern facade, evidently made after the time of the original construction. Near the northwestern corner is a small tricameral annex to the facade, interpreted as a shrine. This construction most likely was functionally connected to the 'theatral' area to the west. At the northwestern corner the facade is broken, and it appears that there may have been a covered portico at this point which connected the West Middle Court with the north-south stairway leading to the upper terrace. It may be of interest that the central column base of this portico is aligned with that of the West Porch to the south. This conjectural portico would have been partially obscured by the construction of the shrine-annex to the northwestern facade. The portico would have stood at the level of the upper portion of the 'theatral' area to the west, part of which may thus have been incorporated into this passageway, but this is unclear.

The 'theatral' area consists of nine shallow treads, about half the number of the Knossian 'theatral' area, but twice as broad. Its northern flank consists of a very finely built ashlar limestone wall, with a continually indented trace along its extant portion. The raised causeway of the Court rises up onto the steps (unlike Knossos) at a slight NW-SE angle, possibly to some missing focus on the top platform (shrine?). At Knossos, the triangular causeway area (dancing circle?) is adjacent to that palace's West Porch entrance; here it is contiguous with the steps of the northern flank of the Court. The principal (widest) causeway here is the north-south one, the others being narrower and less finely constructed. The western walkway is poorly preserved, and its trace can only be followed by an irregular line of flagging which disappears to the southwest. It evidently was slightly curved to join the north-south causeway at the foot of the steps. As at Knossos, the triangular area is adjacent to the sunken *koulouras*.

Within the palace, several cells from the first palace period have been uncovered, as indicated on Figure II.41. These include a set of magazines beneath the back light-well of the second palace 'theatral' area, a room resembling a 'lustral area' to its south, a heavy wall to the southeast of this, evidently the western boundary of the original Central Court, and several wall fragments to the south. Of the latter the most notable is a cell with two square pillar bases, resembling the pillar crypt at Mallia. Unlike the latter, however, this first palace 'pillar crypt' is not positioned at the central bisection line of the Central Court, but is located exactly one-half the distance from the latter to the reconstructed east-west line of the southern facade.[196]

To the east of this chamber is a north-south wall which continues the line of the row of columns forming the western facade of the Central Court of the first palace. Ten columns of the latter colonnade remain — or rather their sunken foundations — and there are two columns on the eastern facade of the Court, indicating that it too was colonnaded, at least in part. The same pattern occurs in the second palace, as we shall see below. In both palaces, the western entrances enter the Central Court near its mid-point, that of the second palace entering the Court north of the mid-point. But seen from the western facades of both palaces, these major palatial entrance systems bisect the palace fabric as seen from the west.

To the north of the Central Court, as shown in Figure II.41, is a double row of alternating columns and piers recalling the ground floor of the 'banquet hall' area at Mallia, but here aligned north-south, as in the pillared hall of Knossos. These columns stand in what was evidently a large hall adjacent to the Court (as at Mallia and Kato Zakro). Only the western, northern and part of the eastern boundary walls of this cluster remain, thanks to their re-use in the structure of the second palace. During that period, as we shall see, all but one of these supports were incorporated into the wall of small rooms.

To the north of this area is a paved court with a diagonal causeway running from a second palace corridor to the northeast (area *E* in Figure II.41). The wall forming the northern border of this later court also dates from the earlier period.

The wall fragments shown to the northeast of Figure II.40 may in part have belonged to auxiliary structures of the first period. These include a fine peristyle portico at whose southern side is a stairway leading up to the Central Court terrace level. It is likely that this earlier entranceway was incorporated into the second palace. To the west of the stairway is a long narrow sunken room, also incorporated into the second palace, which may have been a cold cellar.[197]

As we shall see below in Part Two, the remains of the first Phaistian palace reveal evidence of careful planning and layout, of a character similar to what may be seen both in the later palace here and in other palatial construction. In addition to sharing organizational features with the other palaces, the first palace at Phaistos was planned and laid out in equivalent ways.[198]

Phaistos: Second Palace

After the destruction of their palatial compound, the inhabitants of Phaistos entirely rebuilt their civic megastructure, in contrast to their compatriots at Knossos and Mallia. Evidently, the multiple-terraced first palace at Phaistos suffered earthquake and fire damage much greater than that in other cities, due to its precarious exposure at the edges of its promontory. By contrast, Mallia, standing on flat ground, was largely salvageable, and the basic fabric of that structure was repaired and reused.

The Phaistians leveled the superincumbent remains of the first palace, and laid down a thick concrete platform over the ruins to serve as a solid foundation for the new building. The platform extended over the lowest courses of the western walls of the old palace, and covered over the original pavement of the West Middle Court, leaving but four steps of the old 'theatral' area exposed. The new ground level was thus raised several feet over the level of the old West Middle Court, and the new West Court was continued over the second-storey level of the southwestern quarter of the old palace in front of the new facade (see Figure II.43).

The second palace plan reveals about half the number of cells of the palace at Knossos, but only a portion of the palace is extant. The disposition of the northwestern quarter at the level of the upper terrace is unknown, and at some point in antiquity the entire southeastern half of the palace crumbled to the plain below after the collapse of an entire flank of the promontory. Blocks belonging to the walls of the palace in this area may be seen today below the cliff face, indicating that the original compound entirely enclosed the Central Court. We have no idea of what stood in this quadrant, but the fact that the southern limit of construction to the southwest is as far from the southern limit of the Central Court as the eastern edge of the southeastern tip of the East Court is from the eastern limit of the Central Court makes it plausible that the latter was enclosed on its southern and eastern sides by construction as thick as that to the west, below the western entrance corridor.

In what remains of the second palace, most of this is given over to residential apartments, in sharp contrast to Knossos and Mallia, whose ground-floor residential quarters occupy a fraction of the total mass. In characteristic Minoan fashion, these residential areas command the finest views out over the landscape: to the north, east and south.

The old 'theatral' area in the West Court was replaced, once the latter was submerged by the new platform, by the fine stepped platform built into the northwestern corner of the palace, referred to in the literature as a 'grand propylon entrance'. It is most likely that this construction, which is principally oriented outward, to the West Court, is to be functionally connected to activities in the Court. Its proportions resemble those of the Knossian 'theatral' area, and its position at the northwestern corner of the palace replicates the position of the latter at Knossos. It is *not,* in other words, a 'grand entrance'.

Consisting of a platform with 13 steps adjacent to the bottom of the north-south steps connecting the Court with the West Upper Court, this 'theatral' area has three internal divisions: a stylobate with a large central column between two wall-projections, a double doorway flanking a central pier to the east, and a colonnade opening onto a light-well, the latter forming the eastern end of the cluster. Three small doorways connect the structure to the internal fabric of the palace: two at opposite ends of the 'porch' cell, and one at the southeastern corner of the light-well. The latter leads to a small landing in the midst of a northward-rising stairway leading from the western colonnade of the Central Court up to a peristyle court to the north. The door at the northern end of the 'porch' opens into a stairwell rising to the west, and the door to the south opens into a small cul-de-sac, perhaps a porter's lodge, or more likely a storeroom used in connection with the activities taking place on the stepped platform itself. With the double doors on the north of the porch cell closed, the 'theatral' area becomes entirely an annex of the West Court.

The principal entrance to the palace from the West Court is to the south of the magazine block (corridor 7 in the published plan). On the western facade itself, this entrance consists of a double doorway leading into a vestibule, beyond which is a central pier which would have been originally flanked by a second set of double doors. On the northern side of this vestibule is a door leading directly into the magazine block, via cell 31. To the east of the latter is cell 32, evidently a porter's lodge. Diagonally across the corridor is a doorway giving access to a corridor running south through the southwestern quarter of the palace (cells 12-13-14).

There is a raised causeway running along corridor 7 from its southern door at the west to the colonnade forming the western facade of the Central Court. At this point, reflecting the disposition of the western facade of the corridor, is a third double-door system. While the southern wall of cell 25 to the north most likely continued eastward to meet one of the piers of this double doorway, on the southern side of the corridor is a doorway opening south onto a colonnade fronting on the principal ritual chambers of the palace (cells 24, 23). It is unclear if there was a fourth double-door system to the west of the eastern doors and the southern colonnade door; my own observations of the remains suggest that such a door is likely.

The magazine block (cells 26-37, and the two cells under 70 and 38 in the plan) is organized differently from the great magazine blocks on the western facades of Knossos and Mallia. Rather than having parallel rows of long narrow magazines running east-west, the Phaistian magazine block consists of two rows of storerooms aligned north-south, accessible from a central east-west corridor, cell 26. Bifurcating the magazine block from north to south is a very thick wall, undoubtedly supporting a major structural north-south wall which would have passed over the central pier of the corridor. Such a wall evidently comprised a major wall-division between larger halls on the second storey level (i.e. at the level of the top of the stepped platform) and on a third storey as well.

The organization of the magazine block is reminiscent of

magazine areas of large contemporary mansions (e.g. ML E, ML ZA, and HTR), notably in the cellular proportions of the storage chambers themselves. Shallower than the long magazines of the first palace period at Knossos and Mallia, such a system provides readier access to the contents of each chamber than do the long narrow storeroom systems of Knossos and Mallia.

In one respect, Phaistos reveals a modification of the design of the western magazine zones of the first palaces by incorporating more direct access to the outside of the building (at cell 31, within the controlled vestibule end of corridor 7). A similar type of direct access was, at this same period, cut through the old magazine blocks at Mallia, as we have seen above.[199] Phaistos thus presents a rethinking of older designs, and in this respect certain aspects of its organization resemble design solutions seen in the MM III/LM I period houses examined in detail earlier.

Of the upper storeys here we have no direct evidence, but it seems likely that there existed a series of large halls whose columns would have rested over enlarged portions of the magazine walls.[200] Over cells 68/69 of the stepped platform there was undoubtedly a passageway connecting halls at the (third) level over the magazines with the stairway system to the north of the stepped platform. J.W. Graham thought that the second level over cells 68/69 might be a 'window of appearances' of Egyptian type, for the Phaistian 'monarch' to address his or her subjects, but this seems dubious: more simply, we might suggest that this area was a good vantage point to view ritual activities on the stepped platform itself, below.[201]

A double door leads from the corridor of the magazines to a columned chamber (cell 25) fronting on the Central Court. Within are two columns aligned east-west, bisecting the chamber, between the north wall of cell 32 and a column on the Court colonnade itself. The latter has a curious oval (rather than round) base. It is possible that the Court colonnade was two storeys high at this point, marking cell 25 as an impressive antechamber.[202] On the northern flank of the chamber are two cells beneath 38 and 70, of which the former may have been a lustral area of the old palace incorporated into the new palace.[203] In the northeastern corner of 25 is a door leading to stairway 39, which led to cell 75 to the north, an antechamber to the fine peristyle court

(74) beyond which is the principal hall system of the building.

Given this cell-sequence, and the proximity to the main palace entrance (7), we may suggest that the route 7-25-39-75-74 comprised the formal entrance to the hall system of the palace.[204] The similarities of such a system to that at Mallia will be discussed below; let us now turn our attention to the southwestern quarter of the palace, below the entrance corridor.

This zone comprises three cell-clusters. The smallest (cells 8-9 and 10-11) is an appendage of the West Court, with no internal communication with the palace directly. Evidently a shrine, its use may be connected with West Court activities, and quite possibly with votive behavior connected with formal entry to the palace proper. Its position, next to a major palace entrance, recalls a cluster of cells to the west of the southern entrance at Mallia,[205] as well as West Court construction in the first Phaistian palace (q.v.). Indeed, cells 8-9 and 10-11 stand in a position identical to a doubly entered set of cells adjacent to the West Porch of the first palace.

The southwestern quarter is bisected north-south by a corridor (12-13-14) which divides the shrines fronting on the Central Court from residential apartments to the west. The corridor begins as a passage from the West Entrance (7) at cell 12, opens into a square chamber which was likely a light-well, and then splits into an east-west corridor (14) connecting the religious and residential zones. On the southern flank of 14 are two doors: that to the southwest leads into the residential halls, while that to the east continues the north-south passageway to the southern limit of the remains. At the latter point the corridor evidently connected with an east-west passageway (97').

The apartments — cells 15-21, 95-95' — comprise a series of chambers including two sunken lustral areas (19, 21, one to the north, one to the south), living and sleeping halls (17, 18, 15, 16, and 20), and two halls with PDP systems (95-95'). It seems likely that the quarter comprised two distinct apartments (17, 18, 19 and 16, 20, 21) with a central common room (15). Cells 95-95' may be considered part of the southern apartment. It has been suggested that these were guest suites.[206]

At some point after the initial second palace construction, an additional chamber was added to the west of cell 95, in a recess of the western facade. To the west of the entire apartment area is a jogged retaining wall (hatched in the plan, like the annex to cell 95), whose trace superficially resembles the disposition of the Corridor of the Procession at Knossos. This wall may have served as a balcony or terrace, entered from the southern end of corridor 14.

To the south, at the extreme southwestern corner of the palace, are the foundations of a tricameral cluster, but its relationship to the southwestern quarter is unclear. To its east is a set of foundations aligned east-west (cells 97-97') suggesting a stairwell. Such a stair would be the only access to a second storey in this quarter.

The function and disposition of cells 96, 96', 96" are unclear, being overlain by some later construction. To the immediate north of cell 96 is a large open area within which are traces of a first palace pillar crypt(?), possibly reused in the second palace. But the cell which stands at Phaistos in a position identical to the Knossian and Mallian pillar crypts is cell 24, standing at the geometric center of the central planning grid of the new palace. It does not, however, have a central pillar, but consists rather of a chamber opening onto the western colonnade of the Central Court, around whose walls is a low bench. There is a curious clay base at the center of the room, which may well have been a stand for a ritual object such as a large *labrys* (double axe), or it may have been a statue base.[207] As the plan indicates, this room was remodelled at some point, dividing what was originally a single room into two. Similarly, cell 23 to the south was remodelled, closing off its internal connection with the residential zone within. Like cell 24, it also features a bench along its inner walls.

As noted above, the Central Court, whose pavement is almost entirely intact,[208] is bordered to the west and east by colonnades. The stylobate of the Court is missing in front of cells 23 and 24, as well as along the southern side and part of the southeastern side, so it is unclear as to whether or not the colonnade extended along all three sides. To the north, the Court is bordered by a fine ashlar masonry wall, with symmetrical shallow recesses (and two symmetrical niches) flanking a central doorway (41). Adjacent to both sides of the door are engaged columns. While the shallow recesses surely correspond to windows at higher levels, the purpose of the inward niches is unknown. Recently, J.W. Graham suggested that the two engaged columns were in fact the bases of flagpoles such as may be reconstructed on the pylon-facades of Egyptian temples.[209] Why such an arrangement would occur in a non-Egyptian palatial residence is unclear, however, but a rhyton unearthed at Zakro, evidently representing a peak sanctuary, suggests a possible Minoan prototype.[210] This might make sense if we suppose that the northern facade of the Phaistian Court was the outer facing of a temple of some kind, but in fact it is not: beyond this facade was a 'banquet hall' and the principal hall systems or official residential quarter of the palace.

On the other hand, the special articulation of this facade is unusual and impressive; but its markedness may in fact relate not to the palace fabric itself, but rather to a very prominent feature of the landscape around Phaistos — namely the twin peak of Mount Ida directly to the north, on whose southern slope is situated an important Minoan mountain sanctuary: the Kamares cave.[211] It is also perfectly obvious that the palace at Phaistos is aligned toward the twin peak of Ida, as may be seen by standing at the eastern and western edges of the Central Court. The north-south corridor at the center of the northern facade, however, is skewed in its north-south orientation, due to the incorporation of the alignments of walls of the first palace,[212] so looking north through that corridor toward Ida one gets a false impression of the alignment of the palace.

Thus, if the northern facade of the Court was articulated in some manner to call attention to, or perceptually enhance, the twin peak of Mount Ida and its cave sanctuary — whether by 'flagpoles' or other markers standing above roof-line — we may well refer its organization to an extra-palatial situation. Indeed, if one stands at the center of the Court, directly perpendicular to the shrine room (cell 24), a three-storey roofline at the northern facade would just cut off the lower edge of Ida's double peak, and we might imagine some roof marker 'framing' such an alignment. There is a suggestion of a similar device (a 'horns of consecration') at Knossos which could have served, to judge by its fallen position, to frame the view from the Knossian court to the peak of Mount Juktas to the S-SW. Juktas itself had an important Minoan 'peak sanctuary'. In both cases, such a marker may have served a function similar to the niches in Moslem mosques indicating the generic direction of the distant holy city of Mecca.

The problem of the alignments and orientations of the Minoan palaces is a controversial one,[213] but one which is readily resolvable once we are clear what the issues and variables are, as we shall see in a concluding section in the present Chapter.

To the northeast of the Central Court is another residential zone (cells 63, 63a, 63b, 63c, 63d, and 64), standing in a position similar to the principal hall system of the palace at Kato Zakro. It comprises a series of halls (the main one being cell 63), and a porticoed veranda (or peristyle court: 64). In addition, there was a sunken bathroom area (cell 63d). The main hall was bordered on its western, southern and eastern sides by PDP systems (similar in disposition to halls at Mallia and Knossos); a denuded area on its southern side might be plausibly reconstructed as a small lightwell (as at Mallia). The 'lustral area' is reached through a door in the latter. In the southwestern corner of the same cell is a door which opens laterally onto the eastern colonnade of the Central Court, down a small flight of steps.

The area to the east comprises an L-shaped colonnade which may in fact have originally been an enclosed peristyle court, a more modest version of cell 74 in the northwestern quarter of the palace: pavement traces of its eastern and southern sides may be seen, much denuded. Near the southeastern corner of the latter is a series of steps diagonally cut into the edge of what remains of the hill at this point; possibly leading to a terrace or balcony area or small garden on the hill's edge.

The northeastern quadrant of the palace comprised the principal service areas of the structure. The residential apartment 63/64 (yet another 'guest suite' or seasonal quarters for the permanent residents?) communicates at its northeastern corner with a large open courtyard of trapezoidal shape, at whose center were found the remains of a large baking oven (90). While its eastern boundary conditions are poorly preserved, on the eastern side are a series of storage magazines (54-55), added after the original second palace foundation. The only entrance to the latter is in the northeastern corner, a situation recalling the eastern magazine block at Mallia, but on a much smaller scale. Court 90 communicates with the area of the Central Court through corridor 62, along the northern flank of the apartment suite.

On its northern side is what appears to be an entrance vestibule (cell 53), which provides access to the court itself as well as to corridor 52 to the west, leading on to court 48, to the north of the 'banquet hall' block. Cells 89 and 88 are storage rooms, as is cell 57. Cell 49 is a small courtyard, opening into court 48.[214]

The 'banquet hall' block, cells 58-59-60-61-91-92, is a cluster of service and storage cells built into a first palace pillared hall.[215] It is bisected east-west by a corridor (58) with doors at both ends, connecting north-south corridor 41 with corridors 58 and 56 to the east. To the west of corridor 41 are additional storerooms (44-45-46), entered at 44 from the south, next to the service stair of the block (42-43).

The block reveals the same organizational features that we have seen to the north of the Mallian Central Court: pillared hall, north-south corridor connecting the Central Court with the northern quarter, storerooms, and a service stairway. It has been plausibly suggested that the ground floor here was concerned with food preparation, clearer evidence for which has now been seen in the equivalent cluster at Kato Zakro.[216]

Stairway 42-43 opens, at its mid-flight landing, onto vestibule 75, into whose southwestern corner enters stairway 39. These perpendicularly adjacent stairways recall the complex stair system at Mallia, but the similarity is most likely purely formal.[217]

The area to the north of the 'banquet hall' block and stairway 39 is the principal residential quarter of the palace. To the north of vestibule 75 is a large peristyle court (74), directly to the north of which is a hall, beyond a wide PDP system with six double doors. The seventh door, in the northeastern corner, provides access to a stairway which turns down eastward to reach a corridor separating the two hall systems on the ground floor. It is likely that hall 93 was connected to the northerly hall system at a second level.

Evidently a formal reception area, peristyle court 74 serves as the chief formal interface between the private halls to the north and the entrance system from outside the palace. At the south-western corner of cell 74 is a door leading to a large stairway (71-72-73) leading to a third level. This door also provides access to a long narrow north-south corridor running along the western flank of cells 74 and 93. It probably was a service corridor connected to the hall systems, but its northerly disposition is unknown. Beneath the western stairway (71 *et seq.*) is a closet (73-72).

The stair at the northeastern corner of the peristyle court pauses at a landing, to the south of which is a door leading to the southern hall system, the smaller of the two (cluster 50 on the plan). This hall consists of three cells separated by two porticoes, of which the center cell only was covered: the western and eastern cells are light-wells. In the northwestern corner of the westerly cell (within which is a low bench on its western and southern walls) is a door leading to stairway 51, which rises to the south, and returns upward to the east. The latter flight covers a closet beneath, accessible only from the eastern light-well of the cluster. Stairway 51 evidently provided access to a room above the central cell of the hall system, which would have connected northward to the second storey of the larger hall system.

To the north of the stairway leading to the entrance to cluster 50 is the larger hall system, entered from its central cell (77) down several steps. The system consists of the standard tricameral arrangement: inner hall (79), portico (77), and light-well (78). PDP systems connect cells 79 and 77 with an outer portico to the north (85), bordered by three columns set in a line flanked by projecting walls to the west and east. The system recalls the layout of the northerly portion of the Mallian hall system (see above, Figure II.37), while the parallel alignment of the two hall systems at Phaistos recalls the layout of the Knossian halls with its intervening stairwell.

As at Mallia, there is a sunken bath chamber (cell 83) to the west of the hall system, with an antechamber to the north (81). In both palaces, the bath area can be entered both from the north, off the porticoed veranda, and from the south, from the southwestern corner of the main hall (via corridor 80). Room 82 was most likely a latrine.

The area to the north of the veranda, undoubtedly a private terrace or garden, faced out over the edge of the hill toward the Ida mountain range to the north. To the east of the two hall systems is a north-south corridor (87), which provided more public access to the northern fringe of the palace. A series of cells to the northeast of this corridor (visible above in Figure II.40) were incorporated into the second palace fabric. As noted above, a peristyle court may have served as a principal eastern entrance to the palace via a stairway rising to the south. The latter opens into an area adjacent to cell 53.

The second palace of Phaistos thus reveals many features of design shared by the palatial compounds at Knossos and Mallia, while at the same time presenting us with evidence of new thinking regarding palatial organization. In connection with the latter we may point to the reorganization of the western magazine block system in a more compact and economical fashion, and the incorporation into the structural fabric of the palace proper of the 'theatral' area — stepped platform 67-68-69 — originally part of the old West Middle Court. The older system of a separate 'theatral' construction is retained at Knossos.

Like its brother palaces at Knossos and Mallia, and like most Minoan freestanding structures, the Phaistian palace has a highly articulated and indented outer facade, most highly marked on the western 'front' of the building. In order to understand the proportional articulation of the Phaistian western facade, it is necessary to look in detail at its actual dimensions. The individual facade sections (unlike the older palace facades at Knossos and Mallia) are not laid out as simple fractions and multiples of a decimally expressed modular standard, but instead express whole-number values of a Fibonacci or Summation series (i.e. 1, 1, 2, 3, 5, 8, 13, 21, 34, 55, 89. . .), as illustrated in Figure II.44.

The diagram reveals that, using a modular standard of +0.3400 cm, the designers laid out the sections of the western facade, from south to north, as 21 + 34 + 55 + 89 units, a practice well known in contemporary Egyptian design.[218] Such a proportional harmonic system (in which the ratio between any two adjacent dimensions approximates 2 : 3 or 1 : 1.6) is common in Minoan design elsewhere as will be seen in detail below in Part II; but here at the new palace of Phaistos the harmonic system is employed in a literal fashion ('in clear'[219]).

The western facade, thus, is carved out of the 200-unit grid square upon which the palace as a whole is laid out, and the close correspondence between the dimension of 200 modular units and the 199-unit length of 21 + 34 + 55 + 89 was capitalized upon by the building's designers.[220] Although the 2 : 3 ratio scheme is to be found in the proportional system of many Minoan buildings (including the western facades of Mallia and Knossos, as we shall see), in other instances of its occurrence the Fibonacci ratios are expressed as simple decimally expressed values (e.g. 20 : 30 units, or 40 : 60, etc.). The Phaistian western facade is the only example of the literal application of the numerical ratios as whole-number values.

Thus, the progression of the facade from south to north reveals a patterned increase in the length of each facade section wherein each successive facade piece is increased in size by one increment on the Fibonacci proportional scale. The harmonic system revealed in this and other Minoan designs is itself the simple summation-based system underlying the so-called 'golden mean' harmonic system often attributed to design in various media in the post-Minoan period in Greece.[221] It is not unlikely that Minoan designers and craftsmen learned of such a system through intercourse with Egyptian craftsmen, and there is evidence that Minoan craftsmen participated in some Middle Kingdom building projects.[222] It is important to stress, however, that the Minoan designer applied the *principles* of such a system of proportions to native Minoan architectonic compositions: corresponding Egyptian public construction is invariably rectangular and uniplanar.

The palace at Phaistos provides us with evidence of a clarity, homogeneity, and sophistication in megastructural composition often masked at Knossos and Mallia because of many generations of rebuilding and alteration to existing buildings. At Phaistos, the opportunity to entirely redesign and rebuild a major civic mega-structure provides us with clear evidence that Minoan designers employed the same principles of architectonic organization in their major civic monuments that is patent in the more modest residences examined above.

The following diagram illustrates the cell-cluster organization of the Phaistian palace at its ground-floor levels (Figure II.45).

In contrast to the clustering pattern seen above for Knossos and Mallia (Figures II.30 and II.38), the organization of Phaistos is simpler and more block-like. Each cluster or functional zone tends to be rectangular, in comparison with the jigsaw puzzle aspect of the two other palaces. The closer correspondence between the functional zoning and the principal subdivisions of the modular grid layout are more apparent. This is all the more remarkable considering that the builders of the second Phaistian palace chose to incorporate a number of major walls left over from Phaistos I in laying out their design.[223]

Thus, the block-like or 'insula' organization of the Minoan palace — the microcosmic city-within-a-city pattern proposed by Sir Arthur Evans for the initial state of the Knossian palace – finds its best evidence here at Phaistos (rather than at Knossos).[224]

Within a number of cluster-blocks, however, the antisymmetry and multiple-connective patterns of spatial composition so characteristic of other Minoan design are here in evidence, and it becomes patent that the interpermeability of cells and their often labyrinthine connections are the result of functional requirements specific to given sets of activities. Residential zones are often complexly composed, no doubt to provide a culture-specific balance between privacy and directness of access (e.g. the southwestern residential cluster here), whereas other kinds of activities, such as storage and transport of commodities, are given symmetrical and redundant (i.e. predictable) expression.

In other words, the specifics of cellular composition, in Minoan architecture, are functions of the particular job a given area is to perform, and the patterns of expectation regarding characteristic usage associated with given areas. Such consistencies in the correlation of the formal and functional aspects of a design program are one of the chief hallmarks of the Minoan architectonic code.

All such patterns of consistency and formal/functional correlation are culture-specific, and are expressive of the systems of value and thought peculiar to a given society. What may be seen as 'organic' composition in one society might often appear stilted and rigid to the culture next door. The finely calibrated multidirectional and multidimensional patterns of spatial organization patent in Minoan design — which makes it so attractive to the contemporary eye — are embedded in a cultural system which is abruptly different from our own. In 'reading' Minoan design, we must be forever wary of projecting our own assumptions and predispositions into alien material. We must, in other words, seek to understand Minoan architectonic organization on its own terms, insofar as we can.[225]

Kato Zakro: Palace

Although evidence of an important Minoan settlement was found at Zakro in the last years of the nineteenth century by Mariani and Halbherr, and in 1901 Hogarth excavated a portion of a residential quarter,[226] it was not until 1961 that the palatial compound on the site was discovered by Nicholas Platon, who has headed its excavation since that time.[227] Platon and his associates are in the process of uncovering a remarkable structure mid-way in size between the larger palaces in the center of the island (Knossos, Phaistos, Mallia) and the smaller provincial palace at Gournia. The finds to date suggest that Kato Zakro, standing near the shore of the eastern end of Crete, was an important port city and center of artistic activity in its own right.

Because the excavation is not entirely complete, and because the wealth of information about Minoan culture unearthed here is still in the process of careful evaluation, our observations on the interesting palatial compound will be confined to more general remarks regarding the structure's design and organization, as currently understood.

The palatial compound, on level (and low) ground adjacent to a sheltered cove and beach, stands up against a hill rising to the north, upon which Hogarth's 1901 excavations of the residential quarter were centered. Dating substantially to the Late Minoan I period,[228] the present structure bears a number of salient resemblances to the better known palaces elsewhere, while presenting us with certain unique features of its own.

As the plan in Figure II.46 indicates, the compound is built around a Central Court some 40 by 100 modular units in size,[229] oriented NE-SW (not unlike the orientation of the palace at Mallia). In size, then, the Court is approximately one-quarter the area of the Courts of the major palaces (100 by 200 units), and is close in size to the Court of Gournia.

Unlike the latter, however, the Zakro palace Court is not directly contiguous with the fabric of the city itself, but is a truly internal structure.

The palace shares with its better-known cousins the inclusion of a number of architectonic features, most notably the fine Central Court itself, faced on four sides by carefully hewn limestone blocks, a large and elegant hall system to the east of the Court, a pillared hall to the north of the Court (serving more patently here as a kitchen, with adjacent pantry), light-wells, PDP wall systems, sunken lustral cells, a shrine set deeply within the western block, a colonnade and stairwell adjacent to the kitchen hall, an indented western facade fronting on a West Court at least part of which was paved, as well as other details to be noted in the course of our discussion.

The principal features unique to the palace, or, if echoed elsewhere, are echoed less clearly, are: the round (and likely colonnaded and roofed) bathing pool to the east of the veranda of the hall system, standing in its own walled courtyard; two wells or cisterns entered by means of descending steps, to the south and southwest of the latter; and an elegantly paved double set of halls running north-south along the western side of the Central Court.[230] The subterranean structure to the south of the round bathing pool court could conceivably have served other functions as well.[231]

The fine hall system is more intimately connected with the Central Court than the hall systems of the larger palaces, standing directly on the eastern facade of the Court, beyond a colonnaded portico extending part of the way down the Court facade. On the eastern side, the halls open out, through a veranda, to a private walled courtyard in the middle of which is embedded the sunken round pool. The latter is approached from the southwestern corner of the courtyard, in the area of a cell projecting southward from the line of the southern wall of the court. It is possible that the latter may have in part served as a stairwell to a second floor, returning northward over an adjacent foundation to the west to the level over the veranda.

Within, this large and interesting hall system is divided into two principal parts. To the south is the canonical tricameral hall system, with a light-well beyond two columns at the southern end, a portico at the middle, and a larger main hall to the north. The latter, like its counterparts at Knossos, Phaistos and Mallia, has three of its sides consisting of PDP systems, and its left-hand side (facing from the light-well) is a solid wall. On the eastern side of the hall and porch cells are PDP systems opening onto the veranda (as at Phaistos and Mallia), while on the western side doors from both cells lead out to the Central Court eastern colonnade.

In these respects, then, the hall system, approximately contemporary with the systems at the three larger palaces, is very nearly identical to the latter in nearly every way.

To the north of the hall system proper is an additional hall with indications of internal subdivisons, but oriented inward to the palace fabric: it opens its entire western facade out into the Court portico through a PDP wall system, and half of its northern flank onto one of the major east-west palace corrridors leading to the Central Court. Here, too, the opening consists of a PDP system, with three double doors (evidently there were four onto the Court colonnade to the west). On the Court side, the colonnade facade includes a central, single column, an arrangement which formally resembles the hall system at ML ZA (Figure II.8, above), or even Nirou Khani (Figure II.17. above), although at the latter site we find two columns on the Court facade.

This hall may well have served as a formal reception area for the hall system area to the south. It stands adjacent to one of the principal Court entrances, an east-west corridor on its northern flank, evidently leading eastward to the area of the entrance ramp at the northeastern tip of the palace, itself opening onto a paved area to the north. It seems likely that this northern hall served as a major interface between the private residential quarter and more public sectors of the palace and city beyond. It stands directly opposite another room of a 'vestibular' nature, across the Central Court (cell XXX).

Directly between these two cells is an enigmatic construction in the Court itself, a squared piece of cut stones enclosing a central open space. It has been suggested this was an *eschara* or offering depository, an enclosure for the base of a sacred tree, or an altar of some kind. At the palace of Mallia, as we have seen, there was an altar or offering table at the center of the Central Court, and there evidently was some such object in the Knossian Court, now disappeared,[232] standing to the north of the Court's center in old plans, and slightly to the west. We may also suggest that this stone piece might have served to support and hold some important ritual or heraldic post-like object (such as a large metallic *labrys* or double-axe), not surprisingly destroyed or removed in the destruction of the palace. Such large double-axes are known and pictured

elsewhere,[233] but it should be stressed that there is no direct
evidence of any kind here for such an object. It might even have
been a mast or flagpole such as those pictured on a remarkable
rhyton depicting a peak sanctuary, found here at Zakro nearby
(cell XXIX). The roundness of the central reserved space suggests
some such cylindrical insertion, however.

This Court object stands, as noted above, directly between the
aforementioned north hall to the east, and cell XXX to the west.
The latter has a small central column (recalling the central
[column?] base in Phaistos cell 24). This cell is open widely to the
Court, and the internal column is on axis with the Court stand,
suggesting (as at Mallia) some close connection. It is not entirely
inconceivable, then, judging from its form and position, that cell
XXX could have been a Court shrine; a feature known at every
other Minoan palace. The room is divided internally by an L-
shaped wall to the northwest, which evidently served to close off,
perhaps with doors, the L-shaped passage behind. It is not unlikely
that the latter may have in part served as the foundation of a
missing wooden stair, rising from the northeastern corner, going
westward, and turning upward to the south. The opening out to
the second storey at this latter point would then place such a
route in alignment with a corridor running east-west on the second
storey, along the northern edge of the light-well to the west of cell
XXVIII, to join the upward rise of a complementary stairway
rising north and east from cell XII to the west.

At any rate, cell XXX is clearly oriented out to the Central
Court and its enigmatic base to the east of the wide entrance
threshold. It communicates with the interior of the West Block of
the palace at one point: the southwestern corner doorway, which
would have stood beneath the uppermost rise of our conjectural
stairway, adjacent to what then would have been an under-
stairway closet opening to the north.

Beyond the southern wall of cell XXX is a remarkable and
elegant six-celled cluster of rooms without direct parallel elsewhere except for a partial resemblance to the long hall system of
the so-called Little Palace at Knossos, similarly incorporating a
light-well, and also running north-south along the eastern edge of
the structure.[234] Reading the plan from the north, we find a
square light-well on the northwestern corner, finely paved, sur-

rounded by centered columns on three sides, and a double window to the west, flanking a projecting wall end. This cell gave light and ventilation to five adjacent cells, and secondarily to other cells beyond, toward the center of this West Block.

To the east is a hall with two central columns running north-south, closely aligned with the columns of the light-well itself. To the immediate south of the light-well is a porch, in effect a continuation of the columnar hall to the east, making an L-shaped surround to the well in the hall system proper. This southern cell was evidently closed off by (double?) doors to the west, and by a triple double-door (PDP?) system to the south.

Beyond the latter is a square hall whose eastern wall is a four-bayed PDP system, whose southern wall is solid, and whose western wall is a double door. The two doors to the west open onto small vestibules opening north and south to different areas beyond. To the northwest is cell XV, apparently an antechamber to a sunken 'lustral chamber' or bathroom to its south (cell XXIV). To the southwest are three cells: XXV, evidently the treasury room of the shrine (XXIII) to the north; XXVI, a workshop or atelier; and XXVII, a storeroom.

To the east, the hall opens onto a hall of identical size, itself leading southward, through a PDP wall system, to the largest cell of the cluster (XXIX), considered to have served as a 'banquet hall'. All the halls are paved in geometric patterns.

Although the specific function(s) of this hall cluster is unknown, its formal and topological disposition align it with other large hall clusters known elsewhere. The presence of a light-well illuminating not only the hall cluster itself but, via adjacent windows, other cells as well, recalls a similar situation in the large and elegant mansion TYL A (Figure II.9). The immediate adjacency not only of a sunken 'lustral basin' but an appended large antechamber as well, recalls Phaistos, Mallia, and Knossos (although in the latter case the lustral area opens directly onto one of the halls of the adjacent cluster [the 'Queen's' Megaron], whereas here the approach is indirect).

Both the Mallian and present hall clusters closely communicate with a hidden shrine — at Mallia, a pillar crypt distinct from the larger and more public pillar crypt on the Central Court — here a small shrine back of the 'lustral basin', evidently not a pillar crypt but a room with a table for idols and other ritual appointments. Indeed, if we may draw an equivalence between the Mallian situation and that at Zakro, cell XXX here may then correspond to the more public shrine areas of the Central Court zone at all the other palaces.[235]

Moreover, at both Mallia and Kato Zakro, the position of this hidden shrine is immediately adjacent to an archival cell where Linear A tablets were stored; here, cell XVI beyond the shrine's western wall, and accessible directly from the shrine via two doorways, to the southwest and north, and, at Mallia, the cell serving as the very antechamber to the hall system's pillar crypt.[236] There is also a latrine here, immediately to the south of the archive room (cell XXII).

The conclusion is inescapable: this cluster of cells is organized as a residential hall system of palatial magnitude and topological disposition, incorporating elements familiar elsewhere, even to their patterns of connectivity and placement (e.g. the residential quarter of Mallia). But whether the cluster functioned in the same way as the more canonical formation[237] across the Court is not quite so clear. Indeed, why are there two residential hall systems on opposite sides of the Court?

In one sense, we are back to an issue discussed above in connection with the doubled hall systems of the three major palaces: there we appealed to distinctions in formation and relative position and size which implicated functional differentiations such as seasonal patterns of residence and/or an opposition between more formal (and accessible) and more private (and less accessible) usages.

Here at Kato Zakro we appear to be faced with a similar problem, but here we are presented with two equally elegant, large, and accessible hall systems, differently arranged. But what in fact do these differences consist of?

At first glance, the East Hall System looks like a system of fair-weather living halls (complete with 'swimming pool'[?] and summer veranda), while the West Hall System seems set up for longer stretches of indoor living: its only external direct access is a doorway at its northeastern corner, opening onto the Central Court. It is lighted and ventilated by a large centrally located light-well. It is adjacent to important storage magazines on the western facade of the palace (e.g. cells IX, XII, XXVII), and an office/bookkeeping area (cell XVI). It has a bathroom (cell XXIV), lacking in the East Halls (which, however, have an outdoor bathing tank).[238] It has a shrine (as at Mallia and in private residences, above). It has a latrine (cell XXII), and even an indoor workshop (XXVI).

Moreover, the West Halls and their appendages can be sealed off from outside at several points: by one door on the Central Court side; by adjacent doors to the north of cell IX (a rectangular, large room with a central pavement of brick, a likely entrance vestibule/interface with the northwestern magazine areas); and by the northern and southwestern doors of cell XV, preventing access from the two external entrances into the western facade. Interestingly, one of these facade entrances leads to a cell adjacent to the archives (cell XIII), which is also a reasonable site for a porter's lodge in a standard Minoan house.

It is interesting that the East Hall System, which otherwise resembles its other palatial cousins so closely, is not doubled, as at Phaistos, Mallia,[239] and Knossos, or even as at Haghia Triadha and the Knossian 'Little Palace'.[240] This alone is suggestive of a distinction in seasonal usage between the two hall systems here, for such a distinction can be seen for the palatial examples discussed above: all have a more 'indoor' partner or component. Here, we may plausibly suggest, the 'indoor partner' is the elegant West Hall System. The two are not contiguous or directly adjacent, as elsewhere, or separated by a stairwell-circulatory system (as at Knossos and Phaistos): here the two hall systems are separated by the main circulatory area of the compound, the (relatively small, but proportionally canonical) Central Court.

Closely connected with the residential zones is the pillared hall to the north of the West Halls, and northwest of the Central Court. As noted above, it stands in a position identical to the equivalent formations at Phaistos and Mallia, presenting features of both. Like Phaistos, the columns run north-south. Like Mallia, there are six columns (Phaistos had eight), though the Mallian columns are aligned east-west. There is a small portico to the north of the Central Court itself (or at least for part of it), unlike Phaistos but like Mallia the portico (also) covers a stairwell on the northeastern corner of the Central Court.

The pillared hall (cell XXXII) is taken to be a kitchen, with the smaller cell to the northwest (XXXIII) a pantry. Such an attribution, made only by inference elsewhere, is here apparently supported by the nature of the ceramic finds within. Where is the dining room?

The obvious answer in this context is that it would depend on the season and the formality of the occasion. The finding of amphoras and wine jugs in hall XXIX suggests one such location, while there may well have been a pillared dining hall above the kitchen, as suggested elsewhere.[241] Access from the kitchen rooms to the second storey would have been at the stairway block to the east of room XXXII.

On the western part of the palace, many rooms are given over to storage, a pattern seen in other palatial compounds. Here, cells I through XII were storerooms, five of which (I, II, III, IV, XII) had direct communication with the outside. It seems unlikely then, that any of the six western entrances would have served as a principal formal entry to the palace; although as we have seen at Mallia, one of the major palatial entries (to the northwest) passes through what is clearly a service area (the northern quarter). At Phaistos, the main western entrance (corridor 7, Figure II.43) also provided direct access to the magazine block from the outside.

There is no evident monumentalized West Court here, unlike the other palaces (even Gournia, albeit that is rather small, consisting of little more than an enlargement of a major public street). But the entire western block at Zakro does reveal the now familiar indented trace, on its western and southern facades. Cells XVII-XXI, at the southwestern corner of the block, comprise a semi-autonomous zone with no ground floor communication with the rest of the palace. In fact, this cluster, entered through a single door at the southeastern corner, has the form of a small private residence, complete with a hall system (cells XVII-XIX-XX) in an L-shape, an entry vestibule likely serving as a porter's lodge (cell XXI), a latrine, and an adjacent stairway rising in two perpendicular flights (cell XVIII). The principal part of the hall system is the two larger cells XVII and XIX; to the south of the latter cell is a smaller cell (XX), possibly a light-well(?). To the east of the latter, in a small cul-de-sac, is a partitioned room entered from cell XIX, considered to have been a dyer's works. This separate house (which might have communicated with the rest of the palace at the second-storey level) appears to have been the residence and workshop of a craftsman in the employ of the palace.

To the south of the Central Court is a block of cells given over to workshops and storage. Entered at three points, to the north and west, the southerly section is built at a different orientation than that to the north, evidently following the alignments of the city fabric in that area. In the northwestern corner of the cluster is a stairway, evidently communicating with upper level corridors themselves connecting with the eastern area of the palace itself, over the stepped cistern at the southeastern corner of the Court. The latter appears to have communicated solely with the Central Court in contiguity with the ateliers to the southwest.

The disposition of this block, and the nature of the finds elsewhere in the palace, augment the impression received from other palaces that an important aspect of their function was concerned with the manufacture of various objects: clothing, pottery, furniture, tools, ritual materials, etc. A Minoan civic palace, then, was as much given over to industrial and craft activity as it was to warehousing, residence, worship, and public celebration. Bookkeeping records were kept at all the palaces in the form of clay tablets recording the transshipment of commodities, their storage and disposition.[242] Indeed, it seems patent that the residents of these compounds were deeply involved in business activities of various kinds, including the import and export of commodities such as wine and oil, raw materials, and luxury items such as perfumes, cosmetics, and fine craft goods. It seems likely that the city of Kato Zakro was an important center of Minoan import and export, for it is favorably situated for overseas trade with the countries of the eastern Mediterranean. That it was an important center of island craft manufacture may be gathered from the richness of its products. While we are not yet in a secure position to understand the internal relationships among the various Minoan cities, it is clearly evident that each was an important cultural center in its own region, an urban focus within its own agricultural topography.

Whether the entire island was 'ruled' from a central capital (such as Knossos), or how it may have been ruled, we do not know. We do not know if we are dealing with a confederation of autonomous or semi-autonomous city-states, or a series of urban centers dependent politically (or in other ways) upon a single governmental center.

The increase in our understanding of Minoan culture as a result of the careful and painstaking excavation of the palace at Kato Zakro promises to give us important indications to some aspects of the answers to these and related questions, and we look forward to the appearance of the conclusions of the scholars directly involved in the excavations here. Our remarks concerning the architectonic organization of this remarkable compound must remain similarly tentative, and the speculations offered above must be weighed in this light. While I feel that these speculations are sound, particularly when seen in a comparative light, it must be stressed that our picture of Zakro is incomplete.

Nevertheless it should be understood that whereas the Zakro palace reveals a number of features which are unique or near-unique in detail — such as the fine bathing pool, the disposition of water-supply, and the remarkable West Hall System — it is equally patent that in terms of its formation and architectonic organization, there are strong resonances here with what we have already seen. If there is nothing truly comparable to the West Hall System of Kato Zakro in its details, the geometric and topological disposition of this cluster *vis-à-vis* its auxiliary functional zones is essentially identical to the principal residential quarters not only of major palaces such as Mallia but also of many private residences seen above. There is little at Zakro which is truly surprising in any fundamental architectonic way, in other words, and it may be seen quite clearly that the palace is esentially a contextual variant of invariant patterns of organization manifest in other examples of compatible construction on Crete.

THE MINOAN PALACES: AN OVERVIEW

It will have been seen in the previous discussions that the major Minoan palaces at Knossos, Mallia, Phaistos, and Kato Zakro, as well as the smaller palaces of Haghia Triadha and Gournia, are

essentially contextual variants of the same architectonic organization. We have seen the same (or equivalent) features present in the
design of all of these megastructures, and it seems evident that
they replicate the same patterns — both topological and geometric
— across various transformations of size, materials, positioning of
cells and clusters, and orientations.

The present section comprises a summary tabulation of formative features shared by the palaces. Table II.6 below lists about
a score of features, and indicates their presence (X), absence (0),
or possibility (?). Features noted are annotated by superscript
letters to a key following. The following abbreviations are used:
KN = Knossos; ML = Mallia; PH1 = Phaistos I; PH2 = Phaistos II;
GRN = Gournia; KZ = Kato Zakro; PLT = Plati; HTR = Haghia
Triadha; KLP = Knossos Little Palace; MLE = Mallia House E;
NK = Nirou Khani; PLKB = Palaikastro House B. Of these structures, PLT has not yet been examined; this Late Minoan III (i.e.
post-palatial) 'palace' will be examined below in the Appendix on
Aegean Megaroid Compounds.

Key
1.a. Court bounded on three sides; fourth side missing (off cliff?).
  b. *Idem:* some trace of boundary to southwest; court partly public plaza?
  c. Court bounded on three sides; fourth side unexcavated.
  d. Court bounded on three sides; fourth side unexcavated; partly public?
  e. Court bounded on three sides; fourth side missing.
2.a. Court almost east-west (NW-SE).
  b. Court east-west.
3.a. Small portico above steps on the northern side.
  b. Portico of hall system on court.
  c. No trace on court (= second storey) level remains.
  d. Portico of hall system on court.
4.a. Paved street widens markedly at the western entrance.
  b. Paved court traces to the northwest of the western facade.
  c. Paved court traces behind hall system area.
5.a. No trace for Second Palace; existed in First Palace court.
  b. Fragmented trace of central court causeway (LM III?).
6.a. On the southwestern corner of central court? (Marinatos) Look for at North Plaza?
  b. Small L-shaped stepped platform in the northwestern corner of central court.

Table II.6. *Shared components of formal organization*

	KN	ML	PH1	PH2	GRN	KZ	PLT	HTR	KLP	MLE	OOO
1. Central court	X	X	X	X^a	X^b	X	X^c	X^d	O	O	NK^e
2. Central court NS	X	X	X	X	X	X	O^a	O^b	O	O	
3. Colonnade on court	X	X	X	X	X^a	X^b	?^{b}	O^c	O	O	NK?^{d}
4. West paved court	X	X	X	X	O^a	X^b	?^{c}	O	O	O	
5. West court triangle	X	?^{a}	X	O^a	O	O	O	O^b	O	O	
6. Theatral area	X	X	X	X	?^{b}	O	O	O	O	O	
7. Indented west facade	X	X	X	X	X	X	?^{a}	X	X	X^b	NK?^{f}
8. Indented facades at all	X	X	X	X	X	X	?^{a}	X	X^d	X^e	NK?^{d},PLKB
9. West magazine clusters	X	X	X^a	X	X^b	X	?^{b}	X^c	X^d	X^e	
10. Lustral basin(s)	X	X	O^a	X^a	O^b	X^c	O	?^{c}	X	X	
11. Pillar crypt(s)	X	X	X	X	O^b	O^c	O	?^{d}	O	O^e	NK?^{b}
12. Double axe symbols	X	X	X	X	X	X^b	O	?^{a}	X	O	
13. Central double axe signs	X^a	X	?^{b}	X	X^a	O^d	O	?^{c}	O	O	NK^g
14. Central court altar	X	X	X	?^{c}	O	?^{d}	O	?^{f}	O	O	NK^d
15. West court *koulouras*	X	X	X	O^a	O	O^b	X^e	?.	O	O	PLKB^e
16. Pillared hali N side	X	X	X	X^a	X	X	O^b	O^c	X	?^{d}	NK^e
17. PDP hall system	X	X	O^a	X	?^{b}	X	X^c	X	X	X^d	
18. Double PDP hall system	X	X	O^b	X	?^{b}	X	?^{c}	X	X	?^{d}	
19. Peristyle court(s)	?^{a}	X	?^{a}	X	?^{c}	X^b	O	X	X	X	PLKB^d
20. Central court shrine (W)	X	X	X	X	X	X^b	O	?.	O	O	NK^d

7.a. Not completely excavated to outer boundaries.

8.a. *Idem.*

b. Indented trace on all sides except on the northern street facade; indented northern entrance.

9.a. To the northwest originally long narrow east-west rectangles later remodelled.

b. Magazine-like cells along corridor, fronting on central court. See 8.a.

c. Magazine cells on the western flank of L-shaped building.

d. Magazine rows in the western projecting block.

e. Row of magazines to the northwest of building.

f. Magazines on the northern flank of building, northwest of central court.

10.a. Excavators consider cell under PH2 cell 38/70 as lustral basin.

b. None extant; latrine in the northeastern corner.

c. Possibly obliterated by megaron foundations, on the northeastern corner.

d. Bathroom cells in the southwestern block, not sunken.

e. Lustral basin, sunken, to the northeast of peristyle court area.

11.a. Pillar crypts of PH1 remain in use in the southwestern quarter(?)

b. None extant but shrine in equivalent position off central court, northwest.

c. Internal western block shrine, and shrine(?) off court (northwest), cell XXX?

d. Pillar basement in equivalent position in middle of long flank of central court (= northern side); crypt above, on court level?

e. Cell xxxviii, with *bothros* depression, on east-west axis toward western side?

12.a. No mention in publication; not examined in detail by us.

b. Large store of double axes but no incised symbols on extant walls.

13.a. On east-west axis of tripartite-like shrine off court, on ashlar western facade.

b. Symbol incised on court wall near southwestern entrance to central court.

c. See. 12a.

14.a. Shown in early Knossos plans; later disappears.

b. Court pavement *absent* at exact center of central court.

c. *Idem*; same pavement used in PH2.

d. Square stone object with central round hole towards the northwest of central court.

e. 'Hearth' in central court, opposite hall system entrance, near center .

f. Altar/shrine in central court, dated to LM III by excavators.

g. Pavement alignments, koulouras, directed toward tripartite shrine and horns.

15.a. Those of PH1 apparently unused in PH2 period.

b. Not enough of western court area excavated to confirm or negate presence.

c. LM III 'sacred tree *temenos* (Halbherr, *MRIL* XXI [1905], 235ff).

d. *Koulouras* in central court near tripartite shrine.

16.a. PH1 pillared hall built into PH2 wall, supporting dining hall above(?)

b. Plan of eastern cells off court's narrow end suggests foundations for hall?

c. Four-pillared cell below northwestern corner of megaron foundations.

d. Cell with four columns?

e. Pillared hall resembles KN, GRN, PH1 with square and round alternations.

17.a. None extant after PH2 rebuilding.

b. Hall system to the east of pillared hall area?

c. Like NK, opening directly onto central court on wide court flank.

d. Cell viii (*salle des fresques*)?

e. Like PLT, opening directly onto court on wide flank; see KN 'throne room'?

18.a. See 17a.

b. See 17b.

c. Include long divided cells to the east of hall? See megaroid compounds below.

d. See 17d.

19.a. None extant in canonical form.

b. See 17b.

c. See 17c.

d. At center of building, as elsewhere at PLK.

20.a. See 17a.; cells PH1-XLIV and XLV similar in disposition.

b. Cell XXX?

c. Near opening of second-level (non-extant) pillar crypt by court?

d. Tripartite-like shrine, sacral horns, etc. but on southern end of court.

Clearly, the greatest number of linkages occur among the first six structures (KN, ML, PH1, PH2, GRN, KZ), and among these the first four share the most features. In the case of PH1 and PH2, it may be observed that in a few instances features common to KN or ML will be echoed at either PH1 *or* PH2, not both. Thus, note the following:

1. PDP hall systems are found only at PH2; but then they do not appear at KN or ML (or to my knowledge anywhere else) until the MM III period;

2. PH2 does not include a pillar crypt proper; but then it preserves such a cell from PH1. The correspondent new shrine cell, at the east-west axis of the western flank of the central court, cell 23, may be considered the equivalent ritual chamber, of a different form, but in the canonical position;

3. PH1 has a chamber considered by its excavators to have been a 'lustral chamber' (beneath PH2 cells 38/70);

4. PH2 has no extant causeway triangle in the western court, but PH1 did, as did KN and ML;

5. Neither PH1 nor KN have peristyle courts, but ML and PH2 do.

In the case of GRN and KZ, features common to KN, ML, PH1, PH2 and absent at GRN and KZ are possibly, in the case of the former, to be ascribed to obliteration at the top of the hill; in the case of the latter, to the incompleteness of our knowledge at present.

The structures at PLT, HTR, KLP, MLE have fewer linkages with the first four sites; such linkages that are found are also equally shared with Minoan design in general, i.e. component features 7, 8, 9, 10, 11, 17, 18, and 19. But they also share with the palatial megastructures certain features of modular grid organization (grid squares and sizes in fractions leading up to 100 or 160 units — not a characteristic of nonpalatial construction on Crete — see Part Two below).

Table II.6 above simply lists shared features, and so it presents a fragmented picture of the common properties of the palatial structures; for included in their similarities are equally important topological properties: the relative positioning and connectivity of features. In other words, any comparative analysis of the palatial compounds must incorporate less patent but equally significant similarities of composition of features relative to each other: the fact, for example, that a hall system lies in a certain relationship to an outer (garden/court) facade; that its individual cells are connected in certain patterned ways regardless of their size and absolute orientations. It is clearly such compositional features which help us understand the nature of Minoan design, whose underlying invariant properties have to do as much with the *relationships* among features as with the presence or absence of features themselves. We must remain absolutely clear that relational/topological properties provide us with salient information about the organization of the Minoan architectonic system as fully as does the existence of specific geometric forms.

In the discussions above of the Minoan palatial megastructures an attempt was made to intercalate such relational features by cross-referencing features of one structure with those of another. The picture that emerges is of a certain uniformity of architectonic organization of all the palaces, an underlying conceptual resemblance which transcends size, materials, layout, and details of material articulation. Clearly, certain structures are more similar than others, a situation which may eventually allow us to make a number of inferences regarding the organization of building programs and projects, and even possible evidence for common design by teams of master craftsmen called into service by one civic community after another. Such evidence will be augmented below by our modular analyses in Part Two, where it will be seen that in many cases designers and builders were operating from common constructional patterns in the realization of palatial building programs.

Our analyses of the Minoan palatial megastructures have also revealed that they form a conceptual continuum with other Minoan private construction, particularly the MM III/LM I houses and palatial appendages examined in detail earlier in the present Chapter. Not only do similar and equivalent features of composition turn up among the corpus of forms taken as a whole, but, as we have endeavored to point out, we are dealing here with a fairly homogeneous set of design principles manifest over a wide variety of morphological transformations. We have seen quite clearly, for example, that despite differences of size and absolute placement, all of the examples of the hall system/residential apartment quarters of Minoan builders are variations on a common formal and functional theme. This applies both to private residences and to the palaces themselves: the palatial hall systems are but larger and more finely articulated versions of the common residential systems of the simple private house. Indeed, their relationships to the remainder of their structural fabrics is fundamentally no different from what is to be found in ordinary houses.

As we shall see further in Part Two, the designer/builders of ordinary Minoan houses proceeded according to conventional patterns with respect not only to the placement of residential halls in a structure, but also with respect to the proportional allotment of square-footage given to functional clusters or zones. Indeed, as will become patent below, the planning grid upon which a Minoan building is erected served as a straightforward functional template wherein zones of different usages were mapped. Each Minoan building is conceived as an interwoven set of clusters made up of particular kinds of cells, each cluster given over to specific functions, and each cluster connected to every other by means of a spatial and topological syntax which itself remains constant across its many physical permutations and transformations in response to the particulars of a given building program.

Our analyses have illustrated an important fact not only about Minoan design in particular, but about architectonic systems in general: namely, that at every level of organization, from details of material articulation to the patterns of association among cell-clusters (matrices) in a broad sense, buildings manifest patterns of significance and meaningfulness. *Everything* about a building is meaningul in some way, but not everything (as we have seen) is meaningful in the *same* way. There exist palpable *levels* of organization in a building, and each of these levels exists in an interwoven dialogue with all other levels. Changes on one level affect aspects of composition and organization on other levels.

In this regard it is clear that the conceptual organization of an architectonic formation is inherently *multiple;* what is a whole at one level or from a given perspective on formation is a part at another level or from a different perspective.

It becomes equally clear that a strict dichotomization between 'form' and 'function' is an unwarranted and trivial abstraction: the formal elements of design are elements only insofar as they are simultaneously significant or meaningful. This fact is often difficult to see in dealing with the architectonic system of a nonextant culture, for we inevitably apprehend distinctions in formation which tend to be intuitively meaningful in our own architectonic milieux. It is hard to see what to a Minoan would have comprised a significance of formal articulation and pattern, for we tend to impose our own architectonic perceptions upon this alien material. What we may see as a 'unit' (because it appears to correspond to unities in our own environments) may not have been so understood by a Minoan of the period we are considering (for whom the same form would in fact be merely a subpart of a larger holistic unity).

It is patent that in order to understand the nature of the Minoan architectonic system or 'code' it is absolutely necessary to enter upon a long, tedious, and exhaustive comparative study of the entire corpus of remains. Only in this way can we begin to approach a more realistic and less impressionistic understanding of Minoan architecture. In the next Chapter (III), we will attempt to isolate the elemental meaningful formations serving as (to use a metaphor) a vocabulary or lexicon of forms, in the Minoan corpus. We shall see that it is out of the combination, intersection, and transformation of these base components that the transfinite variety of the corpus arises; a counterbalance to the impression that every Minoan building appears to be a virtuoso piece of its own. As we shall see, such an impression is, on the surface, patently false, for Minoan architectonic design is as rule-governed and conventionally patterned as any other, only in different ways. It will become clearer below (although by now it should already be impressionistically evident) that we have been dealing with certain invariant patterns of systemic organization of which each Minoan building of this MM III/LM I period is a contextual and thematic variant.

Before turning to a consideration of the formative elements of the Minoan architectonic system, we must do two things. First, we shall look more directly at the cluster-patterns of the Minoan buildings examined in the present Chapter. The remainder of the Chapter consists of a series of cluster-diagrams of all the structures analyzed above, presented together so as to clarify the constancies we have noted in the ways cells and cell-clusters or functional zones are composed. Secondly, these diagrams will be augmented by comparative flow-patterns depicting the connectivities among cells in buildings. In both cases, the diagrams begin with the smallest structures and end with the palatial megastructures, in the same sequence these buildings have been examined above. Some of the cluster diagrams have already been seen in our discussion of the major palaces, but are repeated here for comparative purposes. Our aim here is to allow the reader more ready access to direct comparison among the structures described.

Secondly, our consideration of the design of these (by and large) MM III/LM I constructions will be augmented by an examination of a corpus of Late Bronze Age megaroid structures common to the Aegean and Greek mainland which begin to appear on Crete principally in connection with the destructions marking the end of the second palace period. This presentation, made in Appendix A (to the present Chapter), will serve to contrast what we have seen with patterns of organization which become assimilated on Crete in the LM III period, having been introduced from outside the island.

The thorny problem of the alignments and orientations of the Minoan palaces, discussed summarily in the notes to our descriptions above, will be taken up in Appendix B.

CELLS AND CELL-CLUSTERS: MINOAN SPATIAL SYNTAX

Presented below are two types of analytic diagrams. First, a set of cluster or zone diagrams corresponding to the relative placement of cells in Minoan structures, so as to illustrate the ways in which the interior fabric of Minoan buildings is functionally divided up. In each diagram, numbers correspond to cell-numbers employed above in our ground plans, with a couple of exceptions. The reader may compare these diagrams both with each other and with the groundplans above to which they refer.

The second set of diagrams focusses on the patterns of connectivity among cells, numbered according to the schema of the cluster diagrams. Using these diagrams, the reader may take notice of the degree of closeness or separation of cells in terms of accessibility. It will be seen that these patterns of accessibility contrast with the impressions which might have been gained in simply reading the ground plans above, wherein cells *geometrically* adjacent may in fact be quite separate *topologically*. Our aim here is to stress the fact that any building is principally a spatio-temporal construct, a web of cells which unfold not only over space, but — equally importantly — over time. Such an architectonic feature tends to be overlooked if we confine our observations to two-dimensional groundplans alone.

The reader will find that certain additional patterns of organization emerge, for example, the fact that cells of a certain type (e.g. shrines) tend to be positioned in a more or less constant manner *vis-à-vis* entrance(s) to a building. Such patterns represent yet another aspect of the multiplex organization of buildings – and in particular the organization of vast structures such as the large palaces – and must be included in our understanding of Minoan design. In the palatial megastructures, for example, it becomes incumbent upon the designers to incorporate constancies of functional connectivity so as to facilitate intercommunication among the building's parts. In other words, patterns of expectancy are set up such that a user may be able to predict where a certain zone will occur, both in terms of geometric position and in terms of the number of thresholds crossed. In effect, such information is stored or encoded by the *patterns of connectivity themselves:* certain cells are positioned as nodes on a traffic web, and the number of such nodes itself becomes a clue as to what to expect beyond. This aspect of Minoan architectonic organization was alluded to above in our discussion of the traffic patterns in the western magazine block 'shunting yard' at Mallia's palace (q.v.).

Such aspects of organization are hardly arcane or mysterious in any way; indeed they are the very stuff of our own architectural spatial perceptions: any repetition of patterning carries with it maps of expectancy learned by any child in any culture with respect to his own environments. Such patterns of expectancy may be stronger or looser depending upon circumstances which are culture-specific. To our own eyes, it might be easier to predict how many cells from an entrance the master's bedroom in an Egyptian house of the Amarna period may be, in contrast to where the 'lustral basin' in a Minoan house might be. But in the former case, the position of that cell is perceptually cued by an understanding of the essentially bilaterally symmetrical organization of the house overall. In the latter case, we need other information, for the Minoan house is non-bilaterally symmetrical. Here certain constancies of traffic-web patterning come to the fore.

In the cell-cluster diagrams below, entrances are signalled by E, and cells not horizontally accessible from adjacent cells (and only from a second storey) are shown crossed out by diagonal lines.

Within clusters, hall systems are indicated by multiple connecting lines between cells. Heavy outlines denote clusters; cells within are denoted by lighter lines. Omitted are HTR and KZ, which are awaiting publication.

In the traffic lattice diagrams below, the sign E denotes entrance; ζ denotes a stairwell; dotted lines indicate connections from stairwells back down to ground level; open arrows indicate connections to missing cells; and groups of cells surrounded by squares or rectangles indicate positions of hall system. C indicates a courtyard.

The following diagram (Figure II.96) directly compares the central traffic matrix of eight medium-sized Minoan houses (AKHL, KN HCS, KN RV, KN HF, ML DA, ML ZA, TYL A, TYL C). The traffic matrix (in contrast to the organization of the figures in the previous set of diagrams) is shown linearly, so as to directly compare the position of the hall system (H in the diagrams) to the rest of the traffic web. In the diagrams, V = vestibular cell, ζ = stairwell, and a double line with a superscript indicates a 90° change of direction. The porter's lodge is indicated by p.

It will be seen that from the point of view of this main traffic stem toward the hall system, while any number of rooms (r) may be appended, the syntax of connectivity of cells leading to the hall system is constant. Consequently, a definition of the relative position of the hall system includes both a standard number of previous cells of specific functional types, as well as a canonical 90° change in direction, to approach the hall system on its wide flank (as noted in our analyses earlier in the present Chapter).

This syntactic pattern may be generalized as indicated in the next illustration, Figure II.97·

As will be noted, the hall system proper is not a cul-de-sac, but stands between other cells leading to a private stair 'behind'. The more public stairwell near the entrance may be appended either to the vestibular cell or to a corridor cell immediately following the latter. Any number of cells (nR) may be appended anywhere along the main traffic stem. These latter will include service areas such as storage magazines, workshops, or religious shrine areas.

This syntactic pattern appears to be constant for the chronological period under study (MM III/LM I). As more information comes to light, we would necessarily expect this picture to be modified. As may be seen by a glance at other traffic diagrams above, other patterns appear, notably in the large megastructural compounds, which incorporate more functional features than the ordinary middle-sized house.

That this pattern contrasts with those seen below in our examination of Aegean megaroid compounds will be clear when we turn to those buildings. Thus, the present pattern must be seen as largely confined to the present time period. But the pattern also contrasts sharply with those which may be seen elsewhere in the eastern Mediterranean at this time. For example, if we compare the general organization of Minoan houses with comparable private houses at Amarna in Egypt (*c.* 1370-1350 B.C.) (Figure II. 98), it will be seen that the latter contrast in their geometric organization with the three Minoan houses shown.[243]

The Amarna house is bilaterally symmetrical in plan, and its sequence of cells from the entrance vestibule to the innermost private chambers (from north to south) is through increasingly smaller spaces along the central longitudinal axis of the building. The innermost square cell (with a central column), the private common room for the family of the house, gives access to right and left to men's chambers and women's chambers (MBD = master's bedroom; FBD = mistress's bedroom). This pattern of organization tends to be constant in Egyptian villas over a long period of time,[244] appearing half a millennium earlier at El Lahun (XII Dynasty).

What is of interest here is the disposition of the main traffic stem from the entrance to the inner private quarter (which, in contrast to the Minoan hall system, is a cul-de-sac). This pattern of connectivities is revealed in the following diagram, Figure II.99.

Here, two houses, one from the XII Dynasty (El Lahun), and one from the XVIII Dynasty (Amarna) are compared, and both may be seen as contextual variants of the same pattern of spatial syntax. The principal difference between the two houses lies in the manner whereby the women's quarter is appended to the traffic stem. Otherwise the two patterns are equivalent.[245]

The Egyptian and Minoan traffic patterns are compared directly in the next illustration, Figure II.100.

Each system has its own types of constancy. For example, in Crete, there is a compulsory 90° turn into the wide flank of the hall system. In Egypt, the entrance into the residential quarter proper is canonically from north to south. Both patterns underlie variations in the absolute direction of initial entrance to the house proper. In both Egypt and Crete, the residential zones are characterized by different formal components: in Egypt, by the presence of pillared halls and appended bedrooms; in Crete, by a tripartite PDP hall system with appended bathrooms and latrines. In and of itself, each pattern of organization is constant, but between the two patterns, there is an abrupt difference in architectonic realization. In the final analysis, this must alert us that any cross-cultural comparative study of architectonic organization cannot be made on the basis of random features with superficial formal or morphological resemblance. A comparative analysis must always be made holistically between sets of formations understood in their functional significance. This applies equally to comparative study of the corpora of the same geographical area at different points in time, as we shall see below in Appendix A.

NOTES

1. See Arthur Evans, *Palace of Minos* (hereafter *PM*) I: 328-330, 333ff; II: 109, Note 3, 349; III: 234, 290ff, 318ff, Plate XXIV, p. 346; IV: 888ff. Discussed in detail below, see Figure II. 34.
2. *PM* I: 325ff, Figure 238, p. 326.
3. Notably at KN HCS, KN RV and KN HF, discussed below.
4. See Figure II.46.
5. The rest of the house was unpaved, an indication in Minoan construction of the interiority of cells.
6. *PM* II: 391-395, plan, Figure 224, p. 392.
7. A restored view is shown in *PM* II: Figure 225, p. 394.
8. Probably the bathroom of the structure. Paved with gypsum slabs, there may have been a clay bathtub placed within.
9. *PM* II: 396-413, plan, Figure 227, p. 397, section, Figure 226, p. 397; J.D.S. Pendlebury, *Handbook to the Palace of Minos at Knossos* (London, 1933) (hereafter *Handbook*): 62-64; J.W. Graham, *PC*: 52-54. Graham's statement that the RV is ten meters wide east-west is not correct.
10. As suggested by Evans in his reconstructed elevation, Figure 226.
11. *PM* II: 406ff, reconstructed drawing, Figure 235, p. 407.
12. See below under our survey of the Knossian palace.
13. *PM* III: 66ff, colored plate between pp. 66 and 67.
14. *PM* II: 431-476, plan, Figure 251, p. 434; *PC*: 57-58.
15. *Handbook*: 57, map, Figure 4, p. 58.
16. *Etudes Crétoises* IX: 43-48, plan, Plate LXIII; C. Tire and H. van Effenterre,

Guide des fouilles françaises en Crète (Paris, 1966) (hereafter *GFFC*): 59-62; *PC*: 63-64, Figures 21, 22.

17. There exist wall-fragments in the south hall, indicative of modifications to the original plan.

18. A plan of Quarter Delta is given in *GFFC*: Figure 18, p. 57. See also below, Part II.

19. *Etudes Crétoises* IX: 63-79, plan, Plate LXV; *GFFC*: 63-66; *PC*: 64-66.

20. J. Hazzidhakis, *AE* (1912): 197-234; *Dheltion* (1918): 60ff; *id.*, 'Tylissos à l'époque minoenne', *Etudes de préhistoire crétois* (1921), *passim; id., Tylissos: Villas minoennes* (= *Etudes Crétoises* III) (1934): 6-26, plan, Plates VI and XXXIII; J.W. Graham, *PC*: 60-61.

21. See below under our discussion of TYL B and Figure I.3.

22. This break in the wall may in fact have served to provide more direct ground-level access between TYL A and TYL B.

23. The closeness of the 'pillar crypt' to the hall system recalls an analogous situation in the palatial compounds at Kato Zakro and Mallia, as we shall see below.

24. There is some confusion here as to whether this stairwell area might have originally served as a bathroom; a likely place for such a cell, but the evidence is ambiguous.

25. A similar situation is to be seen at Akhladhia (Figure II.3).

26. J. Hazzidhakis, *Tylissos. . .* (1934): 32-47, plan, Plate XI; *PC*: 61-62.

27. See D. Preziosi, *The Semiotics of the Built Environment* (Bloomington, 1979b): 16-37 for a summary of the observations here.

28. The hall system is characterized not by the presence of any one of these cell-types in isolation, but by their characteristic clustering together. Thus, any *one* of these cell-types occurring independently does not signal a residential quarter *per se*.

29. See above, Note 24.

30. See our description of TYL C above in Chapter I.

31. In other words, a 'lustral chamber'.

32. See above, pp. 48-50.

33. See above, pp. 53-54.

34. The square-within-a-square pattern is one of the characteristic structural frameworks in Minoan design. This becomes more patent in our modular analyses below in Part II.

35. In other words, the hall system on the left of the entrance conforming to a tripartite cell-cluster, lying adjacent to the western side of a square-within-a-square cluster of cells.

36. We accept the datings as assigned by the excavators as given.

37. S. Marinatos, *PAE* (1932) [1933]: 76-94, plan, *eik.* 3, p. 82,; *PAE* (1933) [1934]: 93-100; *BCH* LVII (1933): 292-295; *PAE* (1934) [1935]: 128-133; *PAE* (1935) [1936]: 196ff.

38. See *PC*: 69.

39. See Figure II.37.

40. See Figure II.43.

41. *PC*: Figure 76.

42. In contrast to the indication of a single door in the published plan.

43. This cell is filled with rubbish to a height of over a meter.

44. See above under KN RV, and below under KN S and KN SE.

45. In Part II below an attempt is made to indicate the extent of the original plan

on the basis of the indications of the modular arrangements in the extant sections.

46. D. Levi, 'La villa rurale minoica di Gortina', *BdA* 44 (1959): 237-265, plan, Figure 2, p. 238.

47. See the plan of AKHL above for a possible analogue: there the 'stables' are incorporated into the structural frame of the original plan.

48. Such raised pavements are familiar in Minoan construction, occurring in the areas of the major palaces as well as in city streets (e.g. Mallia, Knossos, Phaistos).

49. This suggestion is consonant with the observations of the building's excavators, and a likely place for the bookkeeping activities of the farmstead. Similar arrangements are to be found in Egyptian mansions: see A. Badawy, *A History of Egyptian Architecture* (1966b): 32-36.

50. See above, pp. 48-50.

51. *PM* II: 373-390, plan, Figure 208, p. 375, section, Figure 210, p. 377; *Handbook*: 65-67; *PC*: 55-56.

52. As illustrated in the reconstructed section noted above in Note 51.

53. The conjectured entryway is shown by Evans in his plan, *PM* II: Figure 208, p. 374.

54. Also shown in the aforementioned plan, and restored in the modern rebuilding of the house.

55. At any rate, this is a likely area for food preparation, on analogy with other houses we have seen above.

56. See below, Part II: this is a common harmonic proportion in Crete.

57. *PM* I: 425-430, plan, Figure 306, p. 426; *Handbook*: 64-65; *PC*: 56-57.

58. The ground level of KN HCS is therefore at the second-storey level of KN SE.

59. In his Figure 306, *PM* I: 426.

60. *PM* I: 427; *BSA* (1904): 4ff.

61. *PM* I: 429. There is no direct evidence that the positioning of the pillar crypt was commemorative of this early cave (shrine?), although it seems that the presence of that cave was known to the builders. At any rate, the position of the crypt is consonant with that at the S House in respect to its relationship with the house entrance.

62. See above, Figure II.4.

63. See Evans' discussions in *BSA* (1904): 4ff.

64. *Ibid.*

65. For a similar arrangement, see TYL A above.

66. See the discussion above, pp. 45-59, with associated Tables.

67. *Etudes Crétoises* XI: 7-26; plan, Plates II and III; *GFFC*: 66-70.

68. Which itself is aligned with House ZA to the northwest. As shown in Figure II.16, House ZB and ZG stand at the eastern edge of the paved court to the east of the palace itself. House ZG is thus aligned both with ZA and the eastern facade of the palace.

69. See our discussion below, pp. 75-76.

70. *GFFC*: 68.

71. *PC*: 67.

72. While there is no direct evidence for such a stair, a likely place for a wooden stair would be in cells viii or v.

73. S. Xanthoudhidhes, 'To Minoikon Megaron Nirou', *AE* (1922): 1-11, plan, Figure A, p. 3; measured sectional drawings, Figure B, p. 4.; *Dheltion* (1918): 19; *PAE* (1922-1924): 125ff; Evans, *PM* II: 279-285.

74. See S. Marinatos, *PAE* (1926): 141ff, with map.
75. *PM* II: 279-285. But see *PC*: 58-59, for a contrary view.
76. As indicated by threshold blocks at these points.
77. See below under Knossos.
78. See above, Note 13, for a possible restoration at Knossos, and below under Phaistos.
79. See below under Mallia, Palace, Figure II.37.
80. See the final section of this Chapter below, on Aegean megaroid compounds.
81. At ML ZA (q.v.) the hall system evidently opens onto a private courtyard or garden; a situation replicated, but with differing orientations, at Phaistos (palace) and Kato Zakro. The hall system at Knossos (Hall of the Double Axes) opens onto a veranda: its perpendicular alignment to the latter is similar to that seen here at NK.
82. The remains are unclear beyond this point, so our picture of the western facade of the structure is incomplete. It is very likely, however, that there was an important western entrance near here.
83. It may be of interest, as discussed below in Part Two, that in terms of its modular organization and the size of its planning grid, NK resembles larger 'palatial' compounds more than it does other houses and villas. Its relationships in this regard are closer to the so-called 'little palaces' at Knossos and Mallia (ML E).
84. S. Marinatos, 'To Minoikon Megaron Sklavokampou', *AK* (1939-1941) (published 1948): 69-96, plan, Figure 4, p. 71, measured section, Figure 5, p. 72, reconstructed elevations, Figures 1 and 16; J.W. Graham, *PC*: 70.
85. See below for a discussion of these buildings.
86. R. Bosanquet, 'Excavations at Palaikastro', *BSA* VIII (1901-1902): 286ff; IX (1902-1903): 274ff; XI (1904-1905): 288ff; plan of site in *BSA* VIII: Figure 23, p. 310; J.W. Graham, *PC*: 69-70.
87. *PC*: 70.
88. Discussed in connection with the palaces below.
89. Marked by 'x' in our Figure II.19. A similar peristyle court will be seen below, ML E, and Mallia Houses Delta Beta I and II evidently also had such courts. A very fine, but larger version, is to be seen in the second palace at Phaistos (Figure II.43 below).
90. *BSA* XI (1904-1905): 282-286, plan, Figure 13, p. 282. See also K. Branigan, *Foundations of Palatial Crete* (New York, 1970): 43-44 and Figure 6, p. 44. There are also traces of a massive MM III/LM I building some 19 meters wide, under the western and northwestern corners of PLK X.
91. *BSA* XI (1904-1905): 285. In contrast to the two aforementioned columns, the latter was square in plan.
92. Evidently, at least in part, as storage cellars.
93. J. Hazzidhakis, *Tylissos:* 26-34, plan, Plate VII; Graham, *PC*: 60.
94. On the other hand, a possible analogy may be seen at TYL C, if our conjecture there is accurate; see above, Chapter I. Shrines existing at the center-point of structures may be seen at the major palaces of Knossos, Mallia and Phaistos, below.
95. See below, Part Two.
96. Of which, however, there is no clear evidence. See our discussions below on the subject of the alignment of major Minoan buildings, particularly the palaces.
97. These plans are included below in Part Two.

98. *Etudes Crétoises* XI: 91-154, plan, Plate VII; *BCH* (1932): 514-515; *BCH* (1933): 298; *GFFC*: 70-76; *PC*: 67-68; new chronological survey by O. Pelon, *BCH* (1967): 494-512. The plan presented by Graham (*PC*: Figure 23) is too simplified, removing walls in (his) cells 38, 15, 8, 25, 28, and 6 which are important for understanding the cellular organization of these areas. Graham compares the building to Egyptian mansions at Amarna (1370-50 B.C.), of the type illustrated above in our Chapter I (Figure I.2) (*PC*: 68, Note 16b), a comparison which is unwarranted.

99. Disputed by Graham (*PC*: 68, Note 16c), but a good analogue may be seen in ML ZB, where a stairway is found in an identical position. See above, Figure II.15.

100. See below, Part Two.

101. *PM* II: 513-544, plan, Figure 318, p. 516-517, reconstruction, Figure 317, p. 516; *Handbook*: 57-62; *PC*: 51-52.

102. *PM* II: 543. Evans' north-south dimensions for the building, '84 meters' (*ibid.*: 515) must be a misprint for 84 *feet*.

103. See above under our discussion of TYL B.

104. The restored porch appears in Piet de Jong's isometric reconstruction, *PM* II: 516, Figure 317.

105. See also the palace at Kato Zakro, below (East Hall System).

106. See our discussion above under PLK B.

107. Note that the disposition of this pillared basement recalls the foundations of the 'banquet halls' of the major palaces, suggesting that above this area was a dining room. See the discussions of 'banquet halls' at Knossos, Phaistos, Mallia, and Kato Zakro.

108. *PM* II: 520ff, plan and elevation, Figures 312 and 322. In its original state it was most likely a bathroom ('lustral chamber').

109. Such questions must await a serious understanding of Minoan societal structure.

110. F. Halbherr, *MRIL* XXI, XII della serie III (1905): 238ff; L. Pernier and L. Banti, *Guida degli scavi italiani in Creta* (1947): 28-38, plan, Figure 40. On parallels of the later (LM III) construction with Aegean megaroid compounds elsewhere, see the final section of this Chapter.

111. It is of interest to note that the disposition of this set of halls is paralleled at the palace of Phaistos itself, in its Eastern Hall System; a mirror-reversed image, in large part, of the present hall system. See below under Phaistos.

112. See below under Knossos, Mallia (palaces).

113. See below, pp. 116ff.

114. Discussed in the final section of the present Chapter.

115. To date much comparative discussion has centered upon the purported architectonic similarities among the 'palatial' compounds in Crete and the Levant, without a complementary emphasis upon their important differences. Such discussions are all too often based on purely formal resemblances, without a consideration of equally important functional resemblances or dissimilarities.

116. H. Boyd-Hawes *et al.*, *Gournia. Vasiliki and Other Prehistoric Sites in Eastern Crete* (1908): 24-26, with plan of Town; *PC*: 47-48.

117. Traces of which may be seen in Graham's photo, Figure 63.

118. House H-e, discussed in Appendix A.

119. In this regard, the disposition of houses is not unlike what has been seen above at Palaikastro (see Figure II.19 above).

120. Discussed by Graham, *PC*: 48.

121.   See.below under our discussion of the Knossian palace, and see Figure II.28.

122.   At Phaistos, this Middle Minoan First Palace pillared hall was incorporated into walls dating to the Second Palace: see Figure II.43 below. A similar hall was seen at Palaikastro B.

123.   In other words, a 'banquet hall' (or the 'kitchen' foundation of a second-storey dining hall).

124.   Which would place the hall system in a position overlooking the eastern hill and its surrounding houses below, and which would then cause GRN to resemble Kato Zakro, with its eastern hall systems.

125.   Discussed below in connection with Knossos, Mallia and Phaistos.

126.   The following is a brief bibiographical guide to Knossos:
       A.   Preliminary reports:
            1. A. Evans, *BSA* VI (1899-1900): 3-69; VII (1900-1901): 1-120; VIII (1901-1902): 1-124; IX (1902-1903): 1-153; X (1903-1904): 1-62; XI (1904-1905): 1-26.
            2. D. Mackenzie, *BSA* XI (1904-1905): 181-223; XII (1905-1906): 216-257; XIII (1906-1907): 423-446; XIV (1907-1908): 343-422.
       B.   Final publications:
            1. A. Evans, *The Palace of Minos at Knossos* (*PM*) I (1921); II (1928); III (1930); IV (1936); V (index).
            2. By chronological periods:
               a. MM   I: *PM* I: 127ff; II: 93, 146ff, IV: 50ff.
               b. MM   II: *PM* I: 203ff; III: 356; IV: 61.
               c. MM   III: *PM* I: 315ff; II: 286ff, 547ff; III: 397ff.
               d. LM   I: *PM* III: 280ff; IV: 858.
               e. LM   II: *PM* IV: 291, 901.
               f. LM   III: *PM* II: 335; IV: 734.
            3. Guidebooks:
            J.D.S. Pendlebury, *A Handbook to the Palace of Minos at Knossos* (1939): 39-56; L.R. Palmer, *A New Guide to the Palace of Knossos* (1970). See also J.W. Graham, *Palaces of Crete* (*PC*) (1962): 23-33.

127.   Based in part upon Evans' plans A and B, *PM* II, insert at back of volume. The area of the 'grand stairway' in the southwestern section of the palace is the subject of controversy (see L.R. Palmer, *A New Guide to the Palace at Knossos*); but see our remarks below.

128.   Compare the southwestern corner of Gournia, above, Figure II.27.

129.   It is conceivable that this northwestern porch may also have connected with a bridge leading from the second storey of the palace to a second storey of the Northwest Treasure House (NWTH), a situation analogous to our conjectural restorations at TYL A and B, Evans' conjectures regarding a second-storey connection between the Little Palace and the Unexplored Mansion at Knossos, and our suggestions above for Gournia's western facade entrance system.

130.   *PM* III: 66ff; colored plate between pages 66 and 67. The scene (if indeed it portrays Knossian west court activities) would have been taken from the south, in the area of the West Porch, looking north. On the right side of the fresco is a protruding wall facade, evidently one of the palace's western facade projections. The raised causeway system is clearly depicted, but Evans' illustration (Plate XVIII) is much restored.

131.   Similar triangular areas defined by three raised causeways are also found in the western courts of Phaistos and Mallia (see below), although the latter is rather

smaller than the other two. At any rate, it seems likely that the defined area was a behavioral focus of some kind.

132.   See below, Figure II.37. The Mallia *chorós* is adjacent to a cluster of silos. If there were a 'theatral' area at Mallia, it may have been a separate (and free-standing) structure (like the Knossian construction), possibly standing some-where along the western boundary of the West Court, which is unexcavated. The Phaistian theatral area is a new construction, incorporated into the fabric of the palace itself: the First Palace 'theatral' area is separate, along the northern side of the original West Middle Court (see below, Figure II.40). Unlike Phaistos, the Mallian palace did not undergo a major rebuilding, and so it is conceivable that its original 'theatral' area (if there was one) stood apart from the palace fabric. The only place for it would be out to the west or in The Cour Nord.

133.   Note that at Gournia the stepped area is adjacent to, and possibly intimately connected with, a small shrine along the western facade of the central court.

134.   See below, Phaistos, Second Palace.

135.   In other words, passing eastward from the area of the West Porch.

136.   For a possible analogue at Gournia, see our discussion above. The actual form of the Knossian West Porch is echoed by the West Entrance at Phaistos: both have a central pillar, two doors beyond on the right side, and one door on the left, leading inward to the palace proper. In both cases, the right-hand doors are part of a guard's station. The principal difference is in the orientation of the two porches. See also Nirov Khani.

137.   If it is the case that the NWTH communicated directly with the interior of the palace at a second storey, then it is at least conceivable that the NWTH served some function in addition to storage, since its extreme northwestern and south-eastern corners provide an intimate connection between the palace and the entrance to the theatral area to the north. It may simply have permitted a prominent palace personage to emerge at the N entry in the plan, which looks like a major marked entrance. It is not known how (or if) all the first-floor cells of the NWTH were interconnected, but it is curious that if one enters the struc-ture at either the northwestern of southeastern corner, one could pass through each of the (in some cases tiny) chambers just once, without having to double back: a very nice unicursal maze or labyrinth in its own right! There is, of course, no evidence that the NWTH is the famous Knossian 'labyrinth', despite the bull-fresco visible at the N end of on the outer wall which, like the bull-fresco along the northern entrance to the palace's Central Court, might have been visible to later myth-making Hellenes in the city's ruins.

138.   And, also, as at Gournia. At Mallia the situation is not quite so controlled.

139.   A couple of square paving stones, slightly raised, were found by Evans in the western court near the western facades, which he conjectured might have been altar bases, but the lack of associated finds at these points makes such a conjecture highly speculative.

140.   See below, Figure II.43, and above Note 136.

141.   As already noted, equivalent halls occur at Phaistos, Gournia, Mallia, Kato Zakro, and Palaikastro House B.

142.   See below, Figure II.37, northwestern corner.

143.   Some of these walls connected with work areas in the northeastern quadrant are omitted in our plan: these comprise the so-called 'Royal Pottery Stores' in Evans' plan: *Handbook*: Figure 2.

144.   Even though there were other small buildings in the area of the western court

(visible in the bottom of the *koulouras*), these evidently did not impinge upon the palace fabric proper, and date to an early period.

145. Not included in the present survey, this remarkable structure is discussed in detail by Evans; see *PM* II: 109-139.

146. The actual alignments of the palaces are not identical, although those of Knossos, Mallia, Phaistos and Kato Zakro run generally north-south. It seems evident, however, that the alignments of the palaces are in reference to prominent landscape features, a point saliently made by V. Scully, Jr, in his *The Earth, The Temple and The Gods* (1962). Scully's theses are examined below in connection with our discussion of Phaistos, and below, Workpoints.

147. *Handbook*: 26ff, and Figure 2, pp. 24-25. We must take care here not to confuse a sequential building program (necessary in a megastructure of this size) with evidence for random or agglutinative growth. As is demonstrated in Part Two, there can be no question that the palace was planned as a unit from the start, however long it may have taken to realize the original homogeneous design.

148. See below, 105ff., and compare the plan of the western magazine blocks of Knossos to those extant at Mallia in Figure II.37.

149. L.R. Palmer, *A New Guide to the Palace at Knossos*: 41-51.

150. See the reconstructed schemes offered by Graham, *PC*: Figures 84, 85, and 86. Such halls, whatever their detailed disposition, most likely resembled the halls remaining in the Knossian 'Little Palace': see above, Figure II.23.

151. Cells 12-16, adjacent to north-south corridor 17-11a, comprise an interconnected cluster, entered only at cell 16.

152. The disposition of the walls in this area during the early years of the excavation, shown in plans by Theodore Fyfe as reproduced by Palmer (*A New Guide to the Palace at Knossos*: Plan II), indicates an entirely different arrangement, including a 'megaron' oriented toward the Central Court. No trace is shown of the walls which were to support the stairway reconstructed by Evans over this area. The state of this area prior to the LM III period is unclear.

153. *PM* I: 165-199.

154. At Mallia (Figure II.37) the pillar crypt consists of a single room with two pillars aligned north-south; at Phaistos (Second Palace, Figure II.43) the corresponding room contained no pillar but rather a (statue/ritual double axe?) base.

155. *PM* I: 168ff. Referred to by Evans as an 'envelope-like' design, consisting of a rectangle with two crossed diagonals incised within.

156. *BSA* IX (1902-1903): Figure 18, p. 37. The 'altar base' stands some 11 meters due east of the Tripartite Shrine on the western facade of the Court.

157. See below, Figure II.37.

158. See A. Badawy, *Ancient Egyptian Architectural Design* (University of California Near Eastern Studies IV, 1965), part II.

159. *PM* II: Figure 525, p. 803, Figure 521, p. 799, Figure 523, p. 801.

160. See Graham's discussion of this cluster and its functions, *PC*: 31ff and Note 12, p. 32.

161. For another hall system fronting on a central court, see the East Hall System at Kato Zakro below.

162. As excavated by Blegen; see *Minoica*: 66.

163. *PM* I: 136-139.

164. See below, p. 131ff.

165.   At least in this final state of the plan; the situation may have been different earlier, but this is unclear.

166.   *PM* I: 231-247.

167.   In which case we would expect there to be kitchens either below or adjacent, but the evidence is unclear; see Kato Zakro.

168.   See below, Figure II.37.

169.   Discussed in W. Stevenson Smith, *The Art and Architecture of Ancient Egypt* (1965): 193ff, and Figure 66, p. 196. The plan illustrates the west palace, the more formal structure of the royal compound. The more private residential quarter is across the Royal Road, to the east, connected to the latter by a bridge. That palace is shown in Smith's Figure 65, p. 195. The Amarna compound, dating to *c.* 1370-1350, was built by Amenhotep IV (Akhenaten); his father's palace at Malqata in the Theban district reveals a more irregular plan, at least in overall organization, but its internal blocks manifest a principle of symmetry similar to that seen at Amarna.

170.   Basic bibliography for Mallia (palace and city):
   A.   Preliminary reports:
      1. L. Mariani, 'Antichitá cretesi', *MonAnt* VI (1895): columns 232-241: first mention of the ruins ('*temenos* of Britomartis').
      2. J. Hazzidhakis (discoverer of palace), *PAE* (1915): 108-130; (1919): 50-62; *Dheltion* IV (1918): 12.
      3. *BCH* (Chronique) for 1920, 1921, 1922, 1923, and 1924.
   B.   Final publications:
      Etudes Crétoises I (1928): western quarter, north and east of Court;
      „   „   IV (1936): northern quarters, south and east of Court;
      „   „   VI (1942): completion of northern and eastern quarters;
      „   „   XII (1962): completion of excavation.
   C.   Guide: C. Tire and H. van Effenterre, *Guide des Fouilles françaises en Crète* (*GFFC*) (1966): 5-47. Final reports in press as of this writing.
   D.   Related works:
      1. J. Charbonneaux, 'Notes sur l'architecture et la céramique du Palais de Mallia', *BCH* (1928): 347-387.
      2. N. Platon, *KrKhr* I (1947): 635-636: identification of northwestern quarter (area III) as hall system.
      3. H. Gallet de Santerre, 'Mallia, Aperçu historique', *KrKhr* III (1949): 363-391.

171.   See *GFFC*: 54-56, plan, Figure 17, p. 54, views: Plates XIII and XIV.

172.   Traces of these structural remains may be seen in Figure II.36.

173.   Indications as to the chronological position of various palace sections are given *seriatim* in our description below.

174.   There are, however, Egyptian parallels: see A. Badawy, *A History of Egyptian Architecture* (1966): 32-36, with illustrations, including a plan and reconstruction of a granary court at El-Lahun (Figures 16 and 17) dating to the Middle Kingdom, approximately contemporary with the Mallian granary (XII Dynasty, reign of Senusert (Sesostris) II, *c.* 1906-1888 B.C.). It is known that Minoan craftsmen were at work on the pyramid project of Senusert II at El-Lahun. The Egyptian granaries, unlike the Mallian example, are built into enclosed courts. Badawy (Figure 13, p. 33) illustrates a drawing of a courtyard with two rows of beehive-shaped silos. The excavators of Mallia concluded that the silos were contemporary with the first palace period, though it is unclear if they date to the very foundation of the palace (*GFFC*: 9).

175.   But not by contemporary Egyptian standards, to judge by the representations presented by Badawy (above, Note 174). It may be of significance that there was no paved court on the southern side of the palace: it is certainly conceivable that the area to the south of the palace might have been an agricultural plot at some period, but there is no direct evidence for this. The lack of a bounding wall to the west of the silo cluster (in contrast to all known Egyptian examples) might indicate that the Mallian palace was a more public warehouse than its brother palaces, perhaps serving in part as a public grange or warehouse for the town (an impression augmented by the very open nature of the megastructure). On the other hand, a glance at the plan in Figure II.37 will indicate that the bounding wall of the magazine block immediately to the north of the silo cluster is missing, and so it may be the case that the Mallian granary was also enclosed originally.

176.   See *PC*: 43, for a discussion of the religious nature of this cell-cluster.

177.   Assuming, of course, that there were such similarities to begin with.

178.   S. Marinatos suggests that this may have been the Mallian equivalent of the 'theatral areas' of Phaistos and Knossos: S. Marinatos and M. Hirmer, *Crete and Mycenae* (1960): 137 and Figure 58.

179.   See below, Figure II.43.; see also *GFFC*: 10.

180.   Shown reconstructed in *GFFC*: 16, Figure 5.

181.   Discussed in detail below in Part Two.

182.   See above, Note 156.

183.   See below, Part Two.

184.   See our discussion above for Knossos.

185.   At Phaistos, as noted below, the palace fabric is aligned with its long (north-south) axis directed toward the twin peak of Mount Ida to the north (on the slopes of which is the famous Kamares cave-sanctuary). At Knossos, the palace is not directly aligned toward the peak of the religiously significant Mount Juktas, site of a peak-sanctuary contemporary with the palace. However, as will be discussed further in Workpoints, the principal southern entrance to the Knossian Central Court is not at the center of the southern court facade, but slightly to the east. As may be verified on the site itself, by standing at the center of the Court, in the area of Evans' Central Court altar base (above, Note 156), the peak of Mount Juktas to the south appears directly over the southern doorway, whose position then (by conscious design intent?) *marks* the position of Juktas beyond. My own calculations suggest that the peak would have been just visible over a second-storey roofline. This visual alignment might have been further marked by the placement, at the roofline, of the huge 'horns of consecration' found fallen in this area of the ruins. If this had been the case, then the 'framing' of the mountain peak by a pair of horns would be equivalent to comparable phenomena in Egypt. The question then arises, why didn't the designers of the building make the landscape orientation coterminous with the (ritual?) mountain peak alignment? As discussed below in Appendix A, it would seem that the designers had to accomodate two distinct canonical alignments: a foundation (sunrise) alignment for the palace fabric proper, and a landscape visual alignment, marked by artifactual focussing. It is thus coincidental that the two turned out to be coterminous (i.e. exactly perpendicular) at the palace of Phaistos. Such topographical alignments are hardly unique: a patent correlate would be the niche in Moslem mosques indicating the direction of Mecca; the niche can occur anywhere in the structure, for the fabric of the mosque as a whole generally conforms to the orientation of its urban surround.

186. See *GFFC*: 34-35, 45.
187. *Ibid.*: 46.
188. On the significance of the placement of double-axe symbols in palatial fabrics, see Appendix B below. Recall that double-axe symbols are found incised on the pillars of pillar crypts (at Knossos and Mallia), or on an east-west alignment with a central ritual chamber (Phaistos, see below), as here and at Gournia.
189. *GFFC*: 42. At Phaistos there is a similar close connection between a hall system and a storage for accounts (q.v.).
190. And, as at Phaistos, the lustral cell is immediately adjacent to the west.
191. *GFFC*: 46. It may be of interest that in one of Evans' early plans of Knossos, a cell adjacent to the northern entranceway is labelled a 'tower', an appellation later dropped: see *BSA* VIII (1901-1902): 5, Figure 2. The 'tower' stands immediately to the north of the entranceway, opening onto the northern pillared hall. Such a lookout platform (if indeed it was one) finds correlates in Evans' other 'bastions', such as the East Bastion, but the latter may not have been as high as the one next to the northern entrance, for the ground drops away sharply to the east, whereas it is flat to the northwest: at Mallia, the entire terrain is flat.
192. The following is a brief bibliography relating to both the first and second palaces at Phaistos:
    1. L. Pernier, *RRAL* IX (1900): 631ff; X (1901): 260ff; XI (1902): 511ff; XII (1903): 352ff; *Mon.Ant.* XII (1902): columns 5ff; XIV (1904): columns 313ff; *RRAL* XVI (1907): 257ff; XVII (1908): 642ff; *BdA* I (1907): fasc. viii, 26ff; *Ausonia* I (1906): 112ff; II (1907): columns 119ff; IV (1909): columns 48ff.
    2. F. Halbherr, *RRAL* XIV (1905): 365ff; *MRIL* XXI (1905): 235ff.
    3. L. Pernier, *Il Palazzo Minoico di Festos I* (1935); L. Pernier and L. Banti, *II* (1951) (= *PMF* I, II).
    4. D. Levi, *BdA* (1951): 335ff; (1952): 380ff; (1953): 252ff; (1955): 141ff; (1956): 238ff; *Annuario* XXVII-XXIX, N.S. XI-XIII (1949-1951): 467ff; XXX-XXXII, N.S. XIV-XVI (1952-1954) 483ff; XXXIII-XXXIV, N.S. XVII-XVIII (1955-1956): 289ff; XXXV-XXXVI, N.S. XIX-XX (1957-1958): 193ff; XXXVII-XXXVIII, N.S. XXI-XXII (1959-1960): 431ff; XXXIX-XL, N.S. XXIII-XXIV (1961-1962): 377ff; XLIII-XLIV, N.S. XXVII-XXVIII (1965-1966): 313-399 = final conclusion of excavations of Italian School at Phaistos; final plan, Figure 1, p. 314; *Dheltion* XVI (1960): 267; XVIIB (1961-1962): 297ff; XVIIIB (1963); 'The Recent Excavations at Phaistos', *Stud.Med.Archaeol.* XI (1965).
193. See above, Note 185, and below, Workpoints. Standing in the Central Court facing north towards the twin peaks of Ida, one gets the impression, especially if one's view includes the pavement alignments of the northern entrance corridor bisecting the northern facade, that the orientation of the palace is slightly skewed to the right of Ida. This impression is caused by the fact that that corridor is misaligned (due to accomodations made in the construction *vis-à-vis* earlier wall-fragments of the first palace period), whereas the palace fabric, and the Central Court itself, are directly aligned upon the twin peak, a face which may be verified by standing at either the northern or eastern facades of the Court and facing north. In its original state, the northern corridor would be closed to view from the Court, and the northern facade of the Court would have risen two storeys in height, thereby cutting off all of the mountain peak from view except

for the actual twin peak itself (a situation echoed at Knossos, as noted above in Note 185).

194.   See below, Part Two, for an assessment of the evidence for modular grid planning in the first palace period.

195.   And most likely served in part as a station for a guard or watchman. The arrangement is replicated again in the second palace, and is equivalent in design to the West Porch of the Knossian palace (q.v.), although of a different orientation.

196.   The significance of the positioning of pillar crypts and other ritual cells in palatial fabrics is discussed below in Chapter IV. As will be seen, such cells occupy central nodes in the planning grid itself. Recall that the pillar crypt at Knossos is contiguous with the so-called Vat Room Deposit, evidently one(?) of the foundation-deposits of the palace. Its position, at the geometric center of the western Central Block at Knossos, would thus be generically equivalent to the positioning of commemorative foundation deposits in the 'corner-stones' of our own buildings.

197.   See *PC*: 39, for a discussion of this chamber.

198.   As we shall see in detail in Part Two.

199.   And in this regard the situation here is exactly paralleled by the modifications to the western facade at Mallia.

200.   See *PC*: Figure 83 and 84 for possible reconstructions.

201.   Discussed by Graham in *AJA* 74 (1970): 231-239. A typical Egyptian 'window of appearances' would be on the bridge over the Royal Road separating the western halls of state of the Amarna palace of Akhenaten from the royal domestic quarters to the east (see W. Stevenson Smith, *loc.cit.*). The Amarna complex was built at least two centuries after the palace at Phaistos.

202.   See Graham, *op.cit.*, Figure 1, p. 233.

203.   *PMF* II: 100, 565-566.

204.   The southern wall of cell 25 is ruined, making it difficult to assess whether there may have been a doorway here. The evidence is unclear.

205.   See p. 110.

206.   *PC*: 40, with references.

207.   There are double-axe signs incised on the walls to the west of this area, on axis with the room; an identical situation was noted above for Mallia (hall system pillar crypt area) and Gournia; see above, Note 188, and below, Appendix A.

208.   The pavement proper dates from the first palace period, but it is contained within the borders of the new Central Court, and its adjacent construction.

209.   *AJA* 74 (1970): 231ff, and Figure 1, p. 233. The flagpoles in Egyptian pylon-facades, however, are set into niches cut out of the sloping face of these temple walls.

210.   Illustrated in N. Platon, *Archaeologia Mundi: Crete* (New York, 1966): Plate 47.

211.   For a (conjecturally) similar situation, see our remarks above for Knossos, Note 185.

212.   Noted above in Note 193.

213.   As well illustrated by the reception given V. Scully, Jr, *The Earth, The Temple, and The Gods* (1962) by more literal-minded factions among classical archaeologists. The situation was compounded by the fact that Scully's own photographs in some cases were too obscure to illustrate his (perfectly patent) points that the orientations of Minoan palatial compounds are such as to call attention to, and visually *mark*, the position of ritually prominent Cretan peaks. Scully was of course perfectly correct in his thesis, but the evidence is complex due to the

fact that (in my own view) landscape alignment is one of *two* contributing factors to the overall orientation of a palace fabric. We shall attempt to sort out the evidence below in Workpoints, Part Two.

214. Cell 49, dating from the first palace period, revealed the traces of many cups and plates, evidently thrown down in the destruction of a second palace pantry here.

215. The columns and piers of this first-palace hall were incorporated into second-palace walls.

216. See below under Kato Zakro.

217. In other words, the stairways adjacent to the Mallian pillar hall area. At Phaistos, this connection with vestibule 75 would allow guests to enter directly into the dining hall on the second storey, and to be received formally after entering the palace along the route from the western entranceway.

218. Discussed by A. Badawy, *Ancient Egyptian Architectural Design* (1965), introductory sections.

219. In contrast to its usage elsewhere, by and large, in round-number modular proportions (e.g. 20 + 30 + 50 units, etc.). The phrase 'in clear' is Badawy's.

220. As will be seen in Part Two below, the discrepancy of one unit (200 vs. 199) appears at the extreme southwestern corner of the facade, whose southern wall is misaligned with respect to walls further eastward by *c.* 35 cm (= approximately one unit).

221. See, for example, Jay Hambridge, *The Elements of Dynamic Symmetry* (1967; originally published 1926). A full bibliography of metrological studies is given below in Part Two.

222. Discussed below in Part Two. Evidently there were resident at El-Lahun, in connection with the pyramid project of the Pharaoh Senusert (Sesostris) II, in the 19th century B.C., a group of Minoan craftsmen.

223. As will be seen in detail in Part Two.

224. See the Knossian *Handbook*: 26-32.

225. Chapter III below attempts to elaborate a picture of the elemental constancies in Minoan design, based upon the survey of the remains in the present Chapter.

226. D.G. Hogarth, 'Excavations at Zakro, Crete', *BSA* V (1900-1901): 129-141; L. Mariani, *MonAnt* VI: 298.

227. Reports by N. Platon appear in numbers of *KrKhr* since 1962; see also *BCH*, 1963 onward. The plan used in our description is that by draftsman J. Shaw appearing in *BCH* XCI (1968). The writer thanks Mr Shaw for providing him with excavation measurements of several palace sections.

228. The palace, in other words, was built principally at a time contemporaneous to the beginning of the second palace period seen at Phaistos and elsewhere.

229. See below, Part Two.

230. The only general analogue to the round cistern/pool is a cistern found at Tylissos built against the outer face of the northern wall of house TYL C somewhat later than the foundation of the house itself.

231. Although it is principally considered to be a cistern in function.

232. See above, Note 156.

233. As may be seen for example in *PM, passim.*

234. See above, Figure II.23.

235. Including, for example, the small shrine just off the court at Gournia, similarly near the northwestern corner of the courtyard.

236. See above, pp. 114-115.

237.   Canonical, that is, by comparison with the major hall systems of the palaces at Knossos, Phaistos, Mallia, or Haghia Triadha.

238.   Cell LVIII to the north of the East Hall System is, however, a canonical sunken 'lustral chamber'.

239.   Recall that at Mallia this 'doubling' involves, by our hypothesis, a use of one of the major halls as a focus forming the corner of an L-shaped set of halls.

240.   See above, Figures II.25 and II.23.

241.   See above under Knossos, Phaistos and Mallia.

242.   At Kato Zakro an extraordinary number of fine ceramics were uncovered by Dr. Platon and his team, nicely illustrated in S. Alexiou, N. Platon, and H. Guanella, *Ancient Crete* (1968): Figures 171-196. Figure 192 illustrates the famous 'peak sanctuary' rhyton referred to by Graham in his discussion of the appearance of the northern facade of the Phaistian Central Court (*AJA* 74 [1970] : 231).

243.   In this diagram is included a picture of the modular planning grid organization of the three Minoan houses, discussed in detail below in Part Two. By contrast to the Amarna house, the Minoan houses are interlocked jigsaws of clusters. But even in this regard, note that there are certain morphological patterns: at TYL C (upper left) the residential quarter, an L-shaped cluster, mirrors the storage magazine cluster on the lower left, also an L-shaped area (and, incidentally, of the same square-footage). The main traffic stem is a U-shaped zone in the center of the building. At KN HCS, similar morphological functional patterns emerge: the hall system is L-shaped, as is the entrance corridor. The area between the two, part of the 'lustral area', is a reversed L-shaped cluster. The magazine storage area, on the west of the building (as indeed in many Minoan buildings, including the palaces), is a double-L shaped zone, wrapped around a pillar crypt.

244.   The Egyptian houses noted here are examined in greater detail in D. Preziosi, *The Semiotics of the Built Environment* (Bloomington, 1979b), Chapter II.

245.   D. Preziosi, *loc.cit.* Because El-Lahun is a town house contiguous with other row houses, and because it stands on the northern side of a street, provision is made in the design of the house to bring the entrant round to the north of the structure before the passage to private chambers to the south is made. Houses across the street to the south reverse the composition by eliminating a long corridor to the north which is necessary in the present house: there passage to the private quarters is linear and directly onward to the south.

APPENDIX A: LATE BRONZE AGE AEGEAN MEGAROID COMPOUNDS

After the destruction of the palaces of Crete in the opening phases of the ceramic period LM III, there begin to appear on the island a number of structures whose architectonic organization constrasts sharply with those we have examined above, and which we have noted were characteristic of the opening phases of the new palace period. A wholly new type of house form appears on Crete at this time, in at least one case incorporated into the fabric of an older Minoan palatial compound.

This house form is the so-called *megaron,* a hall-and-porch structure of rectangular outline fronting onto a courtyard, oriented generally north-south. The megaron as a residential form is known principally outside of Crete, and forms the nucleus of the palatial fortresses of mainland Greece and the Aegean islands during the Mycenaean period: the most famous examples are the great halls of state of the Mycenaean palaces of Mycenae, Tiryns and Pylos.[1] But as we shall see, the megaron form has a long history in the non-Cretan areas of the Aegean basin, appearing at the very beginnings of the Early Bronze Age, principally in the northeastern Aegean (e.g. Troy II, Lemnos).[2]

The problems surrounding the chronological sequence of events at the time of the destruction of the major Minoan palaces (and in effect the time of the destruction of most nearly all Minoan settlements) are enormous and controversial, and the present writer claims no expertise in these areas of ceramic inquiry. The principal aim of the present section is to make note of the changes in architectonic design occurring at this time so as to (in part) offer a perspective on this complicated historical period different from that to be had in discussions of chronology based solely on pottery stratigraphy. The observations made below may serve to concretely contextualize the latter discussions so as to arrive at a more realistic understanding of the profound changes in Minoan society taking place during the LM III period. In the course of our observations below, our focus will be comparative in nature, and we shall look at Cretan LM III construction with an eye both to the Aegean basin to the north and to the period on Crete itself just prior to this time.

Gournia: House H-e

After the destruction of the LM I palace of Gournia examined above, the settlement on the hilltop was reoccupied to some extent in the LM III period.[3] Three new buildings appear in the ruins of the old provincial town: a house on the northwestern slope of the hill, adjacent to LM I ruins; a small shrine to the north of the palace but at a different orientation from the latter; and the structure to be examined here, called by the excavators House H-e, built contiguous to the southwestern tip of the old palace fabric, but at a different angle. The three structures may be seen above in Figure II.26; Figure A.1 is a plan of House H-e.

At its greatest extent, the structure is some 17 meters on a side. Its principal focus is cells 31 and 32, a megaron of a canonical type, with an inner hall twice as deep as an outer porch. The porch communicates directly to the outside to the south, across a threshold not extant over the remaining foundation walls. It also gives access laterally to a long north-south corridor lying to the east of the megaron system (cell 33), off which are laterally appended four small cells (34, 35, 36, and 37).

To the north of the latter is a cell enterable only(?) from the exterior back of the building, while to the west of the porch is a wall defining a paved, enclosed area of some kind (cells 38 and 30). The pavement of cell 30 may have extended out to the south, and it is likely that it formed a continuation of a courtyard or paved area to the south of the porch proper. Corridor 33 also communicated directly with the outside to the south. The builders used blocks from the old palace in building.

The plan of House H-e is nearly identical to that of the smaller megaroid quarters of the great mainland palace at Tiryns, a fact noted as early as 1912 by F. Oelmann;[4] indeed the two structures are nearly identical in size.[5]

But the similarity of GRN H-e extends to many other structures of the period as well, as we shall see presently. Most prominent among its similar cousins is a Cretan structure also erected during the LM III period, at Plati on the Lassithi Plateau to the west, near the foot of Mount Dikte (Figure A.2).

Plati: LM III Palace

That Plati was a Minoan palatial compound can hardly be doubted by anyone who carefully examines its plan in detail. The compound was excavated in one season by R.M. Dawkins in 1913,[6] but of the structure today all that remains is Dawkins' excellent detailed plan, for after excavation the ruins were covered over to revert to the property of the landowner of the time. This is indeed most unfortunate, for if it is truly the case that Plati was a single unified compound, its size, to estimate from that of the central courtyard, would have been larger than Kato Zakro or Gournia.

The compound was built at two periods, LM I and LM III, and there are traces of walls of the Hellenic period overlying part of the plan. The construction of LM I is confined mainly to the series of rectangular cells on the southern flank of the courtyard, evidently incorporated into the LM III palace (shown in Figure A.3 in heavier outline). It appears that it was the LM III period construction which made the structure into a palatial compound of the canonical form.

Unlike the other Minoan palaces examined above, the structure's central court is aligned roughly east-west, and the long axis of the court would have focussed attention toward the foothills of Mount Dikte to the southeast and the area of the Diktean cave, legendary site of the birth of the god Zeus.[7] Apart from the LM I walls incorporated into the LM III building, much of the structure lies on bedrock, and so may be considered a largely new foundation.[8]

Within the court, marked by *b* in the LM III plan below, (Figure A.3), is a hearth, possibly akin in function to the central court altars of Mallia or Knossos, or the central court object at Kato Zakro,[9] it stands across from the entrance to the hall system to the south.

The walls of the structure are finely and thickly built, and reveal shallow indentations characteristic of the masonry on the central court at Kato Zakro. Indeed, at point *delta* on the plan above is a shallow jog in the court facade, in a position equivalent to a similar masonry setback on the central court western facade at Kato Zakro.[10] The court as a whole is ca. 18 meters wide, and at least 46 meters in length, larger in size than the Zakro courtyard.

Fronting on the narrow end of the court (block B in Figure A.2 above) are a series of small chambers apparently entered at cell 4, and generically resembling clusters of cells at Knossos and Phaistos.[11] Beyond this, to the west, is a paved court (cell B-1): recall the relationship at Phaistos between the central court and a smaller court to the northern (short) end of the central court, interspersed by the 'banquet' block there. These two blocks are similar in size, though they differ in details of layout.

The central court is entered by a wide gap in the area of blocks B and A, through a corridor coming onto the southwestern corner of the courtyard. The thickness of the walls of all three blocks suggests that the compound was at least two storeys in height, although no indisputable traces of a stairwell foundation may be identified.

The disposition of block A is of most interest here, for even a cursory study of its plan will reveal that its internal organization is equivalent to that of House H-e at Gournia. It is, in other words, a megaroid foundation. Let us compare them directly:

1. Both have a hall system on the left of the block. That of PLT is more 'classically' Minoan in consisting of a PDP hall system, while GRN H-e is a more canonically 'Mycenaean' hall-and-porch megaron;

2. Both compounds are divided such that the halls occupy one-half of the block along its east-west extent (PLT is oriented south-north, however, while GRN H-e is north-south);

3. Both compounds have a north-south row of four small cells to the right of the halls, and in both cases there is an internal entry to the latter from the porch area;

4. In both cases, there is a long north-south corridor contiguous with the four small cells, but at PLT this (paved) corridor is to the *right* of the cells, while that at GRN H-e is to the *left* of the cells:

5. PLT has a row of cells wrapped around the back side of the block; GRN H-e has a single cell beyond the northernmost small cell;

6. Both compounds are square in outline, apart from the northern projection at GRN H-e.

The relationship of the PLT hall system with the central court, however, contrasts with other palatial hall systems, as we have seen above. Indeed, the only close analogues are Kato Zakro's East Hall System, and the hall system at the site of Nirou Khani. But at Kato Zakro, the East Halls are oriented away from the court, and lie parallel with it: here the hall system is perpendicular to the court, and opens directly upon it. At Nirou Khani, the hall system is a simple hall-and-porch affair (see above, Figure II.17) with two columns on the court facade (which might have existed here, but there is no trace over the threshold blocks). Moreover, at Nirou Khani there is no series of parallel cells and corridor as here and at GRN He. Nirou Khani is dated to the LM I period.

Although geometrically the PLT system is equivalent to the block at GRN He, topologically — in terms of the patterns of internal connectivity among cells — the closest analogue is in fact the so-called 'throne room' built into the palace at Knossos not long before its destruction: see above, Figure II.28.

The positions of both clusters are identical, *viz.* at the upper left corner of a central court. In both cases there is a hall which fronts directly onto the court through a vestibular cell. At Knossos, as at Plati, there are four interconnecting small cells on the long flank of the hall, and in both palaces these cells give access at the back to three additional cells wrapped around the back of the hall. At both sites the rank of small cells is bordered by a corridor running from the central court back along the side flank of the block.

Although there is no trace of a 'throne' at Plati, and no real trace of frescoes such as are reconstructed in the Knossian 'throne room', to my eye the Plati block looks like a copy of the Knossian system, but on virgin ground (it is well established that the Knossian block was built into an earlier cluster).[12] Or could it have been the other way round?[13]

At any rate, it is patent that we are dealing with contextual variations of an architectionic composition, although it is unclear if all three examples (KN PAL, PLT, GRN He) served the same functions. The Knossian 'throne room' does indeed appear to be an important hall of state, or the public seat of some official (perhaps indeed a Linear B-speaking mainland overseer?). The compounds at PLT and GRN He seem more modestly domestic in nature (although the halls proper are not all that dissimilar in size).

It may well be the case that the Plati compound is a newer ('third palace period') version of the Knossian system built into an older fabric. In this case, Plati might be seen as an updated version of the older Minoan palatial compound formation, incorporating the latest responses in organization of functions.[14]

The obvious question, then, is: a response to what? To consider this question, we must now turn to evidence from outside Crete itself.

Aegean Megaroid Compounds

The plans of the compounds at PLT and GRN He, and the form of the Knossian 'throne room', while new to Crete in the LM III period, have a long history prior to this period elsewhere in the Aegean basin, appearing as early as the Early Bronze II period in the Troy II/Poliokhni V culture.[15]

Megaroid halls built contiguous with one or more parallel rows of smaller cells appear as early as Troy IIa, if restorations of the Trojan 'Great Hall' complex are accurate.[16] This is shown below in Figure A.4.

Here we find two large megara side by side, with two narrower parallel constructions to the north, each divided into three smaller cells. The entire complex fronted on a large courtyard to the west (ca. 37 meters north-south), apparently walled on all sides.[17] This complex is shown in the upper left of our Figure A.4.

A similar compound, although rather smaller than the first, was erected during the earlier phase of the Troy IIb period, with north-south orientation.[18] It consists of a larger hall-and-porch system to the west, contiguous with a narrower hall system to the northeast; both front onto an enclosed courtyard. This was replaced by the compound shown in the upper right of the illustration in the Troy IIb2 period;[19] here the greater hall has a central hearth (as in Troy IIa), and the smaller megara to the southwest are divided into three chambers each.

Note that in all three of these instances, the depth of the porch is approximately one-half that of the inner hall: a proportion repeated in the examples below. Indeed, as we shall see, these proportions remain • fairly constant in megaroid construction throughout the Aegean during the entire Bronze Age. Recall the plan of GRN H-e above, Figure A.1.

The more famous plan of Troy IIc, on the lower left of our Figure A.4, reveals a compatible arrangement: a large megaron of canonical proportions flanked by side buildings of narrower size, each containing three interconnecting cells. All front perpendicularly upon a wide, walled court to the south, itself entered through a propylon gateway. The court (like those of later Mycenaean palaces) reveals traces of a colonnade interspersed with wall-buttresses.[20]

It is with the following plan, of the period Troy IIg, that we first see a compound resembling those seen above on Crete.[21] This structure, the so-called 'House HS,' is to the west of the main megaron remaining from the previous period, and evidently served as the private residential compound of the Trojan ruling family. House HS is shown at a larger scale on the lower right of Figure A.4.

House HS is a self-contained compound entered from the south by means of a door opening onto an east-west courtyard. The cells beyond divide into four interconnected clusters: that on the far right is a canonical hall-and-porch megaron fronting onto the court (no doubt through a columned portico, now missing). The megaron has a back chamber projecting at a curious angle from the main fabric of the compound,[22] which provides the only access to a rank of four small chambers built parallel to the hall system and contiguous with it to the west. The remainder of the compound consists of a second megaron hall to the west, also containing a back room giving access to a long narrow cell on the western side of the compound (also connected to the courtyard at its southern end).

The eastern half of the compound is patently similar in form to the Gournia house seen above, at least geometrically; but it differs from the latter in the way its cells are interconnected. A somewhat simpler version of the same theme is illustrated by Megaron 605 in the contemporary town of Poliokhni on the nearby island of Lemnos, shown in heavy outline in the town plan below (Figure A.5).[23]

The house is shown in greater detail in the following illustration (Figure A.6).

Like the Trojan example, Megaron 605 is oriented north-south with a megaron hall on the right opening onto an east-west court to the south. There are four small cells parallel to the hall, to the west (as at Troy HS), entered from the back of the main hall as well as from the southwestern corner of the southernmost cell. The compound evidently included additional chambers to the west and northwest, most likely work areas. To the south of the court is a long narrow cell, not unlike the long narrow cell on the western side of Troy HS. The entire compound is entered at a single point: a covered propylon gateway at the southwestern corner.

The proportions of the central part of the compound — the megaron and parallel side-chambers — are the same as those seen at Troy: the porch is one-half the depth of the inner hall, and its width is equal to its depth. In addition, the hall-and-porch comprise exactly one-half the width of the block, for the width of the small cells matches that of the megaron proper. Recall that similar proportions were seen at GRN H-e and PLT if we include their contiguous corridors.

All of these examples of the megaroid compound — consisting of a megaron hall and a parallel row of smaller chambers contiguous with it — date to the Early Bronze Age, and specifically to the Early Bronze II period in the Aegean. Indeed, with one possible exception, none can be found in the Aegean again until the later phases of the Late Bronze Age.[24]

This one possible exception comes from Asine on the Greek mainland, dated to the Middle Bronze II period (Figure A.7).[25]

In plan, the Asine compound consists of a rectangular structure and a trapezoidal structure beside it (D and B in the illustration). The latter is divided into some ten cells resembling in some cases long narrow magazines. The megaroid cluster proper (D) consists of a doubled hall system running in parallel, both fronting on an open area to the north (in contrast to the orientation of the others we have seen). Both halls are entered across a couple of wide steps, and the right-hand (W) hall was divided into two chambers: an inner, longer hall, and an outer porch. Rows of smaller chambers run across the back of both halls (S).

A compound more closely resembling the Early Bronze megaroid compounds comes from the (now underwater) site of

Pavlopetri, off the northern tip of the island of Elaphonisi, itself between the southeastern tip of the Peloponnese and the island of Kythera (Figure A.8).[26]

The compound, shown in heavy outline in the fabric of the early Mycenaean period settlement, is House C-IV. While no thresholds were visible to the excavators, we have conjecturally restored doorways in our plan above. The resultant plan shows a larger hall-and-porch system, to the west, and a series of smaller chambers running parallel to the east; both appear to have fronted onto a courtyard to the south, wider than it is deep. The megaroid cluster proper appears to have had a double porch system, a feature seen in the major Mycenaean megaron palaces such as Tiryns, Mycenae or Pylos.

The plan resembles Megaron 605 at Poliokhni as well as House HS at Troy IIg, but beyond this formal resemblance we cannot go.

Figure A.9 is a plan of a large Mycenaean compound on the island of Delos, considered by its excavators to have been palatial in nature.[27] The remains are too fragmented to allow us to restore the original plan with confidence. What remains of the central portion, however, is of interest to our present discussion, for it would appear that we have here a series of parallel halls (of megaroid form?) fronting southward onto a wide and shallow court. The entrance to the latter is at the southwestern corner, through a gate strengthened by flanking bastions(?).

It is not clear which of the parallel halls was the expected megaron system, for each is rather narrow. Much depends on the conjectural restoration of the original traces of the internal walls: while those restored traces (shown in dotted outline in our plan) appear structurally reasonable, the resultant plan would make for a rather uncanonical megaroid hall system (at least with respect to its proportional allotment of spaces).

In the town of Phylakopi on the island of Melos there was erected during a period known as the Third City a megaroid palatial compound more closely resembling our Early Bronze examples and our Cretan Late Minoan III compounds (Figure A.10).[28] The plan shows the relationship of this compound (in heavy outline) to the fabric of the fortified cliffside town. The palace fronts onto a squarish courtyard walled off from the rest of the town to the west. It is the only structure of its type in the settlement, and it is also the largest in size.

A closer look at the plan will reveal that it is nearly identical in appearance to the compound at Gournia (GRN H-e) (Figure A.11). It comprises a megaron on the western side, with a deeper hall and a shallower porch. At the center of the hall is a rectangular hearth. To the right is a long narrow north-south corridor, giving access to a row of seven small cells aligned north-south all inter-connecting. The northeastern end of the structure projects out beyond the back wall of the megaron (as at GRN), and there are three small cells within. It is unclear how the latter connected to the remainder of the compound.

The megaron system was built into the fabric of an earlier construction (whose walls are indicated to the west and north of the hall proper), so that the new building comprises those sections just described. No connection is shown in the plan between the north-south corridor and the hall system; I suspect that (as at GRN H-e) there was a doorway from the porch's eastern flank, but this cannot be confirmed.

The palace here at PHYL is very close in size to GRN H-e, and both are similar in the proportional allotment of cellular clusters: the megaron hall system occupies in both cases one-half the overall width; the remaining width is divided between the corridor and the small cell row.[29] It is of interest that the width of the PHYL compound, *c.* 13.50 meters, is identical in size to the width of the Delian compound, as well as to Mycenae (±13.60), Pylos (±13.70), and Gla (±13.50).[30] Such correspondences could hardly be seen as coincidental. We will examine these metrological correspondences more directly below.

On the Greek mainland, the contemporary Third Citadel of Tiryns (Late Bronze IIIb/c) includes, on its upper terrace, a splendid Mycenaean palatial compound whose central component is a large megaron hall of elegant proportions (Figure A.12).[31] It consists of a double porch divided by a pier-and-door partition (PDP) system built in the Minoan style and an inner hall twice as long as each of the outer porches. The hall features a large circular hearth surrounded by four columns which would have supported an upper gallery and a clerestory roof beyond. The internal arrangement is replicated in the great megaron halls of state at Mycenae and Pylos, though the latter two are less finely and accurately constructed.[32]

Of interest to our present discussion is the smaller (residential) compound adjacent to the east, shown in the gridded area in the following plan (Figure A.13).

This latter compound, which we shall call Tiryns B, replicates the now familiar Aegean megaroid compounds seen elsewhere, and its plan closely resembles GRN H-e. It comprises a megaron hall and porch to the west, a north-south corridor to the east (as well as a circumferential continuation to the north and west), and *four* small cells beyond. The compound fronts to the south on an enclosed (and partly colonnaded) courtyard twice as wide east-west as it is north-south.

Clearly the domestic or residential quarter of the palace (in contrast to the larger hall of state), this compound is connected with other parts of the palace through circumferential corridors which bypass the main megaron to the west, and connect with a small private entrance through a long narrow north-south corridor opening onto the grand covered propylon entrance to the south. The areas to the east of the compound are built upon a platform whose eastern side consists of an indented series of wall facades higher than the areas further east. Indeed, the outer trace of the palace as a whole resembles the indented trace of a typical Minoan palace building, and it is not unlikely that the Tirynthian compound owes some of its architectonic articulation to Cretan prototypes.

Nevertheless, the structure is thoroughly Mycenaean in internal organization, an organization inherited from prototypes extending back a millennium in the northeastern Aegean.

A comparison with Figure A.1 above will reveal that the measurements of TRN B and GRN H-e are very nearly identical in overall extent, and our analysis of the measurements of both structures indicates that both were laid out on planning grids of identical modular sizes: Tiryns on a grid of squares 2.20 on a side, Gournia on a grid 2.10 on a side. Each grid square represents eight Minoan units of ±0.27.[33] It is of interest that the larger Tirynthian megaron hall was laid out, according to our analyses, on a grid of squares 3.30 on a side (= 12 Minoan units of 0.27). A comparison of the grids of TRN A and TRN B will reveal that the larger megaron is a modular blow-up of the plan of the smaller (12-unit grid squares vs. 8-unit grid squares), while the absolute number of grid squares in each is identical. The plan of TRN B, then, is exactly two-thirds that of TRN A.

It appears inescapable that the same craftsmen — or at least craftsmen working from the same pattern-book — were involved in the construction of Tiryns and Gournia H-e, for there are too many details of organization and modular proportioning of elements shared by the two compounds to be coincidental. The two buildings, in other words, are contextual variants on a common theme.[34]

During the LM III period the site of the LM I small palace at Haghia Triadha was evidently transformed into a Mycenaean palatial citadel of a type closely resembling Tiryns, if we are to judge from the appearance of the LM III remains overlying the HTR villa and settlement (Figure A.14).

A comparison with the plan of Tiryns above (Figure A.13) reveals that in addition to the megaron proper — walls A/B/C/D — both plans include a stoa-like row of magazines or stores (*mercato*) outside the grounds of the palace proper. In both cases, the stoa buildings consist of a north-south row of rectangular cells opening onto a continuous portico: that at TRN comprising a file of columns interspersed by a square pier near the northern end, that at HTR comprising a file of columns and piers in alternation. In both cases, evidently, this row of cells lies along the eastern flank of the main approach to the citadel.

It is of interest that the HTR megaron is comparable in size to TRN A, although its internal disposition is unclear. Its outer porch appears to have been to the east. It may also be noted that the HTR megaron stands over the (filled-in) ruins of the old Minoan villa, whose outer indented trace would then have formed the outer citadel flank to the new Mycenaean-style megaroid palace. In appearance, then, HTR would have resembled TRN, for the latter palace was constructed upon a terraced platform whose outer retaining walls were indented to conform to the outlines of the Mycenaean buildings within, while the indented trace of the HTR citadel would have been a fortuitous survival and incorporation of truly Minoan facades, orchestrated into the present construction.

HTR is the only Cretan settlement which we may plausibly claim was transformed into a large-scale Mycenaean-style palatial compound during the LM III period. But here, only the probable hall of state remains (the counterpart to TRN A), while at GRN, only a residential megaroid compound is known (the counterpart − indeed the near mirror-image of − TRN B). Whether a GRN H-e-type companion to HTR existed here (or, conversely, a TRN A-type companion to GRN He existed at Gournia) is a matter of speculation: we would expect the 'residential quarter' of the HTR megaron to have existed somewhere beneath the unexcavated area to the south (under the chapel of Haghios Gheorghios in the plan).

Before tying up these speculations into a comparative tabulation of features, let us look at one more Cretan construction, at Karphi, on the isolated northwestern rim of the foothills surrounding the Lassithi Plateau, across the plain from the LM III palace at Plati (Figure A.15).

Karphi was evidently a refugee-town, built during the transitional period between the Bronze and Iron Ages.[35] It is not only post-Minoan in date, but in effect post-Mycenaean. The settlement consists of two abruptly contrastive parts: a lower labyrinthine town to the west, and an upper compound to the east.

While the eastern compound is largely ruined, we may see here (if our modular reconstructions are any indication) the pieces of a large unified compound, perhaps 'palatial' in nature. On the northern end is a row of three halls, the two eastern of which are clearly megaroid in inspiration. The halls open onto a courtyard(?) which, if the measurements are any indication, was twice as long north-south as it was wide east-west (100 by 50 Minoan units of +0.34): the canonical proportions for a Minoan-style palace. The cluster of cells to the west of the court also measures 100 units north-south (with the allowances noted in the plan) by (possibly) 50 units east-west.[36] The wall-fragments to the south of the court also measure 50 units north-south. Nothing remains of construction to the east of the court.

By contrast to the remainder of the town, this megaroid palace(?) looks like the residence of the town's rulers (or may simply have been a public civic center). It is of interest that the proportions of the compound replicate those of an old Minoan megastructure while being half its absolute size.[37] In effect, Karphi is the obverse of Plati: whereas the latter puts an Aegean-type compound with Minoan internal articulations into a Minoan palatial framework, Karphi inserts a canonical megaron cluster into a Minoan palatial frame but in a Mycenaean-like courtyard position.[38] The Karphi compound (seen from our Minoan perspective) appears to be a curious blend of old and new elements.

Karphi is half a millennium in time and worlds away in spirit from the built environment of the MM III/LM I period discussed in the text, and stands at the threshold of profound changes in Cretan society which saw the inexorable assimilation of the old Minoan population into a Doric Greek hegemony. But even here we may venture to read traces of a Minoan architectonic sensibility kindled nearly a thousand years before with the foundation of the Minoan palaces.

The processes of assimilation of Aegean architectonic features began in the LM III period with the appearance of megaroid buildings at the close of the second palace period on Crete. The plans above, and their comparative tabulations below, indicate that at least some parts of the island become drawn into a Mycenaean Greek orbit to play a wider role in the military and mercantile activities of the Greek-speaking warlords in the eastern Mediterranean. But if we are to believe Homer, even during this late period Crete remains a powerful and important center of Aegean culture.[39]

The tables below bring together our observations on those features of architectonic organization shared by the megaroid compounds discussed briefly above. It will be clear that the structures noted above are essentially contextual variations on a common structural frame, consisting of a megaron hall (A), a narrow north-south corridor contiguous with it (B) and a rank of four or more small cells arrayed parallel to the latter and opening directly onto each other (C).

Moreover, it will be seen that this pattern of association remains constant despite reversals of the ABC order; in some instances, the megaron hall is to the left of entry into the compound, in other cases to the right of the associated small chambers. In addition it will be seen that the general proportions of the components of the compound tend to remain constant: invariably, the hall is twice as deep as its porch (the latter normally being as wide as it is deep), and the hall-and-porch as a whole occupies one-half the width of the entire cluster.

These proportional relationships become especially clear once we understand a basic fact about Bronze Age construction: namely, that buildings are laid out and constructed on simple planning-grids (the *mammisi* or plan-nets of contemporary Egypt),[40] and that to understand the proportional allotment of spaces in Bronze Age structures it is necessary to understand their modular ground-plan organizations. In the plans above we have included a series of modular planning grids, the evidence for which is derived from our own detailed measurements of these buildings in the field.[41]

The student of Mycenaean architecture will note that such palatial compounds as Mycenae, Pylos and Gla are omitted in our comparative analyses. This omission is intentional, for in many respects what those structures have to add to the present argument is redundant: both Pylos and Mycenae have, in addition to their great megaron halls of state, smaller residential megaroid clusters equivalent in organization to that seen at Tiryns (which we therefore take as our representative example). At Mycenae, the House of Columns to the east of the great megaron is clearly the equivalent Aegean megaroid compound, with a smaller megaron, court, and rank of four small cells. A similar situation may be read at Pylos.[42]

In the tables below, the following abbreviations are used: GRN (Gournia He), PLT (Plati), TR HS (Troy, House HS), LMN (Lemnos, Poliokhni, Megaron 605), ASN (Asine compound BD), PVP (Pavlopetri, Elaphonisis, structure C-IV), DL (Delos, Mycenaean palatial[?] compound), PHYL (Phylakopi, Melos, Mycenaean palatial compound), TRN B (Tiryns megaron cluster B).

Table A.1.   *Megaroid compounds: components and proportions*

		GRN	PLT	TRHS	LMN	ASN	PVP	DL	PHYL	TRNB
1.	porch-to-hall	1:2	1:2[a]	1:2	1:2	1:3	1:2	?	1:2	1:2
2.	megaron-to-whole	½	½	½[b]	½	½	½	?	½	½
3.	ABC pattern	ABC	ACB	BAC	BCA[c]	CBA	BAC	?	ABC	ABC
4.	back rooms?	X	X	X	X	X	X	X	X	X
5.	rear projection	X	O	O[d]	O	O	O	O	X	X

Table A.1. (contd.)

a.   Understanding the 'porch' in this Minoan hall system as the area from the central pillar to the court; if understanding it as from the PDP to the court, then the proportions are 1:1.
b.   One-half of width including small cells to left only.
c.   Corridor (B) not defined strictly except as a passage between the small cells (C) and cells to the west.
d.   Projection possibly fortuitous in shape, to accomodate line of back street.

The suggested standard units employed in the layout of these structures are as follows:

GRN :	0.263	(x 8	= module square of 2.10)	
PLT :	0.310	(x 12 =	,,	3.60)
TRHS:	?		?	
LMN :	?		?	
ASN :	0.275	(x 10 =	,,	2.75)
PVP :	0.350	(x 5 =	,,	1.70)
DL :	0.270	(x 10 =	,,	2.70)
PHYL:	0.340	(x 10 =	,,	3.40)
TRNB:	0.270	(x 8 =	,,	2.20)

A complete discussion of the metrological aspects of modular planning will be found below in Part Two.

NOTES

1.   For Mycenae, see A.J.B. Wace, *Mycenae: An Archaeological History and Guide* (1949) (reprinted 1964); G.E. Mylonas, *Mycenae and the Mycenaean Age* (1966); id., *Mycenae: A Guide to its Ruins and its History,* third edition (1972). For Tiryns, see H. Schliemann, *Tiryns* (1884); K. Müller, *Tiryns, III, Die Architektur der Burg und des Palastes* (1930); C. Karo, *Führer durch Tiryns* (1934); W. Dörpfeld, 'Kretische, Mykenische, und homerische Paläste', *Ath.Mitt* 30 and 32 (1905 and 1907). For Pylos, see C. Blegen and M. Rawson, *The Palace of Nestor at Pylos* (1966).
2.   See the comparative study by J. Mellaart, 'Notes on the architectural remains of Troy I and II', *AS* VI (1960): 131-162. Plans of Troy here are taken from Mellaart; compare C. Blegen, *Troy,* Volume I (1950).
3.   H. Boyd-Hawes, *op.cit.*: 23.

Table A.2.   *Megaroid compounds: dimensions and modular organization*

	Dimensions NS x EW	Hall NS x EW	Porch EW x NS	Module square = x stand. units	Overall modular config. in stand. units
1. GRN	12.30 x 12.60	8.40 x 6.30	6.30 x 4.20	2.10 = 8	64 x 64
2. PLT	14.40 x 14.40	10.80 x 7.20	7.20 x 1.80[a]	3.60 = 12	48 x 48
3. TRHS	15.50 x 15.50[b]	8.00 x 4.00	4.00 x 4.00	?	?
4. LMN	13.50 x 9.00	9.00 x 4.50	4.50 x 4.50	?	?
5. ASN	11.00 x 11.00[c]	8.00 x 5.50	5.50 x 2.75	2.75 = 10	40 x 40[d]
6. PVP	10.50 x 10.50[e]	7.00 x 3.50	3.50 x 1.70	1.70 = 5	30 x 30
7. DL	21.70 x 13.50	?	?	2.70 = 10	50 x 80[f]
8. PHYL	13.50 x 13.50[g]	10.20 x 6.80[h]	6.80 x 3.40	3.40 = 10	40 x 40
9. TRNB	13.20 x 13.20[i]	8.80 x 6.60	6.60 x 4.40	2.20 = 8	64 x 64

a. See above, Table A.1, Note a.
b. Length and width approximate.
c. Dimensions approximate, scaled from published plan.
d. Modular solution, therefore, conjectural.
e. *Idem.*
f. 5:8 proportions overall; plan unclear.
g. Size exclusive of projections.
h. See grid plan: length includes width of wall between hall and porch.
i. Size exclusive of projections, megaron only.

4.   F. Oelmann, 'Ein Achäisches Herrenhaus auf Kreta', *JdI* XXVII (1912): 38ff. The author compares GRN He with the plans of Phylakopi on Melos and of Tiryns on the mainland. Plati had not yet been excavated. Oelmann was more concerned with possible historical/ethnic linkages between Crete and the mainland than with more strictly architectonic implications.

5.   See the tabulations below.

6.   *BSA* XX (1913-1914): 1-13, plan, Plate I.

7.   See D. Hogarth, 'The Psykhró cave', *BSA* VI (1900): 94; N. Kontoleon, 'The birth of Zeus', *KrKhr* XV: 291. On the question of orientation, see the excavation photographs, *BSA* XX (1913-1914): Plate IVb.

8.   See also the comments by J.W. Graham, *PC*: 71.

9.   See our discussion of Kato Zakro above, Chapter II.

10. See above, Figure II.46.

11. At Knossos: the cluster to the north of the Hall of the Double Axes area (above, Figure II.28).

12. Dated (*Handbook*: 36) to LM Ib/LM II. Evans regarded the 'throne room' as a 'revolutionary intrusion' into the palatial fabric. Palmer (*A New Guide to the Palace at Knossos:* 66ff) regards it as being built in the LM III A.2 period, which would make it approximately *contemporary* to the Plati cluster. A glance at the comparable area of Mallia (Figure II.37) indicates what the 'throne room' area at Knossos may have looked like before this later period.

13. Much depends, of course, on which chronological schema we accept: Evans' or Palmer's. There are problems of detail with both. The important point here for our purposes is the architectonic identity of the two clusters.

14. Note that at Kato Zakro, the hall system (east) is situated directly upon the Central Court (although turning its back and side to it); we might (impressionistically) consider the KZ cluster as 'transitional' with respect to the new arrangements at Knossos and Plati, and the old system seen in the earlier (LM I) palace rebuildings at Knossos, Phaistos and Mallia, where the hall systems are situated at the outer borders of the palatial fabric.

15. See above, Note 2.

16. Mellaart, *op.cit.*: Figure 3, p. 137.

17. Preserved mainly to the south and southeast; *ibid.*: 138.

18. Mellaart, *op.cit.*: 139ff and Figure 4, p. 140.

19. *Ibid.*: 141ff and Figure 5, p. 141.

20. Unlike the Mycenaean palatial court arrangements, however, the Troy II court is rather small. Nevertheless we may see in this plan the early seeds of the later Mycenaean organization.

21. Mellaart, *op.cit.*: Figure 9, p. 151, and restored plan, Figure 10, p. 153.

22. It is unclear whether this 'back projection' is isomorphic with that at GRN H-e, for the back walls of the structure appear to have been set so as to conform to a back street coming east-west at a skewed angle. Nevertheless, such a projection need not have been built at all (thereby making the back street even wider), but it was.

23. L. Bernabò Brea, *Poliochni I* (1964): tables 7 and 8; town plan; *BdA* (1957): Figure 2, p. 194.

24. The well-known 'House of Tiles' at Lerna on the Greek mainland (Early Bronze II), and the less well-known, recently uncovered analogue to the latter at Akrovitika in Messenia, while superficially similar in groundplan, are nevertheless not canonical megara: see P. Themelis, 'Protoelladikon Megaron eis Akrovitika Messenias', *AAE* III.3 (1970): 303-311, plans 1, 2, and 3.

25. O. Frodin and A. Persson, *Asine, Results of the Swedish Excavations of 1922-1930* (1938): plan, Figure 42.

26. See *ILN* (February 22, 1969): 22-23, plan, Figure 5, p. 23.

27. H. Gallet de Santerre, *Délos Primitive et Archaique* (1958): 71-87, plan, Plate D; P. Bruneau and J. Ducat, *Guide de Délos* (1965): 85ff, plan, Figure 9.

28. T. Atkinson, R. Bosanquet *et al., Excavations at Phylakopi in Melos* (*JHS* Supplement I) (1904): 55-61, plan II.

29. See our tabulation of measurements in the tables below.

30. D. Preziosi, *MPPAO* (1968): Gla: 587-589, Mycenae: 600-606, Pylos: 624-627.

31. See above, Note 1. Our own measurements of the remains confirm those of the excavators of the palace compounds.

32. Discussed in D. Preziosi, *MPPAO* (1968), *loc.cit.* (see above, Note 30). The watercolor restoration by P. de Jong of the Pylian palace interior (C. Blegen and M. Rawson, *op.cit.*: Figures 418 and 419) is proportionally inaccurate and chromatically fantastic.

33. On Minoan metrology in general, see Part Two below, and our tabulations at the end of this Appendix.

34. Simply because the two structures reveal so many correspondent features is no proof that the two buildings were planned and built by the same craftsmen: our point here is that the two compounds were designed, laid out, and constructed in the same manner. They may in fact have been built generations apart. Indeed, as we are seeing, the Aegean megaroid compound is a highly conservative formation, having been replicated in essentially the same manner for about a millennium. Whether all these megaroid compounds were in fact built by the 'same' ethnic population, speaking the 'same' language is quite another matter. I personally suspect that this was the case, although the evidence is far from unambiguous.

35. J.D.S. Pendlebury, 'Excavations in the Plain of Lasithi, III: Karphi', *BSA* XXXVIII (1937-1938): 57-145, especially 69-98.

36. As we shall see in Part Two, the Minoans evidently used two standard units of measure: one ±0.27, another ±0.34, a shorter 'foot' and a longer 'foot'; comparable situations exist in contemporary Egypt (e.g. standard cubit vs. royal cubit).

37. The Central Courts of the larger palaces (Knossos, Mallia, Phaistos) are, as we shall see below, 100 units EW by 200 units NS.

38. As we have seen, Mycenaean (Aegean) megaroid compounds are situated at the northern end of a courtyard, although Mycenaean courtyards are generally wider east-west than they are long north-south (in contrast to Minoan palatial courts, which are longer north-south – if by 'north-south' we understand a canonical alignment toward some prominent landscape feature. Note that Plati's court is oriented WNW - ESE).

39. Recall the huge contributions of men and ships to the Achaean efforts against Troy during the Trojan War.

40. See A. Badawy, *Ancient Egyptian Architectural Design* (1965), introductory sections.

41. Except for: Plati, Asine, Pavlopetri.

42. At Pylos, it is the *main* megaron which reveals the canonical ABC plan of hall, corridor and four chambers left to right.

III

The Elements of Minoan Architecture

INTRODUCTION

The analyses above have illustrated certain formative organizational features of the Minoan corpus. We have seen that there exist a variety of relationships which forms enter into under specific contextual conditions. Here we shall consider the problem of the nature of such formative units themselves: is there, in other words, a 'vocabulary' of forms specific to Minoan construction, which by their juxtaposition and association generate the spatial compositions we have been considering? What are the basic formative units or elements of the Minoan corpus?

In a general sense, these questions are complementary to those asked and partially answered in the preceding sections of our inquiry. Recall that our definition of the Minoan hall system included the following features:[1]

1. a cluster of three cells of types (a,b,c);
2. aligned longitudinally (a) + (b) + (c);
3. lateral to direction of access;
4. positioned at least one cell removed from primary access;
5. with initial primary access at not more than two points;
6. not forming a cul-de-sac.

If we were to specify the elemental components of the hall system cluster, then, such a specification would include (1) not only space-cells of a particular conformation (types (a), (b) and (c); but also (2) a certain syntagmatic relationship among themselves; as well as (3) certain geometric and topological relationships to other cells or cell-clusters.

What defines a cell cluster or matrix, as our analyses have shown, is principally a *pattern of relationship* among entities of specific types. We have seen that this pattern is constant despite (A) the absolute size of the component units; (B) the geometric configuration of the units; (C) the details of material construction of such units; and (D) the orientation of the cluster of units with respect to other units. Additionally, the number of piers or columns articulating a PDP or a colonnade is variable, as is the absolute internal positioning of the units: as long as the three component cells are aligned in a row, it does not appear to matter if the lightwell cell (a) is on the eastern, western, southern, or northern end.

The definition of component formative units in a corpus is in part a function of the level of organization one is addressing. What is a part at one level or from a certain perspective may be a whole at another level. Thus, from the point of view of the hall system considered as a unit, that unit is seen as being composed of certain component features (cells of certain general types, in certain topological and geometric relationships). From another perspective, the space-cell itself forms a certain kind of unity, composed of sets of contributory elements (walls, floors, ceilings, partitions such as PDPs or colonnades, doorways, windows, internal articulation, and so forth).

It becomes immediately apparent that what constitutes the corpus as a system is not merely a set (whether finite or transfinite) of formal entities, which combine to form larger aggregates, themselves combining with yet larger sets of elemental aggregates; rather, the system includes both *elements* (however formally defined) and *relationships* among elements. But as we have seen, the latter participate as much in the definition of significant entities in the system as do the former. What constitutes a 'hall system' is as much the presence of certain material formations (e.g. PDPs) as a certain diagram or pattern of arrangement of formations. It is clear from our extended study of Minoan buildings in the previous Chapter that merely the presence of a given conformation is insufficient to generate a hall system (or any other notable type of cell-cluster or matrix). Perhaps the principal determinant here is a certain pattern of relationship which transcends particulars of size, color, texture, materials, orientation, alignment, *vis-à-vis* other entities, geometric morphology, etc. We would be wise, then, not to reify unduly our picture of the hall system or any other matrix of cells.

The Minoan hall system, then, can best be defined not as the addition and juxtaposition of geometric forms of invariant types, but rather as a syntactic or syntagmatic pattern *per se,* which alone is constant across a wide variety of material and geometric realizations.

Such a pattern of association among cellular conformations — which we shall henceforth refer to as a *matrix* — must be taken as one of a number of significative units in the system of the Minoan corpus. It exists, as we have seen, in opposition to a variety of other *matrices* characteristic of the system of the corpus.

A matrix may be defined generically as a stable diagram or pattern of relationships among cells, characteristic of a certain time and place in the built environment of a society. Such entities are chronologically or diachronically variable: as has become clear in our inquiry above, and is further elucidated below in Part Two, the Minoan hall matrix changes over time, to be replaced later in the Late Minoan period by another matrix formation, the so-called megaron or megaroid cluster.[2]

For the present we will not be concerned with such patterns of change, but will seek to focus upon the sets of formative relationships manifested synchronically or co-presently during the period in which the data examined above is principally manifest: namely, the so-called Second Palatial period, corresponding to the ceramic phases Middle Minoan III/Late Minoan I.[3]

MATRICES, CELLS AND FORMS

It has been suggested that the matrix, as a component significative element in the Minoan corpus, comprises a pattern of association of cells. What, then, is a 'cell'?

In the most generic sense, we have used the term cell or space-cell to denote a volumetric conformation defined by co-present mass forms. In other words, a space form (normally rectilinear in the corpus) bounded and defined by peripheral mass forms (walls, ceilings, floors, colonnades, etc.). It is clear that every Minoan building comprises at least several such conformations. In the case of the palaces, the plans we have examined contained (e.g. at Knossos) at least several hundred such entities, and may originally have contained two or three times that number.[4] All in all, we have looked at over a thousand such entities, of a wide variety of sizes and internal configurations. Can we specify what is common to all these objects, and in so doing observe certain patterns of similarity, certain cellular 'types' which tend to recur across structures of varying sizes and types?

Clearly, the *cell,* by its omnipresence in the corpus,[5] must be considered as one of the corpus' primary formative entities, one of its fundamental 'building blocks', so to speak. But in this regard, the cell is very nearly universal in any architectonic system, and is one of the primary hallmarks of human environments.[6] Is it then the case that the cell exists as an entity which is simply appropriated by any architectural corpus, achieving differential signification by such contrasting cultural contexts? Is a cell of identical configuration and size (and even materials) in two cultures or two periods of the same culture the 'same' cell?

For a variety of reasons uncovered in the course of our analyses above this cannot be so. Indeed, as is implicit in the foregoing discussion of the hall system matrix, the significance of a cell is at least a coeval function of its internal order and its contextual association among other cells. Two 'identical' cells in different cultures or corpora are not the same entity, for their significance will vary. Indeed, perceptually they will differ, often abruptly.[7]

It must be the case that the significance of a given cellular configuration is in some manner a function of its position *vis-à-vis* the entire set of cells manifest in a given corpus. Ultimately this phenomenon is consistent with what we understand regarding the contextual apperception of simple figure-ground relationships: what is true regarding the variable perception of color in different contexts[8] will similarly be true, in a more complex fashion, for the significative perception of volumetric conformations,[9] a phenomenon well known to many generations of designers, builders and users.

Thus it is clear that the significance of a given cell is to a large degree dependent upon its contextual position with respect to other cells, both contiguous and synchronically co-present in a corpus. Moreover, it is also clear that given space-cells carry a significance established in part by allusory reference to cells of another time and place. Such allusion, additionally, may be perceptually enhanced not only by infrastructural appointments — e.g. furnishings recalling an earlier period or another culture — but also by the very geometric configuration of a cell: consider the contrastive associations adhering to space-cells with standard flat ceilings in contemporary Western buildings and to those with vaulted or semi-cylindrical ceilings.

Such contrastive oppositions are readily apparent in any cursory perusal of the built environment around oneself. Consider two cells of identical configuration (e.g. simple cubes), but with contrastive furnishings, color, surface texture, materials, or position *vis-à-vis* other cells. By the alteration of any one of these features, the significative apperception of the cell may change abruptly.

How then are we to define the 'cell'? Implicit in our usage of the term above is a co-presence of mass and volume, a mutually reciprocal and mutually defining relationship. The perception of a volume as of a particular configuration is inextricably determined by peripheral mass configurations. Conversely, a given mass form is unperceivable without peripheral space. Each is defined and articulated by the other. In a very concrete sense, a cell (understood as the contrastive co-presence of mass and space formation) exists in its own right as a certain *pattern* of relationship. In effect, any architectural structure is made up of linked templates of alternative patterning, a juxtaposition of massive and spatial components.

In architecture, this juxtapositional template is arrayed over three dimensions, themselves consisting of contrastive oppositions (high vs. low, ahead vs. behind, and right vs. left). All of the thousands of forms manifest in the corpus can be seen as occupying equivalent or contrastive positions on a sliding scale of such binarily opposed extremes: cell X contrasts with cell Y next door by being higher, deeper, or wider, whereas ceil Y contrasts with cell Z by being equivalent in height, depth, but not in lateral extent.

The real question here is the extent to which such contrasts, in an architectural corpus such as the one we are examining, represent, when plotted along a tripartite graph, a continual

gradient of change, or clusters of characteristic proportions forming an internally contrastive system in its own right. In other
words, is there a pattern of constancy among the thousands of
cells in the Minoan corpus with respect to geometric configuration? Is there a limited number of such cellular configurations
such that the entire sum of configurations can be seen as contextual variants of some limited set? Or is it the case that there are
no such patterns; that each cell differs from the next by minimal
degrees of internal size and proportion from the smallest to the
largest?

Possibly one of the most important discoveries in connection
with the study of Minoan architecture has been the fact that (A)
all of the cellular configurations found in the corpus can be seen
as simple variants of a small set of basic conformations and proportions, and that (B) this limited set of forms reveals an internally coherent orderliness:[10] the set of forms, in other words,
comprises a system in its own right, in opposition to systems of
other corpora.

Again, it is the case that we come up against a fact of overriding
importance: namely, that what distinguishes this architectural
corpus are the patterns of association and relationship which it
manifests, rather than a material homogeneity of formation. This
becomes increasingly evident at any level of organization of the
corpus: each of its significant unities exists principally as a nexus
or pattern of relationships held in dynamic equilibrium at a given
place and time.

Seen from the perspective of the *matrix,* the *cell* constitutes a
component formation in its own right. Seen from the level of the
cell (which in this perspective exists as a pattern of relationships
of certain types), the individual *form* constitutes a significative
entity. But as we have just noted, a given *form* is itself a bundle
of relationships (with respect, that is, to its geometric morphology).

Let us now attempt to specify the nature of such relationships
at various levels of organization in the corpus.

We may distinguish significative units in the corpus (that is to
say, those unities which are defined by, and reciprocally define,
the overall system manifested by the set of extant formations) at
various levels or scales of organization. Each type of unity exists

to cue the perception of differences in meaningfulness. Each unit of a given type will cue the perception of a certain domain of significance. Such domains may be broad or narrow, depending upon the given corpus. Thus a cellular configuration of a given type will canonically be associated with a certain range of signification and function, in contrast to different configurations which specify contrastive ranges of association.

In the cluster of cells whose characteristic patterns of juxtaposition endow a functional unity among those cells (and which pattern we have termed the hall system *matrix*), each cell may be seen as contrasting with its partners in terms of its function. Cell (a), contrasting with its adjacent partners (formally) by being unroofed and paved, serves to admit light and ventilation to its neighbors, both within and without the system ('lightwell'); 'enclosed court'). Cell (b), which contrasts with the former by being roofed, is furthermore capable of being closed off from cell (c), an entirely interior cell. Cell (b) serves as a transitional cell between inside and outside, comprising a porch or porticoed hall. Only cell (c) can be closed off from its neighbors completely. While we cannot specify the precise range of activities mapped onto each cell, since we are dealing with a non-extant corpus, we can state that there is a significance to this mutable gradation of openness, communication or accessibility. It is clear that this suite of cells comprised a major focus of private activity for the inhabitants of a house, corresponding no doubt to the principal common living spaces of our own dwellings. It is evident by associated finds in some remains that the hall matrix is often serviced by adjacent areas of food preparation and storage; hence it is reasonable to assume that communal dining took place in the system; either outdoors (in cell (a)), on the porch (b), or indoors, depending upon the season and disposition of the inhabitants. We do not know if people slept here normally; most likely sleeping took place principally on the second storey in less communal quarters.

While each cell, both in this particular matrix and throughout a structure, would be associated with a given domain of usage or function, it need not necessarily be the case that such usages could not overlap given formal divisions of a house. We must assume that any such structure would prescribe rather than determine usage or reading, such prescriptions being in some sense a manifestation of attitudes held in common and conventionally by a society. Every house would be a contextual variation on the constancies of such practices. Thus we may speak of the 'function' of a given cell in terms of a dynamic equilibration of dominances of prescription, according to generic patterns of expectancy characteristic to a given society. A building is made to be used (rather than only to be looked at), and it is the patterns of its usage which endow a particular structure with a system of meanings, references and connotations. Such patterns, crystallized by a structure's formal organization, permit a range of usefulness somewhere between completely idiosyncratic appropriation and completely predetermined usage. The structure of a house permits a certain range of affordances, and such affordances are constrained by that structural framework. While one can use any space cell in a building for a very wide range of activities, not every cell will afford every kind of activity. It is precisely this *domain of constraints* which generates a systematicity in the relationships underlying and defining a given structure.

Within the vast and diversified set of relationships manifested by a given corpus, certain patterns or ranges of relationship define a limited hierarchy of organizational levels. While it has been assumed that one such level of organization is the self-contained house structure itself, we should be wary of taking what may well be a principally lexical or verbal category and assuming that it is directly and discretely mapped onto architectonic formation. Considering the complexity of Minoan structures, by now familiar, wherein clusters of cells which are materially contained within a structural framework may not necessarily be part of a functional unity with the remainder of a building, levels of organization beyond the matrix may not be strictly coterminous with our concept of the self-contained 'house'.

In other words, because of the evident fact that in a number of Minoan buildings — both large and small — there exist portions which are only directly accessible from exterior spaces (and, conversely, there are cell clusters structurally contained within adjacent and non-contiguous buildings which are functionally integrated to a given building), the structurally unified building may not *per se* be a significative unity in its own right.

A separate structure, in the Minoan corpus, will characteristically contain groups of semi-autonomous matrices intercommunicating in a variety of ways. As we have seen above in Chapter II, it is evident that there exist certain patterns of association among matrices themselves, as specified by certain formative features. A hall system is accessed only on its side flank; other matrices have other syntactic associations. Certain clusters of cells invariantly stand in certain specifiable relationships both to each other and to an entrance into the structure itself. Indeed, certain cells (e.g. the so-called 'pillar crypts') are invariably at a certain remove from a building's entrance, beyond a minimum number of thresholds (no matter the size, configuration, or absolute placement of the latter).[11]

The point here is that at an increasingly greater scale, the nature of significative unities becomes increasingly diagrammatic and abstract. The patterns of relationship *among* matrices have been seen to be broader and looser than the patterns of relationships *within* matrices. The great variety among Minoan structures as a whole stems from just this very property, making it seem that each Minoan building is a virtuoso piece of its own. At yet as has been demonstrated above, this is in fact a false impression: the simple house at Tou Vrakhnou O Lakkos, the mansion called House C at Tylissos, and the Palace of Knossos reveal identical underlying principles of organization, tendencies toward formative organization operative in various ways at every level of consideration.

That there are constancies in the patterns of relationship among matrices has been clearly seen in our analyses of Minoan buildings of more than one matrix in size (which includes nearly all we have seen). We may term such 'matrices of matrices' *compounds,* and note that one of the salient features of a Minoan compound is that its definition is principally *topological* rather than structural or geometric. In other words, it is *not necessarily the case* that such a unity is coterminous with a geometrically and materially isolable structural frame. Thus, compound ≠ house, even though there *may* be examples where this is in fact the case. Tylissos A-B comprise a single compound, even though they are separate structures.[12] Sklavokampos may have comprised two separate compounds, though it comprises a single freestanding structure.[13]

We may suggest, then, that among the levels of organization in the Minoan corpus there exist (1) compounds; (2) matrices; and (3) cells. At the same time, it is clear that a matrix may consist of a single cell, just as a compound may consist of a single matrix (and in some instances a single cell). In other words, the hierarchy of organizational levels in a corpus is not composed of increasingly 'larger' formal or material entities, but rather of patterns of relationship. In precisely the same manner, an entire verbal utterance, an entire 'text' may comprise a single word, which itself may consist of but a single phoneme (e.g. the Latin imperative / ī / *go*!).[14]

It was observed above in Chapter II that everything about an architectonic formation is significant in some way, but that not everything is significant in the same way. In the present discussion, it has been noted that the significance of a given cell is connected in some way with its formal configuration, which distinguishes that cell from other cells which are contrastively significant. By contrast, the significance of a given matrix lies more in its internal patterns of relationships among its components (cells). What is significant about a matrix, in other words, is its distinctive associative geometry; not necessarily the particular identity and configuration of its component parts, which may be wide or tall, stone or timber, red or yellow, rough or smooth, square or oblong in plan.

With regard to the individual cell, we have noted that its formal organization appears to carry a more 'direct' significance: association with given behavioral domains, connotative symbolism, etc. By this is meant that what constitutes a matrix is *not necessarily* the presence of specific formative details, but rather (and principally) the manner whereby certain ranges of such details are composed. What constitutes the cell as a significative unity in the corpus is the presence of certain formative details in characteristic relationships: in the present corpus, generally a six-sided mass frame delimiting an interior space form. But in a manner analogous to the matrix, what constitutes a cell is *not necessarily* the presence of given formative details, but rather a characteristic pattern of relationship among certain kinds of formative details. A cell may be tall or short, broad or narrow, deep or shallow, stone or brick or timber (or any number of combinations), heavy materials or light materials, colored materials or uncolored, rough or smooth, doors in its walls or in the ceiling or floor, windows or no windows, etc.

But is a *cell* coterminous with a 'room'? Clearly not, or rather *not necessarily*: it is evident that the Minoan built environment incorporates rooms, courtyards, streets, gardens, open-air sanctuaries on mountain tops, and minimally articulated caves in the ground and on the sides of hills. There exists, in other words, a wide range of possible realizations, from the maximally enclosed room to the minimally delimited farm plot. There are no 'empty spaces' within the structure of a built environment, but rather an extended and contiguous web of cellular differentiations associated with contrastive functions and behavioral affordances. While there may be limits to a settlement *per se,* a boundary (fixed or loose) beyond the last farm plot, there may be a peak or cave sanctuary several kilometers removed from the latter, which is topologically and functionally part of the network of architectonic spaces of the settlement zone proper.

Thus the definition of a Minoan settlement is not necessarily coterminous with the extent of its architectural framework.

But how can we specify the nature of the *cell* as a significative unit in the corpus, given such contextual variables? It has been noted above that the minimal properties of a cell include a patterned alternation of mass and space formation. What constitutes a cell, then, is not necessarily four walls, ceiling, floor, and space within, but rather a spatial locus or zone delimited in some way — enough for perceptual affordance within the conventions of a given society — by a mass formation. Conversely, we may assert that a cell may comprise the *obverse* of the latter — namely some distinct and isolated mass formation or locus delimited by a peripheral spatial zone — for example a boundary marker in a field, a votive shrine consisting of an isolated pillar, emblem, or solid mound, etc.[15] even an old and hallowed tree in a field.[16]

Because we are dealing with a non-extant corpus, identifiable manifestations of the latter are minimal: our attention is focussed principally upon space-forms delimited by articulated masses. But our point here is that what constitutes the *cell* as a significative unit in the Minoan corpus, what comprises its chief perceptual hallmark, is an alternative patterning of mass and space formation wherein the material identity and configuration of the mass component is highly variable (within, of course, the limits defined by the corpus itself),[17] and the configurations of the spatial component are also flexible.

Thus while the cell itself may carry a direct signification, it is composed of elements whose composition and interrelationship exist principally for perception: the only significance of the alternation of mass and space is with respect to the perceptual definition of the cell. This is not to say, however, that the particular set of articulations of a mass formation — or of a space formation — may not themselves be directly significative (within the conventional bounds as specified by a given corpus); rather the pattern of alternation and sequential *juxtaposition* universal in all architectonic corpora is itself primarily perceptually significant. It is a device whose architectonic significance is to 'build' units which are themselves directly significative (i.e. cells).

This alternative mass-space patterning constitutes a patterned relationship among mass and space forms. It does not specify which particular mass or space forms are to be sequentially (and tridimensionally) juxtaposed. Rather, it exists as a perceptual bifurcation of the entire set of forms (both mass and space) of which cells are composed. Other aspects of human culture exhibit analogous organizations.[18] What, then, are these sets of *forms*?

A detailed and comprehensive survey of the vast number of cells constituting the Minoan corpus has revealed that there exists a limited number of minimal forms, whose combination, juxtaposition, and transformation generate all possible conformations which characterize the corpus. It is this set of findings which is the subject of the next section.

MINIMAL UNITS IN MINOAN ARCHITECTURE

A perusal of the plans analyzed above in Chapter II will reveal a multitude of particular formations: walls, columns, piers, ceilings, windows, floors, stairs, benches, pavements, recesses, silos, causeways, balustrades, etc. But even a cursory glance will suggest that while the list of such entities is not infinite, there appears to be a very great gradation in size, materials, placement, orientation, colors, and even internal proportions. How can we specify the properties and characteristic features of any one without having our examples blend into any other? Doesn't it appear that the entire corpus consists simply of 'material' *per se,* stretched this way and that under so many possible transformations that to divide any one from any other would be a tour de force on the part of the analyst?

In fact this has not proved to be the case; a fact which is only verifiable by an extensive and thoroughgoing study of large amounts of the corpus itself, focussed upon a specific period of time. While it might well be the case that taken as a whole, over many generations of building, the proportions and conformations of formative entities (however defined) may indeed seem to stretch and blend into each other, to blur and transform into a gradiency of formation, an examination of the corpus at any given point in its history reveals the opposite.

It is through such a comprehensive *synchronic* analysis that the systematicity of an architectonic corpus is revealed, and the dynamic equilibrium of its relationships firmly established.[19] Methodologically, how can such patterns of invariance among these relationships be established?

In order for such constancies to be clearly revealed, we must have at hand some standard measure against which to measure variation: something which will allow us to measure the sameness and difference between portions of an architectonic array. Ideally, such a measure should be compatible with, and in some way derived from, the data at hand.

A useful and powerful way to proceed would be to select portions of that array and to measure variation within such isolable portions. In other words, we may productively proceed by using a context of significative and generally replicated proportions so as to measure variation within it. Such a standard is readily at hand, namely, the space-cell itself, considered as a topological unicum (Figure III.1).

Our measure, then, will be the *cell* itself, superimposed upon the entire range of its contextual manifestations and variations. Such a metaphorical instrument can be held constant to percep-tually enhance whatever contrasts may emerge within its purview. We may then carefully and systematically take note of contrasts in formation as abrupt as those in Figure III.2, or as subtle as those shown in Figure III.3.

Moreover, we will begin to take note that in the corpus the formations in Figure III.4 occur, whereas in Figure III.5 they do not occur, and that the range of variation in the occurrence of the forms shown in Figure III.6 does not occur with respect to those in Figure III.7.

And in a like manner, by systematically isolating all groups of formations which occur in the composition of the cell, we may begin to see that the entire range of subcellular formations in the corpus consists of a fairly limited number of entities or minimal formative units. We will see that certain characteristic patterns of association occur among certain forms, to the exclusion of others, and that it is the patterns of such association which in fact serve to distinguish one cell from another. We will come to understand that not only is it the case that the following two cells, which at first sight appear identical (Figure III.8), are in fact two contrastively significative formations, since they characteristically exist as components of two types of matrices with different functions (Figure III.9).

In connection with this latter point, it will become evident that the set of *forms* so isolated are in themselves primarily significant in an indirect sense. That is to say, each form serves to build larger-scale entities (cells) which are themselves directly significant. Apart from their potential to acquire direct signification in certain contexts such that their isolation from that context may cue domains of meanings otherwise associated with the context itself, such *forms* do not have meanings on their own.[20] We will take up this point again below.

In the process of analyzing the Minoan architectural corpus in this manner, it has been possible to isolate a set of minimal units (Figure III.10).

The chart shows a list of *forms* as isolated by our analysis. Each figure, however, represents not a material entity as such, but is rather an icon for a range of proportional ratios manifested by a class of formations sharing this range. The definition of each range – which stands in contrastive opposition to other ranges – is specifiable on the basis of sets of contrasting perceptual features. Form /D/, for example, is contrastively opposed to form /E/ on the basis of distinctive differences along several dimensions. In a similar fashion, form /C/ differs from /I/ and /J/.

The chart also illustrates the fact that a number of forms occur both in mass and space, and are consequently to be taken as different forms. All told, we may isolate some 18 distinct forms.[21]

The patterns of juxtaposition among forms (in three dimensions) are also specific to the Minoan corpus, and it is these patterns of association which in part contribute to the identity and distinctiveness of the corpus by contrast to other corpora at the same time period, or by contrast to the same corpus at a different point in time.

It will be clear that these *forms* are not a set of 'building blocks' in a material sense. Rather, each form is a characteristic *pattern of relationships* among certain perceptual features, along three axes of perceptual differentiation (higher vs. lower; wider vs. narrower; deeper vs. shallower). It is these patterns of relationship which comprise the minimal units in the Minoan system.

The set of forms given here do not, however, exhaust the set of minimal units in the corpus. To these we must add another set of forms not necessarily of a geometric nature — i.e. materials, coloration, texturing — which are copresent with the former. But because of the nature of the remains, such information is sketchy and minimal: we know a certain amount regarding the use of materials, and something about the Minoan use of color, but in sum not enough to begin to understand the relationships between minimal units of a geometric and non-geometric nature. However, from what information we do have regarding the use of given materials, we can begin to outline at least the nature of the interactions between geometric form and materials.

Figure III.11, for example, illustrates in summary outline the range of different materials present in the corpus.[22] Many of these distinctions, however, derive from current palpable distinctions employed by present-day inhabitants of the island (and from observations of excavators). There is no assurance that Minoan designers and builders would have made similar categories.[23] But we may perhaps try to see if there were significant distinctions in the association of given *forms* and certain materials: do certain *forms* characteristically occur with certain materials?

If we compare the occurrence of *form* /D/ with *form* /E/ with respect to certain materials, as illustrated by the connections shown in Figures III.12 and III.13, where the abbreviations are taken, in sequence, from the names shown above in Figure III.11, then it begins to become apparent that there may be certain consistencies in association among *forms* of a geometric and nongeometric nature.

But it is not yet clear if such a procedure would, given the partial state of our knowledge, succeed in isolating what to the Minoan corpus would have been significant material entities. There is, moreover, a danger here of inadvertently justifying our own lexical categories.

If the Minoan corpus resembles other architectonic systems, then it will likely be the case that certain materials may come to take on more direct signification than is evident to us here. It may turn out that for the Minoan, the use of certain materials may have had connotations of its own. We may imagine, for example, that such is the case with respect to contrasts in texture and finishing of stone; it is generally the case that the major (western) facades of great public structures such as the palatial compounds were composed of finely hewn and squared hard limestone (vs. many private structures). The presence of such material may thereby have perceptually cued (or enhanced the geometric perception of) certain social and functional contrasts.

A similar situation may have existed with respect to color. We may well imagine that there existed a 'code' of coloration which not only was indirectly significant in its own right (providing articulatory contrasts and rhythms, etc.), but may also have had certain direct connotations, such that the presence of a certain color carried more specific information about social status, building function, the function of certain matrices or cells, etc.[24]

This is all information we do not have, and without which our understanding of the organization of the Minoan architectonic system is — and will probably in part remain — incomplete. It may well be that two otherwise identical cells in the corpus — identical in their component geometric forms and materials and relative and absolute proportions — when painted different colors, may have had abruptly different significations, connotations, and usages.

It has become clear in our study of the Minoan corpus that not everything about an architectonic formation is meaningful in the same way. And yet it also becomes evident that everything is not meaningful in *every* way. Each level of organization in the system will carry certain characteristic meanings. Some of this will be redundant: what signifies the existence of a palatial compound may be a whole range of different *kinds* of formative features: colors, the use of certain materials, certain characteristic patterns of relationship among matrices, certain proportions of forms, and so forth. In connection with the nature of its perceptual address, architecture employs visually palpable means to broadcast its messages.

Nevertheless it is equally patent that each architectural corpus transmits its 'messages' in different ways: where one corpus employs color and size to signify social status, another will employ certain types of matrices. In the latter context, the means employed by the former will carry different specific connotations, or not necessarily carry connotations. Indeed, the distinctions in formation patent and obvious to users of corpus A may be imperceptible or meaningless to the users of corpus Z.

Each architectonic corpus must be examined on its own terms, and holistically. It is only in this fashion that we can come to a position wherein we can *begin* to understand the nature of its organization.[25]

NOTES

1. See above, Chapter II, and the discussions of hall systems in the palaces.
2. It will be seen that some megaroid halls — e.g. that of Plati — incorporate features of both, whereas others on Crete replicate the forms of the familiar mainland or 'Mycenaean' megara. Similarly, the great megaroid halls of some non-Cretan palatial compounds — e.g. Tiryns (Megaron A) — incorporate canonical Minoan PDP systems.
3. See above under our discussion of the major palaces, Chapter II.
4. Estimates vary; the number of cells on the second storeys of the Knossian palace may be somewhat less than those of the ground floors if, as Evans suggested, the former consisted of larger halls: see above, Chapter II.
5. At least in terms of what is extant; our knowledge of other structural aspects of Minoan construction — garden plots, farm lands, etc. — is nearly nonexistent.
6. See D. Preziosi, *Architecture, Language and Meaning: the Origins of the Built World* (The Hague, 1979): Chapters III, IV, V.
7. In this regard, see R. Arnheim, *The Dynamics of Architectural Form* (1977): Chapter I.
8. As well illustrated by the researches of Joseph Albers in his series of paintings entitled 'Homage to the Square'.

9. R. Arnheim, *op.cit.*: Chapters II, III, IV; D. Preziosi, *The Semiotics of the Built Environment* (Bloomington, 1979): Chapter II, pp. 9-12.
10. D. Preziosi, *op.cit.*: Chapter III, pp. 38-60.
11. Details discussed above, Chapter II, Table II.4.
12. See above, pp. 53-54, and Figure I.3; and below, Part Two, under Tylissos A and B.
13. Above, Chapter II, on Sklavokampos.
14. A comparative study of architectonic and linguistic systems is given explicitly in D. Preziosi, *op.cit.*: Chapter IV and Appendix B. The example here was suggested by R. Jakobson.
15. D. Preziosi, *op.cit.*: p. 15.
16. This example is suggested on the basis of some evidence for the presence of (sacred?) trees adjacent to the palaces of Knossos and Phaistos, planted in the *koulouras* of the western courtyards: see above, Chapter II, Knossos, Phaistos, Nirou Khani, with references.
17. Once again, our definitions of the *cell* conformation for each corpus must be principally in accord with the range of realizations of that formation by a corpus itself.
18. The most obvious example being, in the linguistic code, the bifurcation of phonemic units into consonantal and vocalic classes, on the basis of these contrastively opposed features. We would suggest, in other words, that just as a linguistic utterance reveals an alternative pattern of consonantal and vocalic units in a syntagmatically sequential stream, so it is the case that in an architectonic system the mass-space alternation of forms (in three dimensions) serves a similar perceptual function. There exists, in other words, a *systemic* similarity between the two systems, beneath the patent and striking differences in material realization of verbal language and built environments. A detailed discussion of this and other comparative problems will be found in D. Preziosi, *The Semiotics of the Built Environment* (1979b), and *Architecture, Language and Meaning* (1979a).
19. This is not to exclude the possibility that the diachronic development of an architectonic system will not reveal its own characteristic patterns of change and cumulative transformation: but it is clear that any serious understanding of the latter must be based upon a thorough going understanding of the former. The two axes must be balanced in a comprehensive study of architectural systems. It has not really been until the present decade that we have begun to understand, in a systematic and comprehensive fashion, the synchronic organization of built environments.
20. As is discussed in detail in D. Preziosi, *op.cit.*, the significance of such *forms* is primarily 'sense-discriminative' – i.e. perceptually discriminating – and secondarily 'sense-determinative' – i.e. simultaneously, in certain cases, carrying direct signification. Again, there are patent analogues to be found in verbal language, notably at the phonemic and distinctive-feature levels.
21. Clearly, as our knowledge of the corpus expands with the uncovery of new remains, this list will undoubtedly expand somewhat, although I suspect not by very much. To such morphological *minima* must also be added distinctive entities based upon material, color and texture, to be discussed below. The primary point to be borne in mind here is that it is out of the combination and juxtaposed sequencing of such entities that a seemingly transfinite number of cellular configurations may be generated by the corpus, in accord with constraints upon cellular types in existence at a given place and time. Thus we may expect that such a set of cellular formations which are manifested by a corpus at any one time is

itself a *subset* of all the possible formations that *might* be generated, but which, for conventional and time-specific reasons, are not.

22. As based on our field surveys. A good introduction to the use of materials in Minoan construction may be found in Graham, *PC*.

23. Such native categorizations, moreover, must be established not merely on the basis of lexical or verbal categories, but principally upon distinctions in *usage*.

24. It is entirely conceivable that in the Minoan corpus there existed certain significant patterns of color coding; given the labyrinthine complexity of many large Minoan buildings, we might expect that the direction of internal traffic − such as coordination and shunting of transport of goods into storage areas − may have been aided by the painting of corridors or doorways in contrastive ways. An excellent example of where such a system might have existed is in the maze of passageways in the western magazine areas of the palaces of Knossos and Mallia. See our discussion above of Mallia, Chapter II. The later Greek memories of Ariadne's red thread are tantalizingly enhanced by the thin red border occurring on the lower section of the walls of the great corridor leading from the western entrance of the Knossian palace to the area of the central court. Such coloration would serve the dual purpose of (a) discriminating one functional zone from another, and (b) connoting the functional identity of a given zone: e.g. red for circulation, blue for passages leading to storage or work areas, etc. In the settlement at Tylissos, it might have been the case that in House C the seven identical doors opening onto the entrance corridor were distinguished from each other by means of contrastive colors: in response to a question by an entrant bringing some commodity to a household, a porter might have responded: 'beyond the green door'.

25. The suggestions as to the formative and significative organization of the Minoan corpus made here are, of course, tentative and in certain places highly speculative, given the nature of the extant remains. But despite the fragmentary nature of our information, we may expect that the patterns of organization evidenced here are not very far from the mark. It will be clear that the remarks in the present section are less hard and fast conclusions and more of an invitation to dialogue. There is little doubt that the observations made here will be subject to continual modification. In another recent volume, I have discussed at greater length the more general implications for a theory of architectonic organization arising out of the analysis of the present data (D. Preziosi, *The Semiotics of the Built Environment*, 1979b).

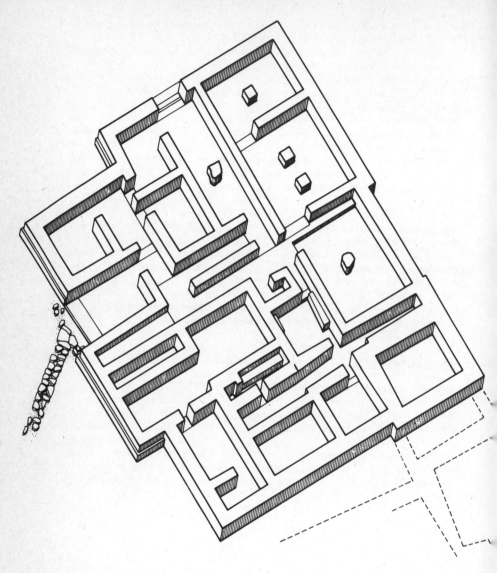

Figure I.1. *Gortyn: plan*

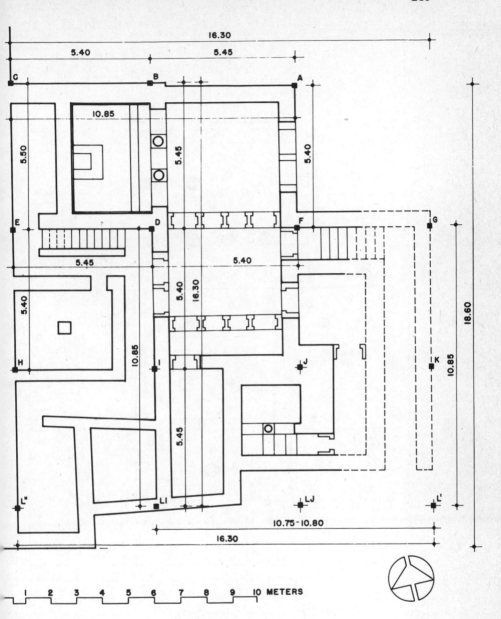

Figure I.2.A. *Knossos: House of the Chancel Screen*

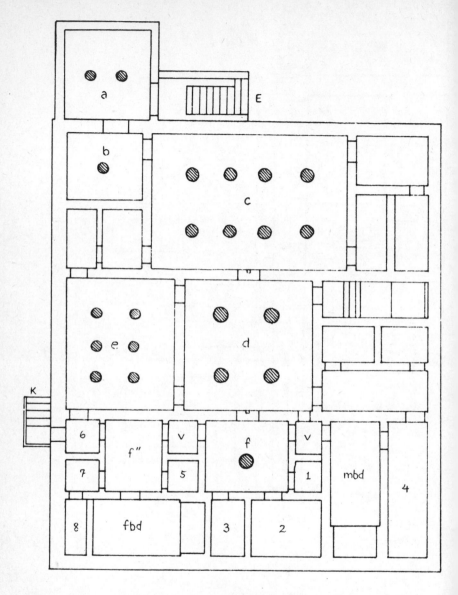

Figure I.2.B. *Amarna: House of the Vizier Nakht*

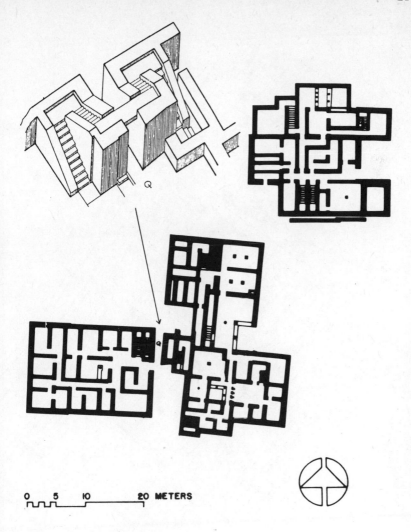

0 5 10   20 METERS

Figure I.3. *Tylissos: Houses A, B, C*

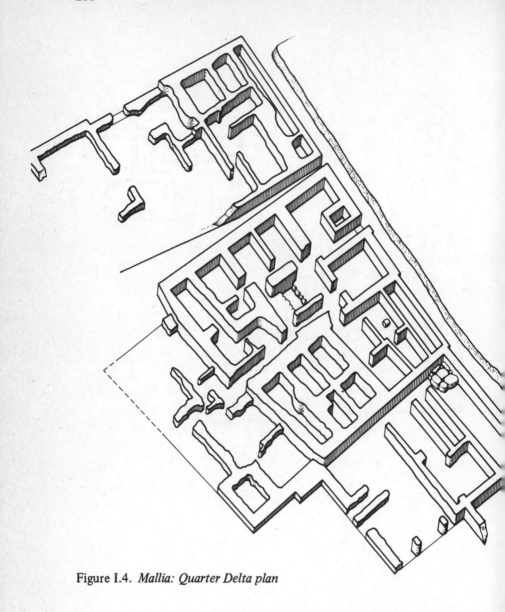

Figure I.4. *Mallia: Quarter Delta plan*

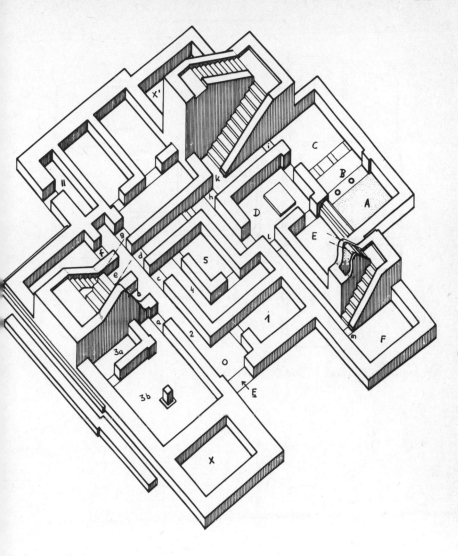

Figure I.5. *Tylissos: House C: plan*

220

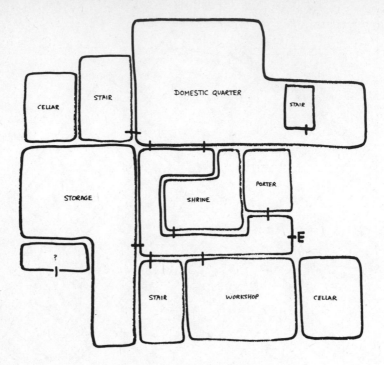

Figure I.6. *Tylissos: House C: functional zoning*

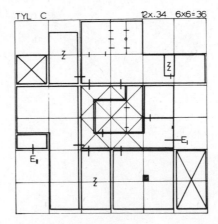

Figure I.7. *Tylissos: House C: areal proportions*

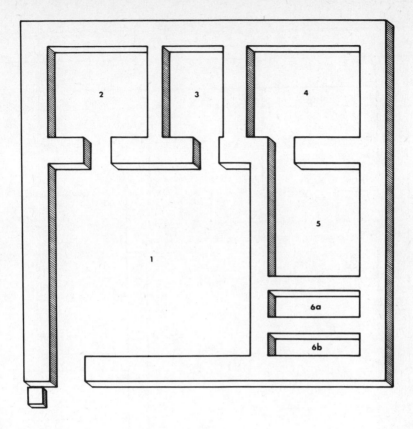

Figure I.8. *Tou Vrakhnou O Lakkos: plan*

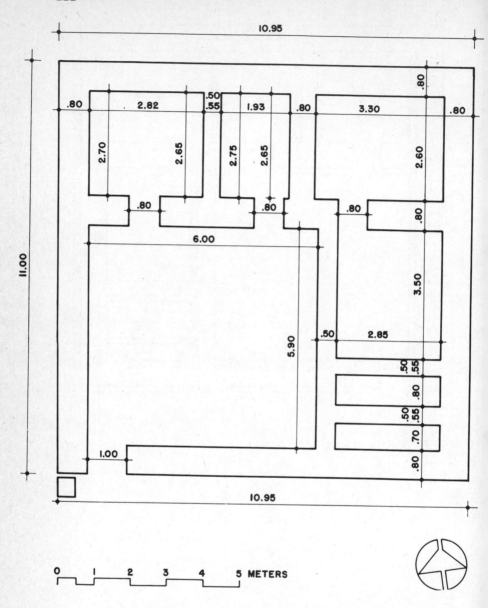

Figure I.9. *Tou Vrakhnou O Lakkos: dimensions of plan*

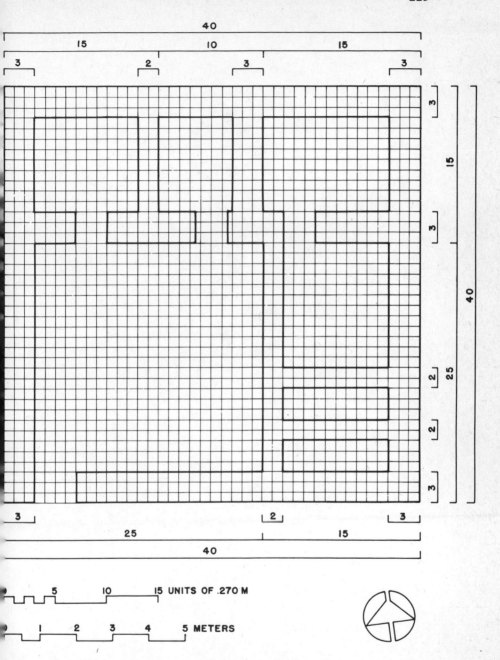

Figure I.10. *Tou Vrakhnou O Lakkos: modular layout*

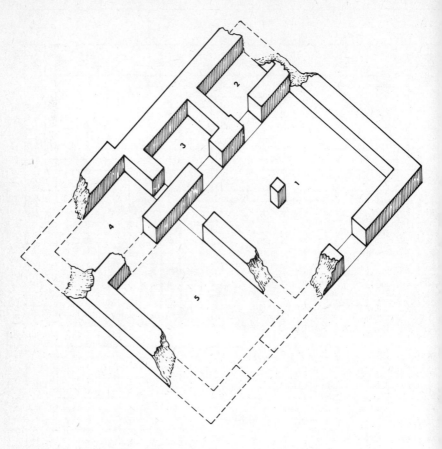

Figure I.11. *Rousses: plan*

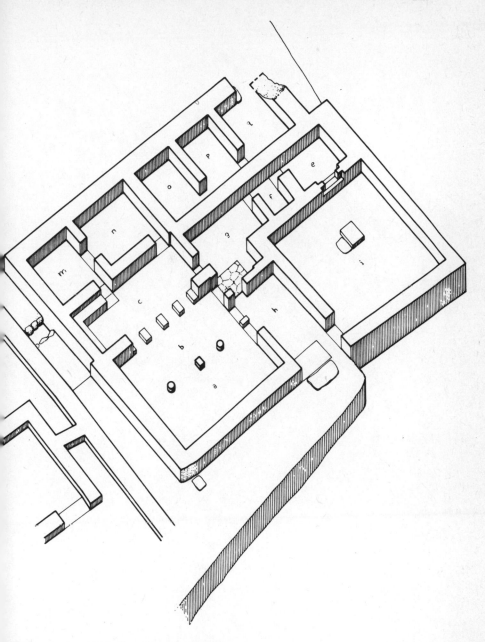

Figure I.12. *Akhladhia: House A: plan*

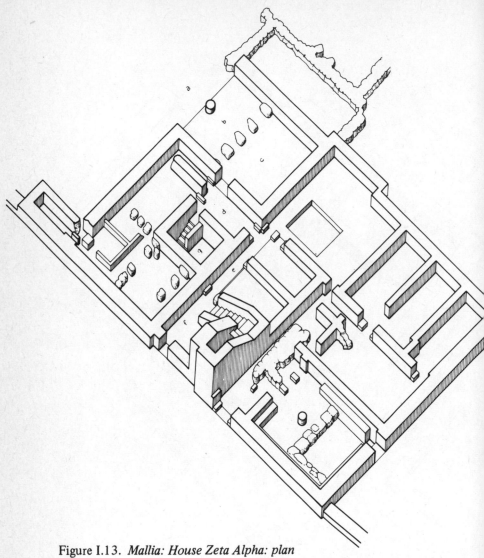

Figure I.13. *Mallia: House Zeta Alpha: plan*

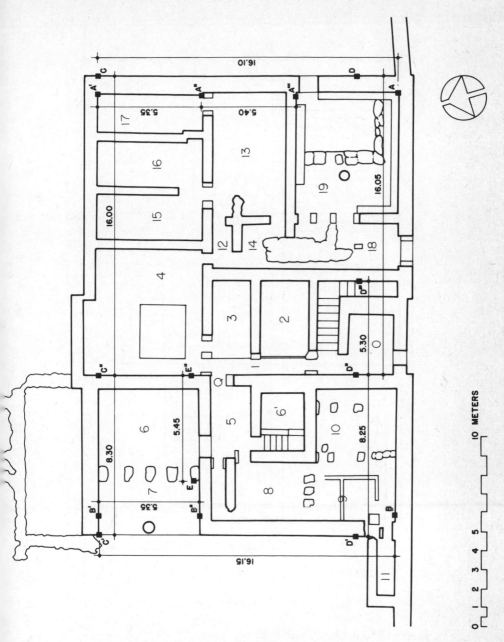

227

Figure I. 14. *Mallia: House Zeta Alpha: dimensions of plan*

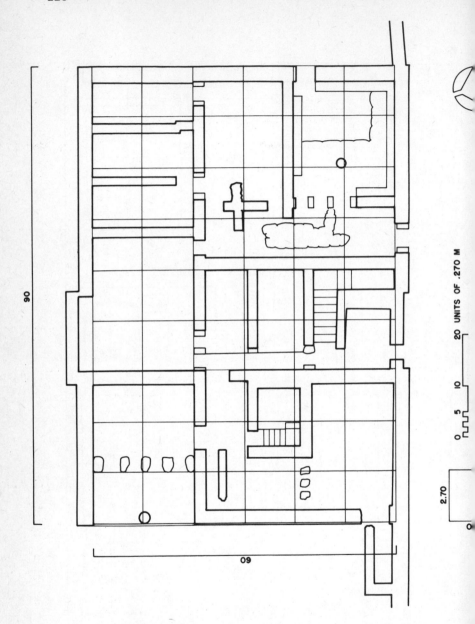

Figure I.15. *Mallia: House Zeta Alpha: modular layout*

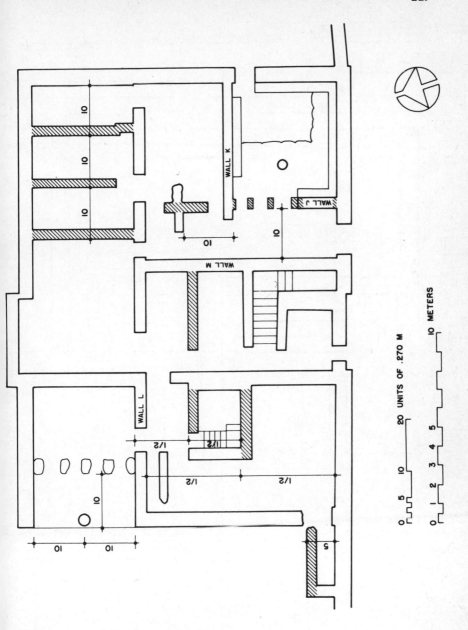

Figure I.16. *Mallia: House Zeta Alpha: construction*

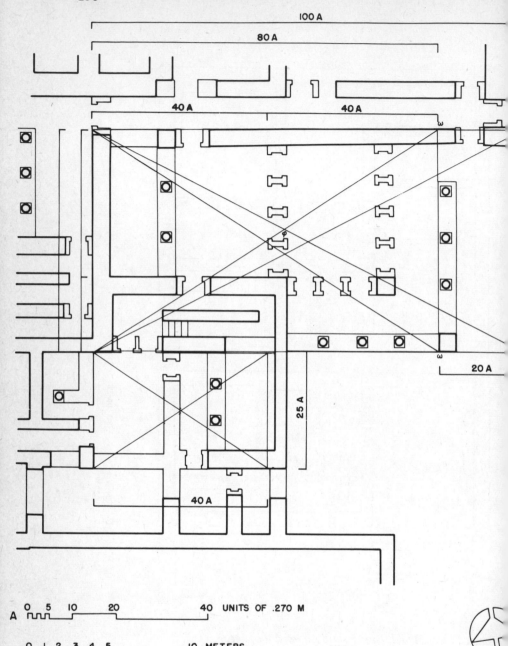

Figure II.1. *Knossos: hall systems*

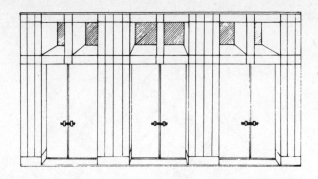

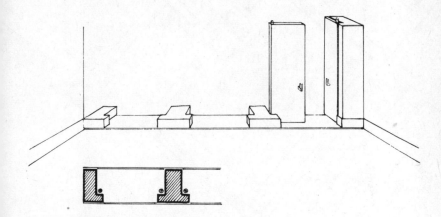

Figure II.2. *Pier-and-door partition system*

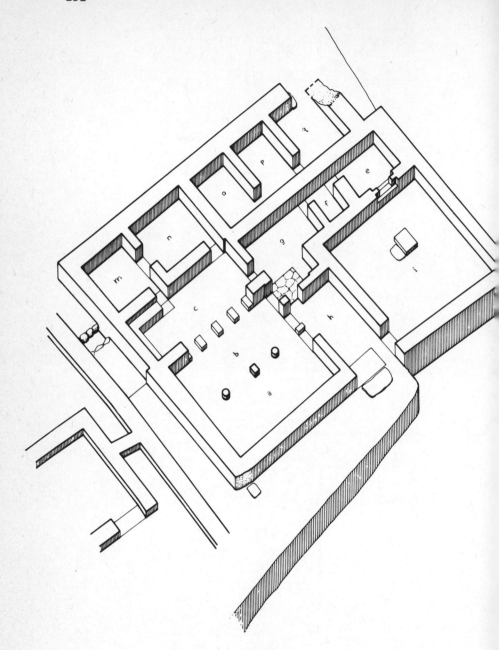

Figure II.3. *Akhladhia: House A: isometric*

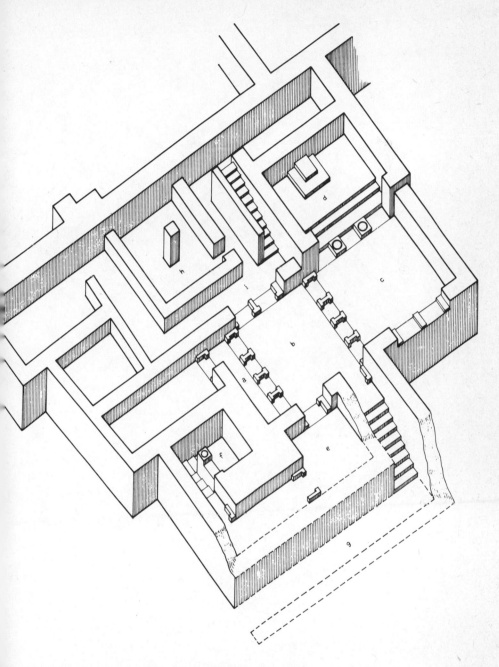

re II.4. *Knossos: House of the Chancel Screen: isometric*

234

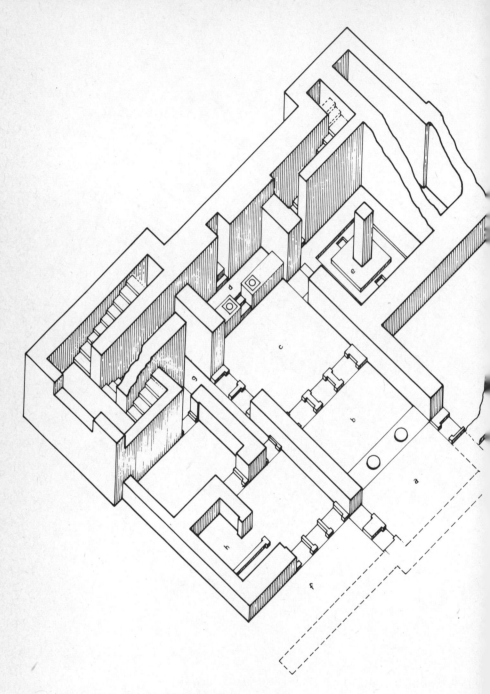

Figure II.5. *Knossos: Royal Villa: isometric*

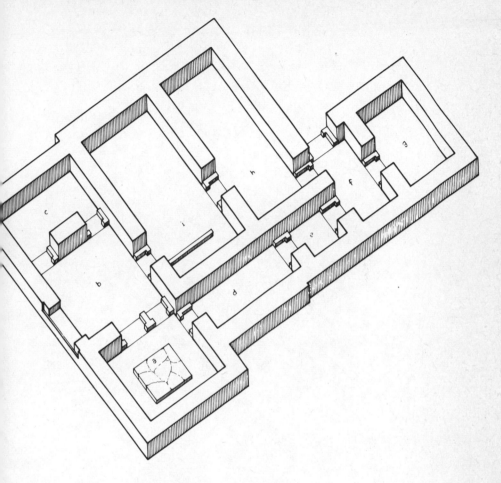

Figure II.6. *Knossos: House of the Frescoes: isometric*

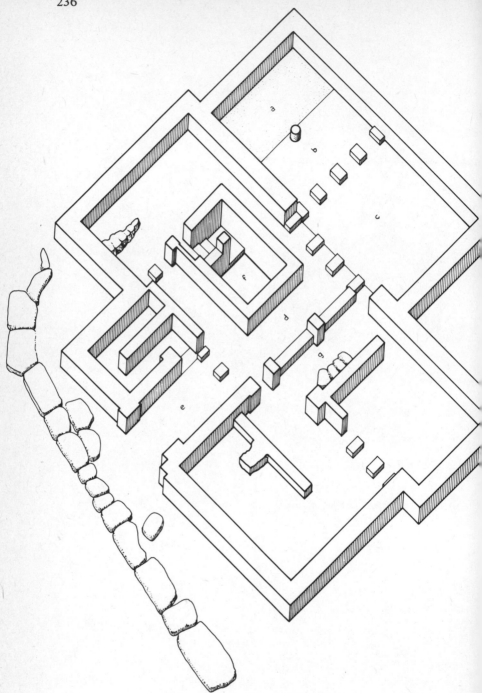

Figure II.7. *Mallia: House Delta Alpha: isometric*

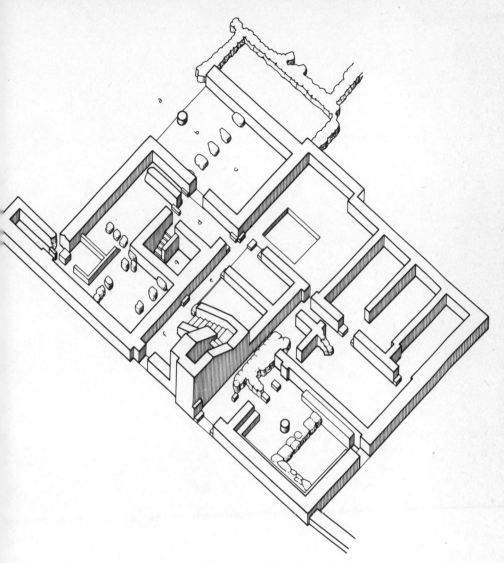

Figure II.8. *Mallia: House Zeta Alpha: isometric*

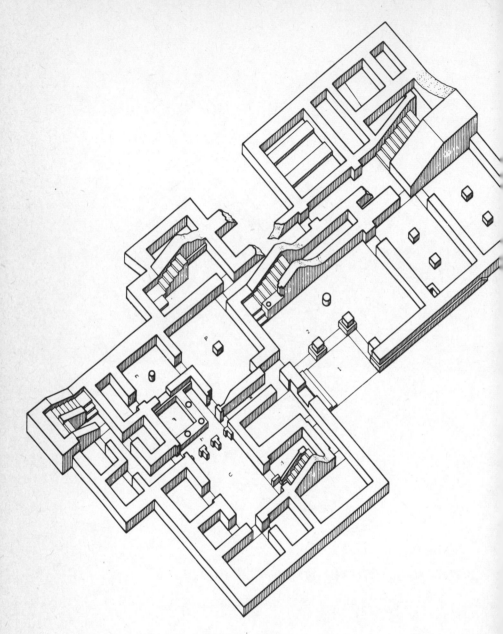

Figure II.9. *Tylissos: House A: isometric*

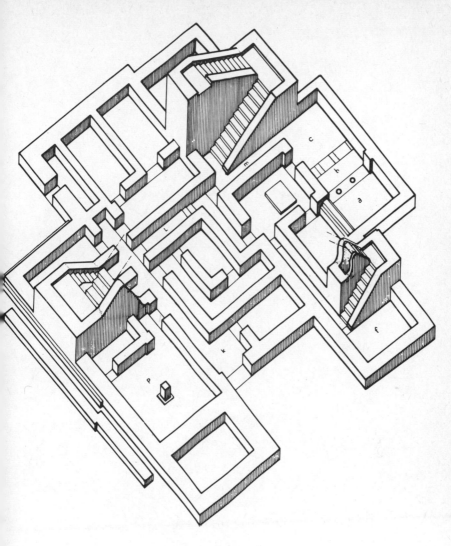

Figure II.10. *Tylissos: House C: isometric*

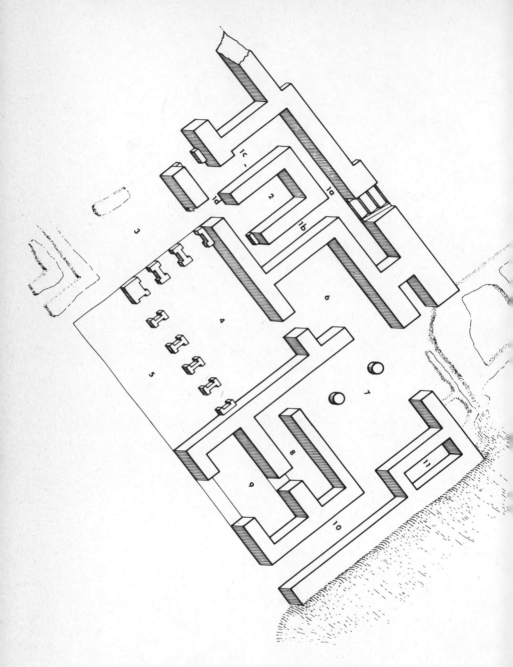

Figure II.11. *Amnissos: Villa of the Lilies: isometric*

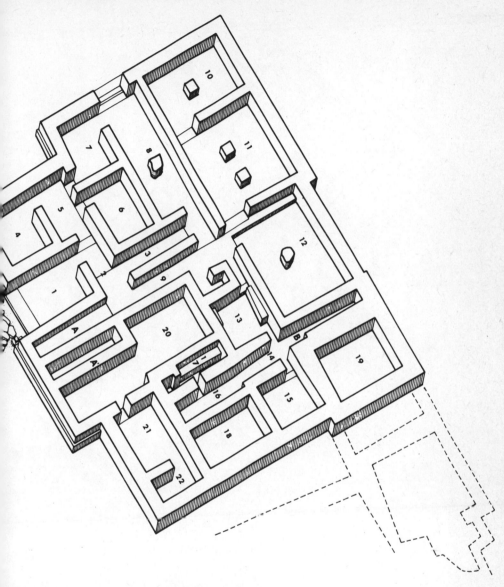

Figure II.12. *Gortyn: Villa Rurale: isometric*

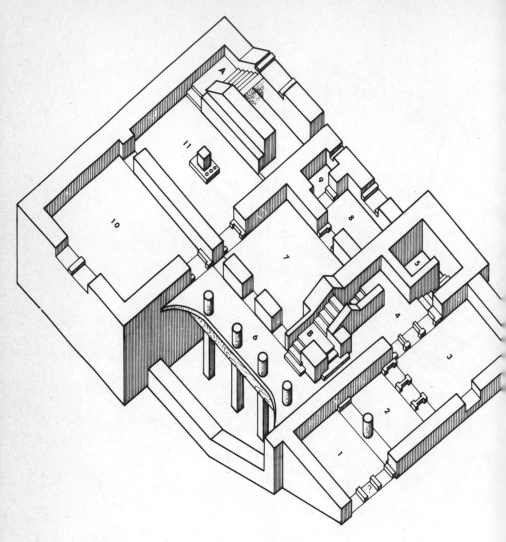

Figure II.13. *Knossos: South House: isometric*

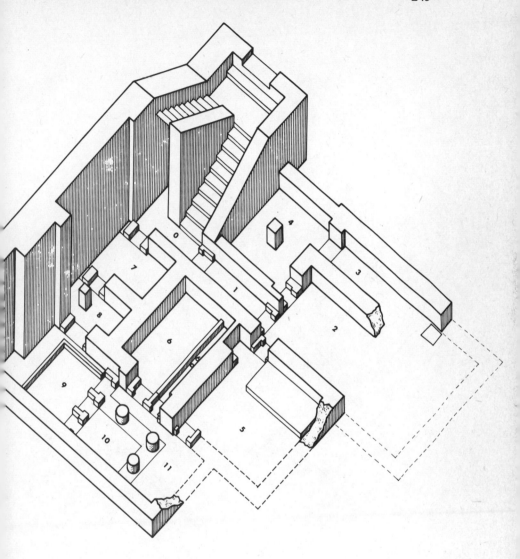

Figure II.14. *Knossos: Southeast House: isometric*

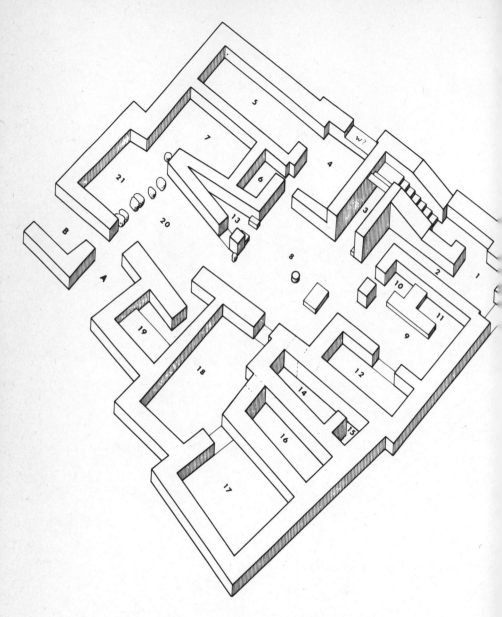

Figure II.15. *Mallia: House Zeta Beta: isometric*

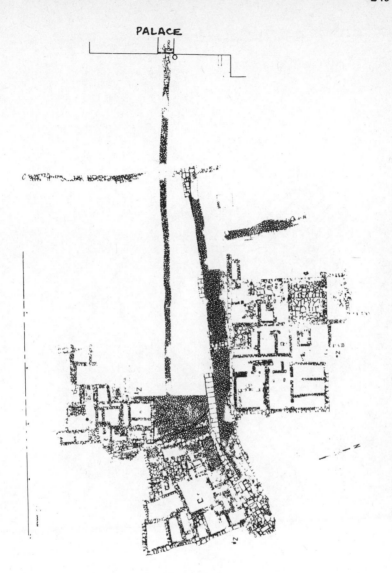

Figure II.16. *Mallia: Quarter Zeta: plan*

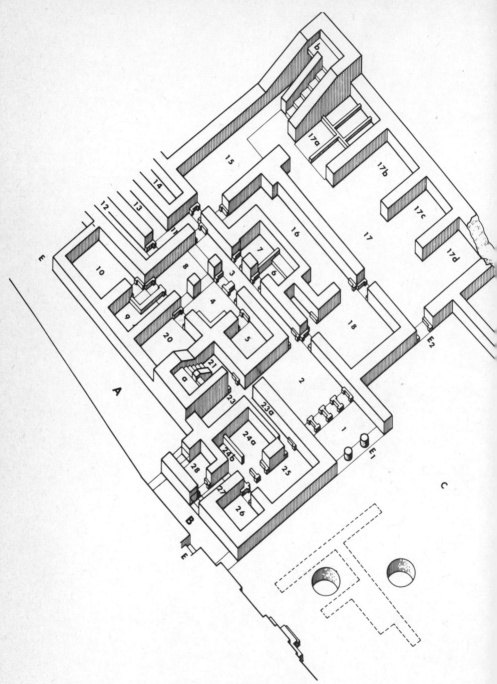

Figure II.17. *Nirou Khani: mansion: isometric*

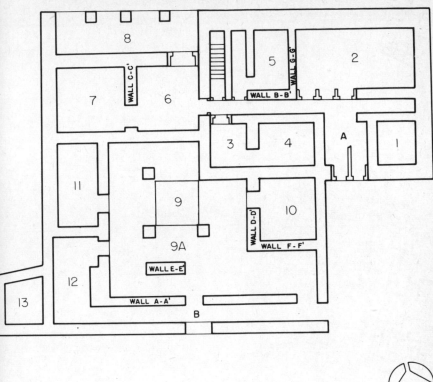

Figure II.18. *Sklavokampos: house: plan*

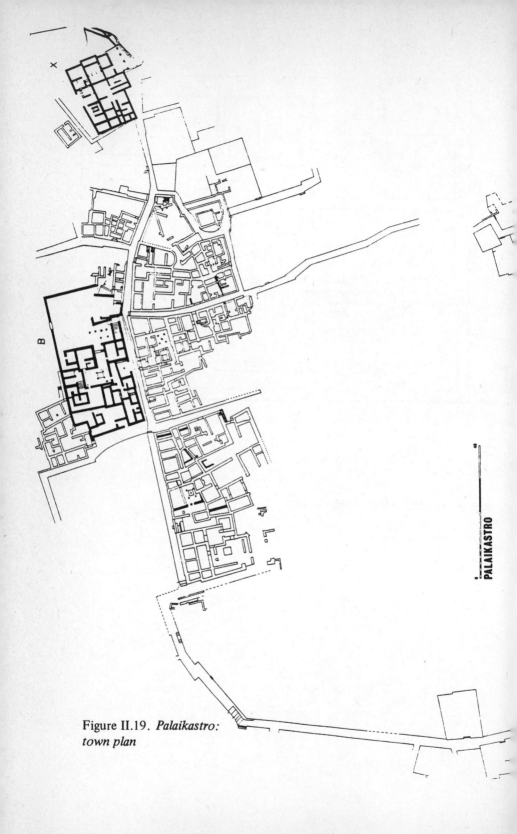

Figure II.19. *Palaikastro:*
town plan

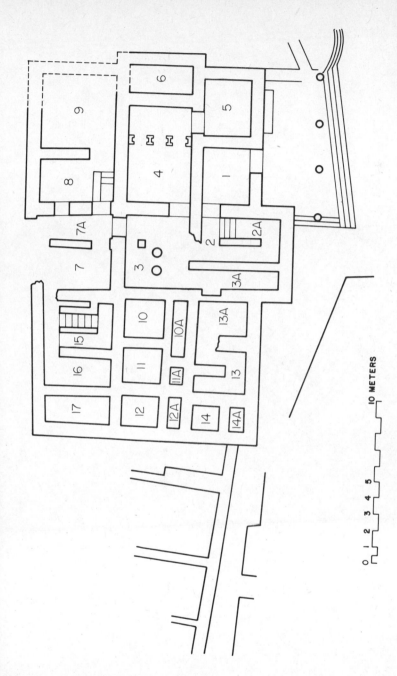

Figure II.20. *Palaikastro: House X: plan*

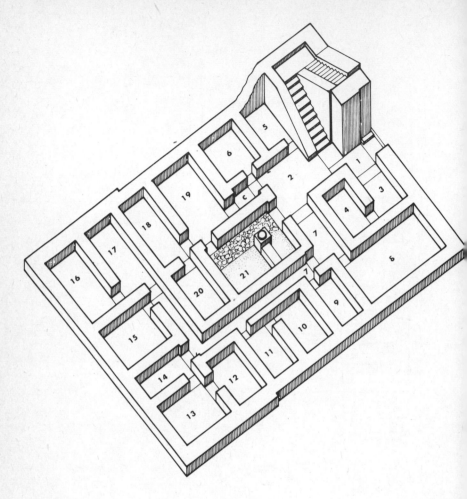

Figure II.21. *Tylissos: House B: isometric*

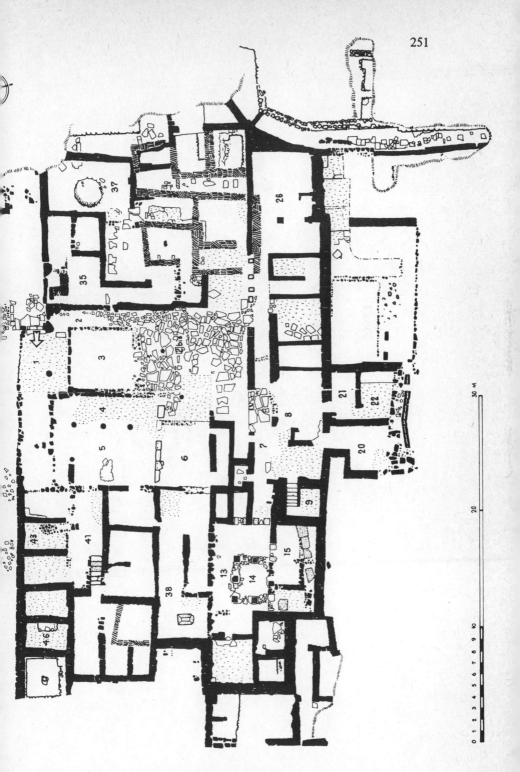

Figure II.22. *Mallia: House E (Le Petit Palais): plan*

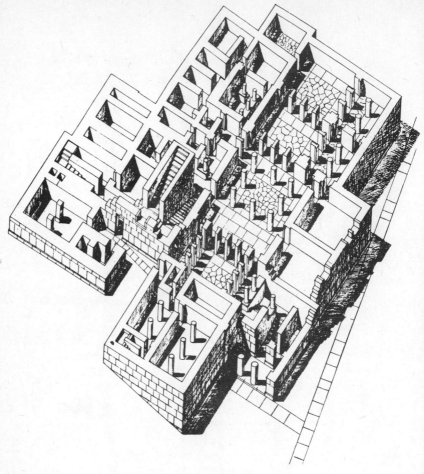

Figure II.23. *Knossos: Little Palace: isometric*

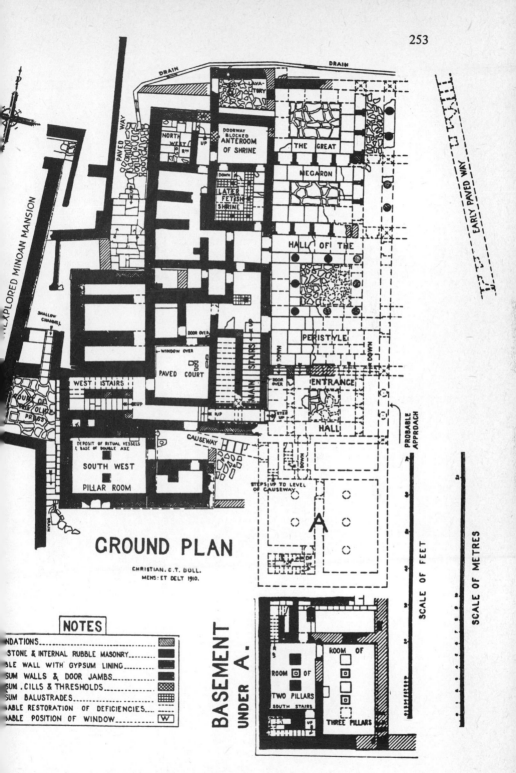

GROUND PLAN

CHRISTIAN. C.T. DOLL.
MENS: ET DELT 1910.

THE GREAT
MEGARON

HALL OF THE

PERISTYLE

ENTRANCE

HALL

PROBABLE APPROACH

EARLY PAVED WAY

SCALE OF FEET

SCALE OF METRES

DRAIN   DRAIN

LAVA-
TORY

NORTH
WEST UP
ROOM

DOORWAY
BLOCKED
ANTEROOM
OF SHRINE

DOWN

LATER
FETISH
SHRINE

DOOR OVER

MAIN STAIRS

WINDOW OVER

PAVED COURT

WEST STAIRS

HOUSE
OF THE
FRESCO

DEPOSIT OF RITUAL VESSELS
& BASE OF DOUBLE AXE

SOUTH WEST

PILLAR ROOM

CAUSEWAY

STEPS UP TO LEVEL
OF CAUSEWAY

A

UNEXPLORED MINOAN MANSION

SHALLOW CHANNEL

NOTES

FOUNDATIONS	
STONE & INTERNAL RUBBLE MASONRY	
RUBBLE WALL WITH GYPSUM LINING	
GYPSUM WALLS & DOOR JAMBS	
GYPSUM CILLS & THRESHOLDS	
GYPSUM BALUSTRADES	
PROBABLE RESTORATION OF DEFICIENCIES	
PROBABLE POSITION OF WINDOW	W

BASEMENT
UNDER A.

ROOM OF

ROOM OF

TWO PILLARS

SOUTH STAIRS

THREE PILLARS

Figure II.24. *Knossos: Little Palace: 1910 plan*

254

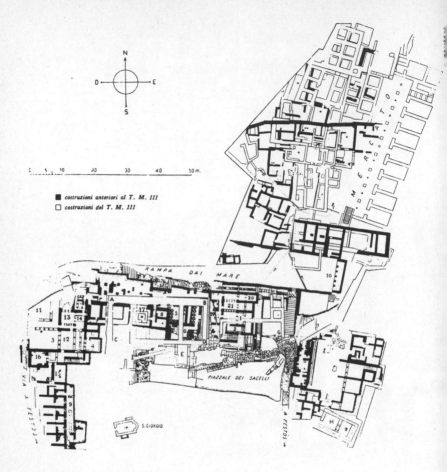

Figure II.25. *Haghia Triadha: villa: plan*

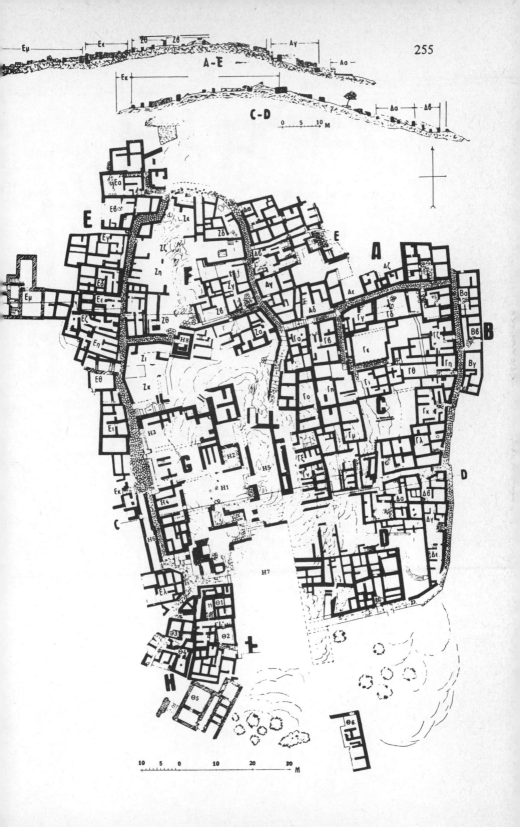

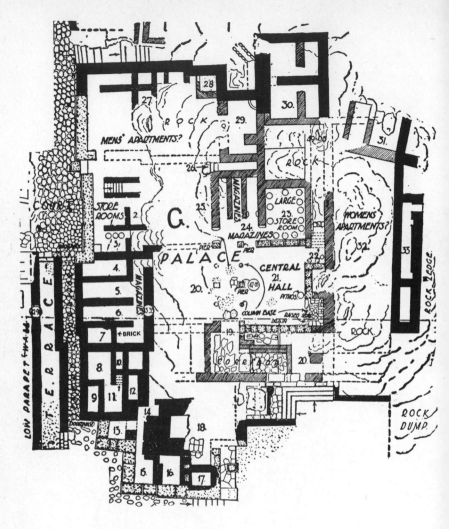

Figure II.27. *Gournia: palace: plan*

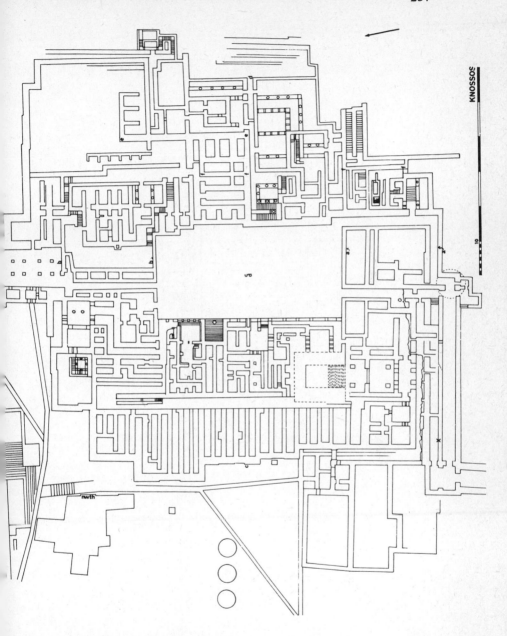

Figure II.28. *Knossos: palace: overall plan*

258

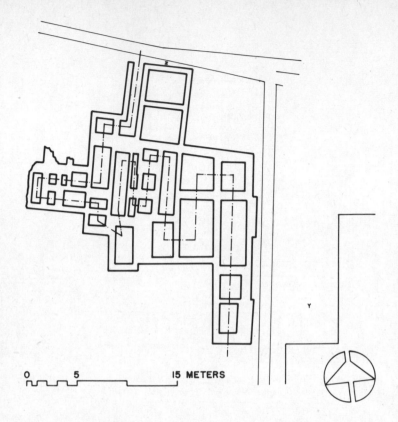

Figure II.29. *Knossos: palace: Northwest Treasure House: plan*

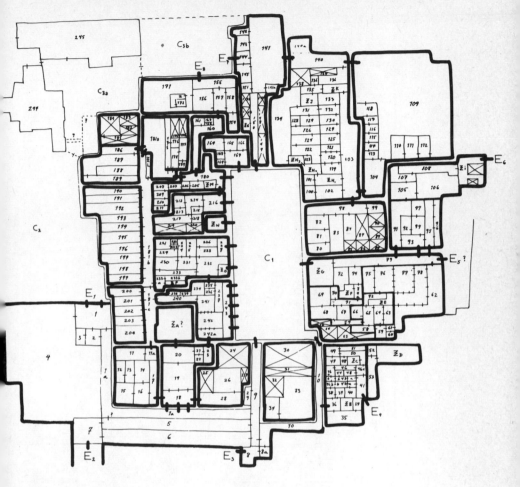

Figure II.30. *Knossos: palace: functional zoning clusters*

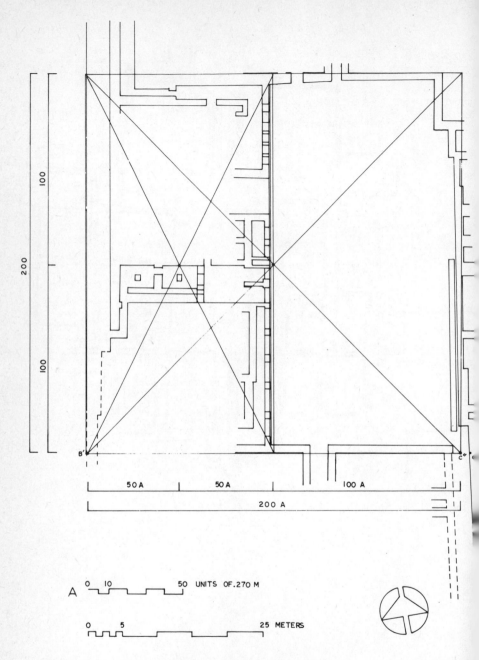

Figure II.31. *Knossos: palace: central modular square*

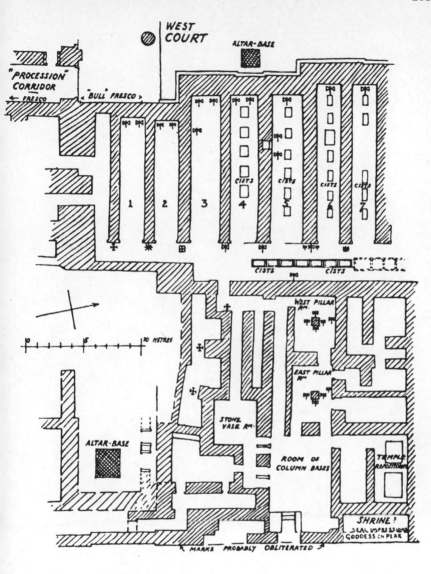

Figure II.32. *Knossos: palace: Fyfe's plan*

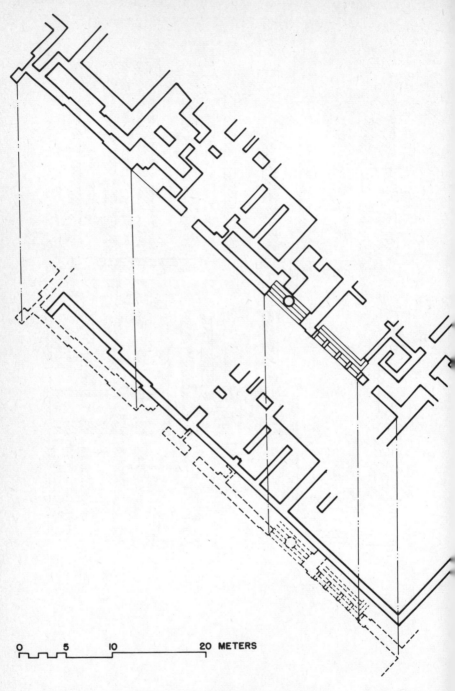

Figure II.33. *Knossos: palace: original court west facade*

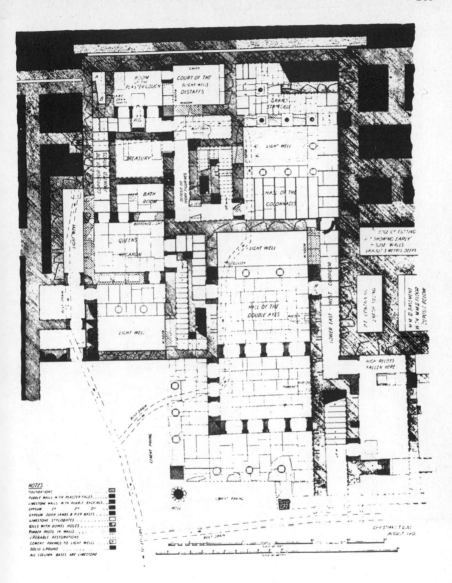

Figure II.34. *Knossos: palace: hall systems: plan*

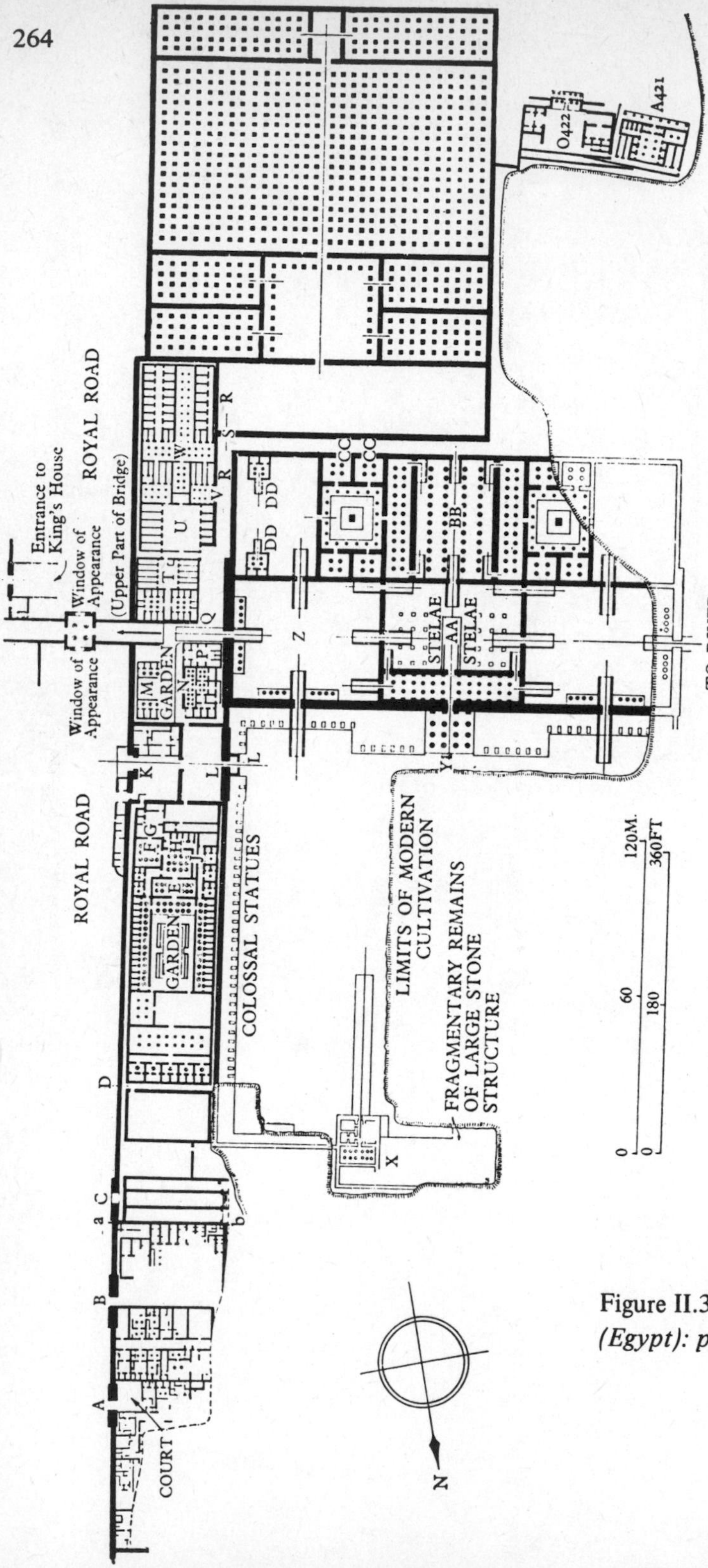

Figure II.35. *Amarna (Egypt): palace plan*

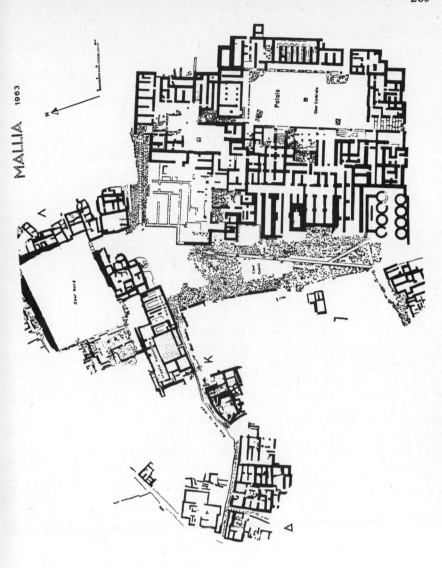

Figure II.36. *Mallia: city plan*

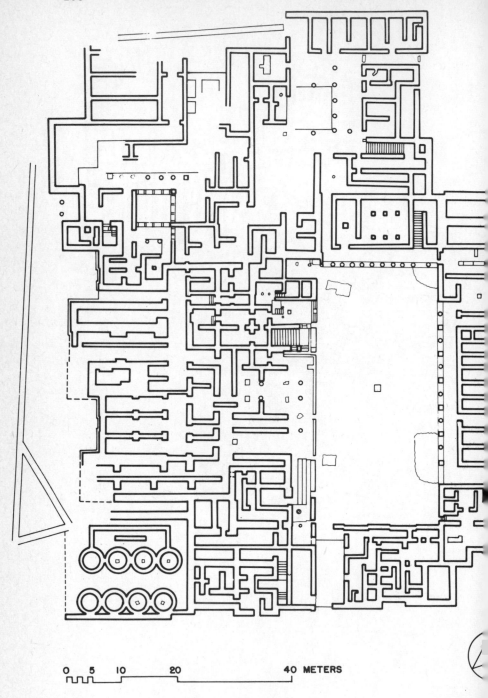

Figure II.37. *Mallia: palace: overall plan*

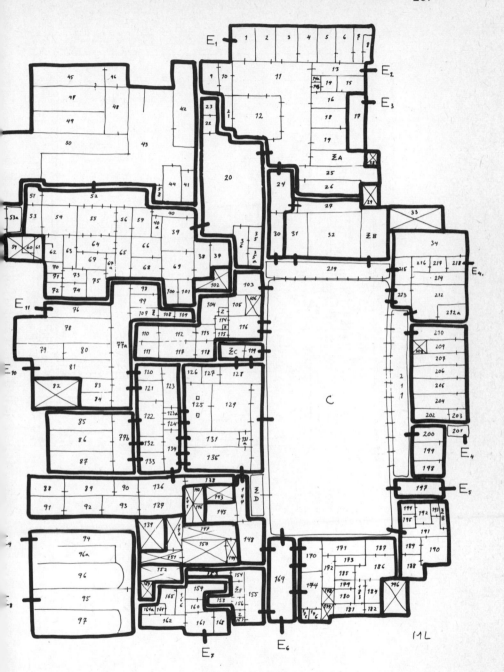

Figure II.38. *Mallia: palace: functional zoning clusters*

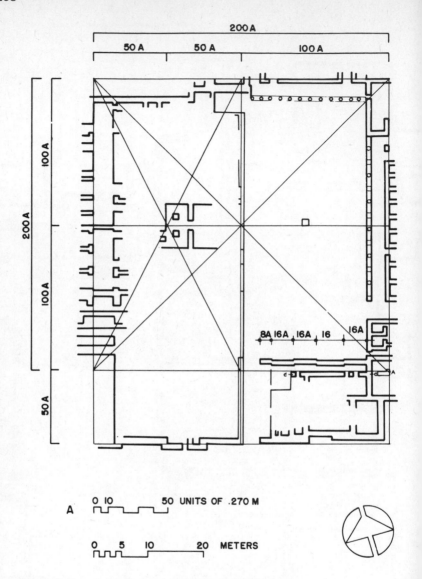

Figure II.39. *Mallia: palace: central modular square*

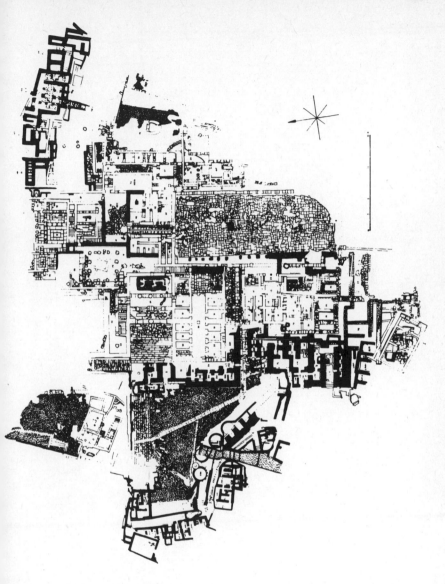

Figure II.40. *Phasistos: site plan*

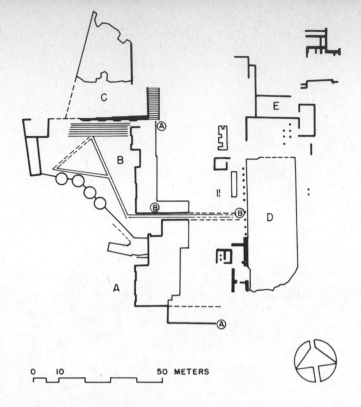

Figure II.41. *Phaistos: first palace remains*

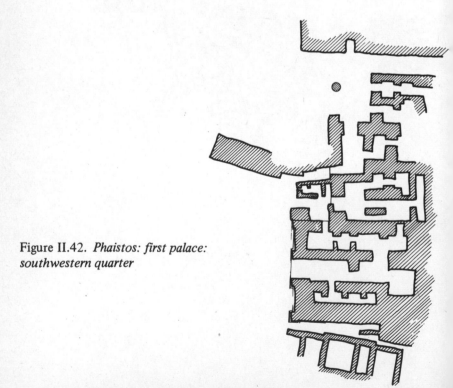

Figure II.42. *Phaistos: first palace: southwestern quarter*

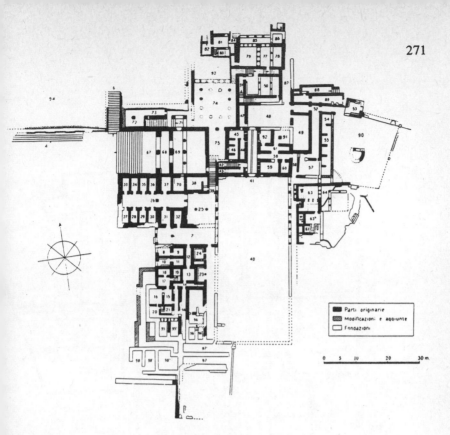

Figure II.43. *Phaistos: Second palace: plan*

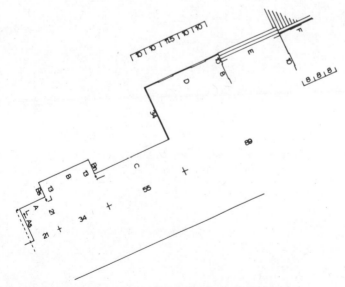

Figure II.44. *Phaistos: second palace: west facade harmonics*

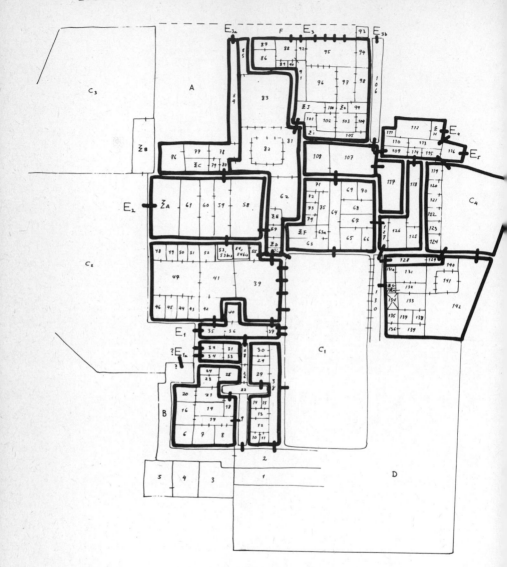

Figure II.45. *Phaistos: second palace: functional clusters*

Figure II.46. *Kato Zakro: palace: plan*

274

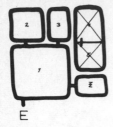

Figure II.47. *Tou Vrakhnou O Lakkos: clusters*

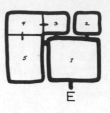

Figure II.48. *Rousses: clusters*

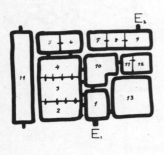

Figure II.49. *Akhladhia: clusters*

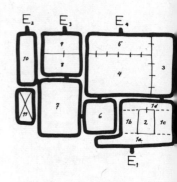

Figure II.50. *Amnissos: cluste*

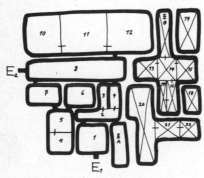

Figure II.51. *Gortyn: clusters*

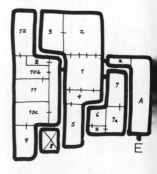

Figure II.52. *Knossos: HCS: clusters*

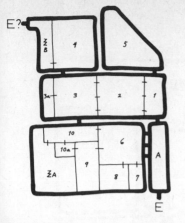

Figure II.53. *Knossos: RV: clusters*

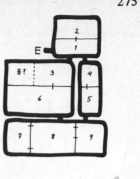

Figure II.54. *Knossos: HF: clusters*

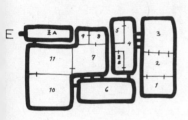

Figure II.55. *Knossos: S: clusters*

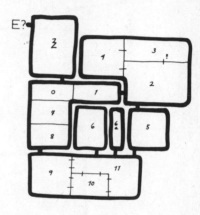

Figure II.56 *Knossos: SE: clusters*

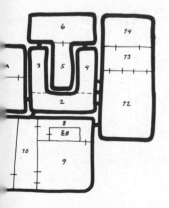

Figure II.57. *Mallia: DA: clusters*

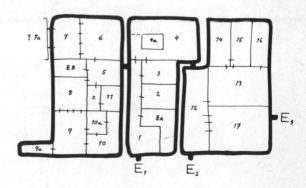

Figure II.58. *Mallia: ZA: clusters*

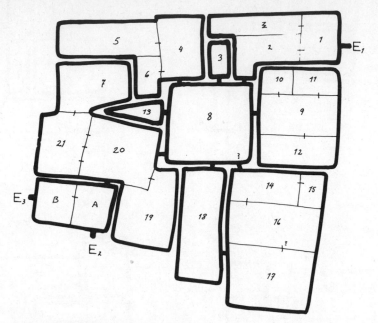

Figure II.59. *Mallia: ZB: clusters*

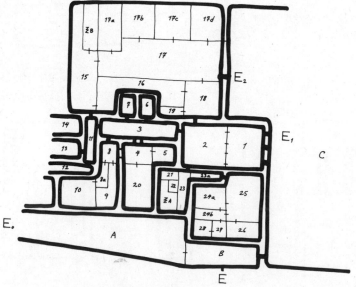

Figure II.60. *Nirou Khani: clusters*

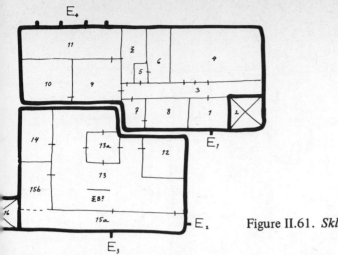

Figure II.61. *Sklavokampos: clusters*

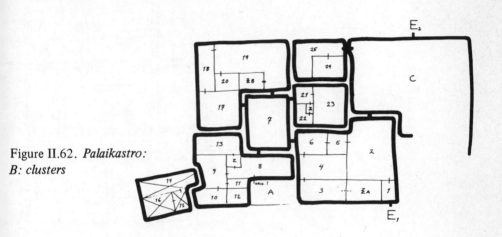

Figure II.62. *Palaikastro: B: clusters*

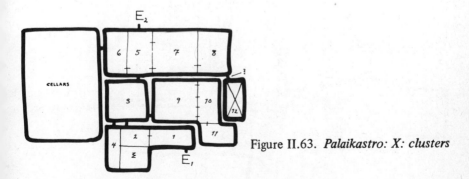

Figure II.63. *Palaikastro: X: clusters*

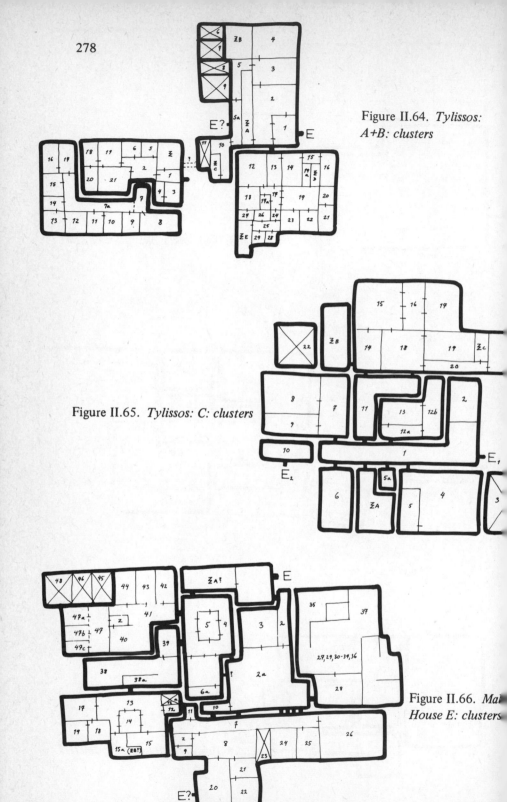

Figure II.64. *Tylissos: A+B: clusters*

Figure II.65. *Tylissos: C: clusters*

Figure II.66. *Mal House E: clusters*

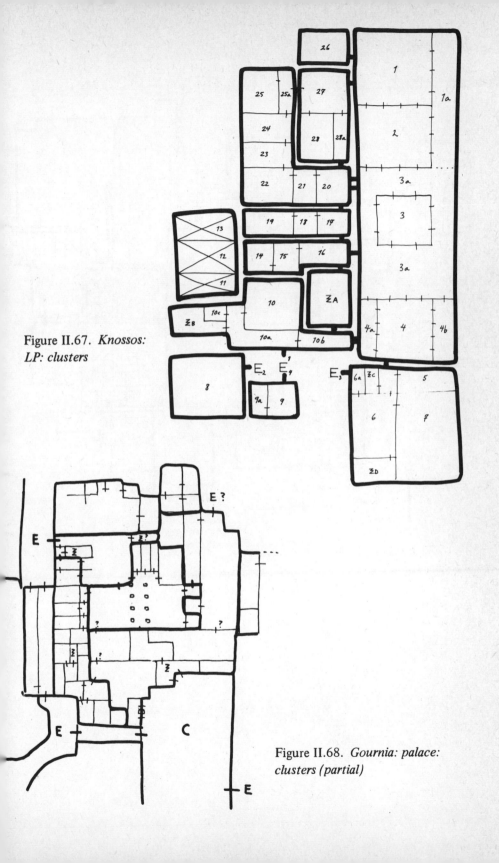

Figure II.67. *Knossos:
LP: clusters*

Figure II.68. *Gournia: palace:
clusters (partial)*

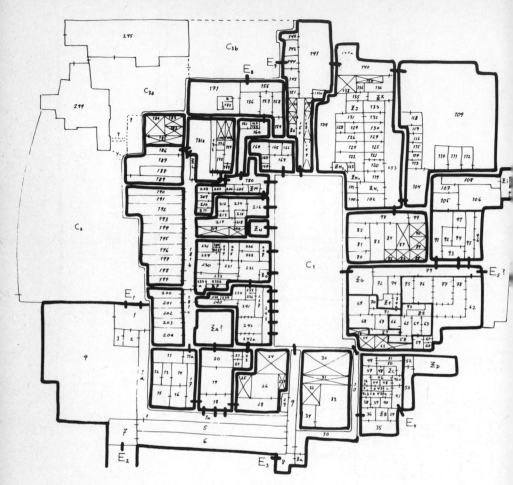

Figure II.69. *Knossos: palace: clusters*

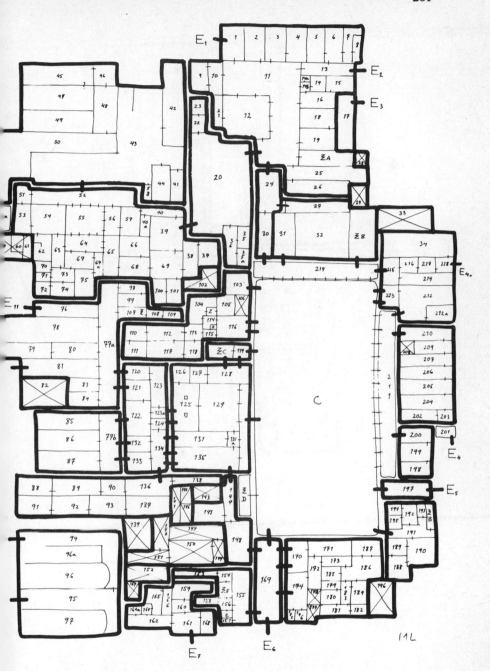

Figure II.70. *Mallia: palace: clusters*

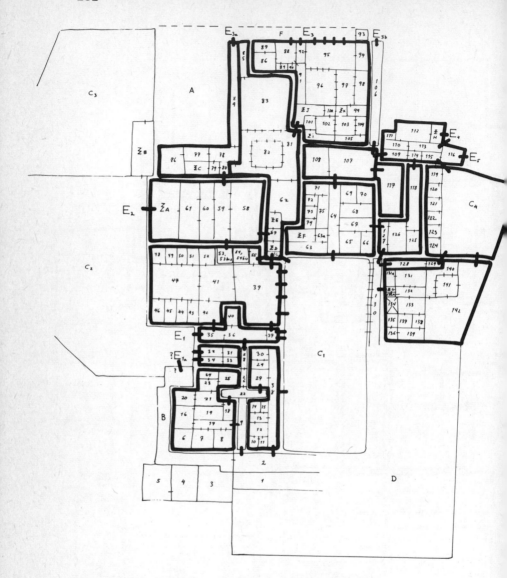

Figure II.71. *Phaistos: second palace: clusters*

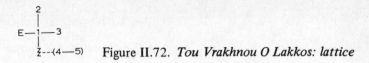

Figure II.72. *Tou Vrakhnou O Lakkos: lattice*

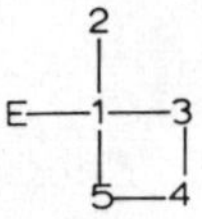

Figure II.73. *Rousses: lattice*

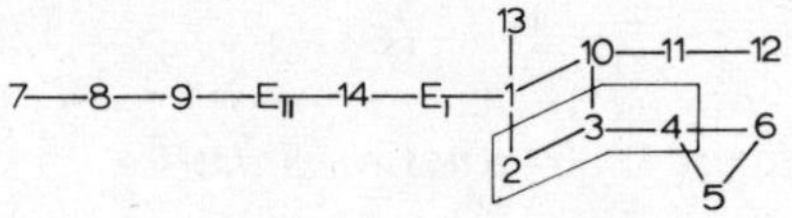

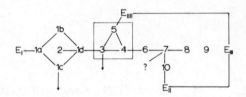

Figure II.74. *Akhladhia: lattice*

Figure II.75. *Amnissos: lattice*

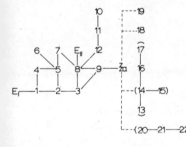

Figure II.76. *Gortyn: lattice*

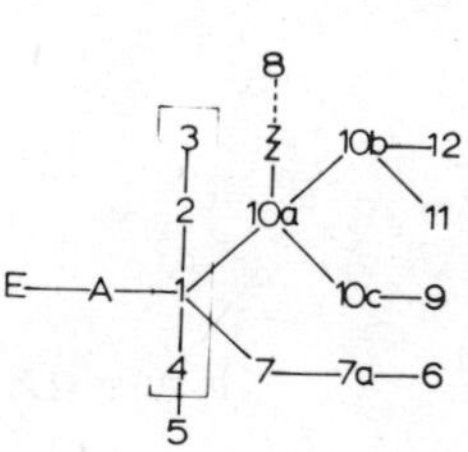

Figure II.77. *Knossos: HCS: lattice*

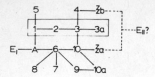

Figure II.78. *Knossos: RV: lattice*

Figure II.79. *Knossos: HF: lattice*

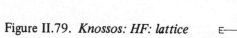

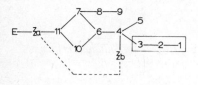

Figure II.80. *Knossos: S: lattice*

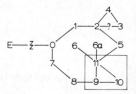

Figure II.81. *Knossos: SE: lattice*

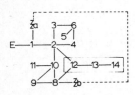

Figure II.82. *Mallia: DA: lattice*

Figure II.83. *Mallia: ZA: lattice*

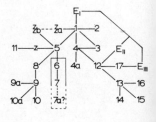

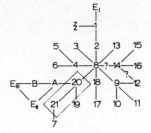

Figure II.84. *Mallia: ZB: lattice*

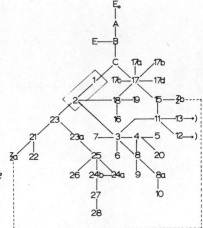

F igure II.85. *Nirou Khani: lattice*

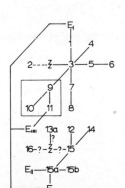

Figure II.86. *Sklavokampos: lattice*

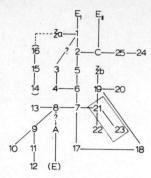

Figure II.87. *Palaikastro: B: lattice*

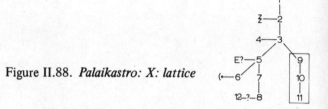

Figure II.88. *Palaikastro: X: lattice*

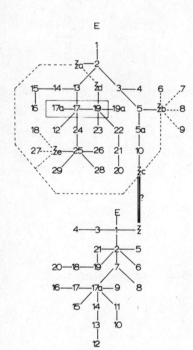

Figure II.89. *Tylissos: A+B: lattices*

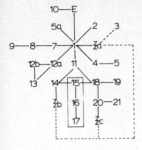

Figure II.90. *Tylissos: C: lattice*

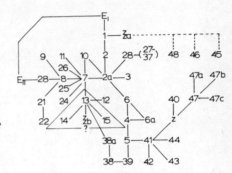

Figure II.91. *Mallia: house E: lattice*

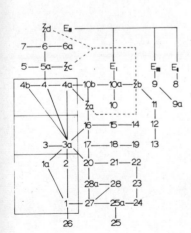

Figure II.92. *Knossos: LP: lattice*

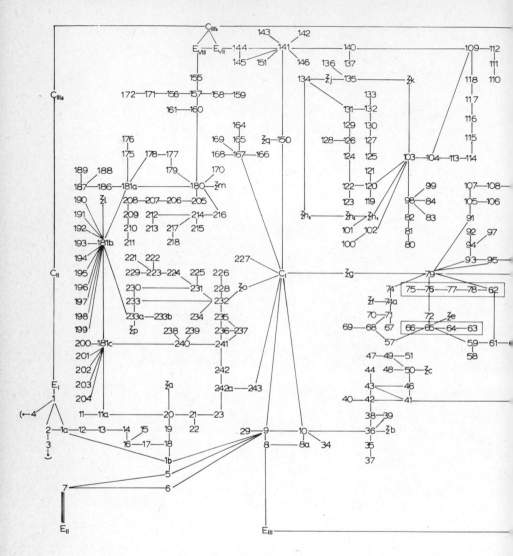

Figure II.93. *Knossos: palace: lattice*

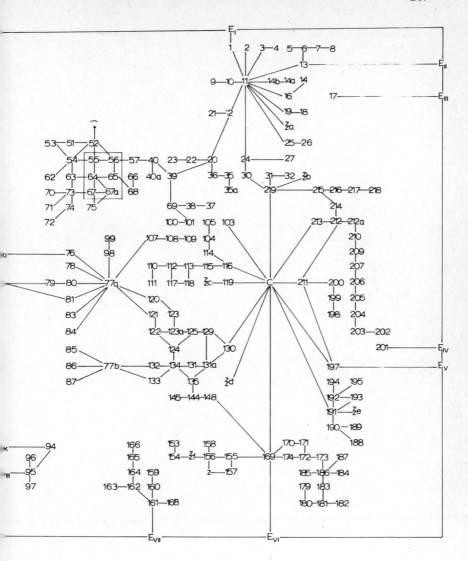

Figure II.94. *Mallia: palace: lattice*

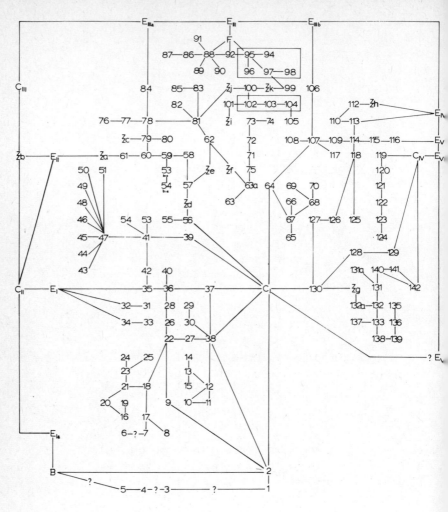

Figure II.95. *Phaistos: second palace: lattice*

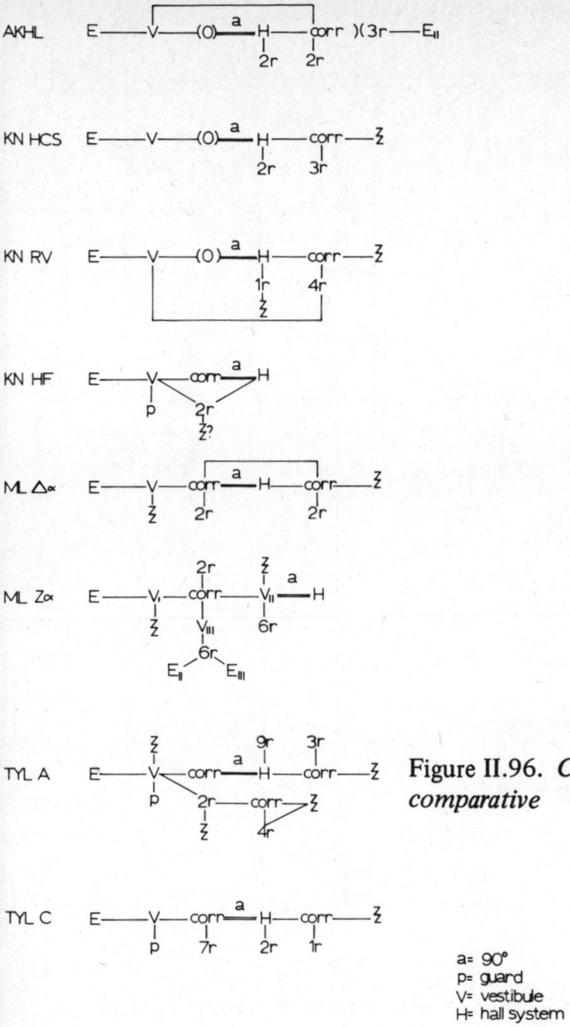

AKHL E——V——(O)—$\overset{a}{\underline{\quad}}$H——corr)(3r——$E_{II}$
2r 2r

KN HCS E———V———(O)$\overset{a}{\underline{\quad}}$H——corr——$\not{z}$
2r 3r

KN RV E———V———(O)$\overset{a}{\underline{\quad}}$H——corr——$\not{z}$
1r 4r
$\not{z}$

KN HF E——V—corr$\overset{a}{\underline{\quad}}$H
p 2r
1
$\not{z}?$

ML Δα E——V—corr$\overset{a}{\underline{\quad}}$H—corr——$\not{z}$
$\not{z}$ 2r 2r

ML Zα E——V_I—corr—V_{II}—H
2r $\not{z}$ a
$\not{z}$ V_{III} 6r
E_{II} 6r E_{III}

TYL A E——V—corr$\overset{a}{\underline{\quad}}$H—corr——$\not{z}$
$\not{z}$ 9r 3r
p 2r—corr—$\not{z}$
$\not{z}$ 4r

Figure II.96. *Central traffic matrices: comparative*

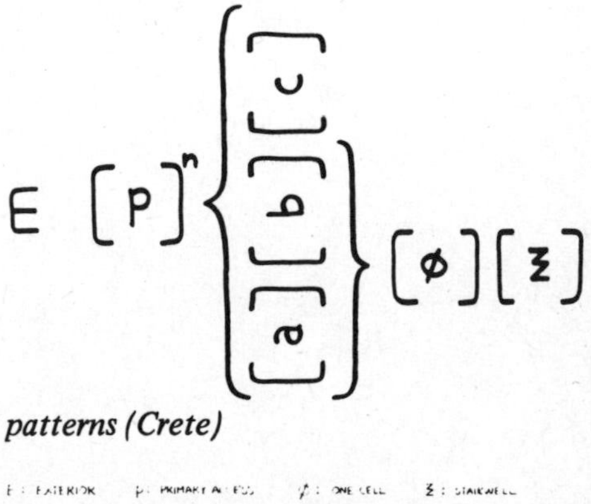

TYL C E——V—corr$\overset{a}{\underline{\quad}}$H—corr——$\not{z}$
p 7r 2r 1r

a= 90°
p= guard
V= vestibule
H= hall system

$$E\ [p]^n \left\{ [a][b] \atop [a] \right\}[\phi][\not{z}][c]$$

Figure II.97. *Generalized syntactic patterns (Crete)*

E = EXTERIOR   p= PRIMARY ACCESS   φ = ONE CELL $\not{z}$ = STAIRWELL

292

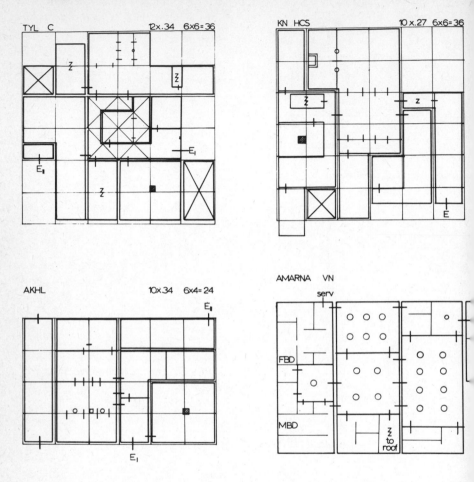

Figure II.98. *Minoan and Egyptian house organization: comparative*

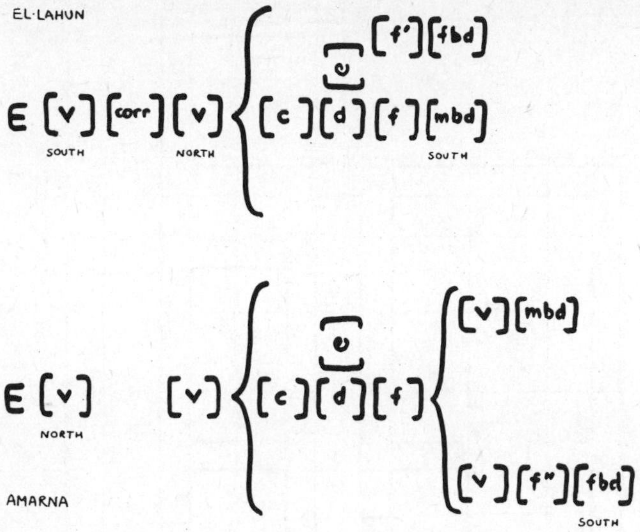

EL·LAHUN

$$E\ [v]\ [corr]\ [v] \begin{Bmatrix} \overline{[e]}\ [f']\ [fbd] \\ [c]\ [d]\ [f]\ [mbd] \end{Bmatrix}$$

SOUTH   NORTH   SOUTH

$$E\ [v]\ \ \ [v] \begin{Bmatrix} \overline{[e]} \\ [c]\ [d]\ [f] \end{Bmatrix} \begin{Bmatrix} [v]\ [mbd] \\ \\ [v]\ [f'']\ [fbd] \end{Bmatrix}$$

NORTH

AMARNA   SOUTH

Figure II.99. *Generalized syntactic pattern (Egypt)*

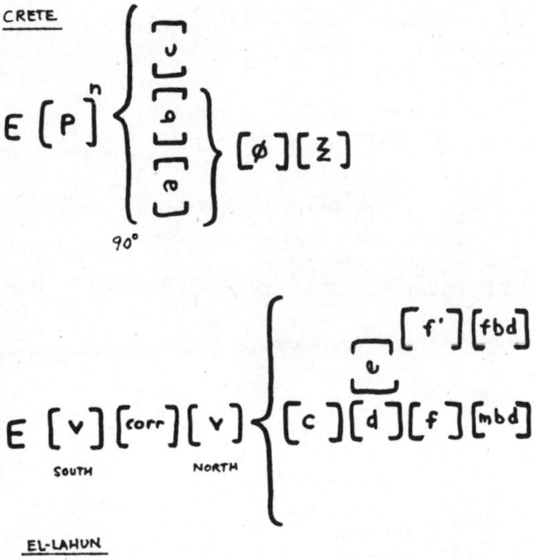

CRETE

$$E\ [p]^n \begin{Bmatrix} [c] \\ [b] \\ [e] \end{Bmatrix} [\emptyset]\ [\genfrac{}{}{0pt}{}{z}{z}]$$

90°

$$E\ [v]\ [corr]\ [v] \begin{Bmatrix} \overline{[e]}\ [f']\ [fbd] \\ [c]\ [d]\ [f]\ [mbd] \end{Bmatrix}$$

SOUTH   NORTH

EL·LAHUN

E: exterior   P: primary access $\emptyset$: one cell $\genfrac{}{}{0pt}{}{z}{z}$: stair
v: vestibule   corr: corridor   fbd: women's quarter   mbd: men's quarter
r, b, c : hall system   c, d, e, f, f' : hypostyle halls

Figure II.100. *Egyptian and Cretan traffic patterns: comparative*

294

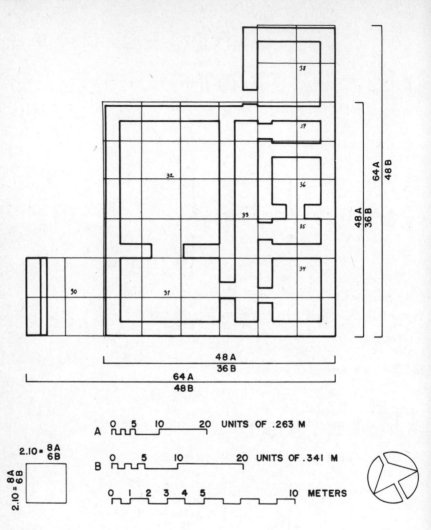

Figure A.1. *Gournia: H-e: modular plan*

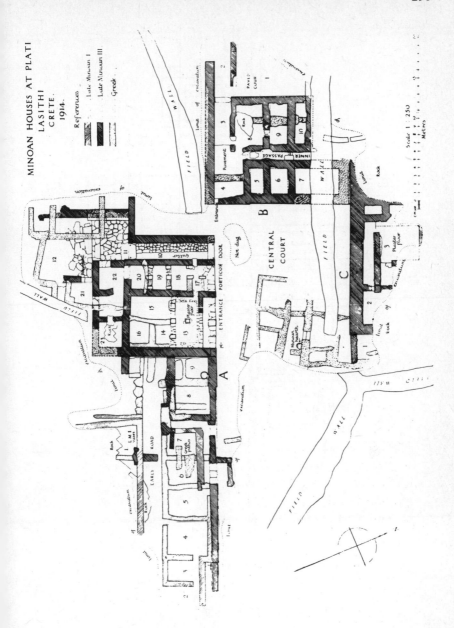

Figure A.2. *Plati: LM III palace: plan*

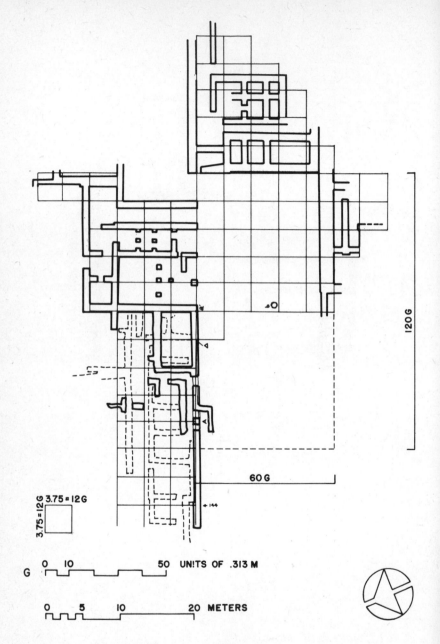

Figure A.3. *Plati: LM III palace: modular plan*

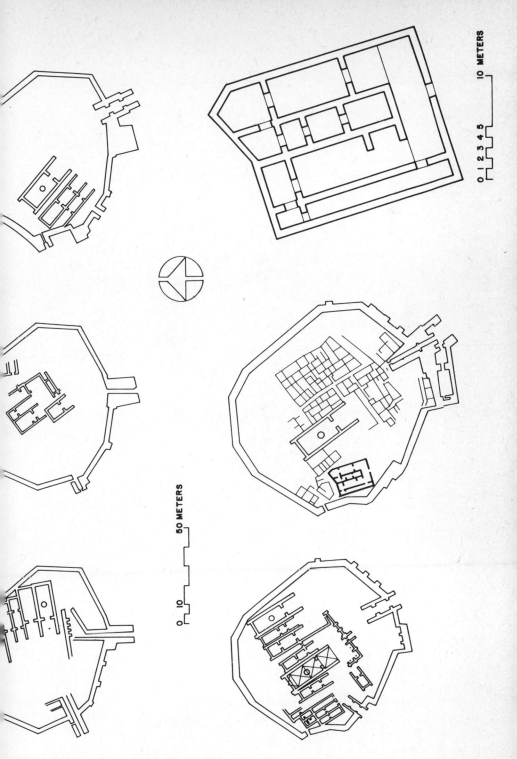

Figure A.4. *Troy: megaroid compounds: Troy II*

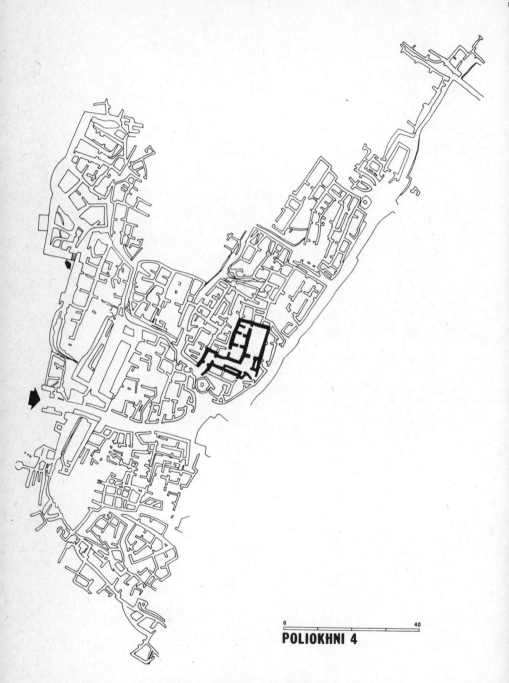

POLIOKHNI 4

Figure A.5. *Lemnos: Poliokhni: town plan*

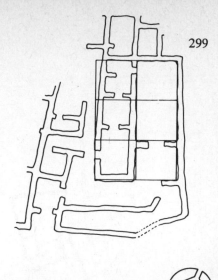

Figure A.6. *Lemnos: Poliokhni: megaroid compound 605: plan*

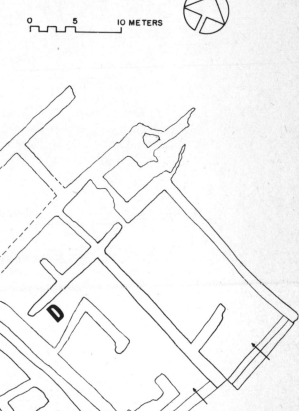

Figure A.7. *Asine: Middle Helladic compound. BD*

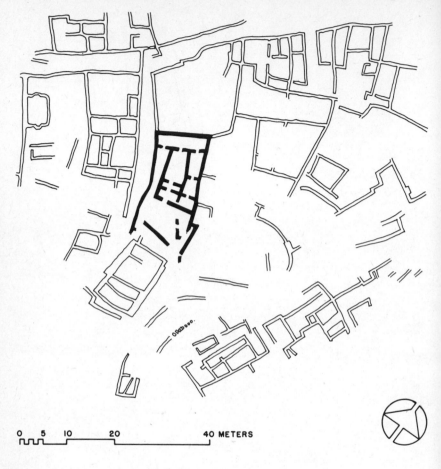

0 5 10   20   40 METERS

Figure A.8. *Pavlopetri: town plan with compound C-IV*

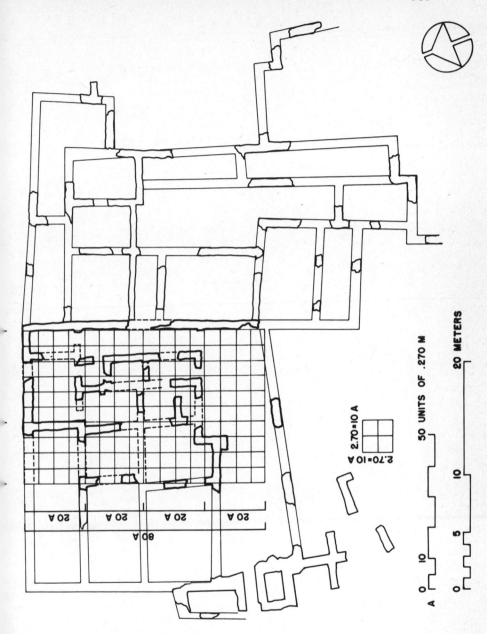

Figure A.9. *Delos: Mycenaean compound: modular plan*

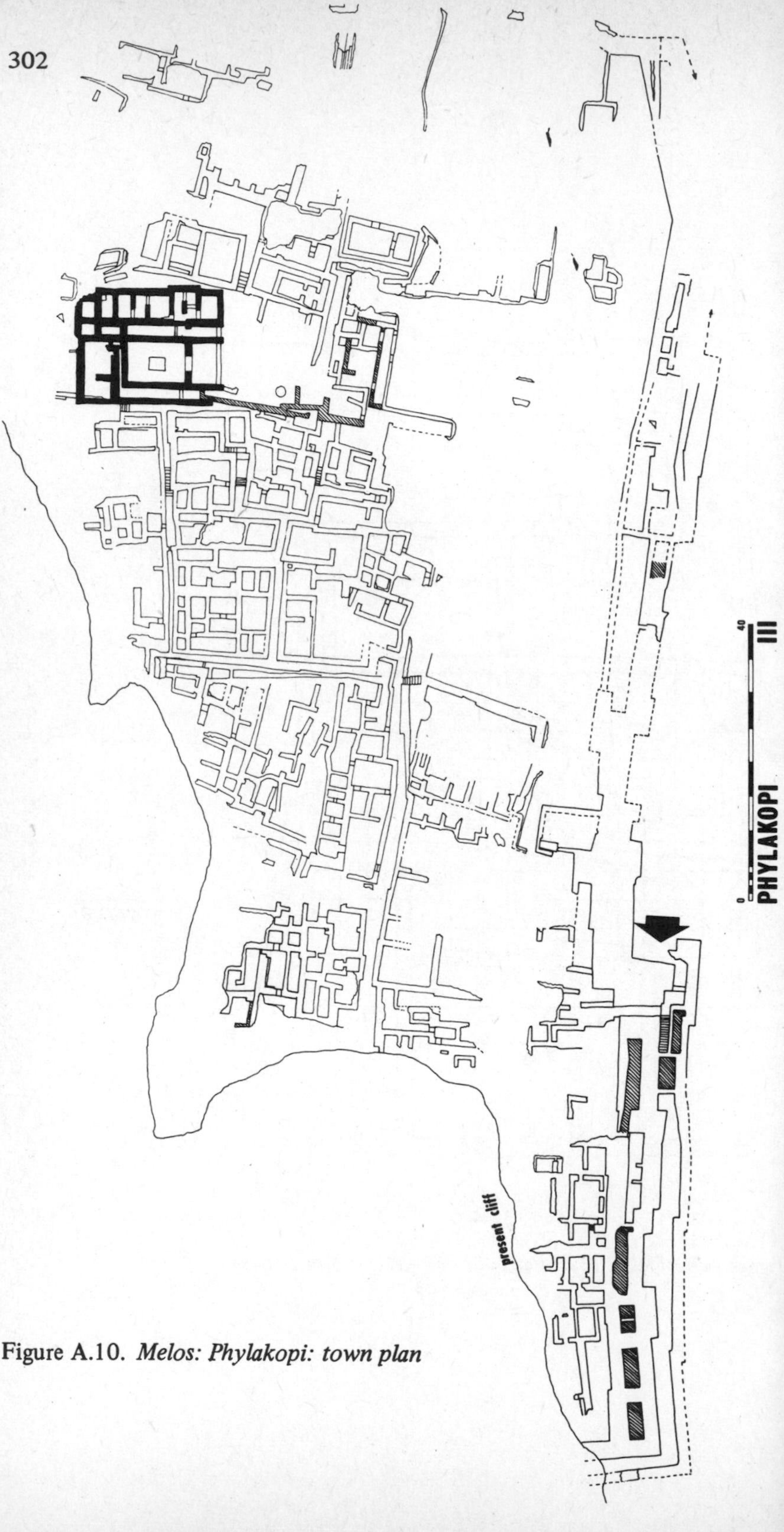

Figure A.10. *Melos: Phylakopi: town plan*

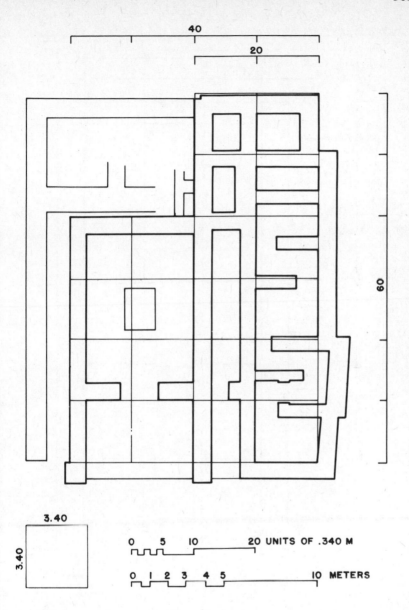

Figure A.11. *Melos: Phylakopi: megaroid palace: modular plan*

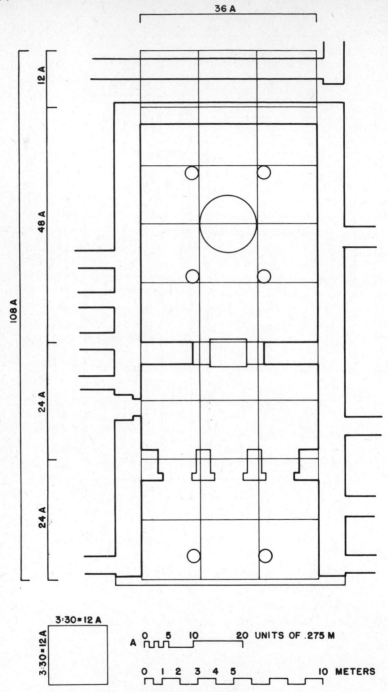

Figure A.12. *Tiryns: larger megaron: modular plan*

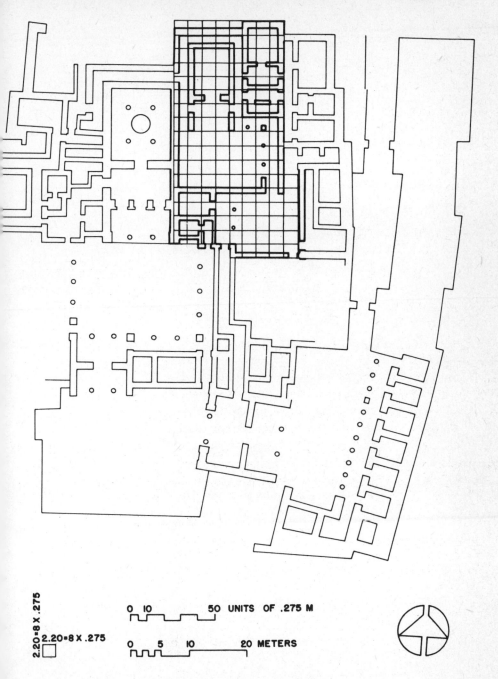

2.20=8 X .275

2.20=8 X .275

0 10   50 UNITS OF .275 M

0   5   10   20 METERS

Figure A.13. *Tiryns: megaroid compound B: modular plan*

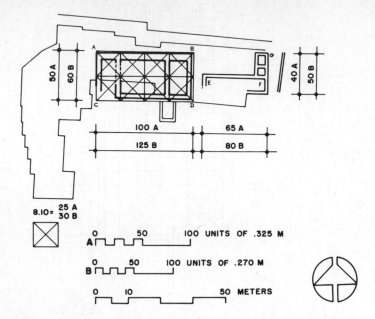

Figure A.14. *Haghia Triadha: megaron: modular plan*

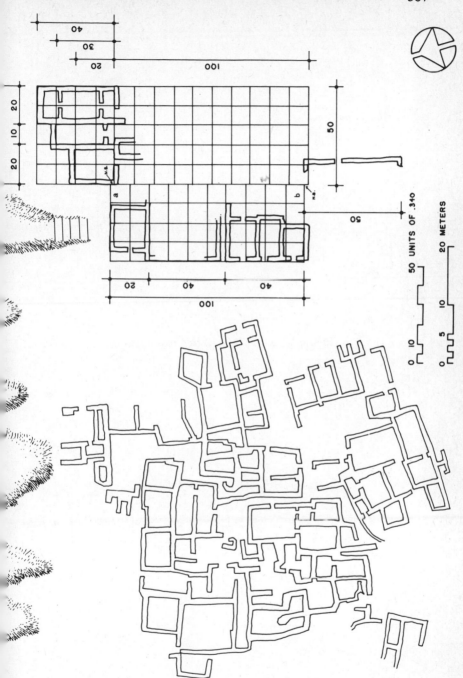

Figure A.15. *Karphi: town plan with megaroid compound: modular*

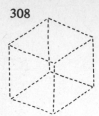

Figure III.1. *Space cell*

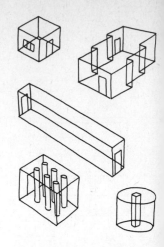

Figure III.2. *Cell types: maximal variation*

Figure III.3. *Cell types: minimal variation*

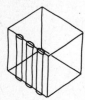

Figure III.4. *Attested cell types*

Figure III.5. *Non-attested cell types*

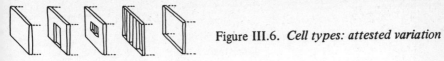

Figure III.6. *Cell types: attested variation*

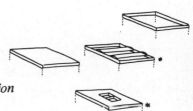

Figure III.7. *Cell types: non-attested variation*

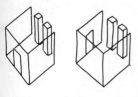

Figure III.8. *Cells: apparent identity*

Figure III.9. *Cells: matrix variations*

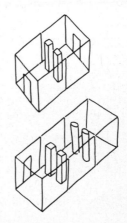

FORMS (clusters of geometric features)		opacity	trans-parency
A	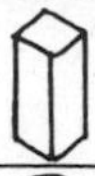	+	−
B		+	−
C	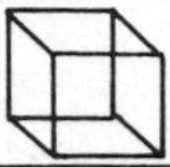	−	+
$D_{1,2}$	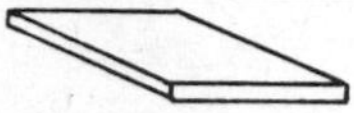	+	+
$E_{1,2}$	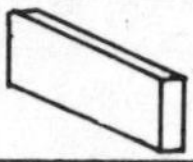	+	+
F		−	+
$G_{1,2}$		+	+
$H_{1,2}$		+	+
I		−	+
J	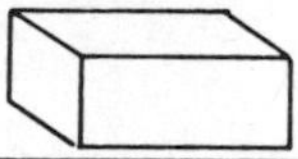	−	+
K	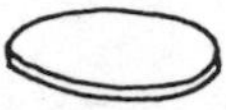	+	−
L		+	−
M		+	−
N	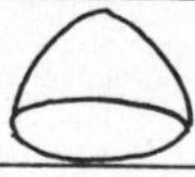	−	+

Figure III.10. *Forms: set of minimal units*

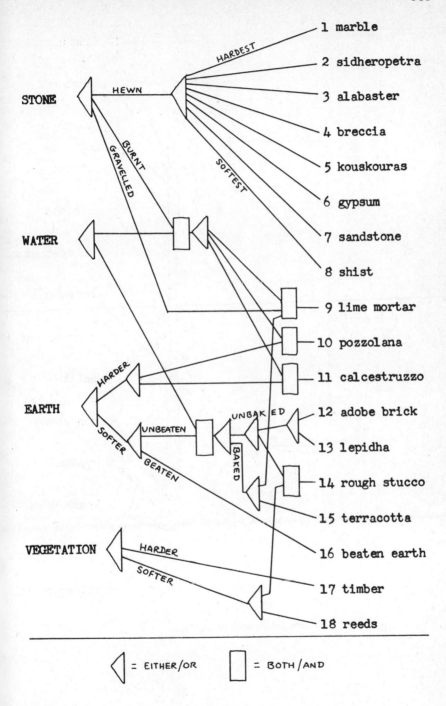

Figure III.11. *Range of materials employed*

312

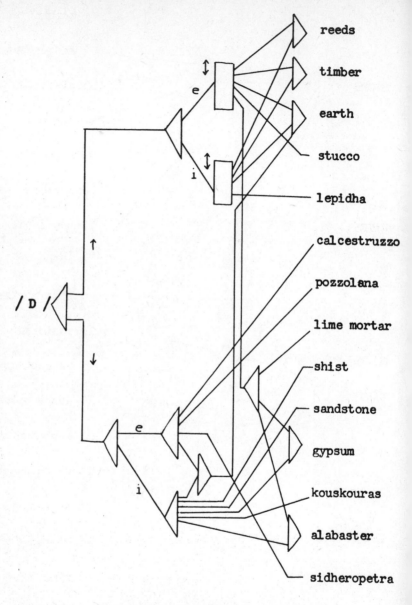

Figure III.12. *Form /D/: material domain*

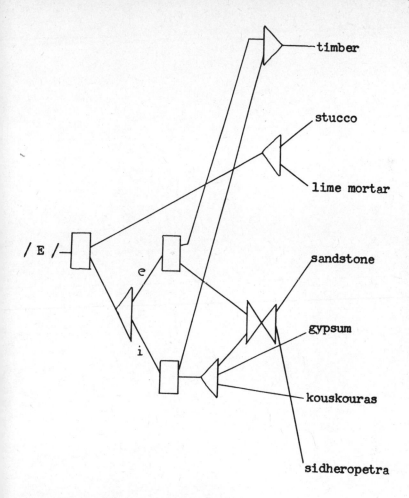

Figure III.13. *Form /E/: material domain*

PART TWO

Modular Organization:
Planning, Layout and Construction

Marco Polo describes a bridge, stone by stone.

'But which is the stone that supports the bridge,' Kublai Khan asks.

'The bridge is not supported by one stone or another,' Marco answers, 'but by the line of the arch that they form.'

Kublai Khan remains silent, reflecting. Then he adds: 'Why do you speak to me of the stones? It is only the arch that matters to me.'

Polo answers: 'Without stones there is no arch.'

(Italo Calvino, *Invisible Cities*, 1972, p. 82)

IV

Modular Analyses

MODULARITY IN PLANNING

Studies of the formative and modular organization of Minoan building design are complementary, interwoven, and mutually supportive. It has become abundantly clear in the formal analyses of the first part of this book that a full understanding of the conceptual organization of Minoan architecture must incorporate an understanding of the processes whereby Minoan builders realized their designs. The orderliness or systematicity of Minoan design is manifest in the ways in which builders divided a building program into component functional parts, ordered those parts according to a proportional allotment of spaces, and mapped these requirements onto a program for construction by means of modular layout grids of regular geometric conformation.

In Chapter I above, we observed a few examples of the manner whereby a given design was planned and laid out on the ground. It was seen that a holistic analysis of the dimensional equivalencies manifested by the extant remains tended to yield evidence for an internal allotment of spaces of regular relative proportions. Such proportions came to be seen as simple fractions and multiples of some basic dimension: some module or standard employed in planning and construction.

Modularity — or replicated regularity — in the planning and construction of buildings is an extremely ancient phenomenon, occurring as early in the history of building as the need for consistency and regularity in the ordering of parts of a structure were required. Such a need was most likely coeval with the earliest origins of environmental structuration among our Palaeolithic ancestors, and was manifested in the ordered selection of raw materials from a micro-ecology to serve as additive components in the construction of frameworks for action and interaction.[1]

Modularity in the strict sense employed here — involving replicated regularity in the geometric relationships of masses and spaces comprising a building, yielding groundplans composed of space-cells whose dimensions were simple fractions and multiples of each other — may well be as old as the early Neolithic period in the Old World. Remarkable evidence for modularity in planning and construction has come to light in the past decade in the excavation of the Neolithic town of Çatal Hüyük in the Konya region of south central Anatolia.[2]

The kind of modular planning evidenced by the groundplan remains of Bronze Age Crete is not unfamiliar to students of contemporary cultures in the eastern Mediterranean, particularly Egypt and Mesopotamia.[3] The extraordinary complexities in spatial organization and the harmonic articulation of masses and planes seen above in our formal study of Minoan design are grounded firmly in approaches to planning and layout widely current during the Bronze Age. These tendencies have hitherto been most clearly apparent in Egyptian architectural design, long the object of detailed metrological study.[4]

Generically similar planning and layout methods were used in Crete and Egypt (but for widely different building programs), and there may very well have been a certain amount of technological intercourse between skilled masons, builders and designers in both societies. There is no secure evidence for such an interchange in the archaeological record as yet, although there is interesting circumstantial evidence uncovered in Egypt for the possible presence of Minoan craftsmen at the building site of the XII Dynasty Pyramid of the Pharaoh Sesostris II, including pottery made locally in Minoan styles, as well as a couple of wooden measuring rods whose internal divisions may very well have replicated a Minoan measuring standard.[5]

But whatever the nature of the technological interchange between Egypt and Crete — and there are any number of possible scenarios[6] — Minoan and Egyptian architectural design are abruptly different in nearly every way. Minoan builders may have seen, admired, and even copied certain Egyptian motifs,[7] but in fundamental formal conception Minoan architectural design is strikingly autonomous.[8] Whatever influence the architecture of Egypt may have had on Minoan Crete seems to be limited (if indeed at all) to some details of decorative articulation and, possibly, to mechanical routines of planning and layout.[9]

We have seen in Part One that a comprehensive and holistic analysis of the dimensions of a Minoan groundplan yields (for those structures sufficiently well preserved) often remarkably clear evidence for modular grid planning and layout. The present Part picks up on the generalized observations made above and presents a detailed modular analysis of each of the buildings studied in Part One. Our aim here is not only to demonstrate the geometric regularity by which each structure was planned, conceived and executed, but also to explore the significance of each modular grid for an understanding of the functional organization of each building. There exists, as we shall see below, a close connection between the organization of functional spaces in Minoan buildings and their modular composition. As will become apparent, a study of Minoan planning procedures yields important information regarding patterns of spatial and functional relationships: certain consistencies in the proportional allotment of space to various functional requirements are observable beneath the often abruptly different formal structures of (for example) Minoan houses, and such patterns resonate with tendencies in the palaces.

The study of modular organization in architecture has often, in the history of art history, been shunted towards the explication of purportedly deep-level harmonics in the surface realization of compositions. In scholarship over the past hundred years or more one inevitably comes upon erudite treatises conclusively demonstrating that the most tumble-down ancient shrine, or the storage granaries of some remote Pacific island, were marvels of harmonic planning which can only be explained by postulating a blood relationship with the planners of the Great Pyramid of Giza.

Not a little metrological study has been based upon the (often hidden) assumption that the geometric patterns of modular organization elucidated in the study of a building have a meaningfulness which is autonomous of the totality, or which somehow stands in relationship to other aspects of formal organization as a deep kernel truth, a uniquely privileged window into the minds of designers.

The plain fact remains that modularity in the organization of an architectural formation exists in a network of formative relations of various types, and its significance can never be more than semi-autonomous of the system within which it is embedded, and of which it is a component and contributing member.

That modularity in the organization of a plan, or harmonic rhythms of facades, or sets of proportions in the array of spaces, or rhythmic patterns of materials, colors, or textures are deeply interwoven among all aspects of architectonic formation is strikingly clear in a detailed and holistic consideration of Minoan architecture. It is the aim of the present part of this study to make explicit not only the modular patterning in Minoan design, but its inextricable relationships to all aspects of the organization of the Minoan built environment, both in formation and signification.

FORMAT

In the following section we shall examine the dimensional regularities of most of the buildings discussed above, in approximately the same sequence. The results of these analyses will be formally tabulated in Chapter V, to be followed by a summary overview of the relationships between modular organization and metrological practices.

In nearly every case, each analysis consists of (a) a tabulation of the dimensions of the given plan, with a suggestion as to the nature of the builders' module employed in construction; (b) a discussion of the implications of patterns of regularity in the structure's dimensions for a picture of that building's modular grid layout; (c) notations of correspondences between regularities of modular subdivision and functional zoning; and (d) notes and cross-references to similar situations seen in other buildings.

Normally, each analysis is complemented by at least two illustrations: (1) a groundplan of the structure under discussion; and (2) a hypothetical modular grid derived from our analysis of measurements, with occasional indication of facade proportioning and modular harmonics.

In the case of the large palaces, several modular diagrams are included in the analysis, pertaining to component palace sections or clusters, as well as an overall modular diagram. Except where noted, and in the case of buildings now destroyed, the metrological evidence for the following modular analyses is derived from the writer's own measurements and surveys in the field.[10]

NOTES

1. The evidence for architectural construction has recently been pushed back to *c.* 300,000 B.C. with the excavation of a seasonal encampment at Nice on the French Riviera, at a site known as Terra Amata. It consisted of an ovoid freestanding structure made of upright and bent sticks embedded in the ground and held in place by a circle of stones, and was approximately 17 meters long. It was rebuilt on the same plan each warm season for about 20 years, on the same spot, and apparently served as a communal house for a group fishing along the ancient coastline nearby. For a discussion of the significance of Terra Amata and its place in the earliest evolution of human architecture, see D. Preziosi, *Architecture, Language and Meaning: The Origins of the Built World* (Mouton, The Hague, 1979a). The site was excavated by H.de Lumley.

2. Excavated by James Mellaart, the remarkable 'pueblo' settlement of Çatal Hüyük flourished from *c.* 7000-5600 B.C. (J. Mellaart, *Çatal Hüyük*, 1964). Individual house units (all of which were contiguous and enterable only from their flat roofs) give clear evidence of careful and regular layout, based upon brick modules.

3. A good introduction to the subject, with useful bibliography, is A. Badawy, *AEAD* (1965).

4. A good bibliography will be found in I.E.S. Edwards, *The Pyramids of Egypt* (1963).

5. The site, now know as Illahun (El-Lahun), was originally excavated by Flinders Petrie; the measuring rods are at present in the collection of University College, London. The latter will be discussed below in connection with our consideration of the value of the Minoan linear standard.

6. It is conceivable that such information was transmitted to Crete by Minoan craftsmen attracted to work on various Pharaonic building schemes (see above, Note 5), or by resident Egyptians in Crete. At any rate, such knowledge may very well have been widespread in the societies of the eastern Mediterranean through any number of possible contacts among craftsmen. Any such contacts, however, remain hypothetical, and evidence for such interactions is extremely indirect.

7. See the discussion by J.W. Graham on possible 'Egyptian' motifs in the articulation of the northern facade of the central court at Phaistos (*AJA* 74 (1970): 231ff): Graham suggests that the two half-columns flanking the central entrance may have continued as tall flagstaffs above the roof line, in the manner of pylon flag poles in similar positions in Egyptian mortuary temple design. This argument is enhanced by enigmatic carvings on a steatite rhyton found at Kato Zakro, depicting (apparently) a peak sanctuary, but the connections remain quite tenuous. Why Minoan builders would have adopted a motif from Egyptian funerary architecture for a palatial compound is unclear.

8.   As is abundantly clear from our comparative analyses above in Part One. As is well known, our knowledge of Egyptian domestic architecture is relatively scanty (in contrast to funerary architecture): hardly anything remains of even great capitals such as the city of Memphis which evidently – again in contrast to funerary architecture – were constructed of relatively transient materials.

9.   The Egyptian connection is explored in great detail by Sir Arthur Evans in the first volume of *PM*.

10. A mention of these surveys, carried out on Crete in 1964-1966 and rechecked in 1972, is made in the Preface, Notes 1-5. Modular analyses of the Late Bronze Age Aegean Megaroid Compounds have been incorporated into our discussions in Appendix A.

MODULAR ANALYSES

1.	TVOL	Tou Vrakhnou O Lakkos (MM I/IIa).
2.	RSS	Rousses (MM III).
3.	AKHL	Akhladhia A (MM III).
4.	AMN	Amnissos, Villa of the Lilies (MM III).
5.	GRT	Gortyn, Villa rurale (LM I).
6.	KN HCS	Knossos, House of the Chancel Screen (MM IIIb/ LM Ia).
7.	KN RV	Knossos, Royal Villa (MM III).
8.	KN HF	Knossos, House of the Frescoes (MM IIIb/LM Ia).
9.	KN S	Knossos, South House (MM IIIb/LM Ia).
10.	KN SE	Knossos, South East House (MM IIIa).
11.	ML DA	Mallia, House Delta Alpha (MM IIIb/LM Ia).
12.	ML DBG	Mallia, Houses Delta Beta and Gamma (MM I).
13.	ML ZA	Mallia, House Zeta Alpha (MM IIIb/LM Ia).
14.	ML ZB	Mallia, House Zeta Beta (MM IIIb/LM Ia).
15.	NK	Nirou Khani (MM IIIb/LM Ia).
16.	SKLV	Sklavokampos (LM I).
17.	TYL A	Tylissos, House A (MM IIIb/LM Ia).
18.	TYL B	Tylissos, House B (MM IIIb/LM Ia).
19.	TYL C	Tylissos, House C (MM IIIb/LM Ia).
20.	PLKJB	Palaikastro, House B (LM I).
21.	PLK X	Palaikastro, House X (LM II).
22.	KZ G	Kato Zakro, House G.
23.	KZ J	Kato Zakro, House J.
24.	ML E	Mallia, House E (Le Petit Palais) (MM IIIb/ LM Ia).
25.	KN LP	Knossos, The Little Palace (MM IIIb/LM Ia).
26.	HTR	Haghia Triadha, Villa (LM Ib).
27.	KN PAL	Knossos, Palace.
28.	ML PAL	Mallia, Palace.
29.	PH I	Phaistos, First Palace.
30.	PH II	Phaistos, Second Palace.
31.	GRN	Gournia, Palace.
32.	KZ PAL	Kato Zakro, Palace.

1. TVOL: TOU VRAKHNOU O LAKKOS (MM I/IIA)

TVOL has been examined in detail above in Chapter I, pp. 27 ff. (Figures I.8, I.9, and I.10.) and thus we will not include it here directly; only a groundplan with dimensions (Figure IV.1.A) and a modular grid solution (Figure IV.1.B) are included to facilitate direct comparison with the analyses below.

TVOL: *NS X EW* : 11.00 x 10.95
     unit   : 0.275
     module : 1.375 (= 5)
     grid   : 40 x 40
     modular
     grid   : 8 x 8

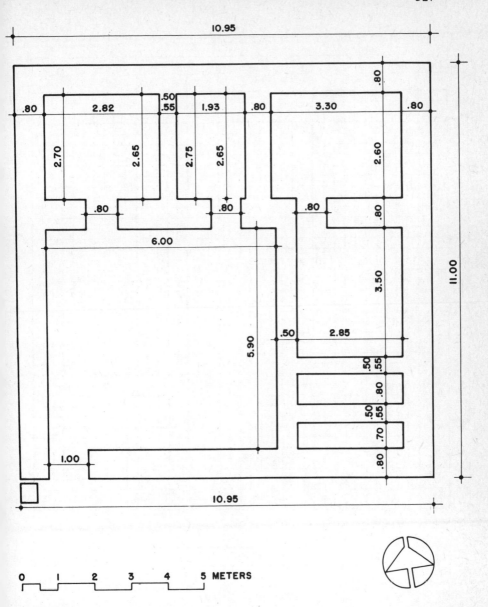

Figure IV.1.A. *Tou Vrakhnou O Lakkos: dimensions*

328

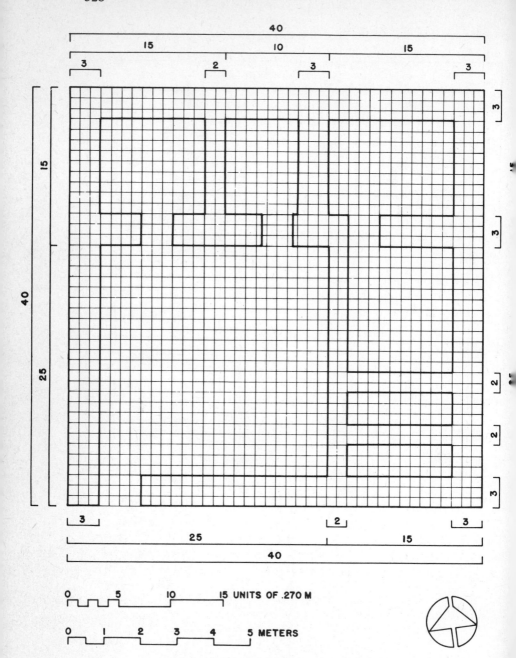

Figure IV.1.B. *Tou Vrakhnou O Lakkos: modular grid*

2. RSS: ROUSSES (MM III)[1]

Although part of its outer walls are ruined, enough foundation traces remain to provide a secure reconstructed plan of RSS. Excavators suggest a second exterior doorway in the southeastern room. Rubble-stone walls generally straight and true, with a slight jog in the western facade near the juncture of the major east-west wall through the building. The plan is the mirror-reverse of TVOL (as noted above in Chapter I), with the exception of the remains of a square pillar base in the largest (northeastern) cell. No trace has been found of a stairway to a second storey. The building is considered to have been used as a small shrine (*hieron*).[2] In contrast to TVOL, all rooms directly interconnect.

RSS: *NS X EW* : 10.95 x 8.10/8.40
      unit   : 0.270
      module : units?
      grid   : 40 x 30
      W facade : 16 : 24 or 2 : 3

NOTES: RSS

1.   Excavated by Dr. N. Platon, near Khondhrou Viannou: *BCH* (1958): 778-779; (1960): 826ff, plan, p. 826, Figure 1.
2.   *BCH* (1960): 826. Note that the proportions of the western facade sections are 16 to 24 modular units, or 2:3; a proportional schema met with frequently in Minoan design, as we shall see.

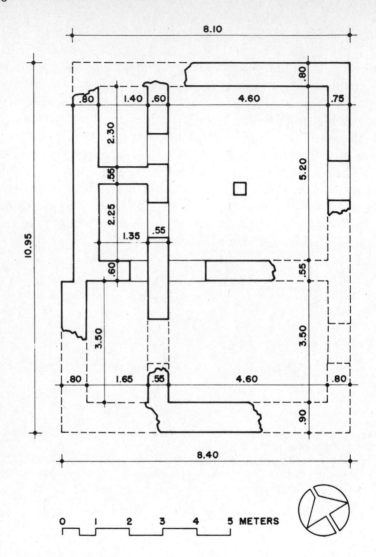

Figure IV.2.A. *Rousses: dimensions*

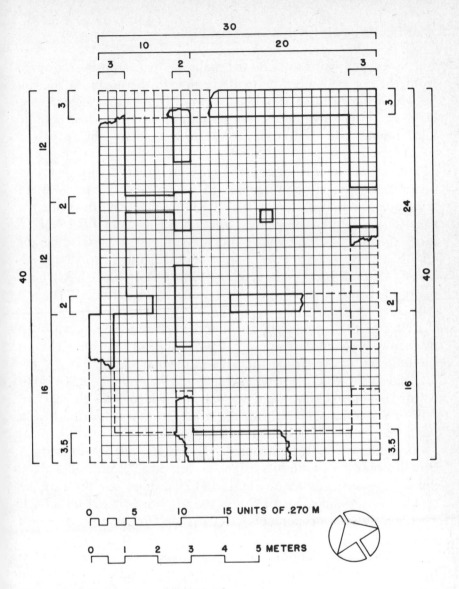

Figure IV.2.B. *Rousses: modular grid*

3. AKHL: AKHLADHIA HOUSE A (MM III)[1]

As shown in Figure IV.3.B, the walls of this farmhouse diverge from the perpendicular, particularly toward the north, as the hill on which the building stands falls away. The misalignments, however, are internally consistent, permitting us to reconstruct the ideal layout grid derived from the measurements shown in the first diagram.

The measurements of the overall layout and its internal subdivisions suggest close adherence to a module of ±3.40, wherein grid squares of 10 by 10 units of ±0.340 generate all the principal functional subdivisions of the structure. Cell-cluster 1-9-10-11-12 (grid squares NOPRSTVWX) replicates the structural frame of TVOL and RSS. Appended to the south of this is a hall system (cells 2-3 in Figure IV.3.A; grid squares FGHJKL), a kitchen/pantry (cells 4-5; grid squares EI), and storage areas MQU and ABCD.[2]

Cell 2 of the hall system is composed of two halves, partitioned by a row of round and square pillars. It appears that the intent of the builders was to divide this area into equal halves, but it is the internal space which is so subdivided, not the grid layout. In other words, it appears that the space was subdivided after the eastern wall of cell 2 was laid out, for the row of piers is equidistant from the latter and the PDP wall system to the west.

As indicated by the grid plan, the house is 40 by 60 units in overall size (4 by 6) modular squares), forming a 2:3 rectangle. The domestic quarter (squares EFGHIJKL) occupies one-third of the structure's ground area, or 8 grid squares out of the total of 24. The hall system proper (FGHJKL) is one-fourth the total grid area.

The proposed planning grid thus served as a straightforward framework for the major and minor functional subdivisions of the ground plan.

The eastern facade is articulated into a recessed portion (the eastern facade of grid squares HLP) and a projecting portion to the north (the eastern facade of grid squares TX): the division is thus 20 modular units and 30 modular units, a proportion of 2 : 3, resonating with the overall proportions of the plan itself.

AKHL: *NS X EW* : 20.00^3 x 14.00
            unit   : 0.340
            module   : 3.40 (= 10)
            grid   : 60 x 40
            facade   : 20 : 30 or 2 : 3

NOTES: AKHL

1. *BCH* LXXXIV (1960): 822ff, plan, Figure 3, p. 824.
2. Alleyway ABCD, including the southern boundary wall, is functionally part of
    House A; walls to the south of the latter are part of the ill-preserved 'House B'.
    On the use of cells 4 and 5 for food storage and preparation, see *BCH* LXXXIV
    (1960): 823. Cell 3, part of the hall system proper, was evidently used as a dining
    area, at least on its southern side, judging from the position of an L-shaped seating
    bench to the south and west.
3. This dimension is an average of the north-south lengths taken across the building
    at the points indicated in the first plan.

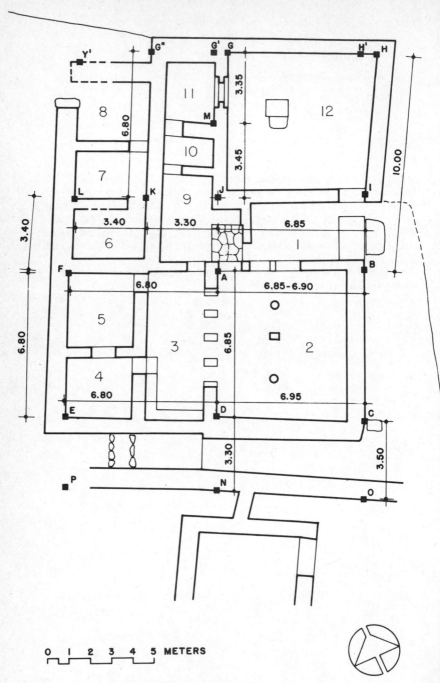

Figure IV.3.A. *Akhladhia: dimensions*

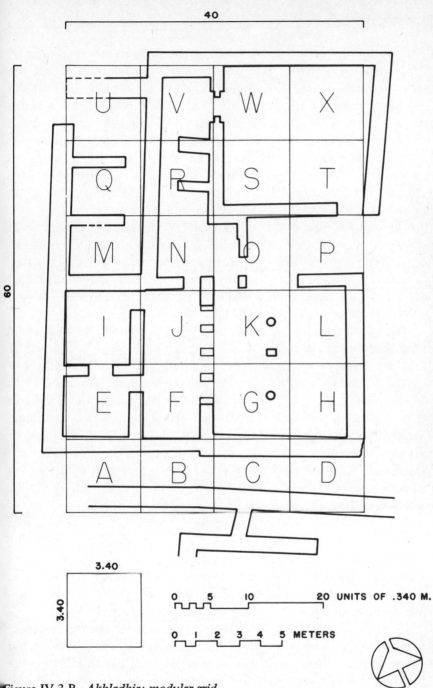

Figure IV.3.B. *Akhladhia: modular grid*

4. AMN: AMNISSOS (MM III)[1]

The northern, western and southern boundaries of the 'Villa of the Lilies' are known, but it is unclear how far to the east the structure extended. The dimensions of the villa suggest the modular layout grid shown in Figure IV.4.B, i.e. grid squares ±2.80 on a side, making the structure five grid squares wide by at least seven squares long. As the diagram reveals, all major walls may be generated by the proposed grid, and the sizes of the various cells coincide with grid subdividions. Walls were constructed on one side of the layout grid lines or another, depending upon *in situ* decisions reached by the builders.

The hall system (grid squares PQRUVWZA' B' E' F'G') resembles those of the palatial compounds at Phaistos or Mallia, with an outer veranda, presumably colonnaded, opening onto a court or garden. To the south of the hall system is a cell (grid squares SX) considered to have been a shrine: its position relative to the hall system recalls the situation at Mallia.[2]

Taking the grid squares to represent ten units of 0.28, the structure as extant is 5 by 7+ squares or 50 by 70+ units. The unit length appears to be corroborated by the ashlar masonry southern facade lengths: that to the south of grid squares OTY is ±7.60 (7.56 = 27 x 0.280), while that to the south of grid squares D'I'is ±5.10 (5.04 = 18 x 0.280). The resultant proportional scheme for the (extant part of the) southern facade is 27 : 18 units, or 3 : 2, a ratio observed above for RSS and AKHL. Here, however, the facade projections are *appended* to the modular layout grid, a situation we shall meet again below.[3]

How far the original structure extended is not known, but if AMN is consistent with other examples, it may have extended to a length of 80 units (yielding a 5 : 8 rectangle, consistent with the facade schema of 2 : 3), or a length of 100 units (yielding a 1 : 2 rectangle); both schemas are known elsewhere, as we shall see. The ruined walls in grid squares EJO to the southwest suggest a possible southward extension of the building in this area.

If this was a self-contained domestic structure, we would expect to find, by analogy with other houses, more extensive service and storage areas: these may have lain to the east (in which case the building must have extended beyond the hypothetical 80-unit length to at least 100 units (or more). It is also possible that the building originally extended further to the west, on a higher level (the present western boundary wall stands at the foot of the Amnissos hill). In any case, it is at least plausible that the presently extant structure might have been the residential core of a larger (palatial?) compound.

AMN: *NS X EW* : 15.50^4 x 19.60^5
          unit   : 0.280
          module : 2.80 (= 10)
          grid   : 50 x 70+
          facade   : 18 : 27 or 2 : 3

NOTES: AMN

1.   S. Marinatos, *PAE* (1932) [1933]: 76-94, plan, Figure 3, p. 82; *PAE* (1933) [1934] 93-100; *BCH* LVII (1933): 292-295; *PAE* (1934) [1935]: 128-133; *PAE* (1935) [1936] 196ff; J.W. Graham, *PC*: 68-69.
2.   See above, Part One, Mallia and Phaistos.
3.   In other words, the articulation of the outer facade is semiautonomous of the grid within; compare the western facade of the second palace at Phaistos above and Figure II.44.
4.   The overall north-south width is exclusive of the southern facade wall.
5.   The overall east-west length as extant to the extent of the grid shown in our diagram.

338

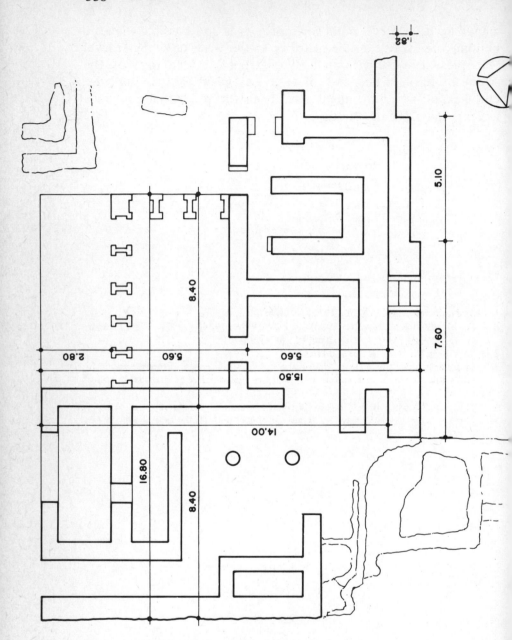

Figure IV.4.A. *Amnissos: dimensions*

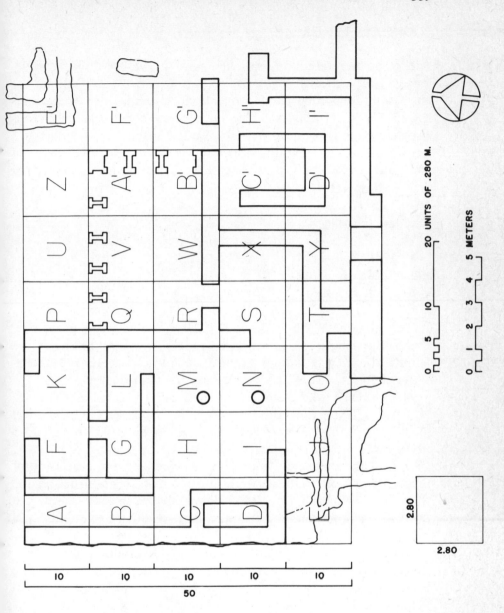

Figure IV.4.B. *Amnissos: modular grid*

5. GRT: GORTYN (LM I)[1]

Although there are many misalignments of walls within the structure, there is enough regularity to permit a reasonable estimate of the structure's modular organization. Overall, the structure is 23.25 EW by 19.90 NS. The outer trace consists of numerous projecting and recessed facades, and a glance at the diagrams below will reveal that the northern facade is a reversed image of the southern facade, just as the eastern facade is a reversed image of that to the west. In other words:

facades	E projected	: A recessed
	F recessed	: L projected
	G projected	: J recessed; and
facades	D projected	: H projected
	B recessed	: I recessed

In the latter case, while D and H project, the length of D approximates the length of I, while the length of B approximates the length of H, even though B and I are both recessed. The dimensions of all facades (A through M) are shown in Figure IV.5.A.

Note that H (6.20) equals one-half of D (12.40) and is twice M (3.10). If we take the dimension of ±3.10 as a hypothetical modular length, the overall dimensions of the structure equal 65 units by 75 units (Figure IV.5.B), or 13 by 15 grid squares. As shown in the diagram, a unit of ±0.310 generates the position of most major walls, but it would appear that in construction the walls of this rural farmhouse did not always exactly follow the idealized grid layout, which specifies grid squares five units on a side (1.55).[2]

Because of the irregularities in actual construction and layout, this solution seems the best, but it leaves much to be desired. The building simply wasn't laid out with the modular precision so often evident in town houses, although a good deal of care was given to the harmonic articulation of facade pieces themselves. The bilaterally symmetric and antisymmetric articulation of the facades are ingeniously interwoven.

A comparison with AKHL above will reveal that, as with that building, the width of a principal entrance corridor (here cell 6) is ten units wide (as at AKHL, but there using a standard of 0.340), in contrast to the proportional allotment of room space adjacent (20 units in both cases).[3] It would appear that the Minoan builder may have conventionally allotted certain standard areal proportions within a layout grid for spaces of particular functions. In other words, distinctions in function appear to have been mapped onto a standard hierarchy of size-allotments. These practices will be further illuminated in examples to come.

GRT: *NS X EW* : 19.90 x 23.25
     unit   : 0.31 (?)
     module   : 3.10 (= 10) or 1.55 (= 5)
     grid   : 65 x 75
     facades : tripartite N + S; bipartite E + W.

NOTES: GRT

1. D. Levi, *BdA* 44 (1959): 237-265, plan, Figure 2, p. 238.
2. This derived unit of ±0.31 closely approximates J.W. Graham's so-called 'Minoan Foot' of 0.3036, to be discussed in a later section. GRT, however, is the only structure whose dimensions appear to reflect that standard (Graham's own examples, taken from the large palaces, are incorrect as we shall see below). As we have seen so far (and as we shall see throughout this series of analyses), the Minoans appear to have employed two standards of measurement: a longer unit whose mean is ±0.34, and a shorter unit whose mean is ±0.27. Each structure analyzed generates modular subdivisions based on approximations of either a longer or shorter unit. The shorter unit is to the longer as 2 : 3.
3. See above under AKHL, corridor NOP in contrast to cells STWX or JKLFGH adjacent.

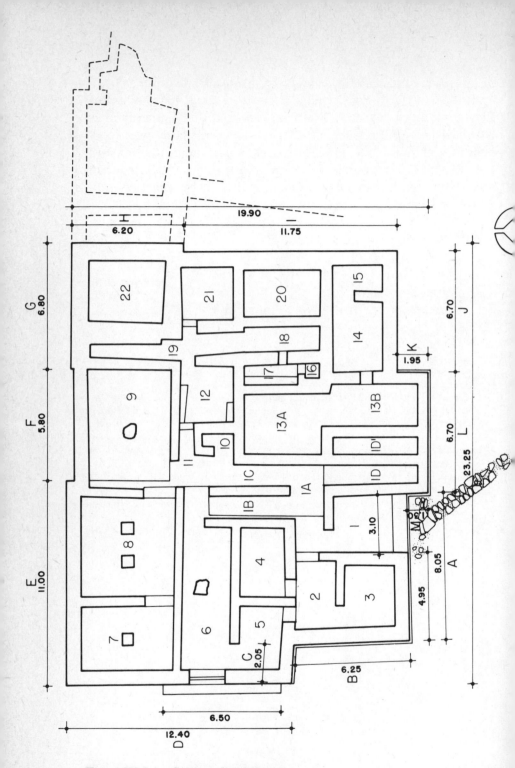

Figure IV.5.A. *Gortyn: dimensions*

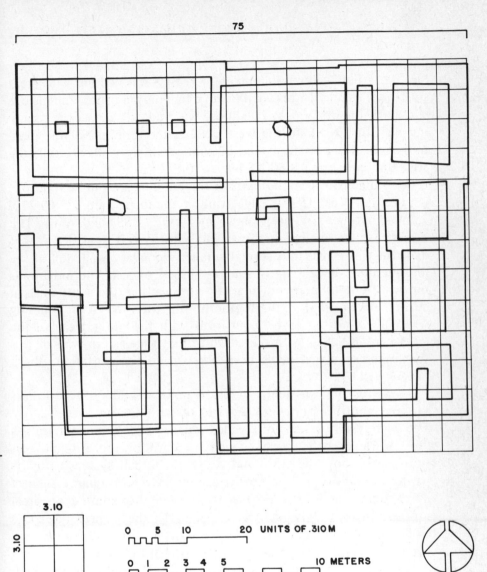

Figure IV.5.B. *Gortyn: modular grid*

6. KN HCS: KNOSSOS/HOUSE OF THE CHANCEL SCREEN (MM IIIB/ LM IA)[1]

Despite a few wall misalignments, KN HCS was laid out with great precision, as may be revealed by an examination of the dimensions shown in Figure IV.6.A. The house was built up against the retaining wall of KN SE to the west, so that the terminus of the planning grid is the eastern face of that retaining wall. Overall, the structure measures 18.60 NS by 16.30 EW.[2]

The dimensions of the parts of the building are simple fractions or multiples of ±5.40, suggesting a modular unit of ±0.270, approximating those seen above at TVOL, RSS, and AMN. The resultant planning grid is shown in Figure IV.6.B. A glance at that diagram will reveal that several smaller secondary walls fall at the midpoint of the 2.70 grid squares (i.e. at ±1.35). The only walls seriously out of perpendicular are the walls in the southwestern corner. In my opinion, the southernmost extension of the building was laid *in situ* so as to align itself with the outer trace of the terrace of KN SE to the west. Note that the eastern wall of this southwestern magazine is perpendicular to the central southern facade wall.

The structure was laid out on a modular grid 60 by 60 units square, subdivided into grid squares of ten units on a side (2.70). The hall system is 20 units wide, while smaller chambers are ten units wide, as is the L-shaped entrance corridor, repeating proportions seen above at GRT and AKHL. The hall system (plus its western extension to the north) occupies ten grid squares, slightly more than one-fourth of the totality: approximating an areal proportion seen above at AKHL. Similarly, the storage magazines and pillar crypt cluster, occupying the entire western flank, occupy ten grid squares, again, one-fourth of the totality.

But it will be observed that the actual construction omits occupation of the four northeastern grid squares, thereby reducing the totality to 32 squares built upon. Seen in this light, the hall system proper (eight squares) is exactly one-fourth of the constructional totality.

The southern facade is articulated into three subsections, progressively recessed from west to east. The facades are situated upon the modular grid in such a way that their *grid-* proportional lengths are, respectively, 10 + 20 + 30 units, or 1 : 2 : 3. This harmonic scheme resonates with that seen at RSS, AKHL, and AMN above.

KN HCS: *NS X EW* : 16.20 x 16.20³
          unit   : 0.270
          module   : 2.70 (= 10)
          grid   : 60 x 60
          facade   : 10 : 20 : 30 or 1 : 2 : 3

NOTES: KN HCS

1.   *PM* II: 391-395, plan, Figure 224, p. 392.
2.   This is the *total* overall size.
3.   This is the modular grid size based on a unit of 0.270; the actual size of the constructed portion of the grid square is 16.30 by 16.30, representing an error of ten centimeters north-south and east-west.

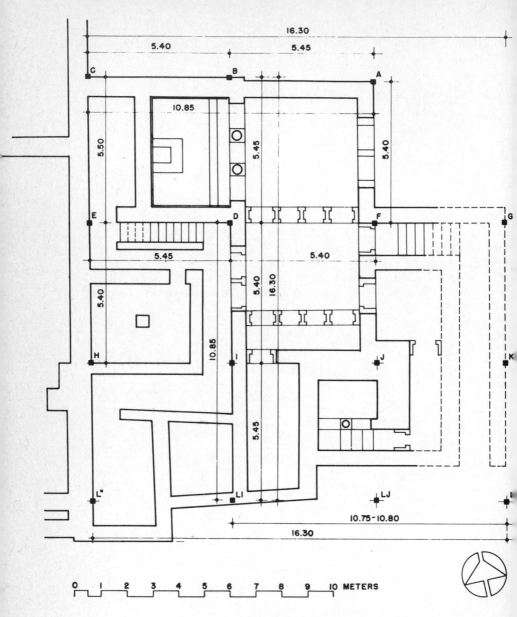

Figure IV.6.A. *Knossos: HCS: dimensions*

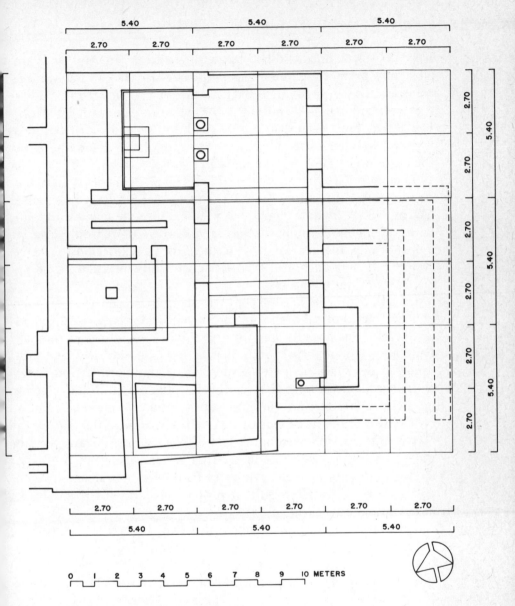

Figure IV.6.B. *Knossos: HCS: modular grid*

7. KN RV: KNOSSOS/ROYAL VILLA (MM III)[1]

KN RV was planned and laid out with great care; interior walls are all nearly perfectly parallel and perpendicular. The overall dimensions (as shown in the first diagram) are ±17.90 NS by ±13.50 EW (between points A-A' and B-B'). As was the case with KN HCS, KN RV is built against a hillside to the west, and the structure's western wall serves as a retainer. The modular grid terminates at the eastern face of this retaining wall (as at KN HCS).

The modular grid shown in Figure IV.7.B indicates that the structure was conceived as a 3 : 4 rectangle, 6 by 8 grid squares EW by NS. A modular length of ±2.24 is suggested, and the resultant grid generates the position of all major walls. We would suggest a unit of measurement of ±0.280, the same as that found for AMN above: but here each grid square is eight units on a side (0.28 by 8 = 2.24) rather than ten.

In terms of the modular grid proper, it is used in a manner identical to that seen above: entrance corridor is one grid square wide, while major cells are two grid squares wide (e.g. in the hall system or pillar crypt); subsidiary rooms are similarly one grid square wide. Thus the layout grid was built upon proportionally in a manner identical to AKHL or KN HCS, the only difference being in the absolute size of the grid square proper (here, eight units; at KN HCS ten units of 0.270; at AKHL ten units of 0.340).

The internal subdivisions reflect a tripartite organization, with the hall system occupying the central zone. This latter, however, is two grid squares wide, while its flanking zones are each three grid squares wide. The resultant proportional schema is 3 : 2 : 3, based upon unit widths of 24 + 16 + 24.

The southern facade is divided into two subsections: a projecting portion to the west (16 units wide), and a recessed portion to the east, 24 units wide (or 32, if the width of the entrance corridor is included). The proportions are 16 : 24 (or 32) or 2 : 3 (or 4). Thus the southern facade reveals a 2 : 3 schema if we exclude the corridor (unlike KN HCS), or a 1 : 2 schema if we include the latter (as we did at KN HCS).

The overall planning grid consists of 48 modular squares; the hall system occupies 12 grid squares (including the western extension), or one-fourth of the totality, an areal proportion seen above.

KN RV: *NS X EW* : 17.90 x 13.50 (ideally 17.92 x 13.44)
        unit   : 0.280
        module   : 2.24 (= 8)
        grid   : 69 x 48
        facade (E) : 24 + 16 + 24 or 3 : 2 : 3
              (S) : 16 + 24 (or 32) or 2 : 3 (or 4)

NOTES: KN RV

1. *PM* II: 396-413, plan, Figure 227, p. 397, section: Figure 226; *Handbook:* 62-64; Graham, *PC*: 52-54. Graham's statement that KN RV is ten meters wide is incorrect.

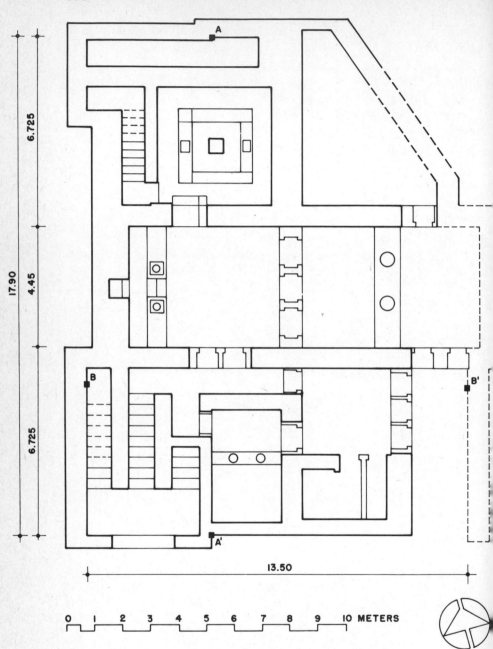

Figure IV.7.A. *Knossos: RV: dimensions*

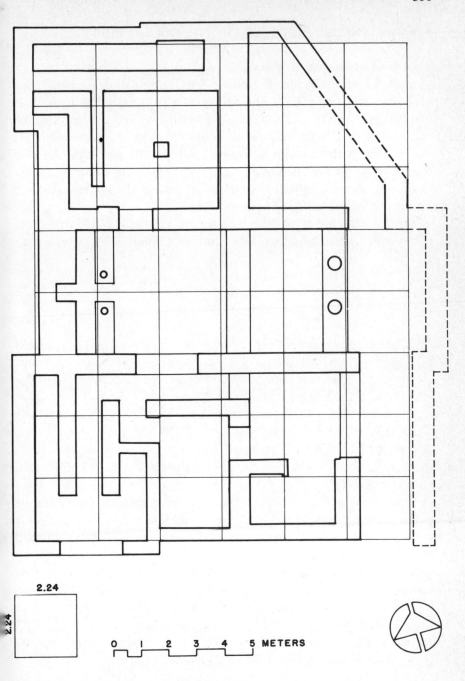

2.24

0 1 2 3 4 5 METERS

Figure IV.7.B. *Knossos: RV: modular grid*

8. KN HF: KNOSSOS/HOUSE OF THE FRESCOES (MM IIIB/LM IA)[1]

The dimensions of this small structure suggest a layout grid of squares ±2.45 on a side (Figure IV.8.B), comprising an overall grid of 24 squares (4 by 6).[2] The hall system (squares UVWX and half of each of QRST) occupies an area equal to six grid squares, or one-fourth of the totality (as seen above). The entranceway (GH) and north-south corridor (LP plus one-half T) are both one grid square wide, as are the smaller cells (CD, IJK). In contrast to the examples above, the hall system is not two grid squares wide but rather one and a half grid squares wide.

To the east and west, the facades are subdivided into three sections, each corresponding to a simple subdivision of the layout grid:

W : 2 + 2½ + 1½ (NS) = 4 : 5 : 3
E : 3 + 1½ + 1½ (NS) = 2 : 1 : 1

The western facade, then, exclusive of the deeply recessed northern section, presents a 3 : 5 proportional scheme, equivalent to the 2 : 3 schemas seen above. Overall, the structure's modular grid forms a 2 : 3 rectangle.

What of the metrological standard underlying the modular dimension of ±2.45? Note that 2.45 x 1/8 = 0.30625, and 2.45 x 1/9 = 0.2722. The latter is already attested in four structures examined above, while ±0.30 approximates the ±0.31 suggested above for GRT.[3]

If the unit employed was 0.30, then each grid square would be equal to eight units, and the overall dimensions of the building would be 48 by 32. If we choose the unit of ±0.27, then each grid square is nine units; a solution which would admit of fractional quantities in describing the width of the hall system (i.e. 13½ units). The 0.30 solution is neater, but the 0.27 solution need not be ruled out. The details of the facade subdivisions (in contrast to their grid-placements) similarly yield ambiguous results: 4.60-4.65 approximates 15 units of 0.306, while 7.30 approximates 24 units (a 5 : 8 proportion), but 3.95-4.00 equals 13 units.

Nevertheless, while the metrological details are unclear, the modular proportions and proportional areal allotment of spaces are consistent with houses already seen.

KN HF: *NS X EW*   : 16.00 x 11.50 (14.70 x 9.80)[4]
        unit   : 0.30625 or 0.2722
        module   : 2.45 (= 8 or 9)
        grid   : 48 x 32 (or 54 x 36) = 3 : 2
        facade (W) : 12 : 20 (= 3 : 5)

NOTES: KN HF

1. *PM* II: 431-467, plan, Figure 251, p. 434; *PC*: 57-58.
2. The same pattern employed at AKHL above.
3. At GRT (q.v.) the suggested unit of 0.31 was isomorphic, decimally, to the modular square size of 3.10.
4. The dimensions in parentheses are those of the proposed modular grid.

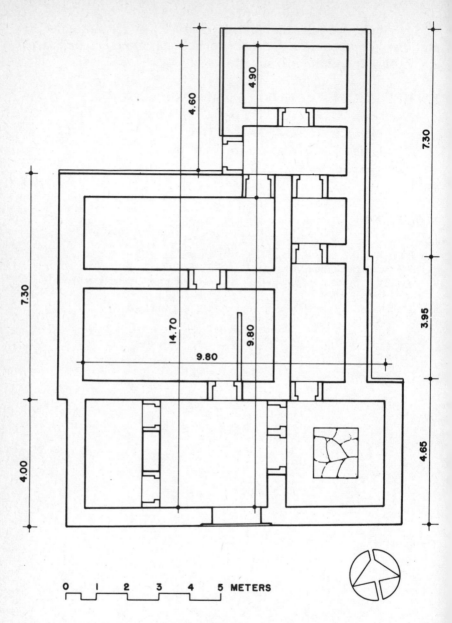

0 1 2 3 4 5 METERS

Figure IV.8.A. *Knossos: HF: dimensions*

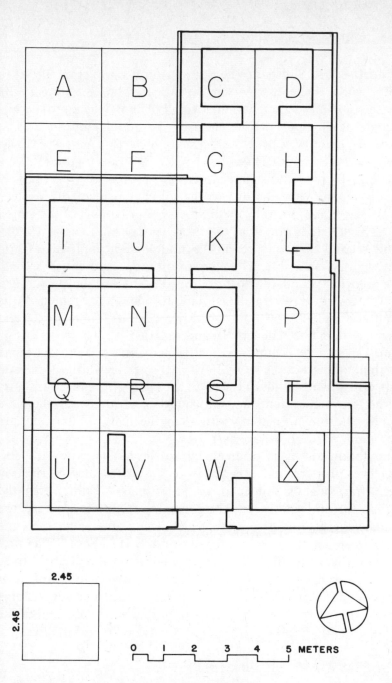

Figure IV.8.B. *Knossos: HF: modular grid*

9. KN S: KNOSSOS/SOUTH HOUSE (MM IIIB/LM IA)[1]

The north-south width of the South House varies from 11.10 to
13.50, while the east-west length varies from 18.55 to 19.20.
Despite some misalignments, the overall plan may be inscribed in a
rectangle of 2 : 3 proportions (four by six modular grid squares, as
shown in Figure IV.9.B). Note that length D'- D''' : A'- A = ±12.28:
±19.20 = 2 : 3. Width D'- D''' = length F-F' (see Figure IV.9.A).
Length F'-F'' = ±6.25, slightly less than one-half of F-F' (12.80).
This discrepancy may be due to the misalignment of the western
wall of the house, for the length A-A' is ±6.40, one-half the length
F-F'. This length is one-third the total length : ±6.40 x 3 = 19.20.

The second diagram presents a modular grid built up of grid
squares ±3.20 on a side. This dimension may represent 10 x 0.32,
a metrological standard close to the 0.340 seen above, or 12 x
0.270, attested in several house layouts. On either standard, the
overall grid is 40 by 60 units or 48 by 72 units. There are 24 grid
squares, as seen above at KN HF and AKHL.[2]

The hall system occupies a smaller percentage of the floor area
here than at the houses seen above, although its width of one and
a half grid squares is identical to that of KN HF, and in absolute
size the two hall systems are similar. Also, as at KN HF, there are
no cells allotted a greater width than the halls, while some are
of the same width; most are narrower.

The southern facade is divided into the familiar tripartite section. The proportional schema is reflected (as at KN HF) by
simple fractions or multiples of grid squares, rather than the
lengths of built wall-traces. Thus, reading from west to east, the
modular lengths are: 20 + 25 + 15 (x 0.320),[3] or 4 : 5 : 3, the same
schema seen on the western facade of KN HF above.[4] The progressive setbacks of this southern facade reflect the diagonal trace
of a paved walkway rising up the slope from west to east. It is of
interest that the major grid breaks in the northern facade, reading
from west to east, are 3½ + 1 + 1½ grid squares, not unlike the
north-south grid breaks at KN HF of 3 + 1½ + 1½ grid squares.[5]

KN S: *NS X EW*   : 13.50 x 19.20[6]
       unit   : 0.320[7]
       module   : 3.20 (= 10)

grid : 40 x 60 (= 2 : 3)
facade (S) : 20 + 25 + 15 (= 4 : 5 : 3)

NOTES: KN S

1. *PM* II: 373-390, plan, Figure 208, p. 375, section, Figure 210, p. 377; *Handbook*: 65-67; *PC*: 55-56.
2. At KN HF, the grid squares are evidently eight units on a side; at AKHL, the grid squares are ten units (of 0.340) on a side.
3. These modular lengths are taken from the western facade to the western face of the first wall (two grid squares); from the latter to the western face of the third wall (2½ grid squares). In other words, the harmonic schema is in this case (as at KN HF) a function of the grid layout itself, rather than the actual built wall lengths. Many other instances of this phenomenon will be seen below, along with examples of coincidence between grid-square breaks and wall-turnings. The two are semi-autonomous of each other, and it appears to be the case that Minoan designers/ builders devised their harmonic schemas coterminous now to one, now to the other.
4. The principal difference between the two examples is the nature of articulation (projection/recession). It is noteworthy that in both houses this tripartite articulation appears on a long facade to the left of a hall system. In both houses the halls occupy identical positions.
5. This ignores the minor jog in the northern facade here adjacent to the waste flue of the latrine.
6. The former dimension, of course, is the actual built width; if our proposal is correct, the layout grid *per se* would have extended to a length of 12.80, thereby excluding the northeastern projection.
7. Or, alternatively, 0.270, as noted above.

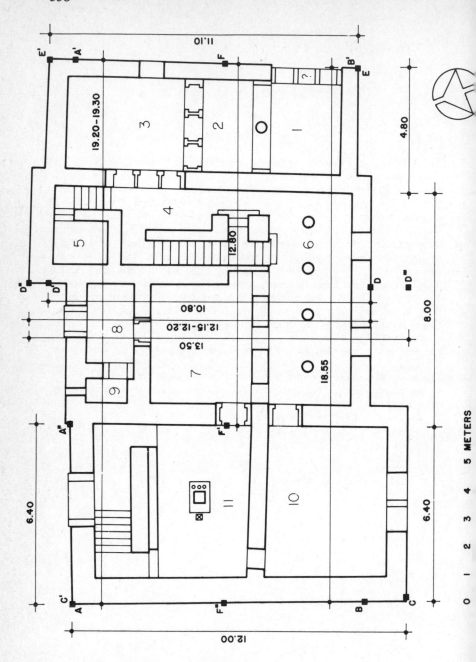

Figure IV.9.A. *Knossos: S: dimensions*

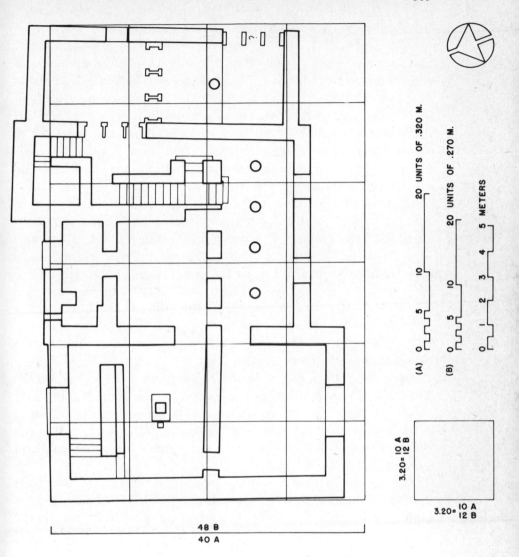

20 UNITS OF .320 M.

20 UNITS OF .270 M.

5 METERS

(A) 0 5 10

(B) 0 5 10

0 1 2 3 4 5

3.20= 10 A / 12 B

3.20= 10 A / 12 B

48 B

40 A

Figure IV.9.B. *Knossos: S: modular grid*

10. KN SE: KNOSSOS/SOUTHEAST HOUSE (MM IIIA)[1]

Our modular analysis, shown in the diagram, is based upon Evans' measurements as published. The structure was evidently laid out as a square 64 units on a side (8 x 8 grid squares of eight units of 0.270 on a side (= 2.175)). The modular unit is derived as one-half the width and length of cell 5, and the resultant grid generates all major walls. If our suggestion is correct, then it should be suggested further that in actual construction the northern and southern boundaries were shortened *in situ*.

While much of the eastern facade is broken away, enough of its trace remained for Evans to reconstruct the positions of facades labelled in our plan as A, B and C; the extension D-E is our own suggestion for the original state of the northeastern corner, based on a reasonable projection of the proportional schema begun to the south. Note that the resultant facade east of the modular grid is related to the adjacent facade of the grid labelled C as 3 : 2, a ratio by now familiar. Facade portion A of the grid is equal to C. Facade B occupies one grid square; according to our reconstruction, facade D would be twice B.

As at KN HF and KN S, the hall system is two grid squares wide, a size matched but not exceeded by a few other cells: 2, 5, 6/6a. Corridor 1 is one grid square wide, or one-half the latter, a situation also seen elsewhere at Knossos, and at AKHL. The hall system occupies ten grid squares, about one-fifth of the total grid squares actually built upon (i.e. 48).

The Southeast House, laid out on a square grid (8 by 8), is built up against the eastern retaining wall upon which KN HCS was later built: the latter is also laid out on a square grid (6 by 6), and the same unit of ±0.270 is evidenced in both.

___

KN SE: *NS X EW*   : 17.36 x 17.36[2]
         unit   : 0.270
         module : 2.175 (= 8)
         grid   : 64 x 64
         facade (E) : 16 + 16 + 24 (= 2 : 2 : 3)

NOTES: KN SE

1. *PM* I: 425-430, plan, Figure 306; *Handbook*: 64-65; *PC*: 56-57.
2. Actual extant east-west width is +15.19; 17.36 = grid reconstruction.

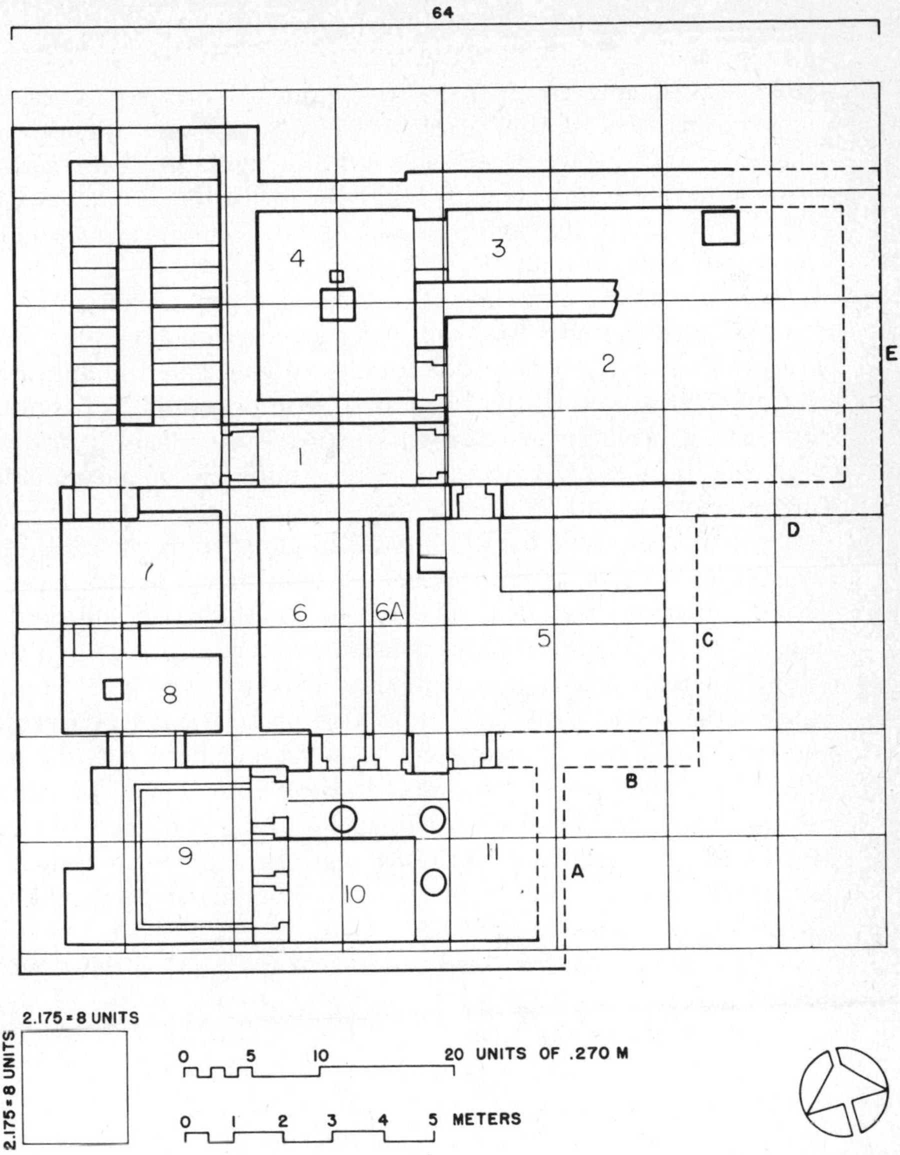

Figure IV.10.A. *Knossos: SE: modular grid*

11. ML DA: MALLIA/HOUSE DELTA ALPHA (MM IIIB/LM IA)[1]

Despite its deeply articulated outer facade, ML DA's ground-plan may be inscribed within a square ±13.50 on a side, exclusive of the wall-widths to the north and south. Furthermore, if this square is divided into eighths (Figure IV.11.B), and further into sixteenths (Figure IV.11.C), the wall positions of the groundplan may all be generated with accuracy.

A hypothetical module of ±1.68 (or 0.84), based on a unit of ±0.280, is suggested.[2] The hall system, occupying 55 grid squares (of 0.84) is one-fourth of the totality of grid squares built upon (ideally 220; in actuality 219), an areal proportion seen above.[3] The actual groundplan is carved out of the overall planning grid, and the facade subdivisions follow accurately simple modular divisions of the grid.

Each grid square of 0.84 equals 3 modular units of 0.280; the overall grid equals 48 by 48 units. As elsewhere, opposite facades are divided into tripartite subdivisions (to the north and south). Figure IV.11.D indicates the relative proportions of facade sections to each other. The eastern side breaks at 15 + 18 + 15 units, the southern side breaks at 18 + 15 + 15 units: the same quantities but with a different arrangement.[4] On the northern side, the grid breaks at 9 + 21 + 15 units, while to the west, reading from north to south, the grid breaks at 9 + 9 + 9 + 21 units. The architectonic effect of the facade articulations suggests a centrifugal, almost spiral progression, calling to mind the curvilinear patterning on some Minoan painted ceramics.

It is noteworthy that the groundplan, carved out of the original square layout grid, balances the reserved area of K on the SE with the combined reserved areas of H + H' to the northwest: 25 reserved grid squares at K, 12 + 3 + 6 (=21) reserved grid squares at H-H'. A similar reserved-balancing will be observed below at TYL C. The progressive setbacks of facade sections to the west follows the diagonal trace of a paved street in a manner reminiscent of KN S.

ML DA: *NS X EW* : 13.50 x 13.50
       unit   : 0.280
       module : 0.84 (= 3) or 1.68 (= 6)

grid   : 48 x 48
facades   : N: 3 : 7 : 5
         E: 5 : 6 : 5
         S: 6 : 5 : 5
         W: 3 : 3 : 3 : 7

NOTES: ML DA

1. *Et.Cret* IX: 43-48, plan, Plate LXIII; *CFFC*: 59-62; *PC*: 63-64, and Figures 21, 22.
2. Note also that 1.68 x 1/5 = 0.336, approximating the modular unit of ±0.340 seen above.
3. Or, 256 − 40 (i.e. including the three grid squares ot the west of the wall facade to the immediate north of the entranceway) = 216; one-fourth of 216 = 54 grid squares (vs. actual 55).
4. Taking as a 'grid break' the principal perpendicular subdivision of the hall system, as indicated in the plan. Overall, this wall facade = 11 x 3 or 33.

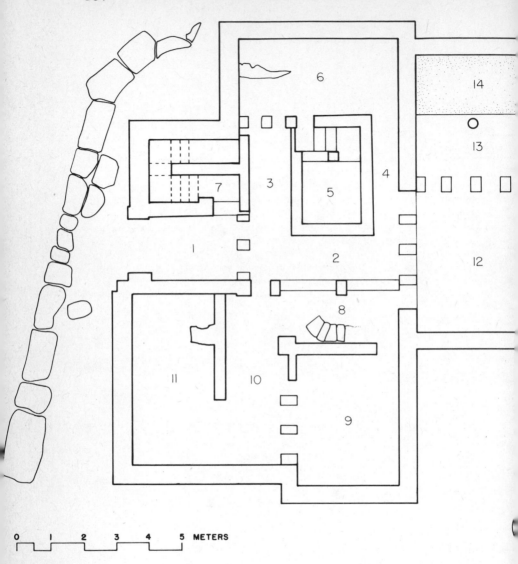

Figure IV.11.A. *Mallia: DA: plan*

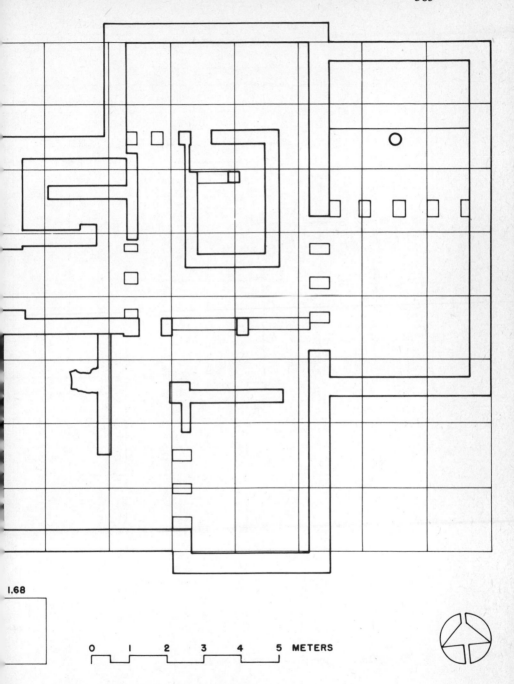

1,68

0   1   2   3   4   5 METERS

Figure IV.11.B. *Mallia: DA: modular grid (1)*

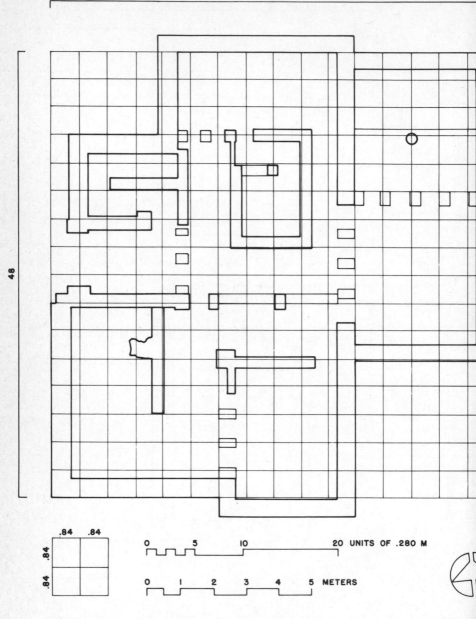

Figure IV.11.C. *Mallia: DA: modular grid (2)*

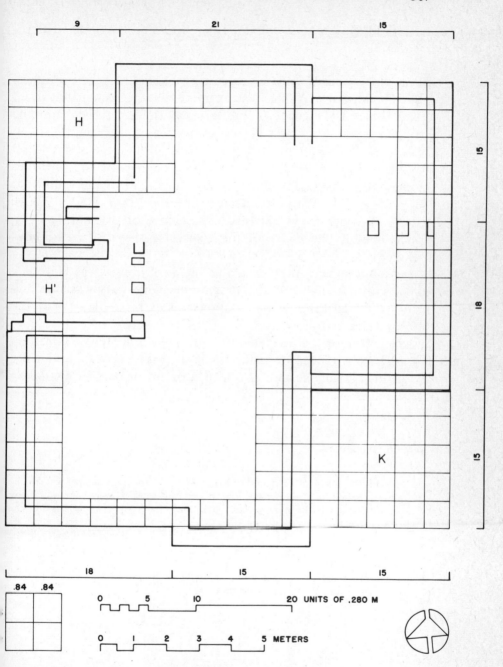

Figure IV.11.D. *Mallia: DA: facade harmonics*

12. ML DB/DG: MALLIA: QUARTER DELTA HOUSES DB AND DG (MM I)[1]

These three houses front on an east-west street along the northern side (House Delta Alpha, just examined, stands across the street from House DG here). Of interest here is the unified harmonic articulation of the street facades, as indicated in Figure IV.12.B. Note that from west to east, the lengths of the facades are: 12.30 + 7.00 + 4.00 + 7.30 + 11.30. These lengths are equivalent to modular lengths based on a standard of ±0.280 of the following: 40 + 25 + 15 + 25 + 40, ideally: 11.20 + 7.00 + 4.20 + 7.00 + 11.20, allowing for a gap in the sequence of five units (1.40), approximately the width of the transverse alley between houses DG and DB-1.[2]

It would appear, then, that this block of houses was built as a unity within a single building programme. This unity was harmonically expressed through the relationships of facade lengths on the public street as follows: A : B : C : D : E : or 8 : 5 : 3 : 5 : 8 ; the same proportional schema seen elsewehere in Minoan construction. The central facade is the smallest; it is flanked on both sides by slightly larger facades, which in turn are flanked by yet larger facade sections.

NOTES: ML DB/DG

1. *Et.Cret* IX: 48-54, plan, Plate LXVII; *GFFC*: 57-58. Built in the first Middle Minoan period, ceramic remains suggest that this block of houses was still in use during the MM IIIB/LM IA period, when House Delta Alpha was built across the street from House Delta Gamma. Bricks found in House DB-1 measure ±0.55 by ±0.40 by ±0.15, or (2 by 1½ by ½) x 0.28, the unit standard employed in the building layout itself. Bricks from Phaistos were found measuring 0.43 by 0.265 by 0.11: *PMF* I: 288.
2. The overall length of the block is 41.90; 0.280 x 150 (40 + 5 + 25 + 15 + 25 + 40) = 42.00, an error *in toto* of ten centimeters.

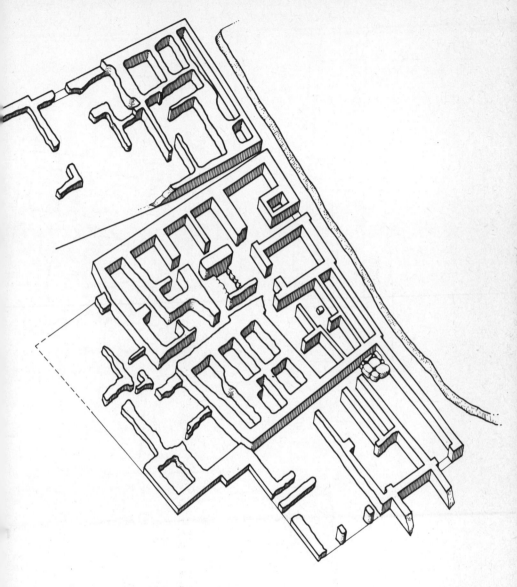

Figure IV.12.A. *Mallia: QD: isometric*

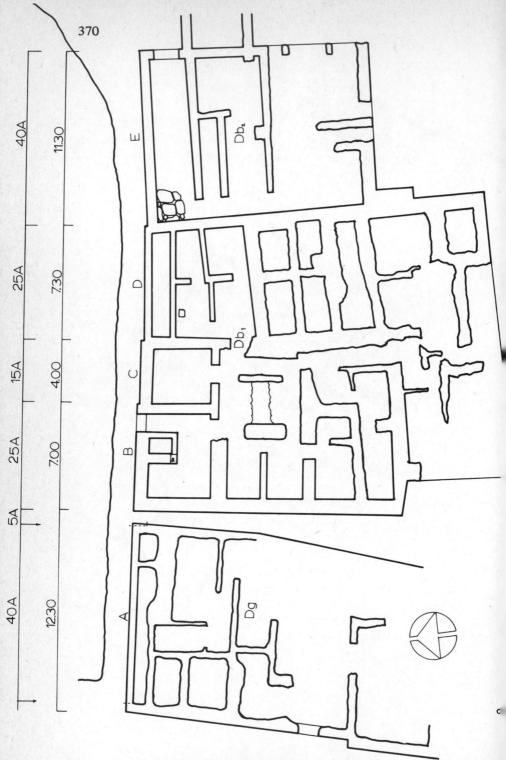

Figure IV.12.B. *Mallia: QD: facade harmonics*

13. ML ZA: MALLIA/HOUSE ZETA ALPHA (MM IIIB/LM IA)[1]

Our measurements of this large and interesting house (some of which are given in Figure IV.13.A) suggest a layout grid based upon a linear standard of ±0.270. The resultant grid is shown in Figure IV.13.B, measuring 60 units NS by 90 units EW. It will be observed that the domestic quarter occupies the western third of the plan net (30 by 60 units), while the remainder is a square (60 by 60 units), within which the area to the south of the magazines describes an inner square, 40 by 40 units.[2]

The hall system proper occupies one-third of the area of the domestic quarter, a smaller proportion than that seen in other houses (where the hall systems occupied approximately one-fourth of the total built area). The hall system opens onto what was undoubtedly a small private garden whose western boundaries are unknown. In a general sense, the plan is organized not unlike that of AKHL: the domestic quarter stands to the left side of a north-south entrance corridor, to the right of which is service and storage space. The proportions of the hall system (2 : 3) reflect those of the house as a whole, and the hall on the opposite (southeastern) corner of the house is the same size. The overall size of the house minus the domestic quarter (16.10-16.15 x 16.00-16.05) is nearly identical to the overall size of KN HCS (±16.30 by ±16.30), which is also laid out on a grid of squares 2.70 on a side, totalling (as here) 36 grid squares.

An examination of Figure IV.13.B indicates that a number of internal walls are not exactly generated by the layout grid. A detailed tabulation of the measurements of the building indicates that these walls were laid out from the faces of already-built primary through-walls, as shown in Figure IV.13.C. Thus, the three magazines in the northeastern corner of the structure were laid out ten modular units in width (2.70) from the inner face of the just-built outer wall;[3] the position of the sunken bathroom in the domestic quarter was set as indicated in the plan, by halving the remaining distance between built walls, and other subsidiary walls (shown shaded in the plan) were measured out as indicated.

Thus, ML ZA would appear to provide us with evidence not only for initial conception and layout, but also for a *sequence of construction*: major boundary and internal structural walls were begun first by masons, who then turned their attention to secondary internal room-dividers.

The northern and southern facades are subdivided into tripartite sections, as elsewhere, with the northern facade showing a central projection and the southern facade a central recession, mirroring the position of the former. The eastern and western facades are uniplanar. Both to the north and south, the relative proportions of the facade sections are similar: seen as functions of major grid subdivisions, that to the north breaks at 30 + 15 + 45 units (= 6 : 3 : 9) as does the southern facade, reading from west to east.

ML ZA:　*NS X EW* : 16.20 x 24.30
　　　　　unit　　 : 0.270
　　　　　module　: 2.70 (= 10)
　　　　　grid　　 : 60 x 90 (= 2 : 3)
　　　　　facade　 : (N and S) 6 : 3 : 9 (= 2 : 1 : 3)

NOTES: ML ZA

1.　*Et.Cret* IX: 63-79, plan, Plate LXV; *GFFC*: 63 -66; *PC*: 64-66.
2.　Recall that this square-within-a-square plan resonates with those of TVOL, RSS and AKHL. In fact, the inner square here is equal in size to the outer squares of the latter:

　　ML ZA　: 10.75 x 10.75
　　TVOL　 : 11.00 x 10.95
　　RSS　　: 8.10 x 10.95
　　AKHL　 : 10.75 x 11.00.

TVOL and RSS were laid out on a unit of ±0.270, while AKHL was laid out on a unit of ±0.340. The positional allotment of usages at AKHL and ML ZA is similar: domestic quarter occupying the left part of the plan, the 'square-within-a-square' service/work/storage areas on the right, with main entrance to the south, between the two major zones.

3.　An identical arrangement will be observed in the layout of the ten-unit wide magazines in the second Phaistian palace below; there the rooms are laid out relative to a just-built outer wall.

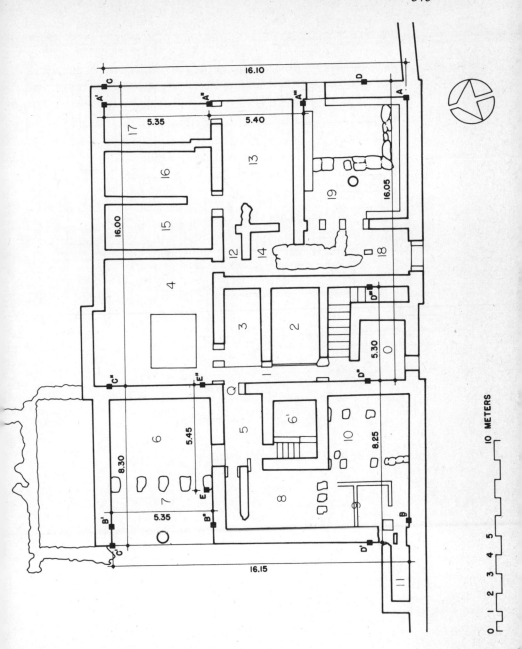

Figure IV.13.A. *Mallia: ZA: dimensions*

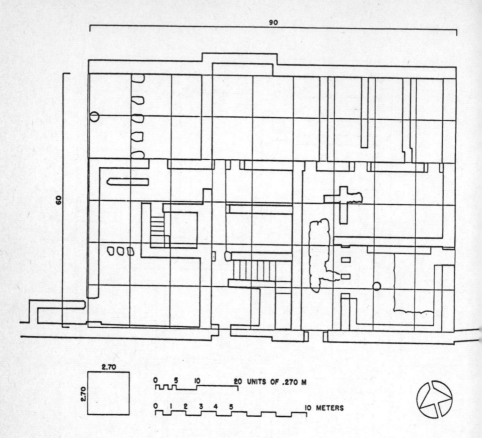

Figure IV.13.B. *Mallia: ZA: modular grid*

375

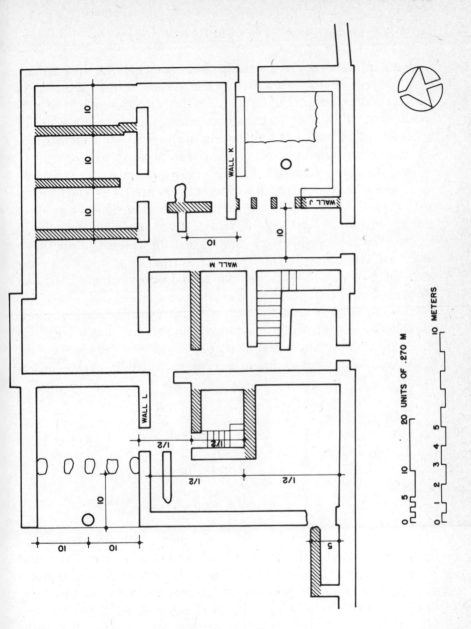

Figure IV.13.C. *Mallia: ZA: secondary layout*

14. ML ZB: MALLIA/HOUSE ZETA BETA (MM IIIB/LM IA)[1]

House Zeta Beta stands across the street from ML ZA, its northern facade opposite the southern facade of the latter (see plan of Quarter Zeta above, Figure II.16). The disposition of the plan recalls that of Quarter Delta above, where the major street facade is carefully laid out and built, while the internal walls increasingly diverge from parallel and perpendicular from north to south.

The structure measures ±17.90 east-west, across the northern face, and ±20.70 north-south, along the eastern face (which fronts onto a side street). The northern facade is divided into three planar sections, ±5.60, ±7.30, and ±5.00;[2] the main entrance is +2.80 from the northeastern corner; and the eastern facade has a recess of ±0.55 at ±11.00 from the northeastern corner. To the west are two facade sections, that to the north being ±5.50; that on the south ±5.30.

It would appear that the plan is too irregular to suggest a reasonable layout grid, and it may have been the case that ML ZB was fitted into the urban fabric as best it could. The facade sections, however, closely approximate a hypothetical unit of ±0.280, as follows:

```
N : 5.60 +  7.30 +  5.00
     20  +  25  +  15  (= 5.60 + 7.00 + 4.20)?
E : 2.80 ; 11.00
     10  ;  40          (= 2.80 ; 11.20);
W : 5.50 +  5.30
     20  +  20          (= 5.60 + 5.60).
```

The ideal modular lengths are given in parentheses above. The hypothetical errors, while small, are not entirely convincing, and we would have to have more detailed information to propose a more secure modular grid layout. It does seem reasonable, however, that the unit employed was somewhere approximating ±0.280, for the resultant facade proportions, using such a linear standard, are consistent with those seen above (e.g. northern facade: 4 : 5 : 3). It may well be that the proportional schema should be referred to grid-breaks rather than actual built facades, as elsewhere.

ML ZB: *modular unit* : ±0.280 (?)
           facade (N)   : 20 + 25 + 15 (= 4 : 5 : 3)

NOTES: ML ZB

1. *Et. Cret* XI: 7-26, plan, Plates II and III; *GFFC*: 66-70.
2. Coincidentally, the dimensions of the northern facade, and its tripartite divisions, recall those of House VI F at Troy VI with similar setbacks: see D. Preziosi, *MPPAO*: 240. But in plan, ML ZB has an internal functional arrangement similar to House E at Mallia, discussed below, and above, Part One.

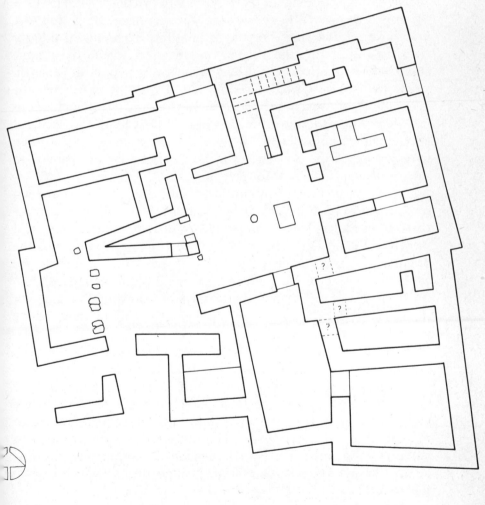

0   5

Figure IV.14.A. *Mallia: ZB: plan*

15. NK: NIROU KHANI (MM IIIB/LM IA)[1]

As indicated in Figure IV.15.A, the overall north-south length of the structure at D-D' is ±26.30; at E-E', ±26.85. Note that D and E are aligned with each other and that this alignment is perpendicular to the eastern facade of the building. The extant east-west length, along line A-A', is ±23.00. The western boundary of the structure is missing; we may conjecture that it stood some three or four meters to the west, thereby making for a square groundplan.

It is noteworthy that line A-A' exactly bisects the north-south width of the building (±13.15 + ±13.15 to the east; ±13.43 + ±13.43 to the west). It appears that the misalignment of wall A-A' may have set the stage for the parallel misalignments of interior walls to the south; the original misalignment could have come about if construction of wall A-A' was begun at opposite ends on *alternative* sides of what was originally a grid line A-A'. Once the builder's error was noted, construction of the wall foundations may have then simply proceeded in a straight line. The resultant misalignments elsewhere in the southwestern quarter would then have resulted from a desire to make the latter closely parallel to the (misaligned) major through-wall.[2]

The width of the projecting cluster 28-27-26, at the eastern end of court/passage A, is 2.75. If we project this dimension as a hypothetical modular length, the result is the modular layout grid shown in Figure IV.15.B, or 100 by 100 units (assuming that the original western boundary was some three or four meters to the west). The suggested linear standard would be in the range 0.263-0.270; it will generate fairly accurately the position of most major walls, taking into account the misalignments noted above, along with *in situ* adjustments.

The hall system thus would be 20 by 30 units, a 2 : 3 rectangle (a now familiar proportional schema). It stands at the center axis of the large eastern courtyard, its width of 20 units flanked by the facade to the south (30 units) and a facade to the north (30 units) to approximately the east-west position of return wall P'Q', north of area D on the first plan. (The double line running east and north from point V in the first diagram is not a wall but a low parapet basis.) The resultant facade proportional schema is (north-south) 3 : 2 : 3.

Within the main court, along its southern facade, are a series of recesses and projecting walls of fine masonry, measuring (west-east) 2.40 + 2.30 + 3.30. These dimensions approximate values of 9 + 9 + 12 units of ±0.270 (ideally 2.43 + 2.43 + 3.24). These articulated facades serve as background for the altar platforms and sacral horns (above dimension 2.30 in the first plan); a reserved pavement area (X-X'/Y-Y'/Z-Z') focusses attention upon the ritual objects at the southern facade. On both sides of this area are two round *koulouras* or lined sunken pits, perhaps serving as stands for trees or containers for votive offerings or ritual debris. The arrangement is in part analogous to the Tripartite Shrine on the western facade of the Central Court at Knossos.

It is not clear if this great court was bounded on the east, and was thereby entirely enclosed. But if the position of the 'tripartite shrine' here duplicated that at Knossos, it may have stood at the center-point of the court facade. Observing that the shrine's central projection is 25 modular units from the western facade of the building proper, we might reconstruct the original eastern facade of the court (assuming there was one) another 25 units further east, thus making the courtyard 50 units wide (13.50): half the north-south width of the building itself. The resultant court would then be very nearly a 1 : 2 rectangle,[3] the same proportion seen for the palatial courtyards of Knossos, Mallia, and Phaistos. That NK was indeed a very special building and not an ordinary mansion is clear both from its plan, its contents, and its dimensions.[4]

NK: *NS X EW* : 26.85 x 23.00+
     unit   : ±0.268-0.270
     module   : *c.* 2.70 (= 10)
     grid   : 100 x 100
     facade (E) : 30 + 20 + 30 (= 3 : 2 : 3)

NOTES: NK

1. *AE* (1922): 1-11, plan, Figure A, p. 3; measured sectional drawings, Figure B, p. 4.; *Dheltion* (1918): 19; *PAE* (1922-1924): 125ff; *PC*: 58-59.
2. See above under ML ZA, where it was observed that construction proceeded

      sequentially, with major structural walls laid first, and secondary internal walls then laid out parallel and perpendicular to the latter's rising wall-faces. We would suggest something similar took place here at NK.

3.   The distance in the first plan from point P to P' is ±24.20, very close to 90 units of 0.270 (24.30), so the actual proportions of the court would have been 5 : 9; assuming the court was in fact 50 units wide, which is uncertain. At any rate, in general appearance the court would have been close to a 1 : 2 rectangle, a schema only seen in palatial design. See Note 4 below.

4.   Only the so-called 'little palaces', and the great palaces themselves, were laid out on modular grids in hundreds or multiples of a hundred, as we shall see below. The modular grid of NK describes a square plan which is one-half the size of the West Central Blocks of Knossos and Mallia. The same modular unit was employed in all three cases. If the 'tripartite shrine' at NK stood (as at Knossos) on the bisection-axis of its court, then the 'palatial' resemblance is all the more striking. If NK was such a compound, we might expect to find more purely residential quarters to the east of the court, as at Knossos and Kato Zakro.

381

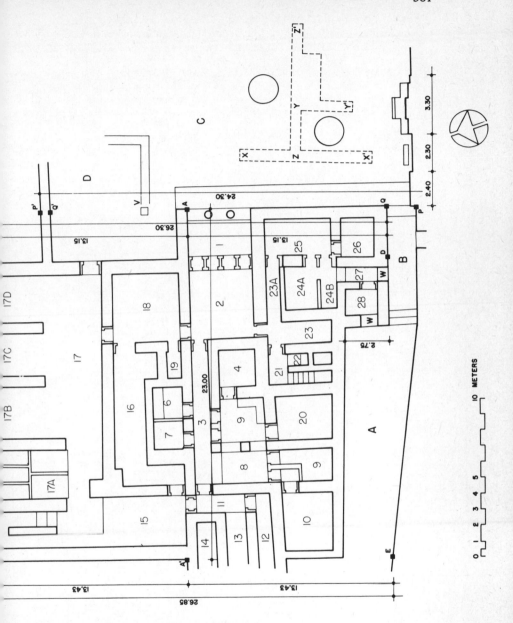

Figure IV.15.A. *Nirou Khani: dimensions*

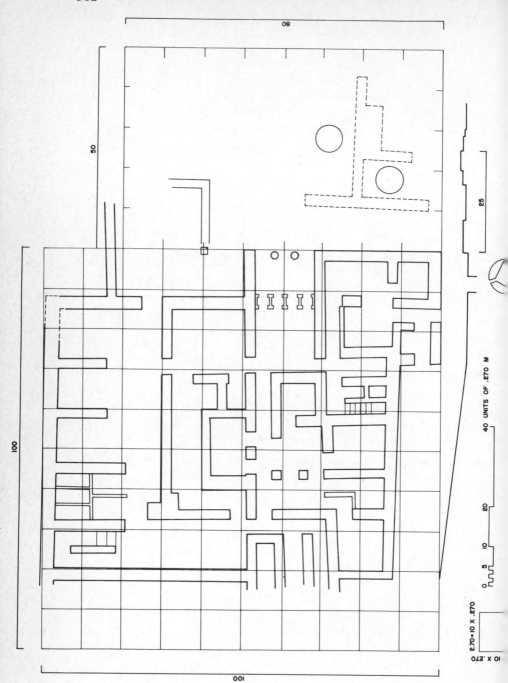

Figure IV.15.B. *Nirou Khani: modular grid*

16. SKLV: SKLAVOKAMPOS (LM I)[1]

The remains of this large house have been largely obliterated some 35 years ago; our plan and dimensions are taken from the excavation publication of S. Marinatos. The plan (Figure IV.16.A) is evidently well laid out, and describes overall a 3 : 4 rectangle. The modular grid shown in our diagram generates most primary walls, except for those subsidiary walls labelled within. The positions of walls A-A', B-B', C-C', F-F', and G-G' are located on halfway points of grid squares, but walls D-D' and E-E' are off axis.

The overall dimensions are ±18.00 by ±24.30; on the face of it suggesting 60 by 80 units of ±0.30, with each grid square ten units on a side. If this were the unit employed, then the position of all subsidiary walls except D-D' and E-E' bisects the grid squares (five units). But other solutions are possible, as suggested by our diagram: 72 by 96 units of ±0.270, or 54 by 72·units of ±0.337. In the case of the former, each grid square would be 12 units on a side; in the case of the latter, each grid square would be nine units on a side.

Only a unit of ±0.337 generates grid squares of even dimension, and we shall very tentatively suggest this standard. The excavators note that the dimensions of the main hall are 3.30 by 6.70 (equals 10 by 20 units). On the other hand, the tripartite division of the stairwell grid square suggests a solution favoring a modular length readily divisible by three (9 x 9).

Whatever the linear standard used, the important point is that the structure was planned and laid out with care, evidently on a modular grid such as the one illustrated. Two points are worthy of note here. First, the areal size of the northern half of the house is identical to that of the southern half, despite differences in cluster arrangement: counting by grid square, the northern quarter occupies 18 squares, the southern side the same.[2]

Secondly, the southeastern cutout of the grid generates wall facades two grid squares wide by three long north-south (a ratio of 2 : 3). It is also of interest that this reserved grid area (six squares) is approximately the same as that reserved to the west (five grid squares): a similar 'balancing' was observed above at ML DA.

SKLV: *NS X EW*   : 18.00 x 24.30
         unit   : 0.337 or 0.270 or 0.30
         module   : 3.00 (= 9 or 12 or 10)
         grid   : 6 x 8 squares (48 in all)
         facade (SE) : 2 : 3 grid squares

NOTES: SKLV

1.   *AE* (1939-1941) [1948] 69-96, plan, Figure 4, p. 71; measured section p. 72.
2.   In actuality the northern section is 19½ squares, the southern side 17¼ squares; the two zones *share* three grid squares south of wall C-C.

385

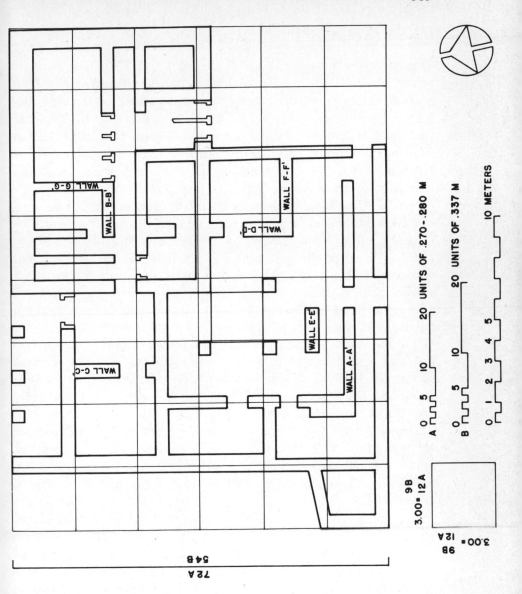

Figure IV.16.A. *Sklavokampos: modular grid*

17. TYL A: TYLISSOS HOUSE A (MM IIIB/LM IA)[1]

This structure measures ±35.00 NS by 22.15-22.90 EW, and its outer trace is deeply articulated by 18 separate facades. The geometric center of the groundplan is at point Z in the first diagram; if projected westward, Z aligns with facade L to the west. Facade A, 12.60 in length, is similar in length to facade O (12.30) diagonally opposite: similar phenomena have been observed at Gortyn, Mallia DA, and Knossos HF. Facade A is also twice the length of adjacent facade R (6.30), just as facade D (5.40) is twice C (2.65). Also, facade D is three-fifths the length of facade B.

Given the overall length of ±35.00, then the east-west width of 22.15-22.90 is slightly too large to be exactly three-fifths; ideally, three-fifths of 35.00 is ±21.00. In fact, however, this is the actual east-west width at K-A to the inner face of facade A (21.25, as shown in the plan).

As indicated in Figure IV.17.B, a grid based upon decimal fractions of the overall length of 35.00 will generate all primary walls and most secondary ones. The resultant grid is 100 by 60 units of a standard of ±0.350, a proportion of 5 : 3. Each grid square is 1.75 on a side, or five units (halved from ten unit squares). The total number of squares is 240, of which exactly two-thirds, or 160, were built upon. The domestic quarter occupies some 63 grid squares, or one-fourth of the total number in the grid.[2] This proportion compares with the allotment of space for hall systems proper in other domestic structures, as we have seen. The northern quarter occupies a similar area as that to the south.

The facades themselves reflect the proportional harmonics of the overall grid plan. To the south, facades F + D + B approximate 10 + 15 + 25 units (ideally 3.50 + 5.25 + 8.75), a proportion of 2 : 3 : 5. Facades A and O approximate 35 units (ideally 12.25);[3] facade Q is 55 units (ideally 19.25); facade P may be 45 units (ideally 15.75);[4] facade K is 15 units; and facade G is 30 units (ideally 10.50).

TYL A: *NS X EW*   : 35.00 x 21.25
         unit   : 0.35
         module   : 1.75 (= 5)

grid   : 100 x 60
facade (S) : 10 + 15 + 25 (= 2 : 3 : 5)

NOTES: TYL A

1. *Tylissos: Villas Minoennes (Et.Cret* III) (1934): 6-24, plan, Plates VI, XXXIII; *PC*: 60-61.
2. Plus five grid squares in the south extension (= 68). Note that the reserved grid areas to the east and west are similar in size overall (33 to the east, 31 to the west), exclusive of the southeastern corner.
3. Note that facade B straddles the grid line, thereby lengthening A.
4. Note that facade O straddles the grid line, thereby lengthening P.

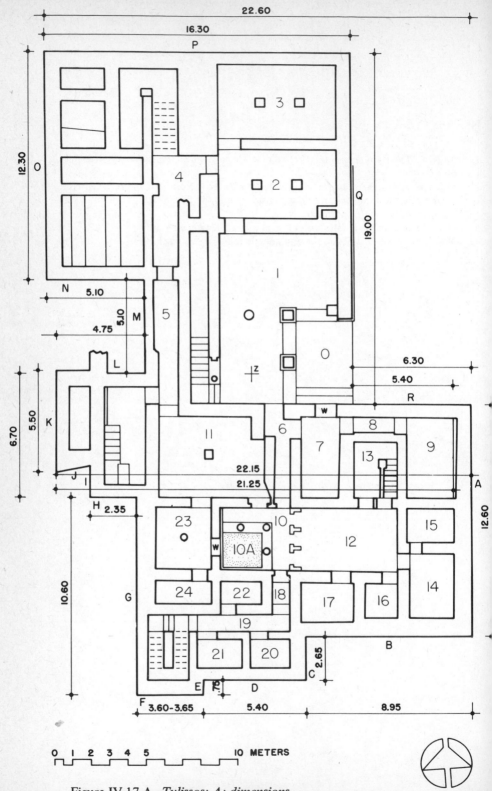

Figure IV.17.A. *Tylissos: A: dimensions*

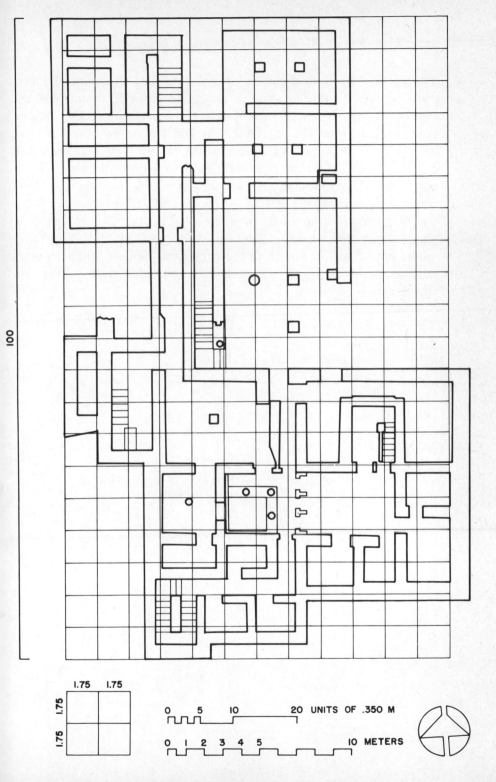

Figure IV.17.B. *Tylissos: A: modular grid*

18. TYL B: TYLISSOS HOUSE B (MM IIIB/LM IA)[1]

Evidently a functional annex of TYL A, TYL B is considerably smaller, and in plan is a simple rectangle some 22 meters EW by nearly 16 meters NS, as indicated in the first diagram. The dimensions indicate that the structure was laid out on a linear standard of ±0.350, the same as that employed for TYL A. The resultant modular grid, shown in Figure IV.18.B, is 40 by 60 units, a 2 : 3 rectangle. The modular grid squares are 1.75 on a side, or five units. TYL B is as long as TYL A is wide (60 units).[2]

The northern and southern walls are articulated by means of a slight projecting plane − 7.10 to the north, 7.20 to the south − each approximately one-third the total (grid) length, and each one-half the grid width of the structure, thus yielding a schema of facades of 1 : 2 : 3.

TYL B: *NS X EW* : 14.00 x 21.00 (grid)
          unit   : 0.350
          module   : 1.75 (= 5 units)
          grid   : 40 x 60 (= 2 : 3)
          facades   : overall: 1 : 2 : 3

NOTES: TYL B

1.   *Tylissos: Villas minoennes* (*Et. Cret* III) (1934): 26-32, plan, Plate VII.
2.   As discussed in Part One, TYL B was probably built before A.   .

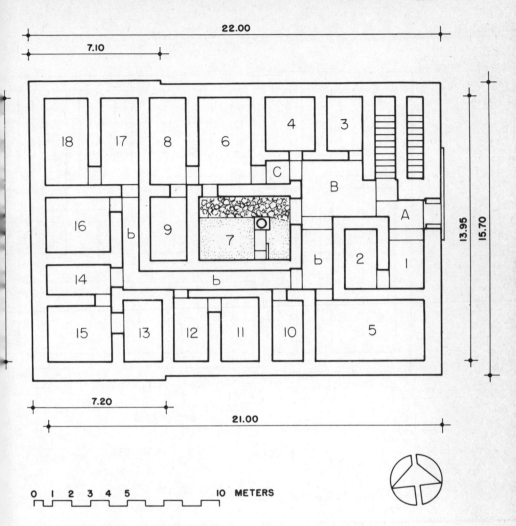

Figure IV.18.A. *Tylissos: B: dimensions*

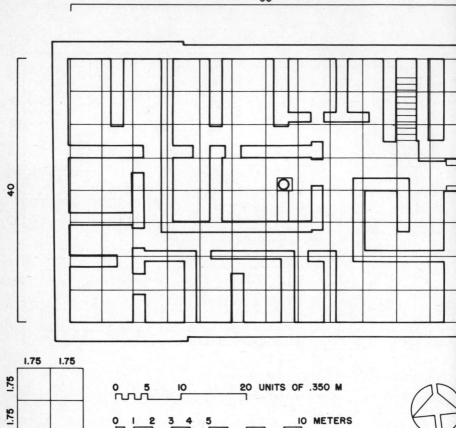

Figure IV.18.B. *Tylissos: B: modular grid*

19. TYL C: TYLISSOS HOUSE C (MM IIIB/LM IA)[1]

The recurrence of dimensions of ±8.00 in the plan of this well-preserved structure suggests a modular layout such as that shown in Figure IV.19.B, based on grid squares ±4.00 on a side. The overall grid describes a square of 6 by 6 by 4.00. Further subdivision of the grid into squares ±2.00 on a side generates the position of nearly every wall in the house. *In situ* adjustments of the positions of walls H and N extended the size of their adjacent rooms within.

Our measurements of the remains suggest a linear standard of ±0.33, resulting in an overall layout grid 72 units on a side. The linear standard is similar to that employed in the two other Tylissan houses (0.350), but its method of articulation is different; here each grid square equals 12 (or six) units on a side, there the grid squares are decimally expressed (ten units on a side).

The square layout grid of TYL C may be compared with that of KN HCS (6 by 6 by 5.40, unit of 0.270), KN SE (8 by 8 by 2.175, unit of 0.270), and ML DA (8 by 8 by 1.68, unit of 0.280) or TVOL (8 by 8 by 1.375, unit of 0.275).[2]

The chief problem with the proposal of a square layout grid is the dating of the separate wall to the south of facade D, which on our plan defines a narrow passage along the side of the house. While there is precedent for a layout grid defining a walled cell not structurally part of a house on the ground floor level (*viz,* AKHL), the excavators of the building suggested in their report of 1909-1913 that this wall belongs to a post-Minoan or Hellenic period.[3] While we are not in a position to dispute their reasoning, the wall in question seems to us by its construction and disposition to have been contemporary with TYL C itself; an impression enhanced by a detailed tabulation of our measurements of the remains. If this wall itself could be securely dated to the post-Minoan period, then we may conjecture that it replaced a boundary wall of Minoan date contemporary with the foundation of the present house.

These suppositions depend in part on our assumption that the house was laid out within a modular grid which defined a perfect square; this need not have been the case: the house could have been laid out as 72 units by 66 units, as suggested in Figure IV.19, C, but our solution seems the simplest, and has precedent elsewhere in Minoan design.

In our discussion of this house in Part One, it was observed that the domestic quarter on the northern side forms an L-shaped cluster of cells, mirroring the L-shaped magazine cluster diagonally opposite on the southwestern corner. In terms of the grid diagram of Figure IV.19.B, the domestic quarter occupies six grid squares (of 4.00 on a side), as does the magazine cluster. This represents one-sixth of the totality of grid squares of 36, but in area this cluster approximates one-fourth of the total built portion of the grid, 28, an areal proportion seen above either for entire domestic quarters, or for hall systems *per se*.[4] (See above, Figures I.6 and I.7.)

As noted elsewhere, the width of the hall system is double that of circulatory corridors or stairway flights. As also seen elsewhere, the square-footage reserved from the layout grid on one side of the building (east) approximates that reserved on the opposite side (west): see for example ML DA or TYL A.[5]

The geometric center of the grid falls within central cell 15 on the first diagram, conjectured to have been a house shrine; such a practice will be observed below in palatial construction.

TYL C: *NS X EW* : 24.40 x 24.40[6]
        unit   : 0.33
        module : 4.00 (or 2.00) (= 12 units or 6 units)
        grid   : 72 x 72 units

NOTES: TYL C

1. *Tylissos: Villas minoennes* (*Et.Cret* III) (1934): 32-47, plan, Plate XI; *PC*: 61-62.
2. On Figure IV.19.C is indicated the set of equivalent values of a standard of 0.286 close to that employed in the four other square house grids just cited. Here, however, use of such a linear standard would yield grid squares seven units on a side, on comparative grounds a less simple solution.
3. *Op.cit.*: notations to Plate XXXIII.
4. In terms of the more detailed grid plan of Figure IV.19.C, this amount translates to 26 grid squares, or one-fourth of the totality of 100 grid squares built upon.
5. With respect to the proportions of the major projecting facades, TYL C does not appear to reflect harmonic practices in evidence elsewhere. Note that facade N is built within five grid squares, facade P along two, facade A along four, facade C along three, facade D along nine, facade E along three (as is facade F), and facade G along four. But note, however, that the *tripartite division* of the eastern facade, with one recessed plane flanked by two projecting planes, *mirrors* the opposite

(western) facade, with a central projecting plane flanked by two recessed planes; a practice observed above at ML ZA, ML DA, KN S, KN HF, KN RV, and GRT. In most of these cases, opposite facades are tripartite, while adjacent (side) facades are articulated differently. This tripartite mirroring (often reversed, often literal) may be seen as one general tendency in Minoan design.

6. Length NS includes width of peripheral S wall.

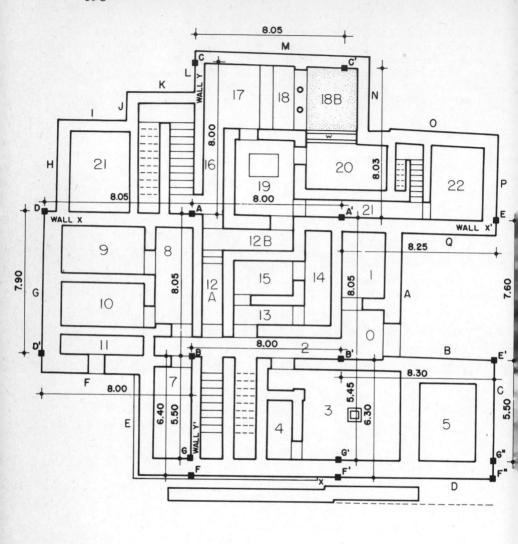

Figure IV.19.A. *Tylissos: C: dimensions*

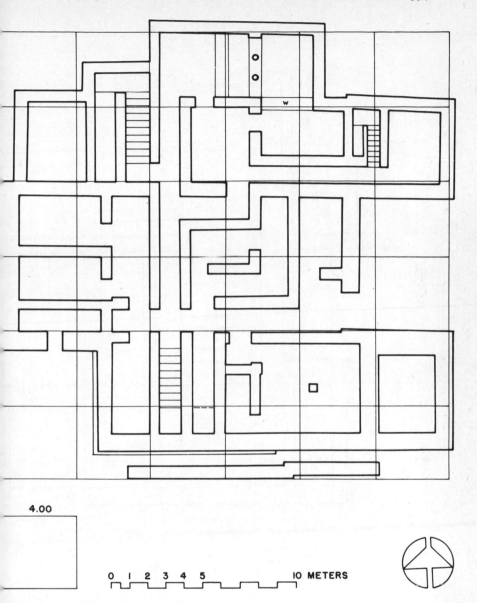

4.00

0 1 2 3 4 5   10 METERS

Figure IV.19.B. *Tylissos: C: modular grid (1)*

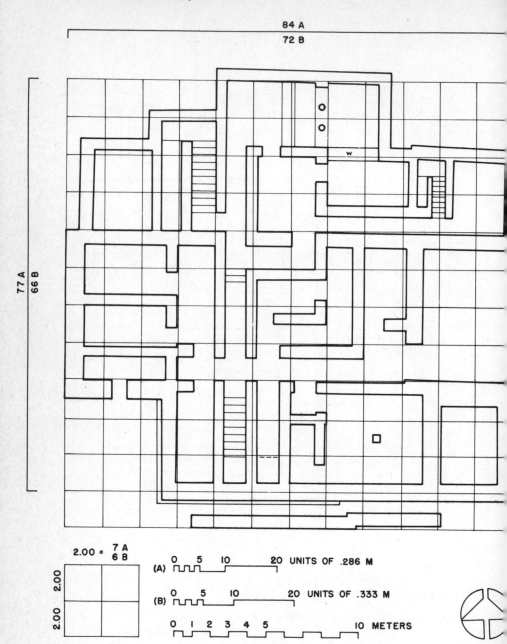

Figure IV.19.C. *Tylissos: C: modular grid (2)*

20. PLK B: PALAIKASTRO HOUSE B (LM I)[1]
21. PLK X: PALAIKASTRO HOUSE X ('LM II')[2]

Because of the near total obliteration of this site during World War II, little remains *in situ* for a detailed survey of the dimensions of PLK B or X. Our evidence for modular planning of these two interesting structures comes entirely from the publications of three-quarters of a century ago.

With regard to PLK B (Figure IV.20.A), while it is clear from the plan that the building was accomodated to some extent to a pre-existent urban fabric, and that it underwent some modifications during its history, by and large this large structure was designed and laid out as a unity. Its southern facade fronts onto the plan that the building was accommodated to some extent to a columned portico which at one time may have served as a principal entrance (former doorway indicated by hatching). To the north of this central axis is a peristyle court, occupying the center of the construction. It is flanked by cell-clusters of approximately equal size; that to the east was a sunken bathroom. Further east is a pillared hall of a type known from the palaces, oriented north-south. To the north and east of the latter is a large court, itself bounded by a perpendicular enceinte pierced by a door in the north.

A study of the plan indicates a number of approximate dimensional regularities: the width of the peristyle court, for example, is about the same as that of the pillared hall. Overall, the structure measures some 22 meters north-south by slightly over 43 meters east-west.

It appears that the building was laid out as a 1 : 2 rectangle (note that $0.270 \times 80 = 21.60; 0.270 \times 160 = 43.20$).

Looking at Figure IV.21.A, our copy of the larger published plan of PLK X indicates a number of simple dimensional regularities, and we may tentatively suggest a planning grid as shown in our diagram for the newer and more regular portion of this house. In general, this part of the building presents a familiar plan, whose prominent feature is a centrally placed hall system occupying the central third of the grid. Scaled dimensions suggest a modular unit of ±2.75, generating a grid of squares whose subdivisions describe the position of all internal and external walls.

It will be seen that the hall system occupies eight grid squares, or exactly one-fourth of the totality of grid squares minus the outer porch. The overall grid consists of 36 subdivisions (minus the four of the porch); the stepped platform is appended to the southeastern corner of the grid.

The plan was clearly conceived and laid out. As elsewhere, the width of the hall is the largest internal width; no other cell is wider, though two are of equal size. This width is exactly twice that of the entrance corridor and porch, and of the stairwell.

As elsewhere above, the eastern facade, fronting onto a north-south street, is divided into three planar sections, with the hall system at the central projecting facade. The southern facade is divided in two, with its shorter projection exactly one-half of the longer facade of the porch.

We would suggest a planning grid based on a linear standard of 0.275, yielding an overall grid 60 by 60 units. Both this dimension, as well as the position of the hall system (occupying the central third of the grid) are identical to the organization of KN HCS (60 by 60 by 0.270): in the latter house, however, the hall is oriented north-south, but in both cases the hall lies parallel to the facade from which entrance is gained. In both cases also the hall system occupies one-fourth of the layout grid.[3]

PLK B: *NS X EW*   : ±22.00 x ±43.00 (= 80 x 160 x 0.270?)
PLK X: *NS X EW*   : ±17.00 x ±17.00
         unit   : 0.275
         module   : 2.75 (= 10)
         grid   : 60 x 60
         facade (E) : tripartite

NOTES: PLK B AND PLK X

1.   *BSA* VIII (1901-1902): 286ff, plan, Figure 23, p. 310; *PC*: 69-70.
2.   *BSA* XI (1904-1905): 282-286, plan, Figure 13, p. 282. The eastern and western halves of the structure were built at different times (the western square is later). The excavators assign the date of the annex to LM II, a ceramic style apparently contemporary with LM IB at Knossos. The area was the site of construction dating back to the Early Minoan II period: K. Branigan, *Foundations of Palatial Crete* (1970): 43-44.

3. In other words, of the built area on the grid, in both cases. The two houses are remarkably alike in planning: same unit apparently employed, same square grid 60 units on a side, same modular subdivision (squares ±2.70 on a side), same tripartite facade subdivisions, same relative positioning of the hall system, similar perpendicular cell-annexing to the innermost cell of the hall system. Also, the grid lines in both cases define the outer walls of the hall systems, and in both houses the halls occupy eight grid squares.

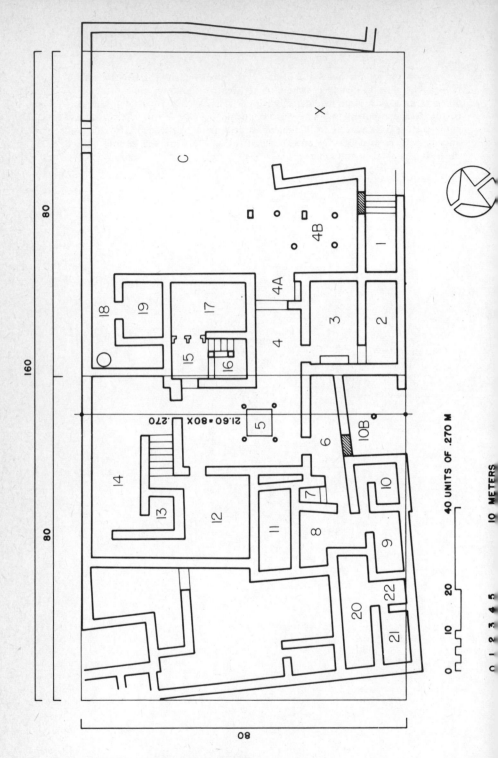

Figure IV.20.A. *Palaikastro: B: plan*

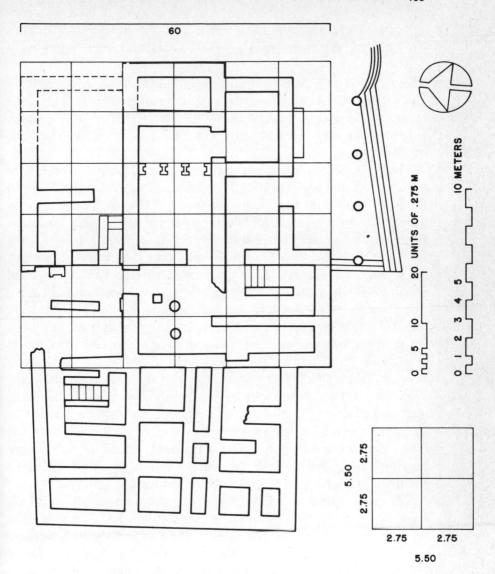

Figure IV.21.A. *Palaikastro: X: modular grid*

22. KZ G: KATO ZAKRO HOUSE G[1]
23. KZ J: KATO ZAKRO HOUSE J[2]

These two Middle Minoan houses stand in the upper town of Kato Zakro excavated by Hogarth at the turn of the century; the recently discovered palace stands tot he south of this plateau (Figure IV.22.A). Both face inward onto the hill, away from the southern slope.

The two houses are essentially similar, and both resemble in a general way the MM IB/MM IIA house at TVOL examined above. Both are square in plan, although House J (Figure IV.23.A) has a projection on the lower left corner adjacent to the only entrance. Both are also nearly identical in size: KZ G is ±17.00 square, while KZ J is ±17.00 NS by ±17.70 EW (excluding the projecting area).

House G is entered on its northeastern side through a small vestibule within which is a small stone seat to the left (as at PLK B). Immediately to the left is the foundation of a stairwell; directly ahead is a second vestibular area, which gives on to a large square chamber to the south and an even larger cell to the west (Figure IV.22.B).

Along the back of the house (south) are four enclosed cells, probably storage basements, at a slightly lower level: the back wall is a retaining wall along the edge of the hillside, extant in Hogarth's time to some 5¼ meters in height. The large cell on the lower right of the plan is paved with rough stones, and thus may possibly have been an internal courtyard. Probably (as at TVOL) the main living halls were on the second storey.

The plan suggests a layout grid based on a module of ±2.00 (possibly 6 x 0.340?), overall 48 x 0.340 square. The suggested layout grid generates the position of all major load-bearing walls.

KZ J (Figure IV.23.A) is similar in design, but contains a larger number of rooms. It resembles KZ G in its square plan, the position of its entrance (which is also adjacent to a stairwell, here to the right), and the position of a large squarish cell directly ahead of the entrance vestibule. In both cases, there is a doorway to the west of the entrance area, leading to a cluster of cells separated from the first large chamber by a long north-south through-wall.

Unlike KZ G, it appears that the major living areas of KZ J were on the ground floor level; here traces of a kitchen and pantry, wine-press, sunken bathroom, and storage chambers were identified. Here the largest cell of the house, to the east, was evidently a courtyard. A small cell in the southeastern corner was a storage cellar, some two meters below grade. Traces of pillar bases along the southern side of the house suggest a pillared hall or smallish hall system.

Figure IV.23.A suggests a modular layout grid which generates major load-bearing walls and many subsidiary walls. As at KZ G, the same modular solution is suggested, i.e. a grid of squares ±2.00 on a side (possibly, again, 6 x 0.340?), overall 48 x 0.340 square. The modular grid of 48 by 48 units resembles our solution for ML DA, there expressed also in six-unit squares, but with a module of +1.68 (= 6 x 0.280).[3]

The modular grids for both houses were generated by halving and quartering the dimensions of the plans. Whatever the actual linear standard employed here, the modular solution seems reasonable. The closest comparison to these two houses may be made with TVOL: a smaller and simpler structure. There, the internal structural frame was a square-within-a-square, neatly articulated. The Kato Zakro houses are more complex internally, but in general the three houses share the following features: (1) entrance near the lower left corner; (2) access (indirect here, direct there) into a large squarish cell, which was (3) a courtyard at TVOL and KZ J, a covered chamber(?) at KZ G; and (4) smaller cells arranged in an L around the latter.

Of the three houses, KZ G and TVOL are closest in design, and may be seen to be contextual variations on a similar design theme.

Both KZ G and KZ J may have had living halls on a second storey along their southern flanks, thereby giving a fine view out over the palace and lower city of Kato Zakro.

KZ G and
KZ J: *NS X EW* (grid) : ±16.32 x ±16.32
           unit   : 0.340?
           module   : 2.04?
           grid   : 48 x 48

NOTES: KZ G AND KZ J

1. *BSA* V (1900-1901): 121-149, especially 137-139, plan, Figure C, p. 138; section, Figure 48, p. 137.
2. *BSA* V (1900-1901): 121-149, especially 140-142, plan, Figure C, p. 138, top; sections, Figure 50, p. 140. In the text of D.G. Hogarth's report, KZ J is referred to as House *I*, in his plan, House *J*.
3. KN SE may also have been laid out on a square grid, but one composed of grid squares eight units on a side (±0.270). The KN SE grid, like those suggested here, was 8 by 8 grid squares overall.

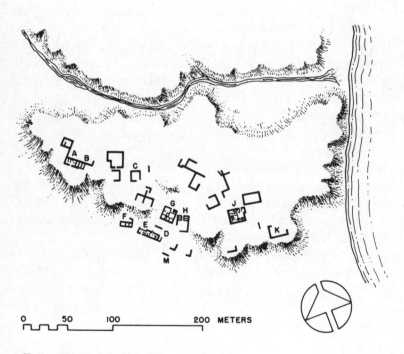

Figure IV.22.A. *Kato Zakro: town plan*

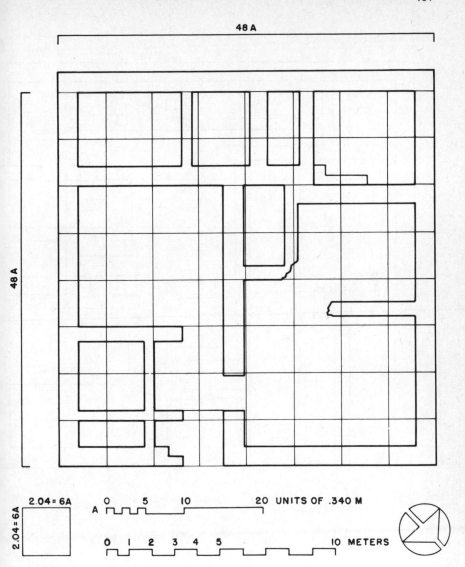

Figure IV.22.B. *Kato Zakro: G: modular grid*

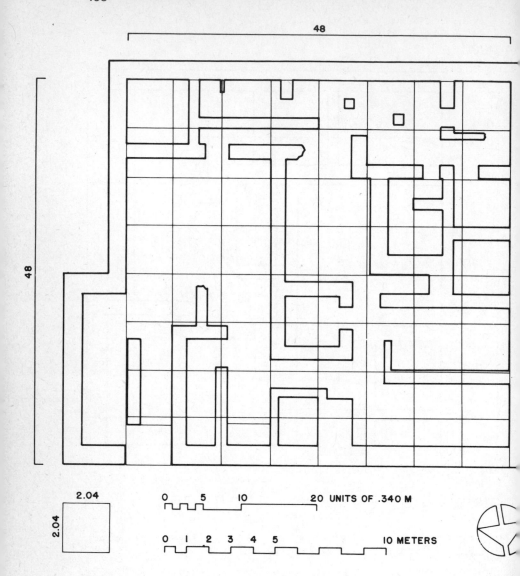

Figure IV.23.A. *Kato Zakro: J: modular grid*

24. ML E: MALLIA HOUSE E ('LE PETIT PALAIS') (MM IIIB/LM IA)[1]

This large and complicated[2] house measures some 54 meters east-west by 34 meters north-south overall (27 meters north-south excluding the southern projection). It is approximately twice as large as NK, and is slightly larger than the Knossian 'Little Palace'.

Our measurements of the remains suggest two possible modular solutions: one based on a module of ±2.70 (Figure IV.24.B), one based on a module of ±3.40 (Figure IV.24.C). Both appear to generate equally plausible solutions, but the first solution takes the southern projection as an appendage to the basic grid, while including the western projection, whereas the second solution incorporates both projections.

Employing a standard of ±0.270, the overall grid is 100 by 200 units built up of grid squares ten units on a side; using a standard of ±0.340, the overall grid is 100 by 160 units, also built up of decimal subdivisions. The first proposal seems the clearest and neatest, and generates a larger number of major internal wall positions. There is precedent elsewhere for the use of either linear standard, and it may be that the two units were employed interchangeably by Minoan builders and masons as a 'shorter' or a 'longer' foot-measure or standard, much in the way that Egyptian designers distinguished between a standard cubit and a longer 'royal' cubit. The two units are related to each other as 4 : 5, and it may be that Minoan builders were well aware of their modular correspondences (e.g. 40 x 0.340 = 50 x 0.270, or approximately 13.5 meters; 80 x 0.340 = 100 x 0.270, or 27 meters, etc.). At TVOL and AKHL, for example, the 'square-within-a-square' plan was laid out in the former case on a standard of 0.275 and in the latter case on a standard of 0.340.[3]

Elsewhere at Mallia, a linear standard in the range ±0.270-0.280 was employed, to the apparent exclusion of 0.340; as we shall see below, a standard of ±0.270 was also used in the Mallian palace. This fact may favor our 0.270 solution here (Figure IV.24.B). Seen from this perspective, the major portion cf the overall planning grid forms a 1 : 2 rectangle, 100 by 200 units in size.

On our analytic grid in Figure IV.24.B, the domestic quarter of the mansion occupies some 52 grid squares, or one-fourth of the total 200 grid squares, a proportion familiar above in more modest structures. The peristyle hall system (cells 13, 14, 15) occupies a total of 13 grid squares, or exactly one-fourth of the overall domestic quarter.

The proposed modular grid also nicely generates the positions of the storage magazines in the northwestern corner, which (like those at ML ZA above) are ten units wide by twice as long, aligned north-south. The *salle aux fresques*, east of 8 in the plan, most likely a standard hall system, is two grid squares wide (20 units), identical to the hall system at ML ZA.

ML E: *NS X EW* : overall: 34.00 x 54.00
                      without southern projection: 27.00 x 54.00
         unit   : 0.270
         module   : 2.70 (= 10)
         grid   : 100 x 200

NOTES: ML E

1. *Et.Cret* XI: 91-154, plan, Plate VII; *BCH* (1932): 514-515; (1933): 298; *GFFC*: 70-76; *PC*: 67-68; recent chronological study: *BCH* (1967): 494-512.
2. Much of the area to the east is confused, due to considerable rebuilding (hatched walls in our first plan). The functional cluster-organization of the building, as we have noted above in Part One, is similar to the smaller house ML ZB. ML E was built into an urban fabric next to the intersection of two streets. It is bordered to the north by an east-west street, but to the south is open ground, evidently a private garden and court; it is not clear how far the latter extended; probably to the south border of the southern projection.
3. In other words, the choice of linear standard was semi-autonomous of a particular architectonic composition, and Minoan builders could use either. Why they may have chosen one over the other is unclear, and may have been due to local crafts-men's traditions or other aspects of a building program about which we can only guess. It is evident, however, that the distinction between the 'shorter' unit and the 'longer' was not directly significant or referential in the same sense as the Egyptian distinction between a standard or shorter cubit measure and a longer or 'royal' cubit, which evidently reflected a complementary distinction between official governmental construction and other construction. By analogy with Egypt, we would expect that the Minoan palaces would be designed and laid out on a 'longer' unit; but as we shall see below, this is not the case.

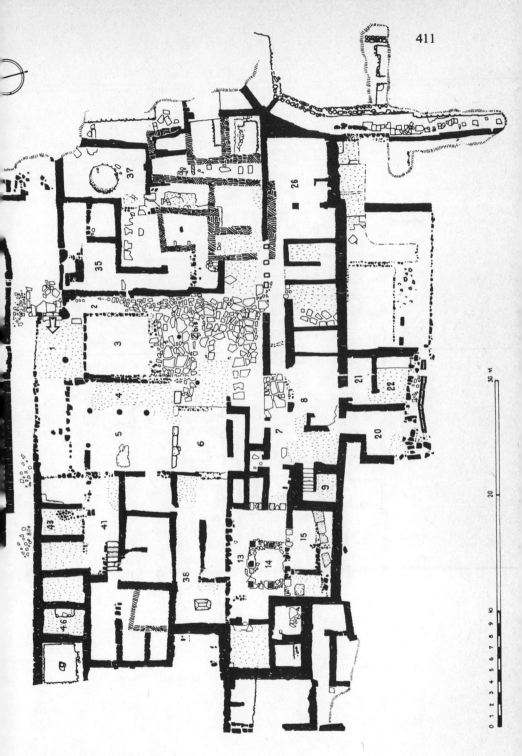

Figure IV.24.A. *Mallia: E: plan*

412

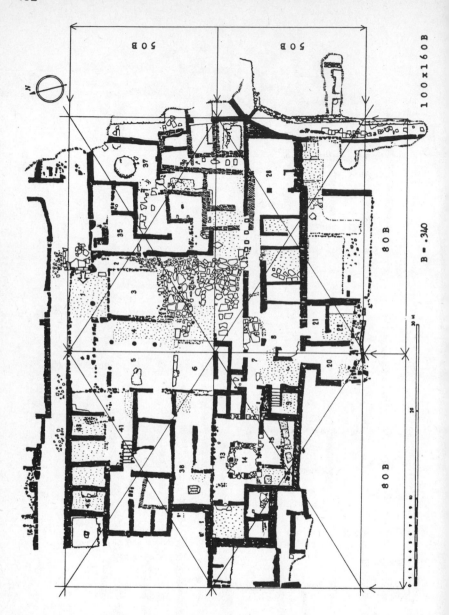

Figure IV.24.B. *Mallia: E: modular grid (1)*

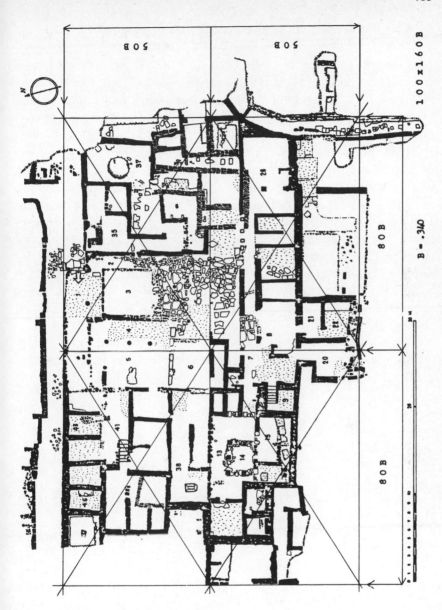

Figure IV.24.C. *Mallia: E: modular grid (2)*

25. KN LP: KNOSSOS 'LITTLE PALACE' (MM IIIB/LM IA)[1]

This elegant mansion is 43.03 NS by 27.46 EW, somewhat shorter and narrower than ML E. It is oriented north-south, like the large mansion TYL A, and like the latter may have had a large annex across the alley to the southwest, connected (as Evans suggested) on a second storey (the so-called 'Unexplored Mansion').[2]

The dimensions of the structure (excluding the highly conjectural restored portion of Figure IV.25.A) indicate that the mansion was laid out on a standard of ±0.270, expressed decimally, as indicated in the second diagram. The overall modular size measures 100 by 160 units, thereby forming a 2 : 3 rectangle, a proportional schema reflected in the interrelationships of major structural parts (e.g. southern facade 40 + 60 units; northern facade 40 + 60 units; relationship of peristyle court north-south length to PDP halls 25 : 40 units, etc.). In this regard, KN LP resembles many other Minoan houses, including all the Knossian houses examined above.

The northern facade presents the familiar tripartite planar subdivision seen elsewhere, with a central projection flanked by two recessed facades.

KN LP: *NS X EW*   : 43.03 x 27.46
        unit   : 0.270
        module   : 1.35 or 2.70 (= 5 or 10)
        grid   : 160 x 100 units
        facade (S) : 60 + 40 (= 3 : 2);
                    tripartite northern facade

NOTES: KN LP

1.   *PM* II: 513-544, plan, Figure 318, pp. 516-517; reconstructed isometric, Figure 317, p. 517; *Handbook*: 57-62; *PC*: 51-52.
2.   *PM* II: 543.

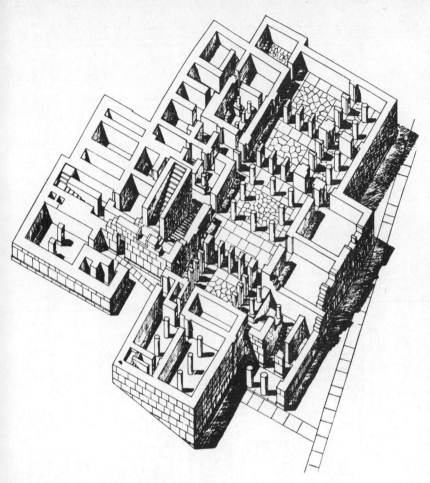

Figure IV.25.A. *Knossos: LP: isometric*

416

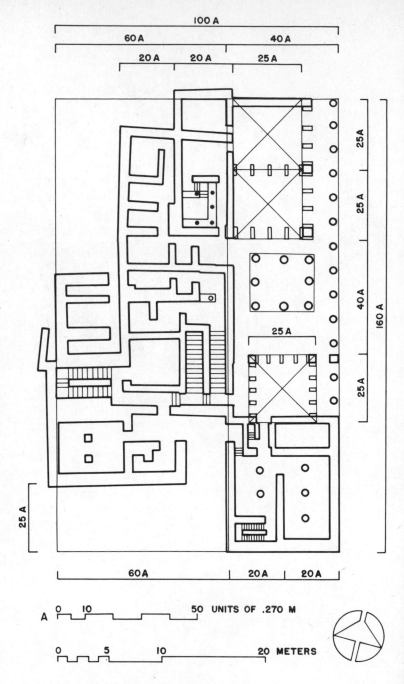

Figure IV.25.B. *Knossos: LP: modular grid*

26. HTR: HAGHIA TRIADHA VILLA (LM IB)[1]

HTR is the largest Minoan structure apart from the palaces themselves, measuring some 55 meters NS by *c.* 85 meters EW. The greatest thickness of this L-shaped building is approximately 27 meters. That the building was planned and laid out with great care may be seen by a perusal of our plan, Figure IV.26.A.

Extensive measurements were not carried out by us, and official dimensions must await final publication of the ruins. As early as 1908, however, F. Noack observed as number of modular regularities in the plan, regarding which, however, he presented no final tabulations.[2]

From whatever measurements were taken of the ruins, evidence points tentatively to a modular grid based on simple multiples of ±0.270, yielding an overall 200 by 300 units (ideally 54.00 by 82.50), a rectangle of 2 : 3 proportions. It is not known what the original boundaries of the courtyard were; the rooms shown on the plan stand on a storey below the court. It is a reasonable assumption, however, that it was of regular rectangular shape, probably somewhat smaller than the present open space in the plan. Our impression is that the court was probably a 1 : 2 rectangle in its original shape, possibly approximating 100 units wide north-south by 200 units long east-west: the size of the central courts of the major palaces, some 27 by 54 meters overall. As we shall see below, the central courtyard width tends to replicate that of major perimetral blocks of 100 units; here the greatest width of the (lower) cells is ±27.00, in the northwestern corner.

HTR: *NS X EW* : *c.* 55 x 85 meters; internal width 27 meters
      unit   : 0.270?
      module : 2.70?
      grid   : 200 x 300 units overall (2 : 3)

NOTES: HTR

1.   *MRIL* XXI, xii della serie III (1905): 238ff; L. Pernier and L. Banti, *Guida degli scavi italiani in Creta* (1947): 28-38, plan, Figure 40.

2.   F. Noack, *Ovalhaus und Palast in Kreta* (1908): Figure 5, p. 30. Noack's diagram gives no dimensions, only a superimposed series of parallel lines indicating internal regularities.

Figure IV.26.A. *Haghia Triadha: plan*

27. KN: KNOSSOS: PALACE[1]

Despite centuries of remodelling and rebuilding, the palatial compound of Knossos (Figure IV.27.A) provides convincing evidence of a unified original conception. Whereas it is apparent that the actual construction of this building took a good deal of time, the actual building program followed principles of composition laid down from the beginning.

We have seen in detail in Part One that the formal and functional organizations of the major Minoan palaces are contextual variants on a common theme. In this section and the ones to follow, it will become apparent that this common architectonic theme is reflected in each structure's modular organization. The features shared by the palaces, in other words, were set out in each case within an identical modular framework, an invariant metrological template.

In what follows we shall examine the layout of major components of the palace, and then present a summary modular grid at the end.

Figure IV.27.B is a diagram of the core of the compound, including the Central Court and West Central Block, containing the principal public/ritual zones of the structure. The entire area (which includes the width of the long north-south Corridor of the magazines to the west) forms a very nearly perfect square; a feature characteristic of Mallia and Phaistos, as we shall see shortly. The dimensions of the square are:

NS: (E) 54.14, (W) 54.16 (including N and S walls)[2]
EW: (N) 54.50, (S) 55.70 (B-C')
       (S) 54.10 (B'-C")

As the diagram indicates, this square is bisected by the eastern facade of the West Central Block, and thereby breaks into two 1 : 2 rectangles. The exact center of the overall square is at the midpoint of the facade of the Tripartite Shrine,[3] and the center of the West Block is at the northern wall of the eastern pillar crypt. Directly to the north of this central point is the Vat Room Deposit, considered to have been the foundation deposit of the entire building: its 'cornerstone', so to speak. The east-west bisection line of the overall square, then, is the southern face of the east-west wall bounding the northern side of the pillar crypts/shrine cluster. The major ritual cells at Phaistos and Mallia are similarly located with respect to their central grid squares.

The central square was laid out on a linear standard of ±0.270, and its overall dimensions are thus 200 by 200 units, bisected at 100-unit points both north-south and east-west. The Court and the West Block are thus 100 by 200 units, and the Vat Room Foundation Deposit stands 50 units equidistant along the east-west bisection line of the West Block. Both the pillar crypts and the Tripartite Shrine occupy the geometric heart of their respective modular grids.

We would suggest that the palace was laid out initially from this core, and that perimetral grid extensions were then appended to that core. This all may have been done simultaneously or in sequence. Perimetral grid squares 100 units on a side were extended to the north and south of the core, as indicated by our measurements of their boundaries.

To the west of the central square was appended the Magazine Block grid (Figure IV.27.C). J.W. Graham noted[4] that the combined north-south length of magazine blocks ABCD is ±60.54, approximating 200 units of his 'Minoan foot' of 0.3036. Note that the combined north-south length of blocks B and C is ±36.24; 36.432 equals 120 'Minoan feet'. Block D is ±13.50 north-south approximating 45 'Minoan feet' (13.662), while the north-south length of A is ±10.70 or 35 'Minoan feet' (10.63). The length of B, ±16.70, approximates 55 of his units (16.698), and that of C (±20.50) approximates 65 of these units (19.734).

On the face of it, Graham's solution seems reasonable enough (35 + 55 + 65 + 45 = 200 'Minoan feet'), but it is not the simplest solution, and it is inconsistent with evidence derived from an exhaustive tabulation of measurements throughout the palace (as well as with measurements of other Minoan buildings, as we have seen above).[5]

The simplest solution in our opinion is the one represented in our diagram, based on decimal values. Each magazine block is essentially square in plan, and a grid based on decimal values of 0.340 defines not only the position of each block as a whole, but the placement of each set of magazines within (each ten units wide, a pattern well attested elsewhere, as we have seen). The solution is as follows:

block X = 150 x   30   NS errors: 0.30, 0.00-0.20
block Y = 150 x 100   0.30, 0.60[6]
block A = 30 x 40   0.50, 0.15
block B = 50 x 50   0.30, 0.10
block C = 60 x 60   0.10, 0.30
block D = 40 x 40   0.10, 0.20
block E = 40 x 50   0.30, 0.00

We would suggest that the West Magazine Blocks were laid out from south to north from the line *a - x* in Figure IV.27.A, a line which is coincident with the southern limit of the central block to the east.[7]

It is noteworthy that on this solution there is an exact decimal correspondence between the modular unities and the number of magazines within each block. Thus,

block A is *30* units NS; it contains *3* magazines;
      B   *50*   *5*   ;
      C   *60*   *6*   ;
      D   *40*   *4*   ;

It is also worthy of note that adjacent magazine facades bear proportional relationships of a type common in Minoan design:

A : B : :   D : C
30 : 50 : :   40 : 60, or
 3 : 5 and   2 : 3.

Graham's 'Minoan foot' masks these clear proportions; the corresponding block proportions in his solution yield (south to north) 7 : 11 and 13 : 9, nowhere else attested in Minoan design.

Of interest here is the fact that the builders used the 'longer' Minoan standard in the layout of the magazine blocks (0.340) vs. the 'shorter' unit employed for the grid as a whole in the palace. In our discussion above of ML E, it was noted that the two standards are coincident at certain modular points (40 x 0.34 = 50 x 0.27). The appearance here in the Knossian palace of the longer unit as a monumental aggrandizement of the standard dimensions of the palace along its major public frontage, and a significant thickening of the palace's outer walls, enhances our impression of the symbolic prestige value of the palatial western facades. It is hardly uncommon in architecture for an increase in size and proportion to broadcast importance within a social scale.

Looking more widely in the palace, it may be noted that the blocks to the north and south of the central grid are a consistent modular extension of it: in Figure IV.27.A, the length *a - a* to the south of the court is 26.85-27.10, while the length *b - b* to the north of the court is 26.85, dimensions which are exactly one-half of the length of the court itself, and which in themselves represent 100 modular units each.

On the eastern side of the palace, the line *f - f - f - f* represents Evans' definition of the original eastern boundary of the structure (from which point the Hall of the Double Axes was built outward in MM IIIB).[8] The width of this original eastern quarter, from *f* to the inner face of the courtyard retaining/boundary wall is 13.40-13.50, or exactly one-half the width of the court, i.e. 50 units of 0.270.

The Hall of the Double Axes system (Figure IV.27.D) extends 27.40 from *f* (including the eastern terrace wall). The larger hall is 13.71 wide north-south, and the smaller hall system is 6.90 NS by 11.12 EW. As indicated in the diagram, these dimensions reflect simple decimal multiples of the unit standard of 0.270: the main hall system is 100 units EW by 50 units NS (80 units east-west excluding the outer veranda), while the smaller hall is 40 units EW by 25 units NS, exactly one-fourth of the area of the larger.[9]

The proportions of these halls are identical; each forms a 5 : 8 rectangle, consistent with the 2 : 3 :: 3 : 5 harmonic system of the palace's West Facade, and in line with practices attested elsewhere.[10]

North of the West Court stands the stepped 'theatral area' whose measurements suggest that (like the West Magazine Block) it was laid out on the longer linear standard. It measures 10.10 wide at the upper platform, which is also ±10.00 long, including the eastern wall. The steps are 10.77 east-west, while the lower walled area is 13.75 east-west. The entire stepped platform is thus 100 x 0.34 long east-west (x 30 x 0.34 wide) (ideally 34.00; actually 34.52) (Figure IV.27.E).

Figure IV.27.F is a diagram of the modular grid of the Knossian palace. The central zone delimits a rectangle 200 units EW by 400 units NS, or 108 meters NS by 54 meters EW. The limits of the grid to the north and south coincide with points *a* and *b* in our first plan of the palace. To the east, the original eastern limit of the grid is at point *b* in the present diagram, later extended with the remodelling of the domestic quarter in MM IIIB 100 units further to the east. To the west, the central grid zone is contiguous with the eastern limit of the magazine block grid, laid out on the longer (0.340) module as described above.

The letters in Figure IV.27.F indicate all known positions of double-axe symbols, as near as can be determined. Although this *labrys* symbol proliferates on the pillars of the pillar crypts (*a*), it is noteworthy that the symbol only occurs at the points in the plan. These are:

a. on the two pillars of the pillar crypts;[11]
b. on the western wall of the Hall of the Double Axes;[12]
c. on the western wall of the northern entrance of the court;[13]
d. adjacent to the northwestern Portico entrance;[14]
e. on the inner faces of the end (western) walls of the magazines;[15]
f. on the eastern face of magazine end walls;[16]
g. on the Stepped Portico entrance to the southeast.[17]

Are these locations fortuitous? While a complete distributional tabulation of the positions of various masons' marks in the palace has not been made, it may be of interest that double-axe signs are placed:

1. to mark entrances to the north and south (*c, d, g*);[18]
2. along the original eastern and western limits of construction (*f, e, b*);[19]
3. on the central pillar crypts.[20]

We may very tentatively suggest that the placement of the double-axe sign may have had something to do with marking significant nodes and boundaries of the modular layout grid. As we shall see below at Gournia, Phaistos, Mallia and Kato Zakro, double-axe signs tend to be clustered at or next to modularly significant points: on bisection axes, at a grid's central point, or on a grid's modular boundaries. Such a procedure is not unknown in contemporary Egyptian architecture.[21]

What of the symbol itself? To be sure, its form suggests an actual instrument (of which many examples are known).[22] But it is also clear that the sign had some important ritual significance as well, judging from its close association with shrines.[23]

It may not be entirely off the mark to suggest that in one of its facets, the *labrys* stood for the modular grid layout itself, a schematic token of the ritual geometry of building foundations. In point of fact, its very form, which hardly varies in proportions over many known examples, is coincident with that of the modular grid with its diagonals (used, if an analogy with Egypt is appropriate, to 'square' a grid of ropes and pegs).[24] The double-axe pattern of modular rope lines would have been constantly before the eyes of the Cretan *harpedonaptae* or rope-stretchers laying out a planning grid.[25] Thus it may be that the Knossian palace was *labyrinthos* both constructionally (by having its very material members hewn with a *labrys*) and symbolically (by having been laid out in the pattern of a *labrys*). It may not be entirely coincidental then, that votive pots found in the Vat Room Foundation Deposit, at point *B* in the grid diagram of Figure IV.27.F bear incised marks perhaps representing the grid square and its center (as shown in the diagram, lower right).[26]

Knossos, then, is surely the 'House of the Double-Axe' (*labyrinthos*) in more than one sense of the term. But as we shall see below, the same practices are attested at the other palaces.

KN: *central grid*   : 200 x 200 (x 0.270)
     perimetral grids : multiples of 50 units; 100 x 200 N + S;
                           50 + 100 E; on W : decimal multiples of
                           0.340
     facades (W)   : 2 : 3 : 3 : 5

NOTES: KN

1. Complete references above, Part One, Chapter II, Note 126.
2. The same dimension is found at Phaistos and Mallia, where also the northern and southern court walls are to be included in the central grid square.
3. A possible analogue may be seen above at NK, which also has a 'tripartite shrine' at the end (mid-point?) of its court.
4. *AJA* 64 (1960): 335-341; *PC*: 224ff. We will return to a close consideration of Graham's hypothesis below under Phaistos.
5. As we have seen, only a couple of buildings may be referred to a layout grid based on ±0.30, but the evidence there is ambiguous (KN HF), or based upon a reading of a plan of a structure no longer extant (SKLV), or not entirely confirmable due to the irregularity of the remains (GRT). Graham's work in this area was important in that he began the process of understanding the regularities in Minoan architectural composition, even if his work did not lead to exhaustive tabulations of the dimensions of whole buildings in order to substantiate his initial impressions; see D. Preziosi, *MPPAO, passim,* and the final tabulations of modular measurements below.
6. Note in the plan the misalignment of the western north-south wall, evidently the source of this large error. This area (Y) is complex in its history, and may not have formed part of the original layout; see *PM* IV: 48ff, and Figure 30 for Evans' conjecture as to the original state (MM I) of this area.
7. Shown as x in the first plan, in line with a further east: representing Evans' placement of the original southern facade limits.
8. See above, Part One, Chapter II.
9. Evidence points to the use of a linear standard here of 0.274, 0.004 larger than that employed in the original layout of the palace. Detailed measurements are given in Preziosi, *MPPAO*: 43, Figure I.A.11.a.2.(b)(1).
10. As a glance at the Knossian houses examined above will reveal; see also our tabulations below.
11. *PM* I: 425, some 39 symbols in all.
12. *PM* III: 346.
13. *PM* I: 394; III: 244.
14. *PM* I: 218.
15. *PM* I: 449 and Figure 322, showing positions of signs in the western areas.
16. *Id.*
17. *PM* II: 145, Note 1, 146. The block on which it occurs, however, is misplaced, but it seems reasonable that it originally stood somewhere nearby.
18. Respectively, northern entrance, northwestern Portico, Stepped Portico.
19. F marks the western limit of the central block grid.
20. Adjacent, also, to the Vat Room Foundation Deposit (*PM* I: 203, Figure 152, 164ff. Pots 4 and 19 in Evans' Figure 118a bear rectangular marks with crossed diagonals within.
21. A. Badawy, *AEAD* (1965): part II. Of interest is Badawy's discussion of the levelling-triangle amulet found in great quantities in Egypt (1965: 40ff), with which the Minoan double-axe sign might be seen as functionally analogous. What we call here a modular grid, Badawy refers to as a plan-net or *mammisi* (1965: 8ff). The author calls attention to the burying of levelling-triangle amulets in foundation pits along bisection-axes of *mammisi* (1965: 42ff).

22.   See the discussion of the *labrys* and labyrinth sign by L.J.D. Richardson, *MycStud* (1966): 285-296. The author rightly notes that despite the high frequency of its occurrence in Crete, the double-axe sign hardly varies in its internal proportions and overall configuration (a situation similar to that of the Egyptian levelling-triangle amulet; Badawy, *op.cit.*: 42).

23.   For one example among many, see the painted sarcophagus from Haghia Triadha with its depiction of an offering-altar between upright double-axes.

24.   In other words, the layout grid would be perfectly square if its diagonals were of exactly equal length; such diagonals for 'squaring' a grid, called in Egypt *remens*, are discussed by Badawy, *loc.cit.*

25.   The Greek word *harpedonaptae* (cord-stretchers, those who stretch [modular] ropes [between pegs]) may possibly derive from the Cretan name *Sarpedon* (brother of Minos and Rhadamanthys). Note that it has been conjectured that Classical Greek initial aspiration /h-/ before vocalic phonemes is derived from an earlier initial /*s-/ (A. Meillet and J. Vendryes, *Traité de Grammaire Comparée des Langues Classiques* (1948): 48ff. Perhaps *harpedon/aptae* is a late echo of *sarpedon*: *cf.* Cantor, *Vorlesungen über Geschichte der Mathematik*: 55-57. A Minoan ruler as an official performing a ritual ceremony of palace foundation by symbolically (or literally) laying out the ropes of a modular grid would be perfectly consistent with contemporary Egyptian practice wherein a Pharaoh ritually served as 'stretcher of the cord' (see Badawy, *op.cit.*: 5-15).

26.   See above, Note 19, with references.

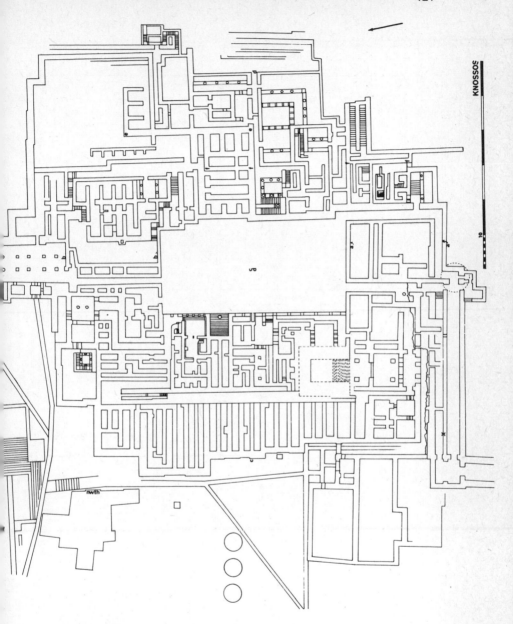

Figure IV.27.A. *Knossos: palace: overall plan*

428

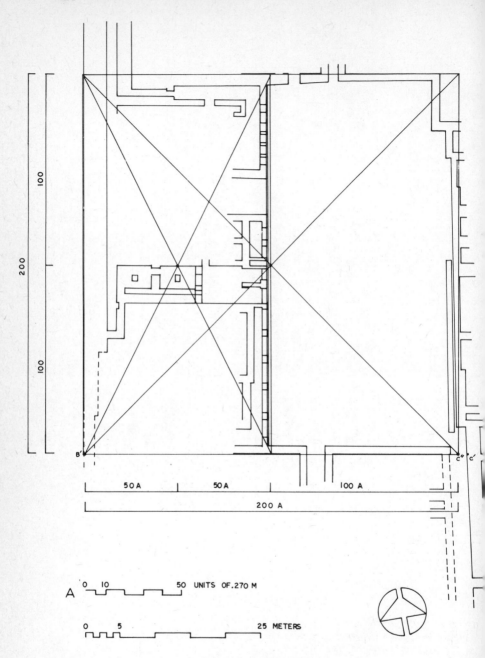

A   0 10   50 UNITS OF .270 M

0   5   25 METERS

Figure IV.27.B. *Knossos: palace: central grid square*

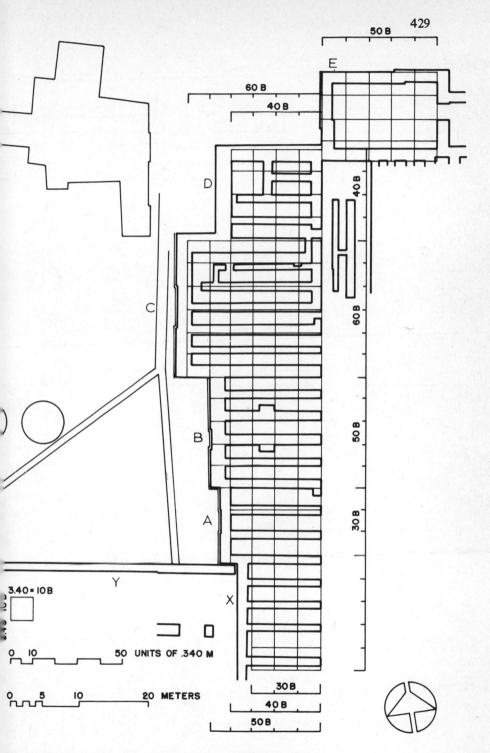

Figure IV.27.C. *Knossos: palace; western magazine grid*

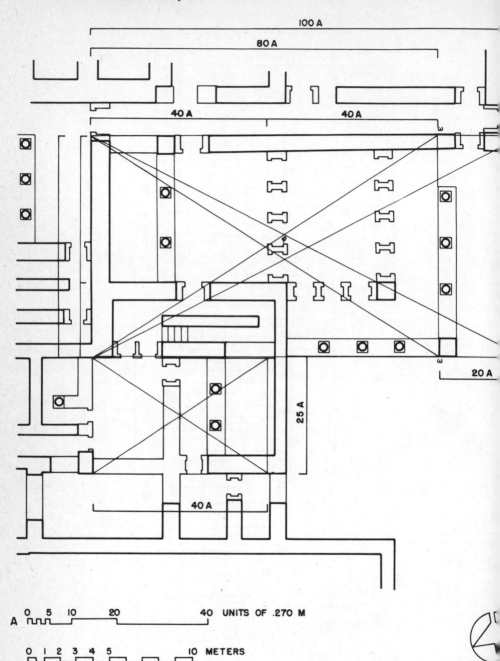

Figure IV.27.D. *Knossos: palace; hall system grid*

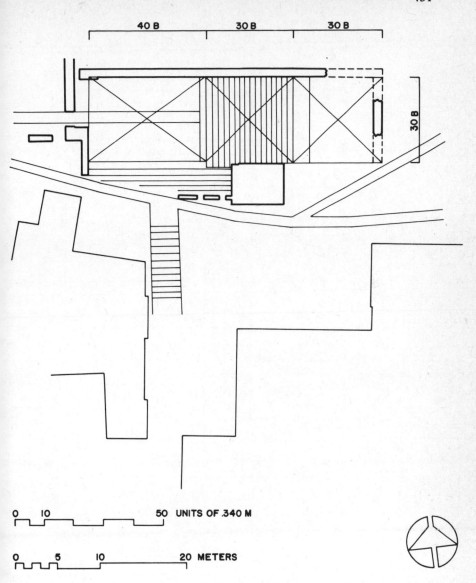

Figure IV.27.E. *Knossos: palace: theatral area grid*

432

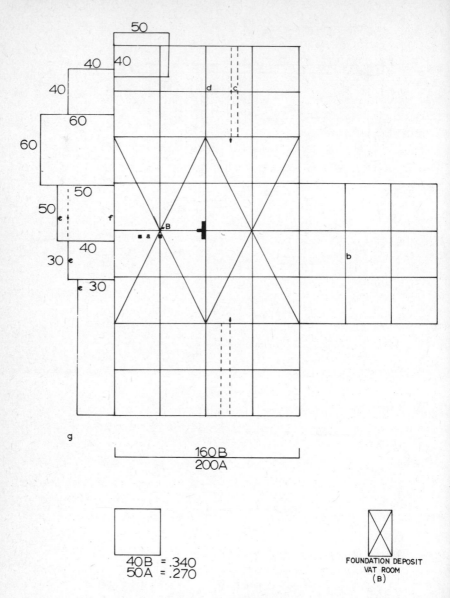

Figure IV.27.F. *Knossos: palace: overall modular grid*

28. ML: MALLIA: PALACE[1]

As we have discussed above in Chapter II, Mallia, while closely resembling Knossos, has had a much less complex history. In certain respects, Knossos at an earlier stage in its history may have more closely resembled Mallia in its extant (final) state (Figure IV.28.A).

The dimensions of the central core of the palace (central court plus western central block) are essentially identical to those of Knossos:

KN : 54.14-54.16 NS by 54.50[2] EW
ML : 54.60   NS by 54.17 EW

However, in its present state the Mallian central court proper occupies a smaller area than that of Knossos, mainly because of the placement of colonnades to north and east, and a remodelled southern wall brought up from the line of the original southern court facade: Figure IV.28.B.

The Mallian central grid defines a square which (as at KN) incorporates the width of the north-south corridor of the magazines to the west, as well as the northern and eastern walls of the court. Once again, a 200 by 200 unit square (x 0.270) is divided east-west by the court and the western central block, and north-south by a bisection line which (as at KN) runs through the centrally positioned pillar crypt. Here at Mallia there is a single cell with two (north-south) pillars, marked with double-axe signs.[3] The crypt stands at the center of its block, as indicated by the intersection of the diagonals in our plan.

In the central court is the foundation of an altar-table, placed exactly on the east-west bisection line of the central grid. But this altar (*cf.* the tripartite shrine at Knossos) does not stand at the center of the eastern half of the central grid proper; rather, it is placed at the exact center of the open area of the courtyard itself. It is equidistant from the eastern colonnade and the western court parapet-boundary. It is thus a reasonable assumption that it was put into position after the erection of the eastern colonnade, on modular grounds; an impression confirmed by the excavators, who see its placement as dating from the second palace period.[4]

The original southern facade of the court is at wall *c-c* in the plan, and the distance from this wall to the southern limit of the palace is 50 units (half that at Knossos). During the second palace period, the southern facade of the court was remodelled, with a wall of recessed and projected planes, each measuring 16 units in length, except for that to the west, which is half as long (eight units).[5] The adjacent width of the paved north-south corridor (whose paving ends to the north at the limit of the original southern court facade) is 5.40 or 20 units.

To the east (Figure IV.28.C), the eastern magazine block is even shallower than the block to the south of the court (±10.90, including eastern and western walls), 40 units wide (ideally 10.80). The southeastern block, fronting onto the southeastern corner of the court, is similarly 40 units wide by 40 units north-south (to the original southern palace grid limit). Between the two blocks is a narrower magazine block, aligned with the eastern facade of the block to the south, across the entranceway. It is ±6.90 wide (6.75 = 25 x 0.270). The plan indicates the modular sizes of these blocks, and their relationship to the central grid to the west.

If the present plan is compared with Figure IV.28.B, a discrepancy will be noted. Here, the modular width of the magazine block is taken to include that block's western wall; there, the central grid's eastern boundary is at the eastern face of the same wall. Evidently, the builders laid out the eastern block from the western face of the foundation courses laid along the original grid ropes rather than from the point where that rope initially stood: a similar idiosyncrasy in layout will be seen in connection with the pillared hall to the north of the central court.

The diagram also indicates that the distance from the northern limit of the central grid to the northern limit of the palace itself measures 160 units; we will examine the northern quarter of the palace in detail below.

Figure IV.28.D is a detailed plan of the pillared hall to the north of the central court. The colonnade to the south is ±2.65 deep (ten units). The width of the hall is 10.80 (40 units), which is the same as its length. The entrance hall is ±4.30 wide (including its western wall) or 16 units, bisected north-south and east-west by the centrally placed pillar (central to the grid, not the actual resultant room). This dimension is repeated to the east of the hall, where the two-flight stairwell is 8 plus 8 units wide (actually: ±4.35-4.45 overall; ideally: 4.32 = 16 units).

The builders also made the northern entrance to the courtyard, to the west of this zone, eight units wide (actually: 2.15-2.25; ideally: 2.16). In laying out the position of the six internal pillars of the hall itself, the builders placed the bases 16 units from the northern face of the northern wall, and eight units apart. But as the plan reveals, there was an error in alignment: the pillar bases are not perpendicular to the northern wall. Nevertheless, the misalignment was consistent, for the six pillars are precisely positioned with respect to each other (eight units apart EW, 16 units apart NS).[6]

The 40-unit width of the hall (identical to that of the block of magazines bounding the eastern side of the court) includes the width of the northern and southern walls. But as we have seen above, the central grid square delimits the northern face of the southern wall of the hall: we thus have a constructional overlap identical to that observed on the eastern block. This most likely indicates (as it might also in the eastern quarter) that the width of the hall was laid out *after* the foundation course of the southern wall was laid, using the southern face of the latter as a guide to later construction. Had this not been the case, the grid of the central blocks and those of the eastern and northern quarters would have been coterminous. The entire situation is reminiscent of the sequenced construction evident elsewhere at Mallia (ML ZA), as we have seen above.

To the north of the pillared hall (Figure IV.28.E), area XXII extends the grid another 40 units to the north (10.90). The remainder, from the northern face of cell XXII-3 to the southern face of the northern palace wall, is 21.60 (= 80 units). Thus, the entire northern quarter is 160 units north-south (43.30; ideally 43.20), measured singly between the arrows of our plan. The width of the northern magazine block (XXVII) is ±26.00, just less than 100 x 0.270. From the eastern face of the latter block to the eastern face of the westernmost projecting western facade of the palace (shown in outline in our plan) is 43.30 (43.20 = 160 units).

To the northwest, the northern facade in its original state probably followed the lines indicated, to join the northernmost western facade. These two northwestern facades measure ±13.20 each north-south (13.50 = 50 units). As shown in the plan, the hall system cluster, built in the second palace period, was laid out on a grid of squares 25 units on a side (varying in size between ±6.50 and 6.70). The hall widths, therefore, are identical to those of the smaller hall system at Knossos.[7]

As at Knossos, the western magazine blocks of Mallia are modularly semi-autonomous of the central layout grid, being laid out in a pattern whose subdivisions are not coincident with major subdivisions of the central grid. In addition, although the same unit (0.270) was employed here (unlike Knossos), it was expressed not decimally (as at Knossos) but in multiples of four (compare the detailed articulation of the pillared hall above): see Figure IV.28.F.

The dimensions of the various blocks very accurately match values of the linear standard of 0.270, as follows:

block F	NS :	9.75	(9.72 = 36 x 0.270)	(0.03) error
	EW :	13.00	12.76 = 48	(0.24)
DE	NS :	17.35	17.28 = 64	(0.07)
	EW :	17.32	17.28 = 64	(0.04)
C	NS :	10.19	9.72 = 36	(0.47)
	EW :	13.00	12.76 = 48	(0.24)
AB	NS :	8.55	8.64 = 32	(0.09)
x-y	NS :	8.55	8.64 = 32 $^{(= 64)}$	(0.09)

The east-west width of AB is uncertain due to the destruction of its western face. The largest error is ±0.47, the north-south length of block C.[8]

The distance x-y, equal to AB, aligns with line a-a, the southern limit of first palace period construction in the West Central Block, somewhat over a meter south of the southern boundary of the central grid square. It is evident that the original intent of the builders was to align the western magazine blocks with the central grid, for the misalignment to the south approximates a misalignment to the north, as indicated in our diagram. Note that:

1. x-y + AB + C (32 + 32 + 36) = 100 (27.32 vs. 27.00);
2. DE + F   (64 + 36)   = 100 (27.10 vs. 27.00);
3. (1) + (2)   (100 + 100)   = 200 (54.42 vs. 54.00);

an error of ±0.42 along the entire western facade. It appears that the western facades were laid out starting from the north, taking the northern face of the northernmost facade's southern wall as origin point, rather than its southern face.

In addition, an error was made in the north-south length of block C, which ideally should have been 9.72 long, rather than 10.19. No doubt the reason for these errors had to do with the fact that in the process of construction itself, the guiding grid ropes were necessarily removed.

The magazine blocks were significantly remodelled during the second palace period to allow for direct access into the north-south magazine corridor from outside. This entailed (as discussed above in Part One) the removal of magazines in block F, to accommodate an entrance corridor as well as the new hall system's southern extension. In block DE, only the northern magazine was left intact. A corridor was put through the center of the block, and a bastion built to replace the two southern magazines. Only block C was left intact. The outer face of block AB is no longer extant. The silos at the southwestern corner of the palace, dated by the excavators to the first palace period, extend 50 units beyond the point *y* in our plan, and thereby protrude further south than the southern limit of the central block grid to the east. Thus the misalignment to the north was increasingly spread forward as construction proceeded toward the south, if our hypothesis is correct.[9]

The overall schematic modular grid of the palace is shown in Figure IV.28.G. It would appear that the non-coterminosities to the west, and the overlapped grid squares to the east and south, were the result of a sequence of construction beginning with the central grid block, and continuing outward along the peripheries. It is not clear what the state of the original layout grid was in the northern quarter of the palace; as noted above, the entire north-western area was substantially altered in order to accommodate the second palace period hall system, which was partially carved out of a pre-existing western magazine area. We have seen above at Knossos that its hall system, similarly built in the second palace period, was simply annexed to the existing grid area to the east of the palace.

Thus it is evident that the palatial compound at Mallia, like its contemporary cousin at Knossos, was designed as a coherent unity. But unlike Knossos, the several steps in its realization failed to mesh precisely with the ideal modular grid plan. These imprecisions are certainly not apparent to the eye within the building itself, and affect the homogeneity of the plan not at all. What they do for us, however, is provide us with interesting evidence for the ways in which a palatial building program was sequentially carried out.

In the original conception of the plan, as we have noted above, the pillar crypt of the palace was positioned at the geometric center of the West Central Block of the central grid square, thereby replicating a ritual procedure carried out at Knossos.[10]

ML: *central grid*   : 200 x 200 (x 0.270)

   perimetral grids : decimal multiples of 0.270: 40 on E; 50 on S; 40 on N; on W: multiples of 4 x 0.270:

   facades (W)   : (NS) 36 + 64 + 36 + 64 (= 100 + 100) or   3 : 4 : 3 : 4

   (S)   : S facades along central grid square Southern extensions: two *tripartite* subdivisions, that on E: one central recess, two projections; that on W: one central projection; two recesses.

NOTES: ML

1. Complete bibliography above, Chapter II, Note 170.
2. Due to the misalignment of the eastern court facade, the southern east-west width at KN is ±55.70.
3. The double-axe sign here occurs twice, along with an incised trident sign and a star (asterisk) sign, the former having worn away since its discovery (*GFFC*: 24).
4. *GFFC*: 20-21. Within the portico in front of the pillar crypt are two stone bases, on line with the pillars to the west, which the excavators suggest may have served as supports for offering tables.
5. We would suggest that this wall was measured and laid out from the eastern side. The planes measure, from east to west:
    4.33 + 4.38 + 4.46 + 4.38 + 2.31, or
     16 + 16 + 16 + 16 + 8   x 0.270; ideally:
    4.32 + 4.32 + 4.32 + 4.32 + 2.16
6. Recall our analysis of the plan of Nirou Khani above, where the misalignment of a major east-west through-wall led to additional (but also consistent) misalignments of adjacent walls to the south.

7. The Mallian hall system, as discussed above in Chapter II, was on its southwestern side partly fit into the boundaries of the original western magazine block facades: see our first diagram here. To the north of this area, the domestic quarter was laid out on a uniform grid 25 units on a side.

8. The significant sizes of the magazine blocks here do not (vs. Knossos) include the perimetral coping stones at ground level, for these do not strictly serve as bases for the walls, but are appendages to those walls, a ground-level trim added to the walls. In other words, it is the dimensions of the wall courses themselves which are metrologically significant at Mallia, rather than their outer ground level articulations. This is a variation on the practice seen at Knossos above. Necessarily, in detailed tabulation of palace measurements, such idiosyncrasies of construction must be taken into account. The wall facades themselves are articulated into tripartite planar subdivisions, with a central recess and two flanking projections. These divide each western facade into three parts, but these parts are not of equal width. They are much ruined today, or in part restored (e.g. block DE). The schema employed by the masons apparently involved making the two outer projecting planes equal in width, with the central recess either larger (DE) or smaller (F, C). We will examine the facade articulations at Phaistos in more detail below.

9. This seems to us to be the simplest solution, enhancing our impression that the blocks were positioned so as to relate, as doubles (36 + 64; 36 + [32 + 32]), to the bisection-axes of the central grid square itself (100 + 100 NS).

10. In the construction of the hall system cluster, a ritual room (pillar crypt) was included in the compound; on a wall to the west was found a double-axe sign, a situation mirroring that of the original *central* pillar crypt of the old central grid square; see above, Chapter II.

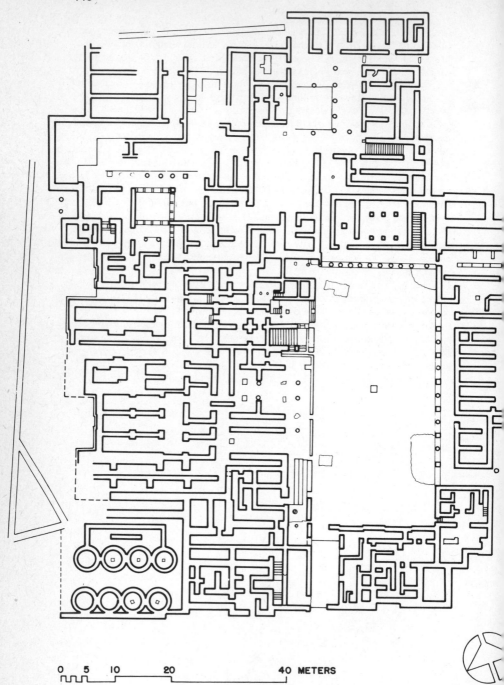

0 5 10   20   40 METERS

Figure IV.28.A. *Mallia: palace: overall plan*

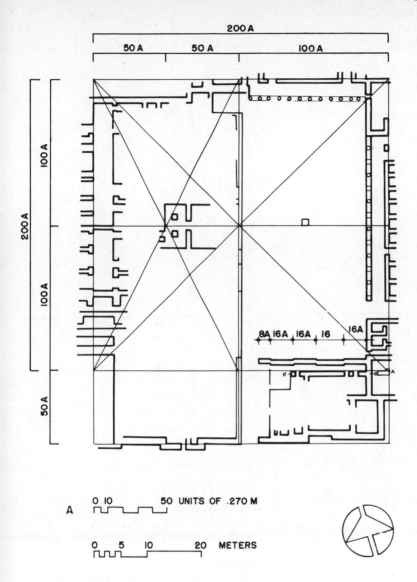

Figure IV.28.B. *Mallia: palace: central grid square*

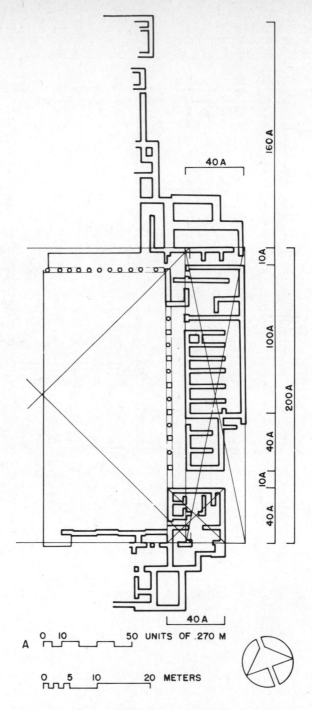

40 A

160 A

10A

100A

200 A

40 A

10A

40 A

40 A

40 A

A   0   10   50   UNITS OF .270 M

0   5   10   20   METERS

Figure IV.28.C. *Mallia: palace: eastern magazine grid*

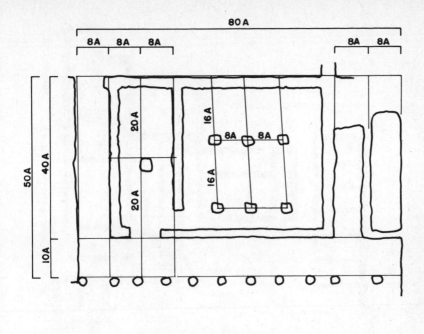

A

0 5 10   20   40 UNITS OF .270 M

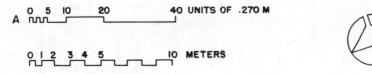

0 1 2 3 4 5   10 METERS

Figure IV.28.D. *Mallia: palace: pillared hall grid*

444

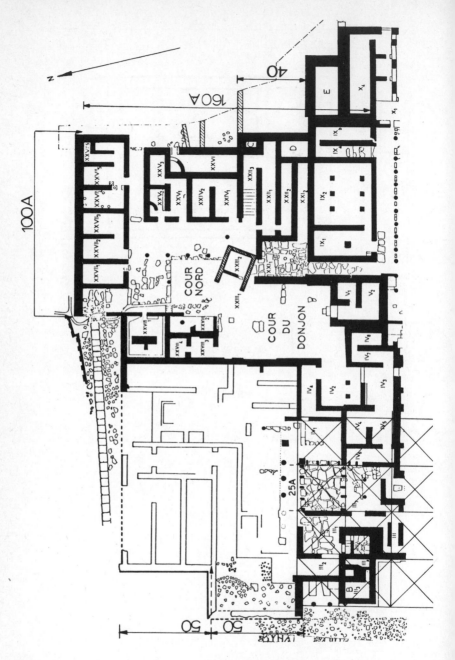

Figure IV.28.E. *Mallia: palace: northern quarter grid*

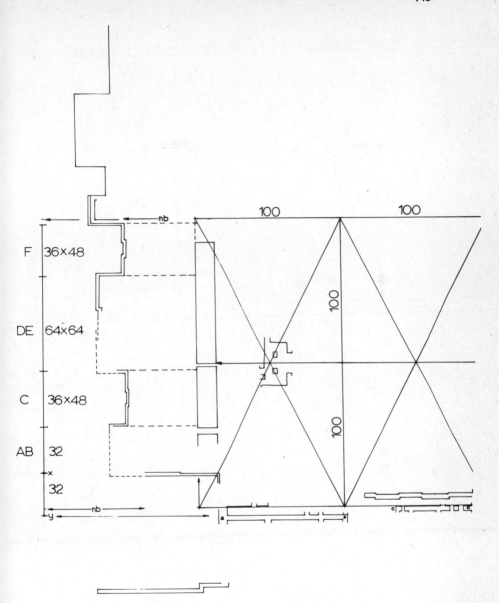

Figure IV.28.F. *Mallia: palace: western magazine grid*

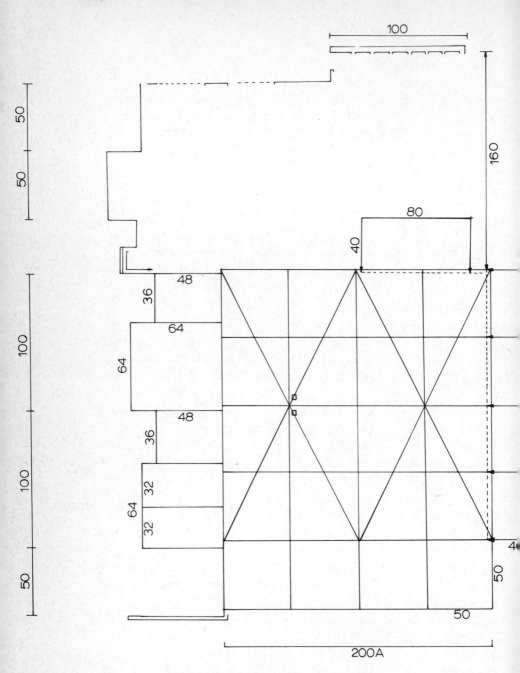

Figure IV.28.G. *Mallia: palace: overall modular grid*

29. PH I: PHAISTOS FIRST PALACE[1]

Although (as with Knossos, Mallia, and Phaistos II) hundreds of measurements were made in our survey of the first Phaistian palace, the greater bulk of the structure lies beneath the concrete platform of the second palace, and is hence unavailable for detailed study. Our modular survey, then, is confined to the outer perimeters of the palace, along with whatever walls were reused during the second palace period (Figure IV.29.A). These remains are indicated in black in our plan.

Figure IV.29.B shows the outer boundaries of the first palace. Unlike Mallia, which was constructed on a more or less uniform surface, PH I was built on a series of terraces rising from north to south (A-B-C).[2] Construction began, as recent excavations have demonstrated,[3] on terrace A, several meters below the level of the second terrace construction (B).

Figure IV.29.C is a schematic diagram of the entire western facade (terraces A and B) and western court. The overall north-south length of the southern half (to point Q) is ±35.00; the remainder, from Q to the northern boundary of the west middle court, is ±35.21. Overall, the north-south length of the west facades is ±70.21. The principal palace entrance is at the bisection line between these two sections, on the level of terrace B (= one storey above the level of construction on terrace A). This entrance scheme was repeated in PH II, as we shall see below.

The northern facade is divided in half again: the southern block measures, at the orthostate level,[3] ±17.51; the remainder is ±17.70. The southern facade, on terrace A, is divided differently: the southern half measures ±13.42, the northern half is ±21.58 of which the West Porch, between points A-A′ in our plan, is ±8.70 north-south. This latter dimension is one-half the north-south lengths of the facades to the north (17.51; 17.70). The remaining section, block B, measures ±12.88.[4] Thus, from south to north, the entire facade measures:

A   B   C   D   E
13.42 + 12.88 + 8.70 + 17.51 + 17.70 = 70.21

Note also that the distance from facade E to the point where the raised causeway intercepts the stepped 'theatral area' is also ±17.50, while the overall NW-SE length of the causeway, as indicated in the diagram, measures ±34.50, bisected in half at the intersection of the east-west causeway.

It will be recalled that the north-south length of block D is nearly identical to that of block DE at Mallia (there: ±17.35; here: 17.51). We saw that that entire facade could be described by values of 0.270, but here a simpler solution comes to the fore if we divide this D length decimally (rather than by multiples of four, as at Mallia), 17.50 x 1/10 = 1.75, which equals 5 x 0.350, the standard unit employed in the layout of TYL A and B above. Thus, 17.50 equals 35 such units. At Tylissos, the module was found to be ±1.70.

Using ±0.350 as a conjectural standard, expressed in multiples of a modular length of five units (±1.70), note that:

A: 13.43; 14.00 = 40 x 0.350 (0.58 error)
B: 12.88; 12.25 = 35 x 0.350 (0.63)
C: 8.70;   8.75 = 25 x 0.350 (0.05).

Because of the difficulty of measuring the southern section, the lengths of A and B are approximate, and the 'error' may be in our measurements, for the walls have buckled slightly here under the weight of later construction.

Nevertheless, the resultant schema is clear and consistent:

A	+ B	+	C	+ D	+	E
40	35		25	50		50
40		60			100	or
	100				100	

Overall, the ideal length of 70.00 is in error by merely 0.21. The resultant schema of 200 units north-south is thus identical to that seen at Mallia and Knossos, although here expressed on a linear standard unit of 0.350 rather than 0.270 as at Mallia.[5]

Block D, as revealed in our first plan, has five internal major magazine subdivisions. It is noteworthy that (although they are not all of identical width, and increase slightly in width from north to south), the number of partitions within the facade is five, numerically matching the proposed modular length of 50 units: an identical situation was seen above at Knossos.[6]

The same modular lengths are found in the west court, as noted above. The overall width of this court, from the facade of block D to the opposite corner, is also 100 units (±35.00). The western third of the causeway triangle, whose paving stones are no longer extant, is ±17.50, or 50 units, making the triangle equilateral.

The retaining wall above the theatral steps is articulated by means of seven (extant) shallow projections and recesses of fine ashlar masonry, measuring east to west: 3.17 + 3.04 + 3.07 + 3.35 + 2.89 + 3.20 + 2.64. All but the fifth and seventh approximate nine units of 0.350 (ideally, 3.15), the remaining two suggest eight units (ideally, 2.80). There is a numerical isomorphism here between the unit-length of the facades and the number of theatral steps (nine), which may be coincidental.

Facade D is divided into three equal sections: a central recessed plane flanked by two projections. From south to north these measure 5.89 + 5.80 + 5.82. It would appear that these lengths are metrologically null, arising out of a simple division of the 50-unit facade (17.51 x 1/3 = 5.836), similar to the situation observed at Mallia. However, the height of the orthostate blocks (first course) is a very precise 1.01 throughout the facade length (1.05 = 3 x 0.350). The euthynteria projects 0.35 out from the wall line (= 1 unit), and the width of the outer wall averages 1.70 (1.75 = 3 units), as shown in our diagram. The depth of the projection of block D from the line of block E is 1.43; 1.40 = 4 x 0.350.

Block A to the south (plan in Figure IV.29.D), measuring 13.42 north-south, is divided in a reverse manner: here a central projection is flanked by two recesses, with slight returns at the corner. The entrance here is a later cutting, not in the original layout.[7] The facade was evidently laid out according to the following modular scheme, from south to north:

a	+	b	+	c	+	d	+	e	+	f	+	g
3		10		3		8		3		10		3

There is an overall error in layout of ±0.58. It may be that this facade was laid out with measuring rods slightly less than 0.350 (note that 13.42 x 1/40 = 0.336). Here, the orthostate blocks are uniformly 0.67-0.68 high (2 x 0.336 = 0.672), and the height of the euthynteria and small projecting blocks of the foundation is 0.33 (equals one unit). The euthynteria projects 0.14-0.185 (0.168 = ½ x 0.336). But while the proportions here are smaller than those of the masonry of block D to the north, the walls are similarly thick (1.70, or five units).

Thus it is clear that the design and layout of PH I is consistent with that of ML and KN, at least on the western magazine blocks. But what of the plan as a whole?

Figure IV.29.E is a diagram of the proposed modular grid of PH I, based on our areal survey of the remains overall. Remains of the palace to the northeast indicate that the overall size of the plan was at least as long east-west as it was north-south: the length *a-a'* in the plan is ±70.00. Dropped down to the south along this eastern side, the lines would form a square 200 units on a side. Note also that the line *b-b'* are aligned with the northern limit of the central court pavement (reused in part in PH II). To the west, *b* is aligned with a colonnade defining the western boundary of the PH I courtyard. Two columns to the east may delimit the original eastern side of that court (it is noteworthy that, as at KN and ML, the dimensions of the court itself are metrological remainders of the planning grid *per se*).

The center of the grid square, point Q, is also aligned with the bisection-axis of the palace, which in turn generates the position of the main western palace entrance. Unlike KN and ML, however, this 'central grid' defines the entire western boundary of the palace, not merely the area to the western limit of a magazine corridor. In addition, the ritual central chambers are here placed differently; not, as at ML and KN, at the center of the western half of the central grid square, but rather (at U and W) at the center of each half of that grid, to the north and south. The positioning of the pillar crypt (W) and lustral chamber(?) U is thus at the center of each of the two (northern and southern) halves of the layout grid. It is of interest that each of these two halves of the palace were built separately (beginning to the south). We may imagine that the placement of each of these ritual chambers reflects a foundation ceremony not unlike that suggested above for Knossos.[8]

The distance from line *b-b'* to the northern face of the PH I archive area is ±35.00, or 100 units of 0.350. Thus the entire extant portion of the remains describes a rectangle of 2 : 3 proportions, measuring 200 units EW by 300 NS (or, overall, a square of 300 by 300, if we include the width of the west middle court). There was undoubtedly some construction along the eastern side of the courtyard, but this has been obliterated through exposure and later remodelling during PH II. It is likely that construction extended some 50 units further east at this point, but this cannot be confirmed. If the palatial compound on this eastern side was shallower than that to the west of the court, then in its original layout the palace would have resembled ML and KN.

PH I: *central grid square* : 200 x 200 (x 0.350)
       perimetral extension : 100 x 200 (N); 100 units W court
       facades (W)   : (NS) 50 + 50 + 25 + 35 + 40
                                tripartite planar subdivisions within
                                each facade (exc. B, C):
                                on N: two projections, one recess
                                    S: two recesses, one projection.

NOTES: PH I

1. Complete bibliography in Chapter II, Note 192.
2. See Chapter II.
3. As at Mallia, the metrologically significant dimension. At the euthynteria level, the blocks measure ±18.24. The projecting euthynteria level, as our analyses here and at ML demonstrate, is a metrological *addition*.
4. This is difficult to measure in detail because of the presence of later construction over the northwestern corner of block A. The original orthostate blocks of B are partly incorporated into later internal walls (rooms LVI and LVII). This later addition was built up near the passageway between this quarter and the bastion/ramp system connecting the two western courts A and B.
5. Recall that at KN our analysis of the western magazine block suggested usage of this 'longer' unit (0.340) here, as an appendage to the central grid square. On the interrelationships between the longer and shorter Minoan linear standards, see our tabulations below, Chapter V.
6. Again, note that the large magazine block DE at Mallia originally contained five magazines. It measures 17.35 north-south. We suggested that the simplest solution there was to see this as 64 units of 0.270. But note that 17.50 = 50 x 0.350, a length at which the two scales coincide. Thus, 17.50 = 50 x 0.350; 17.28 = 64 x 0.270. The fact that there is a numerical correspondence between 50 x 0. 350 and 5 ten-unit internal subdivisions might suggest that the Mallia western blocks might

have been laid out using the longer scale (as at Knossos). But it need not, for if the Mallia western blocks were laid out on the same standard as the coterminous central grid square (0.270), once the outer walls were set in place, the internal subdivision into five chambers could be easily realized by using the longer scale. We saw at ML ZA that internal secondary walls were laid after the outer structural walls were in place.

7.   See E. Fiandra, *KrKhr* 15/16 (1961-1962): 112ff, for a study of the four building periods of PH I.

8.   As far as can be determined, no traces of double-axe signs have been found here in positions where, from our examination of Knossos, they might be expected. However, as we shall see below, the more complete plan of PH II seems to reflect the situation at Knossos: PH II's central ritual chamber is at the geometric center of its central grid square, and double-axe signs are found along its bisection axes. There *is* a double-axe sign in cell U, however; see *PMF* I: 97ff.

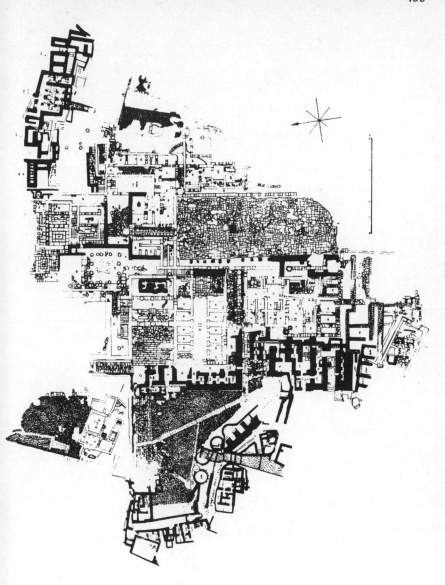

Figure IV.29.A. *Phaistos: palace I: overall site plan*

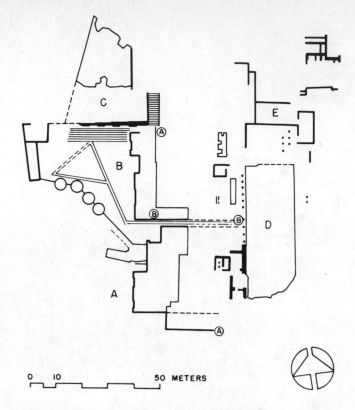

Figure IV.29.B. *Phaistos: palace I: overall plan*

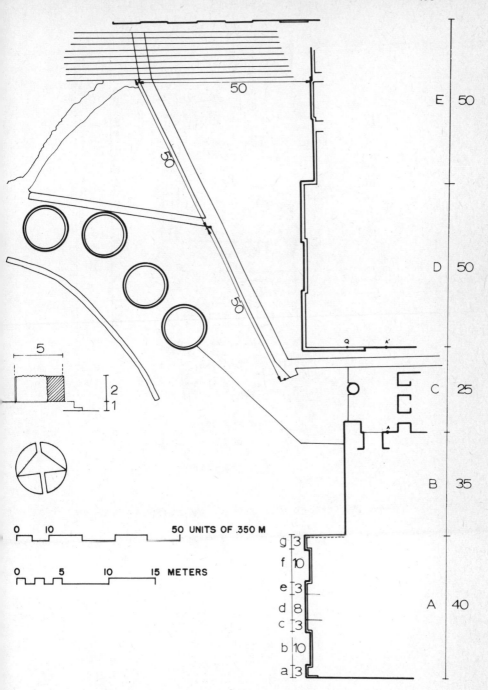

Figure IV.29.C. *Phaistos: palace I: western facade grid*

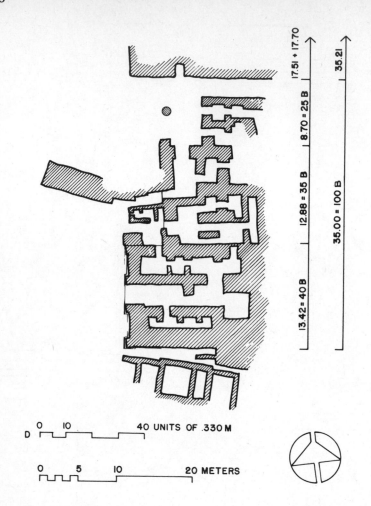

Figure IV.29.D. *Phaistos: palace I: southwestern quarter grid*

457

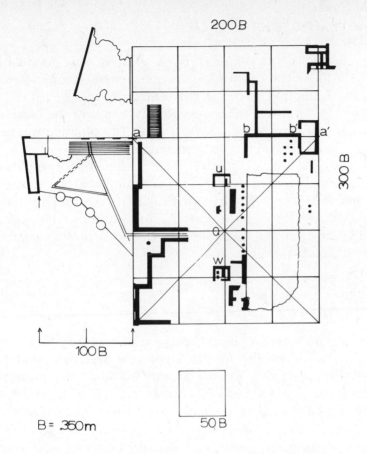

Figure IV.29.E. *Phaistos: palace I: overall modular grid*

30. PH II: PHAISTOS SECOND PALACE[1]

The second palace at Phaistos is an entirely new foundation (Figure IV.30.A), except for such walls as were incorporated in the new construction north of the central court. As such, PH II provides us with an excellent opportunity to study the organization, design and layout of a major palace. The building was very finely and carefully laid out and constructed.

Its dimensions indicate that PH II, in its modular organization, is a contextual variant on the themes presented by Knossos, Mallia and Phaistos I. The eastern half of its central grid square (Figure IV.30.B) defines the central court and its western colonnade. The north-south dimensions of this sector are similar to those of KN and ML:

PH II: 53.88-53.90
KN : 54.14-55.18
ML : 54.60

The north-south length includes the northern boundary wall of the court, the width of the eastern colonnade stylobate, and the western boundary wall, as well as the width of the projected southern wall. The rectangle formed is ±27.10 wide east-west, identical to that of Mallia, and 0.10 larger than that of Knossos.

The center point of the overall grid square falls at point Q in our plan, defining the position of the ritual chamber 24, corresponding to the pillar crypts of Knossos and Mallia. But here, as at Knossos, this center point lies directly on the resultant court (behind its colonnade): a position recalling that of the Knossian Tripartite Shrine. Along the bisection axis of this grid square, on the western wall of cell 24 and along the wall stretching to the west beyond, are found incised double-axe marks (as at Knossos): their position is noted below in Figure IV.30.D.[2]

The grid square itself is 200 by 200 units of 0.270, and this eastern half is exactly 100 by 200 units. Looking at Figure IV.30.C, it will be seen that length *R-r* is 100 units (±27.70).[3] This length is divided in half on the eastern face of the first (W) stylobate, at ±13.85, and divided again in half to the east, at the western face of the innermost stylobate (±6.93). The central stylobate divides the remainder in half again.

The width of this stepped platform, which is the PH II replacement of the buried 'theatral area' of PH I to the west, varies from 13.30 at the bottom step to 13.55 at the top step, to 13.75 at the eastern end. Like the central court grid, the stepped platform is thus a 1 : 2 rectangle, exactly one-fourth of the size of the latter (50 by 100 units vs. 100 by 200 units).[4]

The points *m* and *m'* on the plan are not exactly in alignment: the former stands somewhat to the east of the latter. This 'error' in fact is a result of adjustments made for the incorporation of a misaligned wall from the first palace, as we shall see below.

This stepped platform extends the central grid square 50 units to the north. The northern boundary of the central grid is along the northern face of the magazine block below, as indicated by the diagonal line from central grid point Q on the lower right. The block is divided into three parallel sections running east-west, of which the central portion is the corridor providing access to the magazines to the north and south. As indicated on the plan, the magazines themselves are each ten units wide. They were laid out after the outer (and thicker) walls were placed, from the inner face of that wall.[5]

The magazine block is 17.22 north-south, a dimension replicated on the largest magazine blocks at Knossos, Mallia and PH I.[6] Of this length, only the northern half was extant at the time of excavation; the southern half is a modern rebuilding along symmetrical lines, following the line of extant wall fragments along the southern side of the block. It appears that the western facade was divided among five shallow recessed and projected planes which (as restored) measure 3.34, 3.34, 3.86, 3.34, and 3.34.[7]

To the south of the block, wall *c-c* continues the alignment of the thick internal north-south wall of the magazine block. Had this wall been as thick, it would have been precisely aligned with the former.[8]

Note that along the entire western facade here the modular lengths are (north-south) 50 + 21 + 21 + 21 + 37 (= 50 + 100). The reason for these odd dimensions will become apparent shortly.

Figure IV.30.D is a plan of the southwestern quarter of the central grid square, to the southwestern limits of the palace. To the south, cells *b-b'* may have been a stairwell, and *c-c'-c''* a hall. Wall CD is a high retaining wall; there are traces of a continuation eastward of D at its southern tip. It is noteworthy that the western end of wall C is exactly aligned with the southwestern corner of the magazine block to the north (at *a*), perhaps representing a misalignment of construction along this western flank of the central planning grid. The distance from C to *b* is 13.10, or approximately 50 units (recall the 50-unit addition to Mallia's central grid square to the south).

The western facade of this quarter is divided approximately in half at point *Q*. There is a slight discrepancy in the layout at this half-way point, but it is consistent: gap Y is the same as gap Z to the south. The overall facade is divided into three sub-facades, and the length of facades A + B is ±38.00; 38.60 = 140 x 0.274 or 55 x 0.343 x 2.

The dimensions of these facades are of interest, for they provide evidence of a consistently applied harmonic proportional schema:

facade A: 7.25 (to point *b*)
       B: 11.80 (to point Q)
       C: 19.00 (line Q-*a*)

The dimensions correspond to a harmonic scheme of increasingly larger lengths from south to north (unit: +0.343):

	A	+ B	+ C	+ DE	
	21	+ 34	+ 55	+ 90	(for 89)
ideally:	7.20	11.66	18.87	30.87	(for 30.53),

as shown in the diagram in Figure IV.30.E. In other words, the entire western facade length of 200 units (from the northern flank of the stepped platform) of 0.343 was divided into subsections whose numerical dimensional values represent literal applications of the proportions of the Fibonacci Series of: 1, 1, 2, 3, 5, 8, 13, 21, 34, 55, 89, . . .[9] The precise length of 21 + 34 + 55 + 89 would have been 199 units, or 68.26 (68.60 = 200 units). Here again there is a coincident length on the shorter unit of 0.270 employed in the layout of the grid proper: 250 x 0.270 = 67.50, about a meter short. This meter 'gap' is in fact the gap Z at the southern side of the structure.

Evidently, the builders were aware of the fact that the length of facades D and E, totalling 30.87 (*c.* 150 + 63] x 0.270), approximated 89 x 0.343, 30.53, and continued the articulation of the line of facades to the south by decreasing Fibonacci ratios: 89, 55, 34, 21. They also set back the second facade 11.70 to the east; 11.66 = 34 x 0.343.

Note that the stepped platform block is 50 x 0.270. The magazine block to the south, block D, was laid out as 50 x *0.343*. The length 50 (x 0.270) + 50 (x 0.343) = 90 (x 0.343). For the Fibonacci ratios to have been precise, the magazine block should have been laid out as 49 units of 0.343 (16.81).

Thus we see that at PH II (as at KN) the western facades were articulated by means of the longer linear standard, brought into a coterminous relationship with the central planning grid based on the shorter linear standard. In effect, the PH II western facade of Fibonacci ratios was carved out of a modular grid by taking advantage of the metrological interrelationships of the two Minoan standards of measure.

The Fibonacci system of proportions is well attested in contemporary Egypt.[10] It is also common in Minoan design, as we have seen throughout these analyses, forming the basis of the 2 : 3, 3 : 5, and 5 : 8 proportions seen above on wall facades and in the proportions of modular grid patterns. It is based on a simple summation series of integers:

0 + 1 = 1; 1 + 1 = 2; 1 + 2 = 3; 2 + 3 = 5; 3 + 5 = 8, 5 + 8 = 13; 8 + 13 = 21; 13 + 21 = 34; 21 + 34 = 55; 34 + 55 = 89...

wherein the ratio between any two integers increasingly approximates the proportion 1 : 1.6, the so-called 'golden section'.[11]

Figure IV.30.F is a plan of the eastern quarter of the palace, such as it is. Measurements indicate that this residential quarter was laid out as a square 19.62 EW by 19.50 NS; 72 x 0.270 = 19.44. This was divided into quarters, 36 units on a side, as shown. The colonnade to the west, included in the two western quarters, contains eight (originally nine) pillars, each set an average of 2.43 apart (2.43 = 9 x 0.270). The overall length to the southern face of the northern wall of the court is 21.87 (= 81 units, or 9 x 9). It is of interest that (as at Mallia) the *western* face of the stylobate was used as a base line for layout, thereby creating a grid overlap (the central grid square's eastern limit is the *eastern* face of that stylobate).

The southern face of this cluster is closely aligned with the northern face of the southwestern quarter across the court (see Figure IV.30.A); an identical situation may be observed at Knossos, where the eastern face of the western wall of the northern entrance to the court is aligned with the opposite wall of the entrance corridor to the south.

In Figure IV.30.G is a plan of the northern quarters of the palace. First palace walls incorporated into the construction of PH II are indicated with hatching. Also of this date are the columns and pillars of the lower storey of the 'banquet hall', at Y in the plan.

It appears that the old wall system A-A' and A'-G was used as the base line for the layout of the grid squares to the south and west. The central grid square's northern edge is at point P, 50 units south. The distance from A' to point m in Figure IV.30.C above is ±54.00 or 200 units of 0.270, and the distance from point m'' to m' in that plan is also ±54.00. As we noted above, there is a misalignment to the northwest of the palace, at the western face of the stepped platform, between points m and m'. We would suggest that the latter arose out of an initial misalignment in this area, between the walls at point A' and m''. Evidently what happened was that the builders laid out exactly 200 units from these two points out to the west. The width of the section was kept constant, however, closely approximating 50 units, between 13.30 and 13.77.

The A'-m'' misalignment is also reflected in the north-south misalignment of the north-south corridor bisecting this quarter from the center of the court. This misalignment is visible in published photographs,[11] giving the (false) impression that the corridor (and hence the court) is not directly aligned toward the twin peaks of Mount Ida to the north of the palace.

PH I walls C-C', B-B', and D-D' were used as base lines for laying out the hall systems toward the north. They were laid out on clear decimal multiples of 0.270: the southern hall is 40 by 50 units, as is the larger hall to the north.[12] The east-west subdivisions of both halls were generated by simple halving and quartering. PH I wall B-B' was also used as a base line for laying out the grand peristyle court 74 to the east.

Figure IV.30.H is a diagram of the proposed modular grid layout of PH II. Heavy lines indicate walls from PH I reincorporated in the layout of PH II. Because of these walls, the PH II grid necessarily breaks at the small court north of the 'banquet hall' block.

It will be observed that the modular grids of PH, KN and ML are basically alike, including a central grid square 200 by 200 units (of 0.270), and decimal extensions to the north and south. Not included in our diagram is a projected 50-unit grid extension to the south, discussed above in connection with the southwestern quarters. As at KN and ML, the center point of the central grid square defines the position of the principal ritual chambers of the palace (here cell 24), associated with occurrences of the double-axe symbol, a probable token symbol of the grid square itself. Here at PH II, the center of the *entire* extant grid falls at the east-west bisection axis defining the position of the major western palace entrance (this would be altered if we include the conjectural 50-unit grid extension to the south).

Unlike KN and ML, but like PH I, the 'central grid' here also defines the outer western boundary of the palace: at the two other palaces, the western magazine blocks are *appended* to the western limits of that square. PH II in this regards follows local practice.[13]

PH II: *central grid square* : 200 x 200 (x 0.270)
perimetral extensions : (N): 50 units
(S) : 50 units?
(E): 72 x 72 units
(N): 100 x 100 units
facade (W) : literal Fibonacci harmonic system (in units of 0.343): 21 + 34 + 55 + 89 units, with a 34-unit return, and 13-unit recesses to the south.
five-part planar articulation of main magazine block, western facade.

NOTES: PH II

1. Complete bibliography in Chapter II, Note 192.
2. *PMF* II: 423, Figure 270. Full list of occurrences of this sign given in *PMF* I: 97ff. The signs on the east-west axis here are the only *in situ* double-axe signs found. There is also a double-axe sign in cell 38, dating from PH I (above, PH I, cell *U*). That cell 24 is the chief cult room of the palace is the view of the excavators (*PMF* II: 149ff, Figure 92, p. 152; *PC*: 40). Perhaps the reason that cell 24 is not a canonical pillar crypt (but rather features a single central clay base, perhaps for a statue or an upright double-axe?, is that cell *W* from PH I, a two-pillared crypt, remained in use during PH II. It stands in the empty space in Figure IV.30.A, to the north of cell 96, and south of cell 23.
3. *PMF* II: 306ff.
4. In *PMF* II: Figure 209, opposite p. 336, is a measured sectional drawing of the north-south length of the stepped platform area. The dimensions given in the drawing, confirmed by our survey, are:
    $$2.76 + 1.16 + 2.34 + 1.17 + 2.49 + 0.99 + 2.69 \ (= 13.60)$$
    or $10 + 4 + 9 + 4 + 9 + 4 + 10 \ (= 50 \times 0.270)$
    in other words:
    $$2.70 + 1.08 + 2.43 + 1.08 + 2.43 + 1.08 + 2.70 \ (= 13.50)$$
5. A practice observed in our analyses above: see ML ZA, where magazines also ten units wide were laid out from the inner face of an outer wall.
6. ML: 17.35; PH I: 17.51, 17.70. KN: somewhat less: 16.70-16.90.
7. Evidently the masons divided the wall length according to a longer standard of ±0.34 (0.334), assuming that they divided it into even-unit lengths. The lengths equal $10 + 10 + 11½ + 10 +10$ units. It is not unreasonable to assume that stone-masons employed their own unit measure somewhat different in size from the one employed by the *harpedonaptae* (rope-stretchers). An analogous situation may be seen in the layout of the Mycenaean megaroid palace at Pylos, where the unit employed by the masons and that by the floor-layers were slightly different. See D. Preziosi, *MPPAO*: 624-627.
8. Note the inner alignment to the south, however: the eastern wall of cell 95 (in the first plan) is more closely aligned with the eastern face of the north-south wall in the magazine block.
9. See the discussions below in the next Chapter, and D. Preziosi, 'Harmonic Design in Minoan Architecture', *Fibonacci Quarterly/Journal of Mathematics of the University of California*, VI.6. (1968): 370-384.
10. See next Chapter, and A. Badawy, *AEAD* (1965). Badawy refers to the use of Fibonacci ratios in literal numerals as 'in clear'. This example of its use at PH II is the only literal usage known apart from smaller-number proportions (seen throughout Minoan design above); but see Note 11.
11. Recall that the modular grid of the 'little palace' of Knossos is laid out as 100 by 160 units (= 1 : 1.6).
12. Note that the Hall of the Double Axes at Knossos, 80 by 50 units of 0.270, would be as large as both Phaistian halls combined.
13. J.W. Graham (*PC*: Figure 144) presents a modular analysis of part of PH II, based on a hypothetical unit of ±0.304. The resultant proportions and discontinuities in his grid have no precedent in Minoan design as far as our analyses have been able to determine.

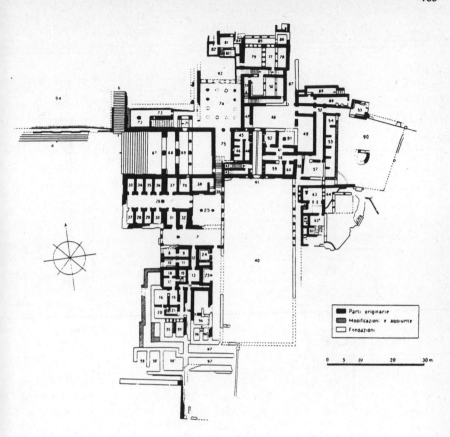

Figure IV.30.A. *Phaistos: palace II: overall plan*

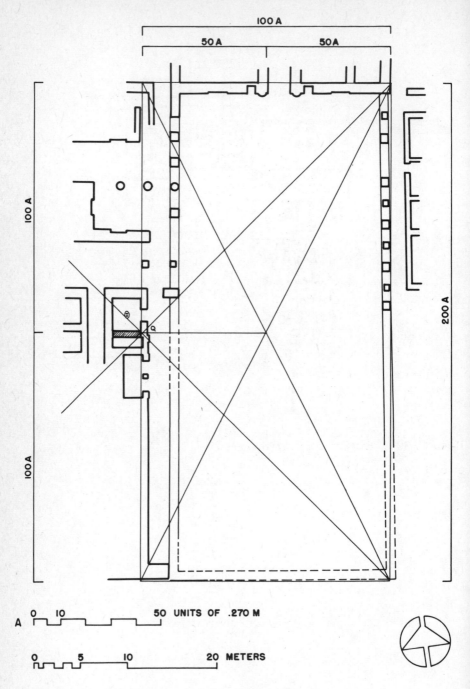

Figure IV.30.B. *Phaistos: palace II: central grid square*

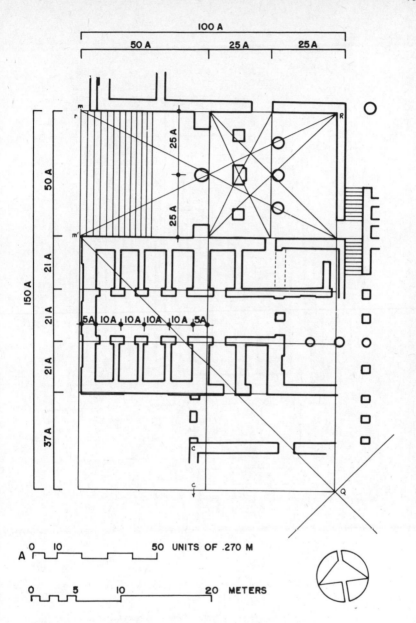

Figure IV.30.C. *Phaistos: palace II: northeastern grid*

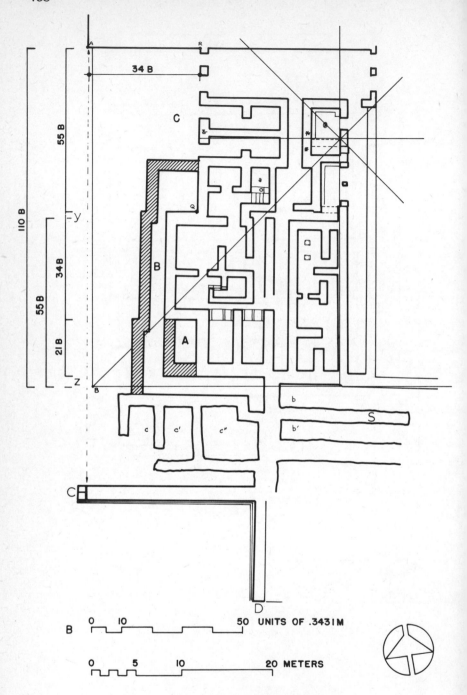

Figure IV.30.D. *Phaistos: palace II: southwestern grid*

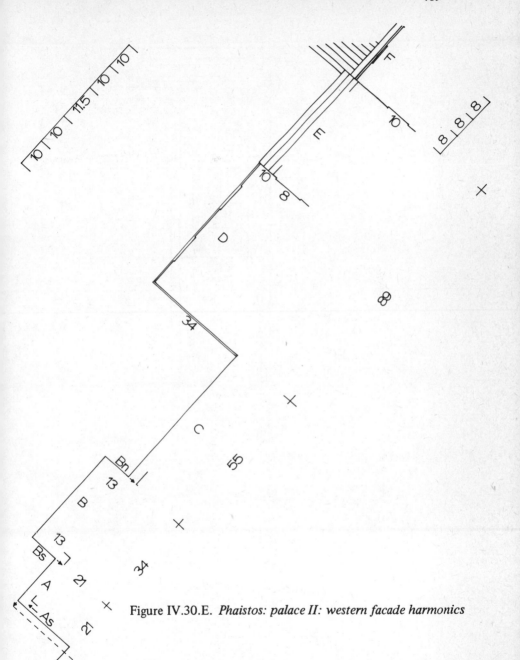

Figure IV.30.E. *Phaistos: palace II: western facade harmonics*

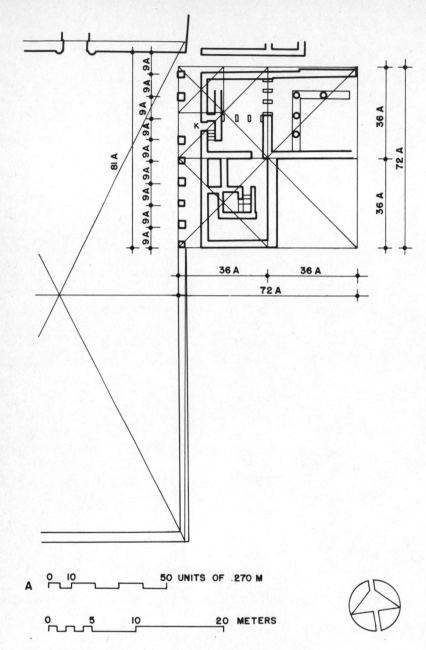

A   0   10   50 UNITS OF .270 M

0   5   10   20 METERS

Figure IV.30.F. *Phaistos: palace II: northeastern grid*

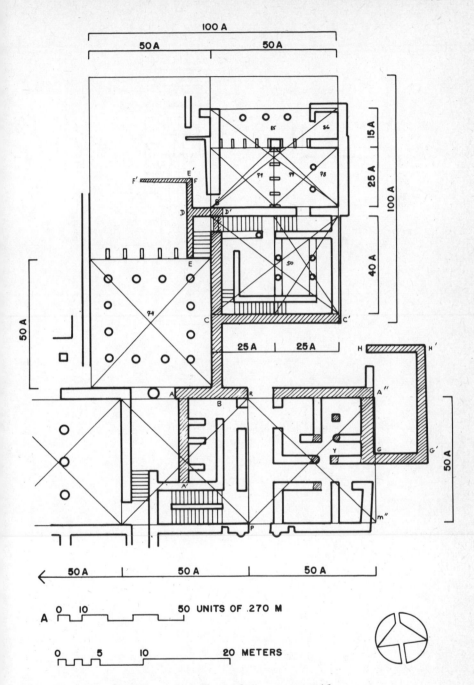

Figure IV.30.G. *Phaistos: palace II: northern quarter grid*

472

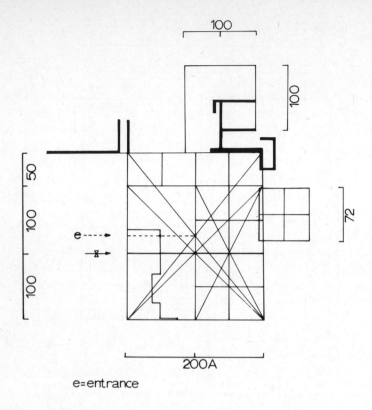

e=entrance

Figure IV.30.H. *Phaistos: palace II: overall modular grid*

31. GRN: GOURNIA PALACE[1]

The crude rubble walls and disturbed topography of the provincial palatial compound at Gournia do not permit extensive modular analysis. It is likely that the palace was fit into a pre-existing urban fabric as best as possible. Our survey was brief, and confined to measurements of articulated facades, and overall long dimensions.

Our (superficial) impression is that the structure was laid out on a unit of ±0.270, with the values as indicated below in Figure IV.31.B. Of interest here is the position of what was evidently a tripartite-type shrine on the western face of the courtyard, at *A* in Figure IV.31.A. Directly to the west of this, incised on one of the western facades of the building, is a double-axe sign, shown in the plan. The relative placement of these two features recalls similar situations at PH II and KN. Nearby is a tiny L-shaped stepped platform, perhaps a small-scale echo of the great 'theatral areas' of the palaces of PH and KN.

GRN: *unit*   : 0.270? Court a 1 : 2 rectangle?
          facade (W) : *tripartite* planar articulation, with two projections flanking a central recess.

NOTE: GRN

1.   H. Boyd-Hawes et al, *Gournia, Vasiliki.* . . (1908): 24-26.

474

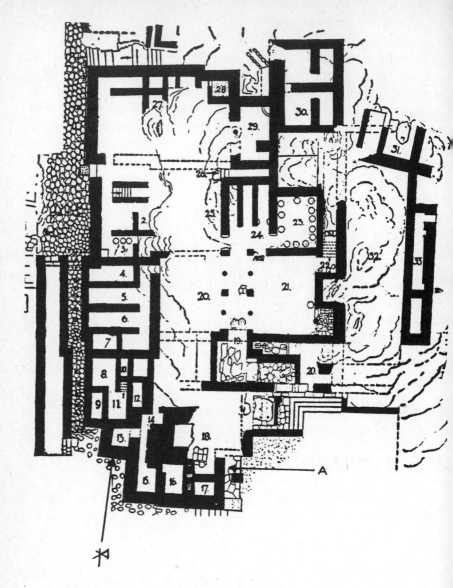

Figure IV.31.A. *Gournia: palace: plan*

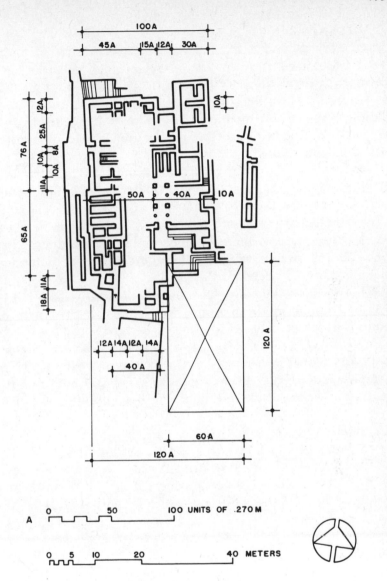

Figure IV.31.B. *Gournia: palace: partial grid*

32. KZ: KATO ZAKRO PALACE[1]

That the palace at Kato Zakro was planned and laid out with clarity and regularity may be seen by an examination of the plan in Figure IV.32.A. Because of the incomplete nature of the excavation, a full *in situ* modular analysis has not been made. Instead, we shall confine our observations to a breif consideration of a few principal dimensions.

The width of the entire compound as indicated in Figure IV.32.B B is ±68.00.[2] The central court altar(?) stands approximately midway between these two limits (±34.00 + ±34.00). The length of the central court from the southern face of the southern wall to the southern face of the colonnade wall to the north is ±33.90, or one-half the overall width of the compound. The colonnade to the north is ±3.25 deep north-south.

The width of the court, including perimetral walls,[3] is ±13.40-13.60. Point Q in the plan is exactly one-half the length of the court plus the northern colonnade, as defined above.[4]

We may very tentatively suggest that the structure was laid out on a grid based on decimal lengths of a unit of ±0.340. Thus, the overall width equals 200 units; the court is 100 by 40 units. In a number of respects, then, Kato Zakro resembles the other palaces.

KZ: *unit*   : ±0.340?
       modular lengths : central court: 100 x 40
                          N colonnade: 10
                          overall width: 100 + 100 units, at mid-point of which is court altar(?).

NOTES: KZ

1. See discussion and bibliography above, Chapter II.
2. This length is chosen because of the (significant?) position of the court object (recalling the modularly significant position of the KN tripartite shrine, ritual cell 24 at PH II, etc. The shrine in the western block stands adjacent to the east-west bisection axis of the central court (marked by Q in the plan). This axis crosses along the northern face of the northern wall of the shrine (cell XXIII), which is at the center of the (entire) eastern compound. Judging from the evident fact that in other palatial compounds the principal shrine stands at a modularly significant

point (see the pillar crypts of KN and ML and PH I), further modular analysis should clarify this relationship here.

3. As at the other palaces, which seems to have been the standard practice.
4. Curiously, point Q stands at exactly the same distance from the main entrance to this quarter, to the north (4.90-5.00) as a similar ashlar wall jog at Plati relative to the portico of its hall (q.v.). We consider the inclusion of the northern colonnade here as metrologically significant by comparison with Mallia above.

Figure IV.32.A. *Kato Zakro: palace: plan*

478

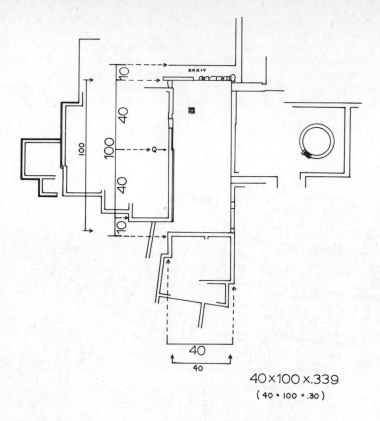

40×100×.339
(40 × 100 × .30)

Figure IV.32.B. *Kato Zakro: palace: modular dimensions*

V

Syntheses

CONCLUSIONS

In Chapter IV above it was demonstrated that in the main, Minoan buildings were planned, laid out and executed with clarity and regularity. We also had occasion to observe that the regularity of modular organization of Minoan structures was closely linked to a variety of other organizational features; notably consistent patterns in the relative deployment of functional areas. What gives Minoan architecture its characteristic identity is more than the corpus of shared formal features examined in Chapters II and III. These features are themselves both consistently associated with each other in characteristic syntactic arrangements, and assigned relative sizes and areal proportions which also tend to be constant.

It was seen, for example, that the Minoan designer/builder assigned various functions to characteristic allotments of square-footage. Thus, in many houses, the living halls occupy roughly one-quarter of the overall internal constructional space. In some cases, these proportions are functions of the actual constructed space (which is often in a sense 'carved out of' a planning grid), while in other examples the proportional allotment of space is a direct fraction of the total modular grid-network out of which a building was constructed.

We have also seen that the modular organization of a structure may have a harmonic significance in its own right. In other words, we have found that the proportional morphology of grid sizes or facade planes provides builders with yet another site for the communication of meaning, along with the syntactic array of formative and functional features.

Modular organization and layout is another aspect of the

material organization of an architectonic system, coexistent with choice of materials, colors, absolute sizes, textures, and so forth. In some cases, the proportional harmonics of facade planes would have been perceptually palpable to a building's users, particularly if the ratios involved were relatively simple, straightforward, and materially enhanced. The overall configuration of Minoan buildings might be quite simple (e.g. squares, 1 : 2 rectangles, or 2 : 3 rectangles), or extremely complex (as in the case of structures with a plethora of deeply articulated facades, e.g. ML DA, TYL A or B, GRT, the Knossian townhouses, or the palaces themselves). In these latter cases we may imagine that some of the complex proportional harmonics manifested in facade articulation would be apprehensible more intuitively than directly, particularly in those cases where the harmonic system employed was a direct function of a modular grid division rather than of the actual dimensions of facades as subsequently built.

As might be expected, it is the largest constructions — the grand villas and palatial compounds — which receive the most sophisticated modular and harmonic attention, although, as we have seen above, the tendencies toward visual and architectonic complexity are manifest in private dwellings as well. Especially note-worthy in this regard are the great palaces, whose western 'fronts' receive a great deal of architectonic and harmonic attention. We may well imagine that these great public facades, fronting onto major public or semi-public plazas, offered the master craftsmen an excellent opportunity to display their Daedalic talents. It is undoubtedly more than merely the accidents of historical/mythological survival that the fame of master architects and designers such as the Cretan Daedalos was later widespread. Whether Daedalos was a person or a guild, an individual or a type, he/they stand alongside justly famed Egyptian cousins such as Imhotep or Senmut, as artist-inventors of the first rank.

In our examination of the modular organization of the great palaces we have a glimpse — veiled but nonetheless convincing — of the close complementarity of Minoan ritual and architectonics. It may well be, as we suggested above, that Minoan religion was deeply imbued with a sense of architectonic order and pattern. The precise centrality of the principal cult room of a palace with respect to the building's modular layout grid, the alignments and orientations of the palaces, the ritual commemoration of the planning procedures of a palace through placement of double-axe symbols on walls at significant modular grid points, indeed the very elevation of the multiple-significative double-axe (*labrys*) symbol itself to a primary religious heraldic sign; all these factors and more persuade us of a close conceptual connection drawn between architectonic and religious ritual.

These associations are hardly surprising or unique, and may be attested to in many societies in both religious and secular environment-shaping, from cornerstone ceremonies in our own buildings to the sacrificial slaughter of a rooster in Greek villages on the occasion of building foundation or completion, from the ritual practices of a Roman priest involved in site planning to the foundation rituals of an Egyptian Pharaoh 'stretching the cord'.

We only dimly understand these practices in Minoan architectural design and building, and can at present simply point to a series of evident interlinkages among a variety of architectonic practices such as those noted above. One of the results of our analyses in the previous Chapter has been an increasingly clear picture of the holistic nature of Minoan architectonic design. Everything about a building, as we have seen, is significant in some way; but each such thing is significant in different ways. Moreover, it has become clear that each aspect of the organization of a building contributes in an integrated way to the totality of what a building has to communicate to its users (and to how users use buildings to create and transmit meaning).

The consistency of ordered relationships among the various components of Minoan design persuades us strongly that such consistencies were intentional. It can hardly be deemed accidental that certain functions were characteristically assigned specific spatial proportions of an overall plan, any more than it was coincidental that a Minoan palatial pillar crypt was positioned at the geometric center of a modular foundation grid. It is undoubtedly the case that some of the patterned regularities in Minoan architecture – for example, the topological invariance of the syntactic association of certain cell-types above and beyond details of materials, size, geometric positioning, or orientation – must be understood as highly conventionalized, perhaps even at times only subliminally perceptible. Our analyses have revealed the existence of patterned regularities which underlie a wide variety of material variation. It is reasonable to assume that the system underlying the Minoan architectonic code comprised more a pattern of expectancy on the part of builders and users than an explicit, verbally articulated set of formulas (though there is no reason to suspect that the latter did not exist as well). Our analyses will have succeeded if a case can be strongly made for a high probability of linkage among a variety of facets of formative organization, so that we can be in a position not to provide hard and fast answers, but rather to begin to ask the right *questions* about Minoan architecture and culture.

It has been my (admittedly personal) impression that the greater bulk of the literature dealing with Minoan architecture has been largely naive and uninformed, and wrongly focussed. In large part this has been the result of a skewed archaeological sensibility which sees the built environment of a society as little more than a passive stage-set for activity, rather than as one of the principal shapers of cultural consciousness, a partner in existential dialogue. It is also my impression that such an attitude has been fostered largely because of the immense difficulties in actually coming to grips with a built environment both holistically and in minute detail. Minoan architecture, as we have noted in the introduction to this study, is (to our eyes) both complex and confusing. It has been the thesis of this study that the only way to begin to dispel this confusion is to discover ways to deal with this complexity on its own terms: to patiently and exhaustively learn the language.

One of the results of trying to deal with Minoan architecture on its own terms is the inevitable uncovering of questions we did not know existed before beginning, and which now loom larger and more pressing. In the final analysis, any book is an invitation to dialogue: the present study has admittedly raised more questions than we can presently answer. But one thing has become abundantly clear: there is an underlying systematicity to Minoan architecture whereby every facet of organization — whether formal, functional, material, or even modular — is related to every other in mutually illuminating ways. We cannot, in other words, seriously understand any aspect of Minoan architecture — no matter how detailed — without understanding its relationship to all other aspects, no matter how seemingly remote and peripheral to our first impressions. The significance of any one architectonic feature is only revealed in terms of its position relative to other features.

One of the things this study has sought to demonstrate is that these relationships are not random, but systematically hierarchicalized, and context-sensitive. It is not accidental that we have focussed our analyses upon a fairly circumscribed block of time in Minoan history, for a synchronic study more than any other can serve to illuminate the conceptual systematicities of an architecture, and their dynamic equilibria. It is this dynamic equilibrium which constitutes the conceptual core of an architecture in any time and place.

TABULATIONS

The present section brings together the observations arising out of the analyses of Chapter IV, so as to enable the reader to more directly compare the modular organizations of the buildings studied. Our focus has been upon the patterned regularity in the deployment of functional spaces within each structure, and only secondarily upon the metrological means whereby such regularities were expressed.

The picture that has emerged from these analyses is one of clarity and consistency in the realization of given building programs. We have seen that the Minoan designer/builder translated the conceptual organization of a building into spatial frameworks which served to communicate design intent. These frameworks comprised areal and dimensional formulas whereby given functions were interrelated and manifested on a geometric grid. In this regard, as noted in Chapter IV, the Minoan builder proceeded in ways similar to those employed in contemporary societies elsewhere in the eastern Mediterranean. The groundplan of a structure was projected upon a grid of squares made up of ropes and pegs, probably a full-scale translation of a gridded drawing.

Along with these graphic methods we should imagine the inclusion of nonvisual sets of instructions and specifications to be followed by craftsmen of various types — rope-stretchers (*harpedonaptae*), masons, woodworkers, painters, labor crews, etc. — no doubt each comprising a guild of craftsmen in their own right. There are many possible ways in which such specifications might have been communicated: from detailed, scale drawings to generic sketches defining the relative placement of component parts of a house. In some cases, we may imagine that these specifications were transmitted wholly verbally by designers to workmen sharing common sets of conventional expectations. No doubt in many cases there was little need to discuss what a given building should include, since such things would have been implicit to all; rather we may imagine that cost, specific quantities, sizes, and relative placement of components would be the primary subject matter of such communications.

Nevertheless, as we have observed throughout this study, each Minoan structure of the period was a unique object, and there is little (if any) exact replication of plans. So we must assume that part of the concern of any designer was the need to fit culturally shared patterns of spatial usage and appropriation to a construct which simultaneously expressed the individuality of a given individual, group, or social station. We must assume that the reason no two Minoan houses are identical is an intentional one, and not accidental. We do not know, and may never know, if this tendency toward architectonic individuation was confined to the tastes of a certain class of client, or if it was a general characteristic in Minoan society at all levels. The evidence is inconclusive, but my own inclination is to favor the latter. The fact remains that no two Minoan buildings of any type are identical. There are no identical 'row houses' in Minoan towns such as Gournia or Palaikastro, despite the fact that there are close resemblances among houses with respect to the kinds of features present. With respect to the syntactic composition of such features, the Minoan architectonic system evidently permitted wide variation in strictly geometric or structural terms. Topologically, however, as we have seen in our study of the hall systems, there exist invariant patterns of relationship, which tend to underlie often striking differences in structure.

Thus, the Minoan designer/builder's task involved the creation of a balance between individuation and socially shared expectation regarding (for example) what a house or a palace should be like. A modular grid would provide a uniform framework or template (or ground) upon which a structure could be composed. By the same token, such a template would serve as a guide for the constructional realization of a design.

We have seen that the Minoan designers during the period studied employed several kinds of templates or frames, e.g. square grids, 1 : 2 rectangles, 2 : 3 rectangles, grids divided decimally or by other means, grids which encoded harmonic articulations of subsequent facade planes, and so forth.

One general principle which seems to be invariant in the creation of a modular grid for design and construction is that such a grid be composed of *equal* subdivisions. Furthermore, such subdivisions are directly tied to the positioning of internal spaces. A grid line defines or generates, as we have seen throughout the previous Chapter, one or another side or face of a wall to be built. In other words, walls are not built over grid lines, but adjacent to and contiguous with grid lines.

We do not know if Minoan builders laid out a grid of ropes and pegs in a complete checkerboard, but it does appear to be the case, to judge from the regularity of dimensions of Minoan buildings, that such a practice may very well have been close to what was actually done. Walls in Minoan buildings (with a few exceptions, as noted in our analyses) are invariably straight and true, and more perfectly parallel and perpendicular than normally achieved by the unaided eye. It seems likely that the aid was a system of carefully measured and controlled grids of ropes and pegs of consistent dimensions.

It is also clear that the system of proportional harmonics manifested by so many Minoan buildings could most easily and economically be achieved through the use of a grid of regular dimensions as a 'ground' for harmonic 'figures' or compositions. Indeed the very system of harmonic proportions uncovered above could only have been realized using careful geometric means. An excellent illustration of this is the harmonic system of the western facade of the second Phaistian palace, articulated as a whole-number Fibonacci series progression of facades $(21 + 34 + 55 + 89)$. In this example, it became clear that a Fibonacci progression along the 250-unit western facade length (unit 0.270) was possible because $250 \times 0.270 = 199 \times 0.340$ (the approximation of 67.50 and 67.66): $21 + 34 + 55 + 89 = 199$. That Minoan builders employed like proportional schemas on a smaller scale in structures of many different sizes and types has become clear through a detailed analysis and tabulation of the dimensions of Minoan buildings.

The following tabulations present a picture of a conceptual homogeneity in the modular organization of Minoan buildings of the period studied, augmenting and enhancing the picture of formal and functional consistency illustrated in Part One.

We have seen that the Minoan builders used several standards of linear measure (or variants of one or two linear standards), ranging in metric value form 0.270 to 0.350. The possible values found are:

0.270 : 13 times
0.275 : 2
0.280 : 5
0.310 : 1
0.320 : 1
0.330 : 1
0.340 : 4
0.350 : 3

Modular lengths — the dimensions of grid squares, in simple multiples of derived linear standards — vary widely, but tend to be most frequent in unit multiples of ten, eight, six, or five. Of these, decimal values predominate, with some 18 examples; the total of non-decimal values is eight.

All of these values are approximated. Closer analysis of the dimensions of the buildings studied will reveal that what may be asserted here as '0.270' may in some cases be 0.269 or 0.271, etc.

Of the range of unit occurrences, by far the largest number cluster about 0.270 to 0.280; at the other end of the continuum, there is a second cluster around 0.340. Within each cluster, the variation is millimetric. What evidence does all this provide us for the value of the Minoan unit of measurement?

In the first place, we should be wary of taking the truly minute differences among the values within the two clusters as indicative of wholly distinct standards of measure. We have no secure basis for drawing a hard and fast line between these found values. Secondly, Bronze Age measuring rods were not stamped out in platinum bars from a central governmental office with an eye on millimetric quality control: they were made of wood, normally,

Table V.1. *Modular grid organization*

	NS x EW	unit	module	grid	shape	m.u.*	squares	F**
1. TVOL	11.00 x 10.95	0.275	1.38	40 x 40	1 : 1	5	8 x 8	X
2. RSS	10.95 x 8.10	0.270	units	40 x 30	4 : 3	1?	[1]	X + f [2]
3. AKHL	20.00 x 14.00	0.340	3.40	60 x 40	3 : 2	10	6 x 4	X + f [3]
4. AMN	15.50 x 19.60	0.280	2.80	50 x 70+	5 : 7+	10	5 x 7+	X + f [4]
5. GRT	19.90 x 23.25	0.31?	3.10?	65 x 75	6½ : 7½	10	13 x 15	
6. KN HCS	16.20 x 16.20	0.270	2.70	60 x 60	1 : 1	10	6 x 6	X + f [5]
7. KN RV	17.90 x 13.50	0.280	2.24	64 x 48	4 : 3	8	8 x 6	X + f [6]
8. KN HF	16.00 x 11.50	? [7]	2.45	48 x 32	3 : 2	8?	6 x 4	X + f [8]
9. KN S	13.50 x 19.20	0.320	3.20	40 x 60	2 : 3	10	4 x 6	X + f [9]
10. KN SE	17.36 x 17.36 [10]	0.270	2.18	64 x 64	1 : 1	8	8 x 8	X + f [11]
11. ML DA	13.50 x 13.50	0.280	0.84	48 x 48	1 : 1	3	16 x 16	
12. ML QD	ca. 42.00 long	0.280	1.40	(40 + 25 + 15 + 25 + 40) = (8 : 5 : 3 : 5 : 8)f		10		X + f [12]
13. ML ZA	16.20 x 24.30	0.270	2.70	60 x 90	2 : 3	10	6 x 9	
14. ML ZB	20.70 x 17.90	0.280?	1.40	(N facade 20 + 25 + 15) = (4 : 5 : 3)f				
15. NK	26.85 x 23.00+	0.270	2.70	100 x 100	1 : 1	10	10 x 10	X + f [13]
16. SKLV	18.00 x 24.30	? [14]	3.00	[15]	3 : 4	[16]	6 x 8	X + f [17]
17. TYL A	35.00 x 21.25	0.350	1.75	100 x 60	3 : 5	5	20 x 12	X + f [18]
18. TYL B	14.00 x 21.00 [19]	0.350	1.75	40 x 60	2 : 3	5	8 x 12	X + f [20]
19. TYL C	24.40 x 24.40 [21]	0.330	2.00	72 x 72	1 : 1	6	12 x 12	
20. PLK B	22.00 x 43.00	0.270?	?	80 x 160	1 : 2	?	?	
21. PLK X	17.00 x 17.00	0.275	2.75	60 x 60	1 : 1	10	6 x 6	
22. KZ G	16.32 x 16.32 [22]	0.340?	2.04	48 x 48	1 : 1	6	8 x 8	
23. KZ J	16.32 x 16.32 [23]	0.340?	2.04	48 x 48	1 : 1	6	8 x 8	
24. ML E	27.00 x 54.00 [24]	0.270	2.70	100 x 200	1 : 2	10	10 x 20	
25. KLP	43.03 x 27.46	0.270	2.70?	160 x 100	3 : 2	10	16 x 10	X + f [25]
26. HTR	55.00 x 85.00 [26]	0.270? [29]	2.70?	200 x 300	2 : 3	10?	?	X + f [27]
27. KN	54.00 x 54.00 [28]	0.270	2.70	(200 x 200)	1 : 1	10	20 x 20	X + f [30]
28. ML	54.00 x 54.00 [31]	0.270	2.70	(200 x 200)	1 : 1	10	20 x 20	X + f [32]
29. PH I	70.00 x 70.00 [33]	0.350	3.50	(200 x 200)	1 : 1	10	20 x 20	X + f [34]
30. PH II	54.00 x 54.00 [35]	0.270	2.70	(200 x 200)	1 : 1	10	20 x 20	X + f [36]
31. GRN	?	0.270?	(W facade dimensions only?)					
32. KZ	? x 68.00	0.340?	(central court 100 NS x 40 EW?)					

*   m.u. = modular unit suggested
**   F = Fibonacci proportions in grid and/or facades: X = grid overall or within; f = facades articulations; $X + f$ = both

---

Notes

1.   Probably laid out in units; decimal divisions (10 + 20) east-west, divisions by fourths north-south (16 + 24).
2.   Western facade proportions 2 : 3.
3.   Eastern facade division 2 : 3.
4.   Eastern facade division 2 : 3.
5.   Southern facade division 1 : 2 : 3.
6.   Southern facade 2 : 3; eastern facade 3 : 2 : 3.
7.   Ambiguously 0.306 or 0.272; module equals eight or nine units.
8.   Western facade 2 : 3; grid 2 : 3.
9.   Southern facade 4 : 5 : 3.
10.   Reconstructed east-west length.
11.   Eastern facade (reconstructed in part) 2 : 2 : 3.
12.   Northern and southern facades 2 : 1 : 3.
13.   Eastern facade 3 : 2 : 3.
14.   Unit ambiguously 0.337 or 0.270 or 0.30.
15.   E.g. 72 x 96 x 0.270 or 54 x 72 x 0.337.
16.   E.g. 12 x 0.270 or 9 x 0.337.
17.   Southeastern faces 2 : 3.
18.   Southern facade 2 : 3 : 5.
19.   Modular size, excluding northern, southern, and western wall thicknesses.
20.   Facades overall 1 : 2 : 3.
21.   As per our suggestions above.
22.   Modular dimensions.
23.   Modular dimensions.
24.   Size excluding southern projection.
25.   Southern facade 2 : 3.
26.   Estimate pending final publication.
27.   Overall grid proportions 5 : 8 (?)
28.   Central grid square only; annexes consistent.
29.   Except for western facade, laid out on 0.340, decimally.
30.   Western facade blocks 2 : 3 and 3 : 5; hall systems 5 : 8, etc.
31.   Central grid square only; annexes consistent.
32.   Western facades 3 : 4 proportions.
33.   Overall estimated limits based on what remains of PH I perimeters.
34.   Overall reconstructed grid (see above) 200 by 300 or 2 : 3.
35.   Central grid square only; annexes consistent.
36.   Fibonacci proportions along whole western facade in progression, 21 : 34 : 55 : 89 (literal numerical values vs. ML QD bove).

and subject to variations in absolute length due to differences in temperature and workmanship. Each measuring rod was a crafts- man's tool, no doubt handed on to apprentices from generation to generation.

The point here is that we should avoid imposing the exacting standards of our own machine technology upon our expectations of the practices of a culture four millennia distant in time, and con- sequently not make too much of the millimetric variations in Minoan linear standards of measure.

All of this is aside from the fact that we have no direct evidence (apart from the consistencies in the dimensions of their buildings) for the exact value of the Minoan metrological unit. Our proposed units in the preceding analyses are derived indirectly from the evidence of constructional consistencies. More secure is our evi- dence for modular (layout) units; moreover, such values are more directly relevant to our purposes here.

Another factor should be brought into play in this discussion. It may not have been the case that the same metrological unit was in use by different groups of workmen constructing a building. Indeed, it is often the case that woodworkers, stonemasons and bricklayers may employ their own standards of measurement for their specific types of tasks.

Nevertheless it is clear that Minoan builders planned and laid out their structures with (often very great) care and precision; and such precision can only have been based upon the careful and consistent usage of uniform modular and metrological standards. While the variations between, say, 0.340 and 0.350 may be insigni- ficant over short lengths, their minute differences will multiply over the dimensions of whole buildings or large sections of a building. In this regard, the buildings at Tylissos are instructive. We have seen above that TYL A and TYL B (the presumed annex to A) were laid out on a unit of ±0.350, whereas TYL C shows evidence of having been laid out on a unit of 0.330. This may be a clue to possible differences in the sequence of building, and/or to the presence of different work crews.

The proposed linear units in Table V.1 are derived solely from exhaustive analyses of the dimensions of each building on its own terms. It is our contention that the absolute value of the standard used is of less interest than the fact that a building was laid out carefully and consistently whatever the actual length of its metro-logical unit.

The millimetric variation observed, however, persuades us that our proposals are on the right track; there is simply too much consistency from structure to structure to allow for coincidence.

It would appear that the Minoan builders used two distinct metrological standards – to judge from the clustering of values around ±0.270 and ±0.340 – a shorter unit and a longer. More-over, in at least two instances (KN and PH II) both were em-ployed: the shorter for the layout of the modular planning grid, and the longer for the proportional articulation of the West Facade. Indeed, it may well be (as we suggested above in connec-tion with PH II) that the shorter and longer units were interrelated in some simple proportional way. It may in fact be the case that we are dealing with variants of some common standard. Evidence for this hypothesis comes not from Crete itself, but from contem-porary Egypt.

Sir W. Flinders Petrie, in excavating the workers' village built at El-Lahun in connection with the construction of the pyramid of Sesostris II (*c.* 1897-1878 B.C.), found evidence of the presence of non-Egyptian workmen, on the basis of pottery since identified as Middle Minoan Kamares ware.[1] He also found two wooden measuring rods, which he published in 1926,[2] which were dis-tinctly different from the cubit measuring rods commonly employed in Egypt. One of these rods, measuring 0.673 in length, was divided by incisions as follows:

1	2	3	½	4	5	6	7

.....].....].....].....].....].....].....].....]

0	0.09	0.19	0.289	0.336	0.38	0.46	0.56	0.673

Figure V.I. *El-Lahun measuring rod*

The rod is a cubit measure divided in sevenths, but somewhat more than the 'Royal' Egyptian cubit of ±0.523-0.525 and the standard (shorter) Egyptian cubit of ±0.449.[3] The former is nor-mally divided into seven palms (or 28 digits), the latter into six palms (or 24 digits).

The actual divisions of the rod are not exact sevenths of the overall length of 0.673; the corrected ideal values would be:

0.096   0.192   0.288   0.336   0.384   0.480   0.576   0.673

Although Petrie's excavation report does not mention if the cubit rods were found in association with the Minoan pottery, the fact that the rods are distinctly different from Egyptian rods suggests a non-Egyptian origin, although not necessarily a Cretan origin.

And yet it will be noted that the half-cubit length, 0.336 (= 0.34) matches the length of a standard derived from the remains of Minoan structures, the 'longer' cluster of values in the range 0.330-0.350. The three-palm length, 0.28, approximates the value of the standard of our 'shorter' cluster of values in the range 0.270-0.280. The El-Lahun rod may be a 'comparative' Minoan/Egyptian rod.

Might we in fact be dealing with evidence for a Cretan metrological standard, i.e. a shorter unit of 0.28 and a longer unit of 0.34 (equals one-half of 0.67)? In other words may the Minoan builders, like their Egyptian counterparts, have employed a longer and a shorter unit? Note that in Egypt, the longer (royal) cubit, was divided into seven palms or 28 digits, while the shorter cubit was divided into six palms or 24 digits. It is plausible to see the Minoan derived standards as bearing a similar interrelation:

longer unit = 0.673   (=cubit; 'foot' = 0.34)
short   unit = 0.56   (=cubit; 'foot' = 0.28)

The two standards would be coincident on the same scale in the following manner:

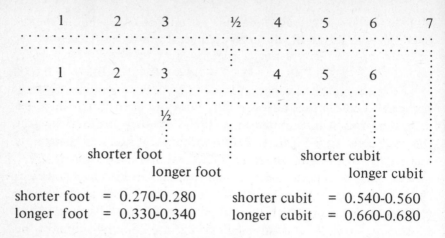

shorter foot = 0.270-0.280   shorter cubit = 0.540-0.560
longer foot = 0.330-0.340   longer cubit = 0.660-0.680

Figure V.2. *Minoan standards of measure*

The conjectural interrelationships would be similar to those of
the two Egyptian standards, but based upon Cretan absolute
lengths. In fact, the two hypothetical standards match the two
ranges of values derived from the dimensions of the Minoan structures examined above. While the actual sample above is fairly
small, the hypothesis is strengthened by evidence for two such
standard lengths from our tabulation of the dimensions of a
couple of hundred Aegean structures studied elsewhere,[4] extending the chronological range of occurrences back into the Early
Minoan period.

While the hypothesis is plausible, the evidence is indirect. No
remains of measuring rods have been identified in Aegean excavations *per se.* There is also no way of precluding the possibility that
the El Lahun rods may have been made and used by craftsmen
from elsewhere in the eastern Mediterranean. Indeed, as will be
seen in the Appendix below, the unit of 0.340/0.670 is similar to
units attested elsewhere (the so-called 'Northern Foot' and
'Northern Cubit').[5] It is also possible that the Minoan unit of
0.270/0.540 may itself be derived from a standard close to (or
derived from) the Egyptian royal cubit of 0.523-0.525.

There is no secure way to decide these issues one way or
another. At best we may claim that on the evidence of Minoan
structures themselves, the Cretan builder employed two distinct
(but possibly interrelated) linear standards. It is also clear that the

Minoan builder planned and built structures distinctly different from those in Egypt or the Levant during the Bronze Age, whether or not he was using a native Aegean or Levantine metrological unit.

This latter point is especially important. There is no necessary or direct correlation between the use of a given standard of measure and a given architectonic style, and whatever metrological evidence may be educed from archaeological artifacts cannot be securely employed to erect scenarios of architectural diffusion. Metrological practices, and the technology of modular planning and layout, bear a semi-autonomous relationship to the architectonic system within which they are employed. In the final analysis, we must address these issues both holistically and realistically. The automobile I drive was assembled from parts stamped out on a metric scale, but for a variety of reasons I am bound to admit that it was built in Detroit.

NOTES

1. W.F. Petrie, *Illahun, Kahun and Gurob* (1891): 14, section 31; excavated before the archaeological discoveries on Crete which revealed the Minoan civilization. Petrie felt that the 'Kamares' pottery, despite its non-Egyptian style, was made in local clay. It is plausible that Cretan craftsmen employed in the El-Lahun building project would have made their own domestic ware, in their own style, using materials at hand.

2. W.F. Petrie, *Ancient Weights and Measures* (1926): 40, section 90, numbers 13 and 14. The writer acknowledges the kindness of the Egyptian Collection of University College, London (where the rods were brought), and of its Keeper, Mr. I.E.S. Edwards, and Mr. D.M. Dixon, for providing him with detailed measurements and a photograph. The second rod can no longer be found; it evidently had the same measurements.

3. A. Badawy, *AEAD*: 2. The shorter cubit of ±0.45 was apparently used in crafts; see E. Iversen, *Canon and Proportion in Egyptian Art* (1955): 19-22, and the Appendix to Chapter V below.

4. D. Preziosi, *MPPAO* (1968); measurements taken from a wide variety of structures throughout the Aegean Basin, dating from all periods of the Bronze Age. See above, Preface.

5. 'Measures and Weights', in F.G. Skinner, *A History of Technology* Volume I., (1954), 774-784.

APPENDIX B: MODULAR DESIGN IN THE ANCIENT WORLD:
CHRO NOLOGICAL AND GEOGRAPHICAL PATTERNS

The problems concerning evidence for metrological diffusion in the ancient world are quite complex.[1] The simple identity or near-identity of standards of linear measure in different geographical areas is not in itself productive of useful derivational models. This may be demonstrated by the following.

It will be found that the metrological system found in use on Minoan Crete is nearly identical to the system employed contemporaneously in the Indus civilization,[2] as evidenced from fragments of measuring rods from Mohenjo-daro and Harappā.[3] There, a 'foot' of 0.330-0.336 was derived from a graduated fragment of a measuring rod made of shell;[4] a fragmentary bronze rod from Harappā yields a 'cubit' of 0.518-0.530.

In addition, the system of weights employed at Harappā, notable for their constant accuracy over a very wide range of examples,[6] is identical to systems employed (?) at Malthi-Dorion on the Greek mainland during the second millennium B.C., contemporary with the Indus civilization.[7]

No direct links of a material nature exist between the cultures of the Indus Valley and the Aegean.[8] But clearly some explanation seems required for the existence of this metrological identity, extending even to the use of decimal and sixteenth divisions.[9] One would wish to find some (even merely geographical) intermediary.

F.G. Skinner notes that the major standards of linear measure used in antiquity (and mediaeval Europe) were the following:[10]

1. Egypt: Royal Cubit: 0.542 ±0.005 (seven palms or 28 digits)
2. Egypt: Short Cubit: 0.449 (six palms or 24 digits)
3. Palestine: Cubit: 0.447
4. Greece: Athens: 0.316 (Foot); Aegina: 0.315
5. Etruria: 0.316
6. Mediaeval England: 0.31675; Mediaeval Germany: 0.314[11]
7. Rome: Foot: 0.292, 0.294
8. 'Northern Cubit': 0.676 (range: 0.660-0.686)
9. 'Northern Foot': 0.333-0.335 (range up to 0.343)

The latter two units (essentially 8 = 2 x 9) are clearly identical to what has been found above for Crete and the Aegean, as well as the Indus Valley. On the use of the 'Northern Foot' in the ancient world, note the following (documentable) usages:[12]

1. Sumeria (1) Gudea statues[13] (±2300 B.C.)   0.330.
           (2) Babylon City Wall.[14]
2. Egypt   (1) Kahun wood rod[15] (XII Dynasty)   0.336.
           (2) Kahun wood rod[16] (XII Dynasty)[17] 0.338.
3. Anatolia (1) Çatal Hüyük bricks (6070-5950 B.C.) 0.320.[18]
           (2) Beycesultan bricks (4000-3000 B.C.) 0.320-
              0.340.[19]
4. Aegean (1) Messara tombs[20] (Early Minoan)[21] 0.325-
              0.340.
           (2) Early Helladic I construction.[22]

The above appear to be the earliest documentable usages in the several geographical areas. This suggests the following 'diffusionist' model:

   A. Protoneolithic (Çatal Hüyük).
   B. Chalcolithic (Beycesultan).
   C. Early Bronze Age (Crete, Greece, Anatolia, Babylonia, Indus).[23]
   D. Middle Bronze Age (Aegean, Egypt).

There is no secure way of determining if the appearance of the Northern Foot in XIIth Dynasty Egypt represents a 'diffusion' from the Aegean or the Levant; workmen from both areas are known to have been present in the workmen's village at Kahun.[24] A similar problem may be seen with regard to the Indus and Mesopotamia.[25] The basic problem lies in our inability to document the very first occurrences of the Northern Foot in theses areas;[26] the diffusionist schema above is essentially a fiction.[27] Perhaps the most we can say at present is the following:

1. The standard of measure used in Crete and the Aegean during the Bronze Age has antecedents in absolute value in Anatolia in the previous (Chalcolithic) periods (and perhaps traceable back as far as the Protoneolithic period at Çatal Hüyük);[28] it appears to

be identical to units used contemporaneously in Mesopotamia and the Indus Valley.

2. This unit was one of four[29] employed during the Aegean Bronze Age, frequently manifesting a usage based on proportional ratios of the Fibonacci series, a system known to have been used (albeit differently) in contemporary Egypt.[30] The earliest apparent occurrence of the canon in Egypt is during the IIIrd Dynasty (*c.* 2780-2680 B.C.),[31] which contrasts with proportional canons seen contemporaneously in Mesopotamia.[32] It occurs about a century later in Anatolia (West),[33] and forms one of the bases of modular design in Minoan architecture.[34]

It should be obvious from the above that a diffusionist model based *solely* on the presence or absence of a modular unit in the architecture of contiguous or non-contiguous areas means next to nothing. Any such comparative study will have to incorporate more fundamental aspects of architectural syntax to have any significance; it must seek to relate the usage of such units to patterns in formal organization, spatio-temporal syntax, and so forth. It might be found in one area, for example, that the proportional canon employed in the layout of facades compares with rhythms in circulatory lattices within a structure.

NOTES

1.   As W.M. Flinders Petrie rightly notes (*Ancient Weights and Measures*, 1926: 41, Section 94); the cautious comments of R.V. Nicholls (*BSA*: 53-54, 1958-1959: 101ff) are equally relevant. The first corpus of ancient writings on metrology and related subjects is F. Hultsch's, *Metrologicorum scriptorum reliquiae*, Volume I (1864); II (1866): the first deals with Greek sources, the second with Roman. Unlike the previous major source book (A. Böckh, *Metrologische Untersuchungen*, 1838), Hultsch's work is related to the modern metric system (see his *Griechische und römische Metrologie*, 1882), as are most modern works, except those of Petrie, after the 1860s. See also R. Lepsius, *Die Langenmasse der Alten*, and J.-A. Decourdemanche, *Traité pratique des poids et mesures des peuples anciens et des Arabes* (1909). On Egypt, see Petrie, *op.cit.*: especially Chapter XVI (sections 87-94); and also his *Illahun, Kahun and Gurob* (1891): 1-15; *cf.* F. Chabas, *Recherches sur les poids, mesures et monnaies des anciens Egyptiens* (1876). Apart from references to studies by Dörpfeld, Caskey and Graham in our text above, no comparative study of Bronze Age Aegean metrology has appeared, although the writer's (unpublished) dissertation attempts to deal with the question to some extent (ms., Harvard University Library). Valuable recent material

includes R.V. Nicholls, *op.cit.*: 101ff; Note 108, p. 105, who notes the comment by E.B. Wace that the houses of Mycenae seem to have been laid out with a unit of 0.49 (= 'the *ell* of the 0.327 foot', Note 108). Miss Wace's suggested unit is taken by Nicholls as representing a function of a unit known later at Smyrna (*loc.cit.*), for which, at the time of Nicholls' publication, no evidence had yet been found. In the writer's dissertation it is noted that (as a result of our surveys at Mycenae), a unit of *c.* 0.330 was in use in some Mycenaean construction. This might corroborate Miss Wace's comment above, to my knowledge as yet unpublished. On the Anatolian side, see R. Naumann, *Architektur Kleinasiens* (1955), especially his chart of comparative brick dimensions used in Anatolia from the third to the first millennium (p. 46), which incorporates a list of relative proportions.

2. *C.* 2500-1500 B.C. The classic chronological study is C.J. Gadd, *Proceedings of the British Academy* XVIII (1932).

3. M, Wheeler, *The Indus Civilization* (1962): 66-67.

4. E. Mackay, *Early Indus Civilizations* (1948) I: 404: the establishment of the value of the Indus foot-unit at Mohenjo-daro.

5. M.S. Vats, *Excavations at Harappā* I (1940): 365: the cubit at Harappā approximates the value of the Egyptian Royal Cubit of 0.524 ±0.005 (*v.infra*). The author states (p. 366) that the use of these two units is supported by the results of 'over 150 checks which have been applied to the buildings of Harappā and Mohenjo-daro, comprising measurements of various well-planned houses, rooms, courtyards, streets and platforms'. '150 checks' hardly represent a thorough metrological analysis, despite the appeal to the existence of the measuring rods (if indeed they are accurately restored); see Wheeler, *loc.cit.*, and Graham, *AJA* 64 (1960): 336, Note 17.

6. Mackay, *op.cit.*: 447; Marshall, *Mohenjo-daro and the Indus Civilization* II (1931): 461ff, 589ff; III: Plates CXXX-CXXXIV, and CLIV.

7. N. Valmin, *SME*: 377ff, 386; thereby corroborating Wheeler's (much later) statement (*op.cit.*: 66) that the Indus system 'is unlike any other in the ancient world'. Wheeler (p. 35) notes that '... in most Indus buildings [the] architectural history has never been worked out, and the published plans are inadequate'. Excavation measurements are made in English feet and inches, making quick comparative analysis difficult.

8. Stylistically the two architectural corpora are quite distinct, differing in formal syntax and material usage, as may be observed in Wheeler, p. 27ff.

9. *Ibid.*: 66; a comparison is made with modern Indian usage of a 16-part *rupee*.

10. 'Measures and Weights' in *A History of Technology* I (1954): 774-784.

11. The Carolingian Foot (±0.34: K.J. Conant, *Speculum* XXXVIII (1963): 5; at Cluny the module appears to have been 0.295: *id.*, 'Measurements and Proportions of the Great Church at Cluny', *Beiträge zur Kunstgeschichte und Archäologie des Frühmittelalters* (1961): 238) may have been a derivative of the Drusinian foot of 0.333, which according to the *agrimensor* Hyginus (*De Limitibus constituendis*: 210) *Item dicitur in Tungris pes Drusianus, qui habet monetam et sescunciam*; i.e. was in use in the territory of the Tungri in lower Germany; it was apparently so well established there by tradition that the Romans under Drusus (38-9 B.C.) adopted it for use in the northern Roman provinces instead of their own unit of ±0.296. Its length appears to have been two *digiti* longer than their own unit with its 16 *digiti* (0.296 + 2 x 0.185 = 0.333; Skinner, *op.cit.*: 778). W. Horn and E. Born (*Art Bulletin* XLVIII (1966): 285-308, 'The Dimen-

sional Inconsistencies of the Plan of St. Gall and the Problem of the Scale of the Plan') suggest that the 'Carolingian foot' had a number of regional variants (0.34, 0.3329, 0.333-0.335); one of these 'variants' is given as 0.292-0.297/0.300 (in use apparently in the Novitiate and Infirmary, as well as Guest Areas, at St. Gall); we might suggest that this 'variant' is a module of nine-tenths of a Carolingian (0.34) foot, or simply a reflex of the Roman unit of 0.296. The latter was employed in Cluny III, the unit of 0.34 at Cluny II.

12. Unfortunately, Skinner gives no bibliography, in contrast to other articles in the same volume.

13. Two statues of Gudea of Lagash (B and F) now in the Louvre represent the monarch seated holding a tablet in his lap, on which are tools of the architect's trade (stylus and measuring rod); Statue B (E. de Sarzec, *Découvertes en Chaldée*, (1884): Plate 15, Figure 1) includes on the tablet an incised temple-plan. The ruler on Statue F (*ibid.*: Plate 15, Figure 2) has 16 subdivisions. The rulers represent full-scale versions of the Sumerian cubit of 0.495, and its foot (= two-thirds cubit) of 0.330. Skinner (*op.cit.*: 778) notes that this cubit is three-fourths of the 'Northern Cubit' of 0.676 (specifically, three-fourths of its lowest occurring manifestation, 0.660).

14. B. Meissner, *Babylonien und Assyrien* I (1920): 289ff, Figure 111, p. 300 shows a plan of part of the City Wall; the curtain-lengths are ±33.64, the tower lengths are 8.39-8.36 (=. 100 Northern Feet and 25 Northern Feet). Note also that 2.5 brick lengths = ±0.85 (*ibid.*: 296); one brick = 0.34. That '2.5 brick lengths' occurred frequently as a modular unit is suggested by its mention in extant ancient texts (L. Messerschmidt, *Keilschrifttexte aus Assur historischen Inhalts*[3]: text no. 3, verse 38ff.

15. Petrie, *Ancient Weights and Measures* (1926): 40, section 90, numbers 13 and 14; 41, section 93. This rod, discussed above in our Chapter IV, is now in the collection of University College, London (cat. no. U.C. 16747). See *Illahun, Kahun and Gurob* (1891): 14, section 31. It measures 0.673 overall, and is divided into two halves and seven palms.

16. This second rod is now apparently missing (correspondence 11 January 1967).

17. Skinner, *loc.cit.*, notes occurrences of the Northern Foot on two horizons: (1) 1550-250 B.C., five Egyptian wood and stone rods at Turin, Alexandria, Florence, Leiden and Cairo, made as *reference* standards showing also the Egyptian Royal Cubit of 0.524 ±0.005. The Northern Foot is *marked off at or near the 18th Digit of the Cubit*, or 0.338. The ratio is thus 9 : 14, making the Northern Foot a rather unlikely derivative of the Egyptian Royal Cubit; (2) 300-100 B.C.: cut on wooden rods or stone slabs found in Egypt. I take the latter to refer to the limestone slab found by Petrie in Memphis (Petrie, *op.cit.*: 40, section 91) measuring 0.68072 in length, from a Ptolemaic or Roman horizon. The author apparently omits the two Kahun rods discussed above in our fourth Chapter.

18. J. Mellaart, *Çatal Hüyük* (1967): 67. An entire structure in Level VIA (shrine E.VI.10) has survived to its roofing; it has an interior height of 3.30; the walls are one-tenth of this in thickness, or one brick thick (*ibid.*: 63); bricks from this level measure 0.08 x 0.16 x 0.32. The excavators suggest (*loc.cit.*) that hand and foot were the standards of measure, with four hands of 0.08 to a foot of 0.32. The bricks, sun-dried, were apparently formed in a wooden mold (*ibid.*: 55); the author gives a chart on the page quoted of brick-sizes found in the various archaeological strata. The early appearance of the 'Northern Foot' in Protoneolithic horizons here is rather extraordinary, being (apparently) the earliest metrological

evidence known at present; this is not, however, inconsistent with the clarity and orderliness of the architecture at Çatal Hüyük, where in addition the first known 'town plan' is portrayed on a wall fresco (q.v.).

19. S. Lloyd and J. Mellaart, *Beycesultan* I (1962): 19-26. It is of interest that the dimensions of late Chalcolithic bricks here are nearly identical to those mentioned above in our Note 17.

20. Surveys of the Messara tombs made by the writer reveal an alternation between the use of units of c. 0.27 and c. 0.33: Dhrakones (0.27); H. Irini (Epsilon, 0.338, Eta, 0.27); H. Triadha (0.325); Kalathiana (0.34 or 0.275); Kamilari (0.275); Leben (subneolithic/E.M.I, 0.27); Koumasa (A: 0.338; B: 0.338; E: 0.275); Moutsokero (0.277); Platanos (A: 0.3275; B: ?; G: 0.27); Porti (0.332); Salame (0.338).

21. All are Early Minoan, although Dhrakones yielded only Middle Minoan objects.

22. For example, Eutresis, House I (0.27); see D. Preziosi, *MPPAO, passim,* on Greek units.

23. Contacts between the Indus and Mesopotamia are discussed in Wheeler (*op.cit.*: 90ff) on Knossos and Harappā, *ibid.*: 81.

24. Petrie, *Illahun. . . , passim;* H.J. Kantor, *AJA* 51 (1947): 1-103; *PM* I: 290. 'Kamares' pottery found by Petrie is shown in his Plate I, Figures 3-8, 10-15.

25. Wheeler, *op.cit.*: 71ff. There is a possibility of an export trade in beads from the Indus to points west (*ibid.*: 80).

26. It is possible that the value of the Northern Foot may occur as early as 2500 B.C. in the Temple at 'Ubaid (First Dynasty of Ur): P. Delongaz, *The Temple Oval at Khafajah* (1940); the quadrangular terrace measures 33.00 by 26.00.

27. At best we might speak simply of potential zones of diffusion; see now W.F. Leemans, 'Mesopotamië en de Indus Cultuur', *Phoenix* VII (1961): 2.

28. Needless to say there exist wide gaps in our knowledge; resemblances between such sites as Hacilar, Aspipetra Cave on Kos, Ayio Gala Cave on Chios, Sesklo, Kato Ierapetra on Crete can be made, without finding direct or indirect architectural linkages. Certainly a complete survey of the earliest architecture of Anatolia is needed, on the scale of W. Nagel's *Die Bauern- und Stadtkulturen im vordynastischen Vorderasien* (1964).

29. See Preziosi, *op.cit.*: 739-761.

30. Badawy, *AFAD, passim; id.,* 'The harmonic system of architectural design in Ancient Egypt', *Mitt.des Inst. für Orientforschung* III (1961): 1-14. Similarities between Minoan and Egyptian practice might prove rather detailed; a statement by Badawy in *A History of Egyptian Architecture* (1954): 57, to the effect that 'in the process of surveying the axis (of the Mortuary Temple of Nebhepetre Mentuhotep at Deir el Bahari, XIth Dynasty) was marked by a line of a dozen holes, in which flat triangular loaves of bread were deposited' seems analogous to the situation discussed under Knossos in Chapter III regarding the 'Vat Room Deposit' and double-axe sings along the nodules and axes of the design-grid; perhaps the lined-up small holes in the pavement of the northwestern court at Phaistos refer to a foundation ritual similar to the Egyptian one described by Badawy (see Phaistos in Chapter IV above).

31. *JNES* 11 (1952): 113-123; W.S. Smith, *The Art and Architecture of Ancient Egypt* (1965): 256; Badawy, *AEAD*: 183.

32. Badawy notes in *Architecture in Ancient Egypt and the Near East* (1966): 117, that the Babylonian system appears to be quite different, as evidenced by the rhythms of wall-recesses, for example, of Kish (see Watelin, *Kish* III: 10): 2.5 :

2 : 2.5 and 1.5 : 2 : 1.5 and 2.5 : 3 : 2.5. A good deal of work is needed on the Mesopotamian side.

33.   Namely at Karataş Semayük (Preziosi, *MPPAO*). On relations between Egypt and northwestern Anatolia, note the gift of a wooden throne inscribed with the name of Pharaoh Sahure' of the Vth Dynasty (*c.* 2563-2420 B.C.) found at Dorak (J. Mellaart, 'The Royal Treasure of Dorak', *ILN* (Nov. 28, 1959): 754ff.); many foreign contacts are known for this Dynasty; see W.S. Smith, *op.cit.*: 75.

34.   As we have seen extensively in our analyses in Chapter IV, tabulated in Chapter V. A good recent discussion of the affinities between Minoan and Near Eastern palatial design is J. Graham's 'The Relation of the Minoan Palaces to the Near Eastern Palaces of the Second Millennium', *McyStud* (1964): 195ff, and *PC*: 229ff. Note the cautions of M. Mellink in *AJA* 63 (1959): 295.

Orientation and Alignment of the Minoan Palaces

Any building placed in a landscape will bear palpable visual relationships to features of that landscape, by virtue of its geometric and tectonic organization. Any rectilinear structure will ordinarily have four (or more) fronts, each of which 'faces' some portion of the local topography. Windows or doorways in these faces will consequently 'frame' a view of a section of the landscape. Some of these framings will be fortuitous, while others may capitalize upon an orientation or alignment toward some landscape feature so as to 'mark' or 'point' to that feature.

To what extent are Minoan palatial compounds oriented so as to call attention to — even deliberately focus upon — significant features of the Cretan landscape? Are the palaces deliberately aligned toward important points in their landscapes?

In our examination of the formal organization of the palaces of Knossos, Mallia and Phaistos, we noted the fact that the orientation of the central court called attention to a prominent mountain view:[1] at Knossos, southward toward Mount Juktas; at Mallia, southeastward toward Mount Dikte, and at Phaistos, northward toward Mount Ida. It was suggested that such orientations were deliberate rather than fortuitous. From the central court at Knossos, there is a fine view of Mount Juktas, on which was located a peak sancturary. From the Mallian court, one's view is directed toward Mount Dikte, in whose cave the Minoan Zeus was born. At Phaistos, the view northward is dominated by the twin peaks of Mount Ida, on whose southern slope is a cave sanctuary, the cave of Kamares.

While it is obvious that such orientations exist, it is necessary to ask a number of interrelated questions so as to clarify the problem of palatial alignments, and their purportedly deliberate nature.

We need to ask the following questions:

1. Is there unambiguous evidence that such orientations are deliberate?

2. Are there formal clues in the structure of the palaces which visually 'mark' or focus upon:
   a. peak sanctuaries or caves;
   b. mountain peaks or summits themselves?

3. Are there equally significant alignments aside from the aforementioned?

4. Are we dealing with one phenomenon or two? In other words,
   a. landscape visual *alignment*; and/or
   b. solar or celestial *orientation*.

5. If the orientation of a palatial courtyard provides a visual focus upon a religiously significant mountain peak or sanctuary, is it then proper to consider the orientation of the palace courts as not necessarily north-south but primarily in the direction of that landscape feature?

The last question is raised because of the fact that the courtyard orientation of Knossos, Phaistos, Mallia and Kato Zakro is generally north-south, but that of the court of Plati, the LM III palace on the Lasithi Plateau just below Mount Dikte, is more generally NW-SE, i.e. in the direction of the Diktaean cave.[2]

Would it then be more proper to say that the palatial court, insofar as in at least one of its functions it served as a locus of religious activity, is oriented toward a religiously significant point in the landscape?

These questions were first seriously raised by V. Scully, Jr., nearly 20 years ago in a sensitive and persuasive study of the landscape siting of Greek temples and Bronze Age palatial buildings.[3] In that study, Dr. Scully suggested that the Minoan palaces were situated so as to frame a view of religiously important points in the Cretan landscape, in particular the principal mountain peaks of Ida, Dikte and Juktas.

Scully was patently correct in his observations, but the questions raised have yet to be conclusively answered to the general satisfaction of students of Minoan architecture. In part, the hostile reception given Scully's theses has confounded the issues, and by and large the subject has been laid aside.

In my view, speculation on the subject has been too hastily and recklessly put aside. The subject is an important one for the purposes of the present study, for if it can be shown persuasively that Minoan palatial compounds were deliberately aligned with certain features of the local landscape, then such a feature must be incorporated in the set of formative features of Minoan architectural design, i.e. a building's *situation* in a landscape; its external relationships. Our study above has focussed primarily on *internal* formative organization.

It is also my view that Scully's thesis has implications for two distinct (but interrelated) phenomena: *viz. structural orientation* and *visual alignment* or *marking*. The two phenomena need not coincide, and where they do coincide, such coincidence may be itself fortuitous. Let us try to be clear about these two phenomena.

By *structural orientation* will be meant here the generic orientation of the structural fabric of a building with respect to cardinal points of the compass. In this respect, the structural orientations of Knossos, Phaistos, Mallia, Gournia, Kato Zakro, and Plati differ. Of these, only Phaistos II is structurally oriented north-south by east-west. We may then ask if part of the building program of a palace was a *generic* or *specific* cardinal orientation.

By *visual alignment* or *marking* will be meant the specific channeling of one or more views from a palace to a significant point (or points) in the external landscape. In this respect, we can point to architectonic features in the organization of the areas peripheral to the facades of the central courtyards of Knossos, Phaistos, Mallia, and Plati which can be said to frame, focus, or point to religiously significant external landscape points, i.e. the evidently sacred peaks or peak sanctuaries associated with Mounts. Ida, Dikte and Juktas.

We must try to be very specific about what such 'architectonic features' are, and we must seek to demonstrate that these features are in some evident way equivalent from one palatial compound to another. One such feature has already been noted above: the actual alignment of the palaces' central court. The long axis of these 1 : 2 rectangular plazas may be seen to 'point' to or channel vision upon an external landscape prominence.

But what does such 'pointing' or focussing actually consist of? As we have observed above in Chapter II, it is only in the case of Phaistos II that the central court is *exactly* aligned upon the twin peaks of Mount Ida to the north. At Knossos and Mallia, the courts are *generically* aligned, i.e. Mounts Juktas and Dikte lie beyond the southern facade of the central courts, but the structural frame of these courts is not strictly aligned upon the mountain peaks. What does this mean?

In considering the question of central-court alignment, we must be aware of a very important fact, viz. that the palatial central courts were surrounded by peripheral facades, in some cases rising two or even three stories in height. What does this fact do to the hypothesis that the central courts 'framed' or focussed on a sacred mountain peak?

At Phaistos, Mallia or Knossos, the effect of peripheral construction would be to cut of those mountains from view with the exception of their summit peaks; which would then ride above the court facade (to the possible exclusion of other landscape rises in other directions). The three summits would be visible to a person standing at the center of the court; at a point, in other words, directly opposite the principal court shrines to the west. At Phaistos, this position is directly in front of cell 24; at Knossos, the position is directly in front of the Tripartite Shrine and the pillar crypts beyond; at Mallia, the position is at the point of the centrally situated court altar, and (again) opposite the pillar crypt to the west. Such a position, in other words, would be at a point on the east-west bisection axis of the central modular grid square of the palaces, as we have seen above in Chapter IV. We may imagine, then, that a worshiper at the prescribed position would directly face the peak (or peak sanctuary)[4] while standing exactly perpendicular to the principal palace shrine.[5]

But we do not know *why* he or she would so orient him/herself. Would such a person recreate the ritual siting procedures of the palace foundation itself? Is the position a commemoration of the latter? Is the person offering prayers and/or votive goods to (a) the sacred peak, and, turning to face (b) the chief palace shrine, then performing equivalent actions?

We do not know, and may never really know. All that remains to us is the architectonic frame within which ritual behavior took place.

It was noted above that it is only at Phaistos that the structural orientation and visual alignment are coterminous. At Knossos, the peak of Mount Juktas is off to the southwest, a few degrees off the north-south axis of the court. At Mallia, the peak of Mount Dikte is (if one stands at the center of the court, at the altar or *bothros*) is above the southeastern corner of the court, directly above the diagonal axis of that open area. Why is it the case that at Knossos and Mallia the structural axes and visual alignments are not coterminous?

It may be that Knossos provides a clue here. A glance at the plan of the palace will reveal (Figure II.28) that the southern facade of the court is primarily interrupted by a large doorway which is *not* at the center of that facade; indeed, it is several meters to the west. We shall assume (as we must) that this placement is not accidental, but deliberate, especially considering the care given the placement of component parts of the palace — e.g. the Court Shrine — in other quarters. There is no obvious reason why this sole interruption of the southern facade plane could not have been placed at the center point (and hence be more directly aligned with the position of the northern facade court entranceway).

We may suggest a reason for this displacement, having to do with the position of the peak of Mount Juktas beyond the southern court facade: standing at the center of the court, the doorway is so positioned to focus the eye upon Juktas beyond. We have noted above that a large 'horns of consecration' was found fallen from an upper storey in the debris of this area, it is conceivable that this object stood on the roofline, perhaps serving to 'frame' the Juktian peak itself.[6]

We do not know if the pair of 'horns' stood in that position, but there is pictorial evidence for such 'horns' standing along the rooflines of Minoan buildings.[7] It is thus possible (though not provable) that these (otherwise unusually huge) 'horns' stood on the southern court facade roofline, above the doorway, at a second storey roof height. *If* this is the case, then the resultant feature would present us with a sculptural version of an interesting Egyptian pictorial motif representing the disk of the sun framed by two mountain peaks: the shape of which is identical to the Minoan 'horns of consecration'.[8]

But if we accept this 'framing' or focussing hypothesis, we must then answer the question as to why the palace fabric of Knossos was not simply laid out in *direct* alignment with the peak of Mount Juktas. It could hardly have made a difference; the structure could simply have been turned a few degrees more to the southeast in its initial modular layout and construction.

It is my hypothesis that this was not possible — not because of topographical constraints, which in all the palaces are insignificant[9] — but because the palace, for some as yet unknown reason, *had* to be laid out as it was, with the structural orientation it reveals.

It may be that the reason the palace has the orientation it does is connected with the particular techniques of its original layout procedure. As we have demonstrated in Chapter IV above, the palaces were laid out on a modular grid featuring a central square grid at whose center axis were situated the principal ritual chambers of the building.[10] If we take it as a reasonable assumption that such a modular grid square was laid out by means of ropes and posts or pegs, then it may very well have been the case that the grid ritual was begun at sunrise.

The reason for this assumption is that each upright post or *gnomon* would cast a shadow westward, and that such a long sunrise shadow may have been employed as an initial guide to the orientation of the east-west ropes of the subsequent grid.

The resultant structural orientation of a palace would therefore be a function of the particular position on the horizon at which the sun rises on a particular day during the year. Since this position changes throughout the seasons (rising *due* east only on the Vernal Equinox or Autumnal Equinox) — and, since the eastern horizons of the palaces are not flat but themselves mountainous — the resultant structural orientations of the palaces would differ. It may also be the case that because the eastern horizons of the palaces are not flatly uniform, even if each palace were laid out on the same day of the year, the emergence of the sun above the eastern mountains would cast slightly differing east-west shadows from modular *gnomons* at each palace site, for the sun would not be rising perpendicular to the earth's horizon, but rather at a sloping angle.[11]

Thus it becomes clear that *three* factors are involved in palatial orientation:

1. solar sunrise alignment determing the east-west axis of the modular layout grid;
2. generic courtyard alignment with respect to the prominent landscape feature; and
3. specific framing of the latter within the resultant structural fabric of the building as built, at a point marked within a court facade.

We have said nothing here about Kato Zakro, Gournia or Plati. Plati is no longer visible, but there we may surmise that the second factor above is also present (which belies the initial assumption that a palatial court must face north-south on its long axis, for the Plati court would have *generically* pointed to Dikte and the Diktaean cave off to the southeast). We do not know (because excavation of this compound was halted before its limits were uncovered) if factor (3) was also in evidence here. At Kato Zakro, we do not know exactly what peak sanctuary in the hills to the northwest may be generically pointed to by the court's long axis.[12] This leaves Gournia, but there the situation is the same as that of Kato Zakro: the court does point to a range of peaks to the southwest, but we do not know what peak may have had a religious significance. In addition, the siting of the Gournia palace may have been in part constrained by (a) the long north-south axis of the hilltop on which it stands, and (b) by the fabric of the town in which it was embedded (assuming the latter antedated the former, which is unclear).

As noted above, it is only at Phaistos that factors (1), (2), and (3) were coterminous in their effects.

These aspects of site-planning are neither bizarre nor unusual in the history of architecture in many cultures, and no more strange than the placement within an Islamic mosque of an architectonic *marker* such as a niche to focus attention upon the geographical position of the holy city of Mecca, often hundreds of kilometers distant, and quite invisible. Indeed, the orientation and alignment of a Minoan palace would in a number of respects recall those for an Islamic religious building. In the latter, the feature within the fabric of the building marking the position of direction toward Mecca (*mehrab*) is compromised with the structural orientation of the mosque, which may be constrained by other factors (such as a pre-existent urban grid, etc.) It may, in other words, be off-axis with the orientation of the structural frame of the building proper, in the same way that Minoan visual peak (-sanctuary) alignment does not necessarily coincide with structural orientation.

These conjectural points are strung together in a delicate web, and many of our assumptions may be incorrect. We simply need more information before we can make more positive assertions regarding the nature of Minoan palatial site-planning. Nor is the end result of these observations the postulation that the practices at Stonehenge have now found a Mediterranean counterpart.[13]

By the time that the present volume appears in print, the writer will have made a detailed survey in the field of Minoan orientations and alignments,[14] and the provisional answers suggested above may have been supported or disproven. For our present purposes, it can be asserted that any thorough consideration of the formal organization of the Minoan palaces cannot omit a consideration of the important external relationships of these remarkable megastructures. Scully's observations are, in the main, patently correct: and we must now answer the challenge of his insights.

NOTES

1. See above, Chapter II, p. 162, and Notes 185, 193, 211; Chapter II, Appendix, p. 112 and Note 7.
2. Chapter II, Appendix, p. 162 and Note 7; photographs in *BSA* XX (1913-1914): Plate IVb.
3. V. Scully, Jr., *The Earth, The Temple, and The Gods* (New Haven, 1968, second edition, with references to the present writer's observations, Introduction).
4. In all cases, on the facing slope of the peaks involved; thereby involving the same alignments.
5. On the positional significance of the major palace cult cells, see our discussions above in Chapter IV under Knossos, Mallia and Phaistos. At Knossos, the principal Foundation Deposit of the palace, the Vat Room Deposit, lies adjacent to the pillar crypt and along the east-west bisection-line of the modular grid square.
6. See above, Chapter II, p. 162.
7. See for example the remarkable rhyton unearthed at Kato Zakro depicting, apparently, a peak sanctuary itself (see above, Kato Zakro, Chapter II, Note 240).

8.   Discussed and illustrated by S. Giedeion, *The Eternal Present: The Beginnings of Architecture* (1964): 342.

9.   It is only really in the case of the hilltop palace at Gournia where the topography (or a pre-existent(?) urban fabric) may have provided significant constraints on orientation.

10.   See above, Note 5.

11.   Discussed by F. Hoyle, *On Stonehenge* (1977), perhaps the most sensible and lucid examination of the problems of solar alignment.

12.   Although excavators of Kato Zakro note the existence of cave deposits (and burials) in the gorge known as the 'Valley of the Dead' inland from the palace proper; see references above, Chapter II, Note 225.

13.   See above, Note 11.

14.   Completed during 1980; to appear.

Bibliography*

* This bibliography is a list of major references pertinent to problems discussed in the text, as of 1979. In some instances, the titles of reports in archaeological journals have been abbreviated or standardized (e.g. Preliminary Report or Archaeological Report), particularly in cases where a single author has published a number of consecutive site reports.

Arnheim, R. (1977), *The Dynamics of Architectural Form.*

Atkinson, T. et al. (1904), Excavations at Phylakopi in Melos, *Journal of Hellenic Studies,* Supplement 1.

Badawy, A. (1954), *A History of Egyptian Architecture: From the Earliest Times to the End of the Old Kingdom.*

___ (1961), 'The harmonic system of architectural design in ancient Egypt', *Mitt. des Inst. für Orientforschung* III.

___ (1965), *Ancient Egyptian Architectural Design.*

___ (1966a), *Architecture in Ancient Egypt and the Near East.*

___ (1966b), *A History of Egyptian Architecture: The First Intermediate Period, the Middle Kingdom, and the Second Intermediate Period.*

Blegen, C. (1950), *Troy* I.

___ (1958), 'A chronological problem', *Minoica, Festschrift zum 80. Geburtstag von Johannes Sundwall.*

Blegen, C., and M. Rawson (1966), *The Palace of Nestor at Pylos.*

Böckh, A. (1838), *Metrologische Untersuchungen.*

Bosanquet, R. (1901-1905), 'Excavations at Palaikastro', *Annual of the British School of Archaeology at Athens* VIII.

___ (1901-1905), 'Excavations at Palaikastro', *Annual of the British School of Archaeology at Athens* IX.

___ (1901-1905), 'Excavations at Palaikastro', *Annual of the British School of Archaeology at Athens* XI.

Boyd-Hawes, H. (1908), *Gournia, Vasiliki and Other Prehistoric Sites in Eastern Crete.*

Branigan, K. (1970), *Foundations of Palatial Crete.*

Brea, L.B. (1964), *Poliochni I.*

Bruneau, P., and J. Ducat (1965), *Guide de Délos.*

Calvino, I. (1972), *Invisible Cities.*

Cantor, M.B. (1965), *Vorlesungen über die Geschichte der Mathematik.*

Chabas, F. (1876), *Recherches sur les poids, mesures et monnaies des anciens Egyptiens.*

Charbonneaux, J. (1928), 'Notes sur l'architecture et la céramique du Palais de Mallia', *Bulletin de Correspondence Hellénique.*

Conant, K.J. (1961), 'Measurements and proportions of the great church at Cluny', *Beiträge zur Kunstgeschichte und Archäologie des Frühmittelalters.*

____ (1963), 'Medieval academy excavations at Cluny, IX: systematic dimensions in the buildings', *Speculum* XXXVIII.

Decourdemanche, J.-A. (1909), *Traité pratique des poids et mesures des peuples anciens et des Arabes.*

Delongaz, P. (1940), *The Temple Oval at Khafajah.*

Dörpfeld, W. (1905), 'Kretische, Mykenische, und Homerische Paläste', *Mitteilungen des Deutschen Archäologischen Instituts/Athenische Abteilung* XXX.

____ (1907), 'Kretische, Mykenische, und homerische Paläste', *Mitteilungen des Deutschen Archäologischen Instituts/Athenische Abteilung* XXXII.

Douglas, M. (1974), 'Symbolic order in the use of domestic space', in *Man, Settlement and Urbanism,* ed. by Ucko and Tringham.

Edwards, I.E.S. (1961), *The Pyramids of Egypt.*

Evans, A. (1899-1900), 'Preliminary report', *Annual of the British School of Archaeology at Athens* VI.

____ (1900-1901), 'Preliminary report', *Annual of the British School of Archaeology at Athens* VII.

____ (1901-1902), 'Preliminary report', *Annual of the British School of Archaeology at Athens* VIII.

____ (1902-1903), 'Preliminary report', *Annual of the British School of Archaeology at Athens* IX.

____ (1903-1904), 'Preliminary report', *Annual of the British School of Archaeology at Athens* X.

____ (1904-1905), 'Preliminary report', *Annual of the British School of Archaeology at Athens* XI.

____ (1921), *The Palace of Minos at Knossos* I.

____ (1928), *The Palace of Minos at Knossos* II.

____ (1930), *The Palace of Minos at Knossos* III.

____ (1936), *The Palace of Minos at Knossos* IV.

Fiandra, E. (1961-1962), *Kretika Chronika* 15/16.

Frödin, O., and A. Persson (1938), *Asine, Results of the Swedish Excavations of 1922-1930.*

Gadd, C.J. (1932), 'Seals of ancient Indian style found at Ur', *Proceedings of the British Academy* XVIII.

Gallet de Santerre, H. (1949), 'Mallia, Aperçu historique', *Kretika Chronika.*

___ (1958), *Délos primitive et archaique.*

Giedeion, S. (1964), *The Eternal Present: The Beginnings of Architecture.*

Glotz, G. (1925), *The Aegean Civilization.*

Graham, J.W. (1956), 'Archaeological report', *American Journal of Archaeology.*

___ (1957), 'Archaeological report', *American Journal of Archaeology.*

___ (1959), 'Archaeological report', *American Journal of Archaeology.*

___ (1960), 'Archaeological report', *American Journal of Archaeology.*

___ (1961), 'Archaeological report', *American Journal of Archaeology.*

___ (1962), *Palaces of Crete.*

___ (1964), 'The relation of the Minoan palaces to the Near Eastern palaces of the second millennium', *Mycenaean Studies.*

___ (1970), 'Archaeological report', *American Journal of Archaeology.*

Halbherr, H. (1905a), 'Archaeological report', *Memorie delle Reale Istituto Lombardo XXI,* XII della serie III.

___ (1905b), 'Archaeological report', *Rendiconti della Reale Accademia dei Lincei* XIV.

Hambridge, J. (1967), *The Elements of Dynamic Symmetry.*

Hazzidhakis, J. (1912), 'Archaeological report', *Arkhaiologiki Ephemeris.*

___ (1915), 'Archaeological report', *Praktika tis en Athenais Arkhaiologikis Etaireias.*

___ (1918), 'Archaeological report', *Dheltion* IV.

___ (1919), 'Archaeological report', *Praktika tis en Athenais Arkhaiologikis Etaireias.*

___ (1921), 'Tylissos à l'époque minoenne', *Etudes de préhistoire crétois.*

___ (1934), *Tylissos: Villas minoennes* (*Etudes Crétois* III).

Hochberg, J. (1978), *Perception.*

Hogarth, D.G. (1900), 'The Psykhro Cave', *Annual of the British School of Archaeology at Athens.*

___ (1901), 'Excavations at Zakro, Crete', *Annual of the British School of Archaeology at Athens.*

Horn, W., and E. Born (1966), 'The dimensional inconsistencies of the plan of St. Gall and the problem of the scale of the plan', *Art Bulletin* XLVIII.

Hoyle, F. (1977), *On Stonehenge.*

Hultsch, F. (1864), *Metrologicorum scriptorum reliquiae* I.

___ (1866), *Metrologicorum scriptorum reliquiae* II.

___ (1882), *Griechische und römische Metrologie.*

Iversen, E. (1955), *Canon and Proportion in Egyptian Art.*

Kantor, H.J. (1947), 'The Aegean and the Orient in the second millennium B.C.', *American Journal of Archaeology.*

Karo, G. (1934), *Führer durch Tiryns.*

Kontoleon, N. (1970), 'The Birth of Zeus', *Kretika Chronika* 15.

Lawrence, A.W. (1957), *Greek Architecture.*

Leemans, W.F. (1961), 'Mesopotamië en de Indus Cultuur', *Phoenix* VII.

Lepsius, R. (1884), *Die Längenmasse der Alten.*

Levi, D. (1949-1951), 'Archaeological report', *Annuario* XXVII-XXIX.

— (1951), 'Archaeological report', *Bolletino d'Arte.*

— (1952), 'Archaeological report', *Bolletino d'Arte.*

— (1953), 'Archaeological report', *Bolletino d'Arte.*

— (1953-1954), 'Archaeological report', *Annuario* XXX-XXXII, N.S. XIV-XVI.

— (1955), 'Archaeological report', *Bolletino d'Arte.*

— (1955-1956), 'Archaeological report', *Annuario* XXXIII-XXXIV, N.S. XVII-XVIII.

— (1956), 'Archaeological report', *Bolletino d'Arte.*

— (1957-1958), 'Archaeological report', *Annuario* XXXV-XXXVI, N.S. XIX-XX.

— (1959a), 'Archaeological report', *Bolletino d'Arte.*

— (1959b), 'La villa rurale minoica di Gortina', *Bolletino d'Arte.*

— (1959-1960), 'Archaeological report', *Annuario* XXXVII-XXXVIII, N.S. XXI-XXII.

— (1960), 'Archaeological report', *Dheltion* XVI.

— (1961-1962a), 'Archaeological report', *Annuario* XXXIX-XL, N.S. XXIII-XXIV.

— (1961-1962b), 'Archaeological report', *Dheltion* XVIIB.

— (1963), 'Archaeological report', *Dheltion* XVIIIB.

— (1965), 'The recent excavations at Phaistos', *Studies in Mediterranean Archaeology.*

— (1965-1966), 'Archaeological report', *Annuario* XLIII-XLIV, N.S. XXVII-XXVIII.

Lloyd, S., and J. Mellaart (1962), *Beycesultan I.*

Mackay, E. (1948), *Early Indus Civilization.*

Mackenzie D. (1904-1905), 'Preliminary report', *Annual of the British School of Archaeology at Athens.*

— (1905-1906), 'Preliminary report', *Annual of the British School of Archaeology at Athens.*

— (1906-1907), 'Preliminary report', *Annual of the British School of Archaeology at Athens.*

— (1907-1908), 'Preliminary report', *Annual of the British School of Archaeology at Athens.*

Mariani, L. (1895), 'Antichita cretesi', *Monumenti Antichi* VI.

Marinatos, S. (1924-1925), 'Mesominoiki Oikia en Kato Mesara', *Dheltion* IX.

___ (1926), 'Archaeological report', *Praktika tis en Athenais Arkhaiologikis Etaireias.*

___ (1932), 'Archaeological report', *Praktika tis en Athenais Arkhaiologikis Etaireias.*

___ (1933a), 'Archaeological repot', *Praktika tis en Athenais Arkhaiologikis Etaireias.*

___ (1933b). 'Archaeological report', *Bulletin de Correspondence Hellénique.*

___ (1934), 'Archaeological report', *Praktika tis en Athenais Arkhaiologikis Etaireias.*

___ (1935), 'Archaeological report', *Praktika tis en Athenais Arkhaiologikis Etaireias.*

___ (1948), 'To Minoikon Megaron Sklavokampou', *Arkhaiologiki Ephemeris.*

___ (1968a), 'Archaeological report', *Arkhaiologika Analekta ex Athinōn.*

___ (1968b), *Excavations at Thera* I.

___ (1969), 'Archaeological report', *Arkhaiologika Analekta ex Athinōn.*

___ (1970), 'Archaeological report', *Arkhaiologika Analekta ex Athinōn.*

___ (1973), *Excavations at Thera* VI.

Marinatos, S., and M. Hirmer (1960), *Crete and Mycenae.*

Marshall, J.H. (1931), *Mohenjo-daro and the Indus Civilization* I and II.

Meillet, A., and J. Venryes (1948), *Traite dé Grammaire Comparée des Langues Classiques.*

Meissner, B. (1920), *Babylonien und Assyrien* I.

Mellaart, J. (1959), 'The royal treasure of Dorak', *Illustrated London News.*

___ (1960), 'Notes on the architectural remains of Troy I and II', *Anatolian Studies.*

___ (1964), *Çatal Hüyük.*

Mellink, N. (1959), 'Archaeology in Asia Minor', *American Journal of Archaeology.*

Messerschmidt, L. (1911-1922), *Keilschriftteste aus Assur historischen Inhalts.*

Moore, C. (1977), *Body, Memory and Architecture.*

Müller, K. (1930), *Tiryns, III, Die Architektur der Burg und des Palastes.*

Mylonas, G.E. (1966), *Mycenae and the Mycenaean Age.*

___ (1972), *Mycenae: A Guide to its Ruins and Its History.*

Nagel, W. (1964), *Die Bauern- und Stadt-Kulturen im vordyn astischen Vorderasien.*

Naumann, R. (1955), *Architektur Kleinasiens.*

Neisser, U. (1976), *Cognition and Reality.*

Nicholls, R.V. (1958-1959), 'Old Smyrna: the Iron Age fortifications and associated remains on the city perimeter', *Annual of the British School of Archaeology at Athens.*

Noack, F. (1908), *Ovalhaus und Palast in Kreta.*

Palmer, L.R. (1970), *A New Guide to the Palace of Knossos.*

Pendlebury, J.D.S. (1933), *Handbook to the Palace of Minos at Knossos.*

___ (1937-1938), 'Excavations in the Plain of Lasithi, III: Karphi', *Annual of the British School of Archaeology at Athens.*

Pernier, L. (1900), 'Archaeological report', *Rendiconti della Reale Accademia dei Lincei.*

___ (1902a), 'Archaeological report', *Monumenti Antichi* XII.

___ (1902b), 'Archaeological report', *Rendiconti della Reale Accademia dei Lincei.*

___ (1903), 'Archaeological report', *Rendiconti della Reale Accademia dei Lincei.*

___ (1904), 'Archaeological report', *Monumenti Antichi* XIV.

___ (1906), 'Archaeological report', *Ausonia* I.

___ (1907a), 'Archaeological report', *Ausonia* II.

___ (1907b), 'Archaeological report', *Bolletino d'Arte.*

___ (1907c), 'Archaeological report', *Rendiconti della Reale Accademia dei Lincei.*

___ (1908), 'Archaeological report', *Rendiconti della Reale Accademia dei Lincei.*

___ (1909), 'Archaeological report', *Ausonia* IV.

___ (1935), *Il Palazzo Minoico di Festos* I.

Pernier, L., and L. Banti (1947), *Guida degli scavi italiani in Creta.*

___ (1951), *Il Palazzo Minoico di Festos* II.

Petrie, W.M.F. (1891), *Illahun, Kahun and Gurob.*

___ (1926), *Ancient Weights and Measures.*

Platon, N. (1947), 'Archaeological report', *Kretika Chronica.*

___ (1958), 'Archaeological report', *Bulletin de Correspondence Hellénique.*

___ (1960), 'Archaeological report', *Bulletin de Correspondence Hellénique.*

___ (1966), *Archaeologia Mundi: Crete.*

Platon, N., S. Alexiou, and H. Guanella (1968), *Ancient Crete.*

Preziosi, D. (1967), 'Minoan architectural planning methods', *American Journal of Archaeology.*

___ (1968a), 'Harmonic design in ancient architecture', *American Journal of Archaeology.*

___ (1968b), 'Harmonic design in Minoan architecture', *Fibonacci Quarterly: Journal of Mathematics of the University of California* VI.6.

___ (1968c), '*Minoan palace planning and its origins*'. Unpublished dissertation.

___ (1970), 'Formal and functional analysis of Minoan architecture', *Labrys* I.

___ (1971a), 'The conceptual organization of the Egyptian house', *American Journal of Archaeology*.

___ (1971b), 'Modular design in Minoan architecture', in *Studies Presented to George M.A. Hanfmann*, ed. by Mitten, Pedley, and Scott.

___ (1979a), *Architecture, Language and Meaning*.

___ (1979b), *The Semiotics of the Built Environment*.

Richardson, L.J.D. (1966), 'The Labyrinth', *Mycenaean Studies*.

De Sarzec, E. (1884), *Découvertes en Chaldée*.

Schliemann, H. (1884), *Tiryns*.

Scully, Jr., V. (1962), *The Earth, the Temple and the Gods*.

Skinner, F.G. (1954), 'Measures and weights', in *A History of Technology* I.

Smith, W.S. (1965), *The Art and Architecture of Ancient Egypt*.

Snijder, G.A.S. (1936), *Kretische Kunst*.

Themelis, P. (1970), 'Protoelladikon Megaron eis Akrovitika Messenias', *Arkhaiologika Analekta ex Athinōn*.

Tire, C., and H. van Effenterre (1966), *Guide des fouilles françaises en Crète*.

Tuan, Yi-Fu (1975), *Topophilia*.

Valmin, N. (1938), *The Swedish Messenia Expedition*.

Vats, M.S. (1940), *Excavations at Harappā* I.

Wace, A.J.B. (1949), *Mycenae: An Archaeological History and Guide*.

Watelin, L.C. (1924), *Excavations at Kish*.

Wheeler, M. (1962), *The Indus Civilization*.

Xanthoudhidhes, S. (1922), 'To Minoikon Megaron Nirou', *Arkhaiologiki Ephemeris*.

Index of Sites
(items italized = illustrations)

Guy Ankerl

Experimental Sociology of Architecture

A Guide to Theory, Research, and Literature

1981. 15 x 23 cm. 550 pages.
Hardback. DM 125,—; US $57.00 ISBN 90 279 3219 0
Paperback. DM 50,—; US $22.75 ISBN 90 279 3440 1
(New Babylon Studies in the Social Sciences, 36)

This first sociology of architecture results from research carried out in the USA, Canada, and Switzerland under the direction of the author, who is a sociologist as well as an architect.

It is a systematic, internationally grounded, comprehensive work, oriented methodologically to an experimental, and conceptually, to an objective (hard-science) approach. In fact, it provides a first conceptual and paradigmatic framework for this new field of specialization.

Communication as the empirical basis of all social phenomena supplies the unifying viewpoint to Ankerl's sociological theory of architecture. Architecture is explored in its specificity as a medium. Since the architectural space system affects most directly the network and structure of the face-to-face communication of user groups, these aspects of communication are also studied. In the discussion of architecture as a medium the contributions of semiotics and linguistics are also put to use.

In methodology, he demonstrates how research in objective sociology can be reinvigorated by the application of experimental designs. In sum, the author shows why the sociology of space creation is an excellent starting point for the development of an objective and experimental sociology.

Prices are subject to change without notice

mouton publishers

Berlin · New York · Amsterdam